Mindfulness

Mindfulness-based approaches to medicine, psychology, neuroscience, health-care, education, business leadership, and other major societal institutions have become increasingly common. New paradigms are emerging from a confluence of two powerful and potentially synergistic streams of inquiry: one arising from the wisdom traditions of Asia and the other arising from post-enlightenment empirical science.

This book presents the work of internationally renowned experts in the fields of Buddhist scholarship and scientific research, as well as looking at the implementation of mindfulness in healthcare and education settings. Contributors consider the use of mindfulness throughout history and look at the actual meaning of mindfulness whilst identifying the most salient areas for potential synergy and for potential disjunction.

Mindfulness: Diverse Perspectives on its Meaning, Origins and Applications provides a place where wisdom teachings, philosophy, history, science and personal meditation practice meet. It was originally published as a special issue of *Contemporary Buddhism*.

J. Mark G. Williams, Ph.D. is Professor of Clinical Psychology and Director of the Oxford Mindfulness Centre at the University of Oxford, UK. His research focuses on how best to alleviate depression and suicidality. Previous publications include *Mindfulness: A Practical Guide to Finding Peace in a Frantic World* (2011) and *The Mindful Way through Depression: Freeing Yourself from Chronic Unhappiness* (2007).

Jon Kabat-Zinn, Ph.D. is Professor of Medicine Emeritus, and Founder of MBSR and the Center for Mindfulness in Medicine, Health Care and Society at the University of Massachusetts Medical School, USA. He teaches mindfulness meditation as a systematic mind/body approach to help people cope with stress, anxiety, pain and illness. Previous publications include *Mindfulness for Beginners: Reclaiming the Present Moment – and Your Life* (2012) and *The Mind's Own Physician: A Systematic Dialogue with the Dalai Lama on the Healing Power of Meditation* (2011).

Mindfulness
Diverse Perspectives on its Meaning, Origins and Applications

Edited by
**J. Mark G. Williams and
Jon Kabat-Zinn**

Routledge
Taylor & Francis Group

LONDON AND NEW YORK

First published 2013
by Routledge
2 Park Square, Milton Park, Abingdon, Oxon, OX14 4RN

Simultaneously published in the USA and Canada
by Routledge
711 Third Avenue, New York, NY 10017

Routledge is an imprint of the Taylor & Francis Group, an informa business

This book is a reproduction of *Contemporary Buddhism: An Interdisciplinary Journal*, volume 12, issue 1. The Publisher requests to those authors who may be citing this book to state, also, the bibliographical details of the special issue on which the book was based.

British Library Cataloguing in Publication Data
A catalogue record for this book is available from the British Library

ISBN13: 978-0-415-63096-2 (hbk)
ISBN13: 978-0-415-63647-6 (pbk)

Typeset in Helvetica
by Taylor & Francis Books

Printed and bound by CPI Group (UK) Ltd Croydon, CR0 4YY

Publisher's Note
The publisher would like to make readers aware that the chapters in this book may be referred to as articles as they are identical to the articles published in the special issue. The publisher accepts responsibility for any inconsistencies that may have arisen in the course of preparing this volume for print.

Contents

CONTENTS

Citation Information

The chapters in this book were originally published in *Contemporary Buddhism: An Interdisciplinary Journal*, volume 12, issue 1 (May 2011). When citing this material, please use the original page numbering for each article, as follows:

CITATION INFORMATION

Notes on Contributors

Ruth A. Baer, Department of Psychology, University of Kentucky, Lexington, USA

Martine Batchelor, Buddhist teacher and author, South West France

Ven. Bhikkhu Bodhi, Chuang Yen Monastery, New York, USA

Mirabai Bush, Center for Contemplative Mind in Society, Williamsburg, USA

Michael Chaskalson (Kulananda), Centre for Mindfulness Research and Practice, School of Psychology, Bangor University, UK

Georges Dreyfus, Department of Religion, Williams College, Williamstown, USA

John Dunne, Department of Religion, Emory University, USA

Christina Feldman, Co-founder and Guiding Teacher, Gaia House Meditation Retreat Centre, Devon, UK

Melanie Fennell, Oxford Mindfulness Centre, University of Oxford Department of Psychiatry, Warneford Hospital, UK

Rupert Gethin, Theology and Religious Studies, University of Bristol, UK

Paul Grossman, Department of Psychosomatic Medicine, Division of Internal Medicine, University of Basel Hospital, Switzerland

Jon Kabat-Zinn, Center for Mindfulness, University of Massachusetts Medical School, USA

Willem Kuyken, Mood Disorders Centre, School of Psychology, University of Exeter, UK

Edel Maex, Psychiatrist, Ziekenhuis Netwerk Antwerpen, Belgium

Andrew Olendzki, Executive Director and Senior Scholar, Barre Center for Buddhist Studies, Massachusetts, USA

Sharon Salzberg, Insight Meditation Society, Massachusetts, USA

NOTES ON CONTRIBUTORS

Saki F. Santorelli, Center for Mindfulness in Medicine, Health Care and Society, University of Massachusetts Medical School, USA

Zindel Segal, Centre for Addiction and Mental Health, University of Toronto, Ontario, Canada

John Teasdale, retired scholar; formerly Research Scientist, Medical Research Council's Cognition and Brain Sciences Unit, Cambridge, UK

J. Mark G. Williams, Oxford Mindfulness Centre, University of Oxford Department of Psychiatry, Warneford Hospital, UK

Nicholas T. Van Dam, Department of Psychology, University at Albany, SUNY, New York, USA

Preface

How shall we define 'mindfulness'? Is there one unified view or definition of it in the cultures from which it originally stems, or diverse perspectives on it? Where do current 'secular' applications of mindfulness in mainstream settings come from? Why might it be important to know and understand this history and the source of these practices and their classical expressions in different cultural streams? These are some of the vital questions that are addressed in this volume.

This book first appeared as a Special Issue of the journal *Contemporary Buddhism*. It appeared as Volume 11, number 1, 2011, and was distributed to its regular subscribers, libraries and individuals throughout the world. It soon became the most popular and sought after issue of the journal, with more downloads of individual articles in the first three months than had happened in the lifetime of the entire journal. Many people told us that it should be issued as a book to reach an even wider audience.

Its popularity and impact represent the continuing interest that scholars, scientists, instructors and practitioners alike are taking in mindfulness. We provide some background to this extraordinary phenomenon in our introductory chapter.

Yet there are still reasons to be surprised by its popularity. The chapters here are not, for the most part, clinical or practical in tone, nor do they steer away from difficult or controversial topics. People are reading these contributions because they go beyond the introductory texts on mindfulness, important as these are for many. Indeed, difficult issues are tackled head-on, often in riveting and compelling fashion. The popularity of this volume when it was a Special Issue of the journal represents a maturing of a field that seeks now to understand both the origins and deep history of mindfulness as well as its wider contemporary applications, and in this way, nourish the practice itself and its embodiment in teaching within a broad and growing range of professional endeavors.

More and more, those who practice and especially those who seek to teach mindfulness are realizing something hugely important: namely, that there are untold riches to be found in being exposed to and coming to understand both the ancient teachings and newly emerging insights from the philosophy, history and science of mindfulness; especially when these insights are held within the context of one's own day by day cultivation of mindfulness under the guidance of an experienced meditation teacher and wise mentor.

PREFACE

This book provides, for us all, a place where wisdom teachings, philosophy, history, science and personal meditation practice meet. We hope you enjoy exploring it and discovering both the richness and the challenges of these offerings for yourself.

Mark Williams & Jon Kabat-Zinn

MINDFULNESS: DIVERSE PERSPECTIVES ON ITS MEANING, ORIGINS, AND MULTIPLE APPLICATIONS AT THE INTERSECTION OF SCIENCE AND DHARMA

J. Mark G. Williams and Jon Kabat-Zinn

The editors introduce this book on Mindfulness, explaining its rationale, aims, and intentions. Integrating mindfulness-based approaches into medicine, psychology, neuroscience, healthcare, education, business leadership, and other major societal institutions has become a burgeoning field. The very rapidity of such growth of interest in mainstream contemporary applications of ancient meditative practices traditionally associated with specific cultural and philosophical perspectives and purposes, raises concerns about whether the very essence of such practices and perspectives might be unwittingly denatured out of ignorance and/or misapprehended and potentially exploited in inappropriate and ultimately unwise ways. The authors suggest that this is a point in the development of this new field, which is emerging from a confluence of two powerful and potentially synergistic epistemologies, where it may be particularly fruitful to pause and take stock. The contributors to this book, all experts in the fields of Buddhist scholarship, scientific research, or the implementation of mindfulness in healthcare or educational settings, have risen to the challenge of identifying the most salient areas for potential synergy and for potential disjunction. Our hope is that out of these interchanges and reflections and collective conversations may come new understandings and emergences that will provide both direction and benefit to this promising field.

We are delighted to introduce this book that first appeared as a special issue of the international journal *Contemporary Buddhism*. The book is devoted exclusively

to invited contributions from Buddhist teachers and contemplative scholars, together with mindfulness-based professionals on both the clinical and research sides,
writing on the broad topic of mindfulness and the various issues that arise from its
increasing popularity and integration into the mainstream of medicine, education,
psychology and the wider society. That two scientist/clinicians, neither of whom
identifies himself as a Buddhist, and neither of whom is a Buddhist scholar, were
invited to be guest editors, is itself an event worthy of note, and a sign of the good
will and spaciousness of view of the journal's outgoing editor, John Peacocke. We
thank him for the profound opportunity, and the faith he has placed in us.

For many years, from the early 1980s until the late 1990s, the field we might call
mindfulness-based applications went along at a very modest level, at first under
the aegis of behavioural medicine. The number of papers per year coming out
followed a linear trajectory with a very low slope. Someplace in the late 1990s, the
rise began to go exponential, and that exponential rate continues (Figure 1). Interest and activity is no longer limited to the discipline of behavioural medicine, or
mind/body medicine, or even medicine. Major developments are now occurring in
clinical and health psychology, cognitive therapy, and neuroscience, and increasingly, there is growing interest, although presently at a lower level, in primary and
secondary education, higher education, the law, business, and leadership. Indeed,
in the UK, the National Health Service (NHS) has mandated mindfulness-based
cognitive therapy as the treatment of choice for specific patient populations suf-

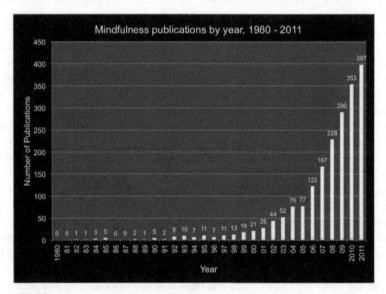

FIGURE 1
Results obtained from a search of the term 'mindfulness' in the abstracts and
keywords of the ISI web of knowledge database on March 19, 2012. The search
was limited to publications with English language abstracts. Figure prepared by
David Black, MPH, Ph.D., Cousins Center for Psychoneuroimmunology, Semel
Institute for Neuroscience & Human Behavior, University of California, Los
Angeles.

fering from major depressive disorder. What is more, at a scientific meeting on mindfulness research within neuroscience and clinical medicine and psychology in Madison in October 2010,[1] delegates from the National Institute of Health reported that NIH alone funded more than 150 research projects in mindfulness over the preceding five years. The growth of interest in mindfulness in the past 10 years has been huge, and in many ways extraordinary.

From the perspective of 1979, when mindfulness-based stress reduction (MBSR) came into being in the Stress Reduction Clinic at the University of Massachusetts Medical Center in Worcester, Massachusetts, the idea that mindfulness meditation would become integrated into mainstream medicine and science to the extent that it already has, that the NIH would fund mindfulness research at the levels that it has, as well as hold a day long symposium on its campus in May of 2004 entitled Mindfulness Meditation and Health, and that the NHS in the UK would mandate a therapy based on mindfulness nationwide, is nothing short of astonishing. This interest is not confined to North America and the UK. It is occurring worldwide.

Indeed, given the zeitgeist of the late 1970s, the probability that Buddhist meditation practices and perspectives would become integrated into the mainstream of science and medicine and the wider society to the extent that they already have at this juncture, and in so many different ways that are now perceived as potentially useful and important to investigate, seemed at the time to be somewhat lower than the likelihood that the cosmic expansion of the universe should all of a sudden come to a halt and begin falling back in on itself in a reverse big-bang . . . in other words, infinitesimal. And yet, improbable as it may have been, it has already happened, and the unfolding of this phenomenon continues on many different fronts. In the large, it signals the convergence of two different epistemologies and cultures, namely that of science and that of the contemplative disciplines, and in particular meditation, and even more specifically, Buddhist forms of meditation and the framework associated with their deployment and practice. Since Buddhist meditative practices are concerned with embodied awareness and the cultivation of clarity, emotional balance (equanimity) and compassion, and since all of these capacities can be refined and developed via the honing and intentional deployment of attention, the roots of Buddhist meditation practices are de facto universal. Thus, as Kabat-Zinn argues in the closing contribution, it is therefore appropriate to introduce them into mainstream secular settings in the service of helping to reduce suffering and the attendant mind-states and behaviours that compound it, and to do so in ways that neither disregard nor disrespect the highly sophisticated and beautiful epistemological framework within which it is nested, but on the contrary make profound use of that framework in non-parochial ways consistent with its essence.

The emergence within science and medicine of interest in Buddhist meditative practices and their potential applications represents a convergence of two different ways of knowing, that of western empirical science, and that of the empiricism of the meditative or consciousness disciplines and their attendant frameworks, developed over millennia. The world can only benefit from such a convergence and intermixing of streams, as long as the highest standards of rigor and empiricism native to each stream are respected and followed. The promise of deepened insights and novel approaches to theoretical and practical issues is great when different lenses can be held up to old and intractable issues.

At the same time, such a confluence of streams and the sudden rise in interest and enthusiasm carries with it a range of possible problems, some of which might actually seriously undermine and impede the deepest and most creative potential of this emergent field and hamper its fullest development. It is in this context that we hope this special issue will spark ongoing dialogue and conversation across disciplines that usually do not communicate with each other, and equally, will spark an introspective inquiry among all concerned regarding the interface between what has come to be called 'first person experience' and the 'third person' perspective of scientists studying aspects of human experience from a more traditional vantage point (Varela and Shear 1999). The promise of the convergence and cross-fertilization of these two ways of understanding the world and human experience is large. It is presently becoming a leading current of thought and investigation in cognitive science (Varela, Thompson and Roach 1991; Thompson 2007) and affective neuroscience (Lutz, Dunne and Davidson 2007). In a parallel and overlapping emergence dating back to 1987, the Mind and Life Institute has been conducting dialogues between the Dalai Lama and scientists and clinicians, along with Buddhist scholars and philosophers on a range of topics related to the confluence of these streams (see Kabat-Zinn and Davidson 2011; www.mindandlife.org).

If increasing interest and popularity in regard to mindfulness and its expressions in professional disciplines might inevitably bring a unique set of challenges and even potential problems—the stress of 'success,' so to speak—then questions to ponder at this juncture might be: Are there intrinsic dangers that need to be kept in mind? Is there the potential for something priceless to be lost through secular applications of aspects of a larger culture which has a long and venerable, dare we say sacred tradition of its own? What are the potential negative effects of the confluence of these different epistemologies at this point in time? Do we need to be concerned that young professionals might be increasingly drawn to mindfulness (or expected by their senior colleagues to use or study a mindfulness-based intervention) because it may be perceived as a fashionable field in which to work rather than from a motivation more associated with its intrinsic essence and transformative potential? Can it be exploited or misappropriated in ways that might lead to harm of some kind, either by omission or commission? Might there even be elements of bereavement and loss on the part of some, mixed in with the exhilaration of any apparent 'success', as often happens when success comes rapidly and unexpectedly?

If we can ask such sometimes hard or even uncomfortable questions, and if we can discern elements of both possible danger and promise that we have not thought of before, and if we can stay in conversation and perhaps collaboration across domains where traditionally there has been little or no discourse, perhaps this confluence of streams will give rise to its maximal promise while remaining mindful of the potential dangers associated with ignoring the existence of or disregarding some of the profound concerns and perspectives expressed by the contributors to this special issue. The very fact that a scholarly journal devoted to Buddhism would host this kind of cross disciplinary conversation is itself diagnostic of the dissolving of barriers between, until recently, very separate areas of scholarship and inquiry.

This book thus offers a unique opportunity for all involved in this field, as well as those coming to it for the first time, to step back at this critical moment in history and reflect on how this intersection of classical Buddhist teachings and Western culture is faring, and how it might be brought to the next level of flourishing while engendering the least harm and the greatest potential benefit.

Our first task as Editors was to draw together an international team to contribute original essays, including authors who might raise issues of which some of us may not even be aware either from the scholarly or cultural perspective, issues that might shed some light on how this field could be enriched and deepened. To that end, we invited scholars of Buddhism, scientists, clinicians and teachers who we thought would be able to speak deeply to two audiences: first, to those in the Buddhist community who may not be so familiar with the current use and growing influence of mindfulness in professional settings, or who may be a little puzzled or anxious about it; second, to teachers and researchers within the Western medical, scientific, psychotherapeutic, educational or corporate settings, who would like to be more informed about current areas of debate within Buddhist scholarship.

With this aim in mind, we have organized the essays in a certain sequence, starting from scholars of Buddhism who can help us situate the contemporary debate in an historical context, then moving to teachers and clinicians/scientists for their perspective, before finally coming back to the historical context and the question of how best to honour the traditions out of which the most refined articulation of mindfulness and its potential value arose, yet at the same time, making it accessible to those who would not seek it out within a Buddhist context.

From Abhidharma to psychological science

In the first essay, Bhikkhu Bodhi examines the etymology and use of the term sati in the foundational texts to help convey the breadth and depth of mindfulness. He explores the differences in treatment of sati pointing out how those systems that give greater emphasis to mindfulness as remembrance require re-interpretation in the light of those that place greater emphasis on what he calls 'lucid awareness.' He examines passages from Nyanaponika Thera to show the dangers of using 'bare attention' as an adequate account of sati. Against this background, his article focuses on both the beauty and the challenges inherent in bringing mindfulness into modern healthcare, education and neuroscience. His article lays important groundwork for understanding the meaning and use of words relating to mindfulness in the texts, and offers a unique perspective on what is and is not important in bringing such practices to the West.

Georges Dreyfus' essay explores the potential hazards of an incomplete understanding of mindfulness, both from the theoretical perspective but also, of major concern, on the experiential level as well. In particular, he argues that current definitions of mindfulness that emphasize only one of the themes present in the historical traditions—present-centred non-judgmental awareness—may miss some of the central features of mindfulness. He explores the implications for current practice of taking fuller account of those Buddhist texts that present mindfulness as being relevant to the past as well as the present, including a capacity for sustained attention that can hold its object whether the 'object' is present or not.

Andrew Olendzki continues this examination of the same issues using first the Abhidharma system as found in the Pali work Abhidhammatthasaṅgaha in which mindfulness is seen as an advanced state of constructed experience, and wisdom as arising only under special conditions; contrasting it with the Sanskrit Abhidharmakośa, where both mindfulness and wisdom are counted among the 'universal' factors, and thus 'arise and pass away in every single mind moment.' This has important implications for what we understand about what we are doing in meditation, for the latter approach assumes that, although mindfulness and wisdom are hidden most of the time by attachment, aversion and delusion, the mind is fundamentally already awakened and inherently wise. As Olendzki says 'The practice becomes one of uncovering the originally pure nature of mind.' He suggests that it is the latter approach that provides a basis for an Innateist model of development, and he critiques this model from a constructivist perspective.

What is the contemporary teacher of a mindfulness-based intervention to make of this debate? What are its implications?

John Dunne's article speaks directly to this issue. He focuses on 'non-dual' practice in relation to the more mainstream descriptions found in Abhidharma literature, examining Buddhist non-dualism, including attitudes to and theories about thoughts and judgments and how these arise and are affected by practice. He takes up the arguments made in Georges Dreyfus' article, pointing out how Dreyfus's analysis, though an excellent presentation of a 'classical' Abhidharma approach to mindfulness, may not be a good fit for the non-dual Innateist approaches to mindfulness that are the more immediate forebears of the mindfulness practiced by clinicians and studied by many scientists in the West, as discussed by Jon Kabat-Zinn in his description of the range of Buddhist influences on the development of MBSR.

John Teasdale and Michael Chaskelson have contributed two essays that take up the challenge of bringing together Buddhist theory and clinical practice. The first article offers a way of looking at the first and second of the Four Noble Truths from the perspective of the question: 'what has this to do with those who come to an MBSR or MBCT class?' After all, they say, participants in classes are primarily looking for relief from the stress and exhaustion of their illness, or they want to stay well after depression. They do not come asking for resolution of existential suffering.

6

The authors take this question head on: How are the Four Noble Truths relevant to clinician's concerns? Their article emphasizes the way in which our minds are constructed in a way that makes it very difficult to see clearly the nature of our own suffering, and how we add to it by the way we react to moment by moment experience. They also show the compulsive quality to our attachments, expressed in the very language of 'shoulds' and 'musts' and 'if onlys' — how absorbed we are in wishing things were different from how we find them. In so doing, the authors give a deeper meaning to the notion of a 'cognitive' therapy, beyond the cartoon images that are so often mistaken for real knowledge and understanding of the approach. Not only this, but their analysis reminds us how much emotional pain in the Western world arises from the same conditions that have always operated, and how, as the authors express it 'the patterns of mind that keep people trapped in emotional suffering are, fundamentally, the same patterns of mind that stand between all of us and the flowering of our potential for a more deeply satisfying way of being'. Finally, the article talks directly to teachers of mindfulness-based interventions: why do teachers need to know these truths at all? They point out the dangers of attempting to teach without the 'road map' both of understanding and of experience.

Teasdale and Chaskelson's second article unpacks classical Buddhist teachings from the perspective of underlying psychological processes and, in particular, the way that working memory (already referred to in Georges' Dreyfus' article) operates. They revisit and re-state Teasdale and Barnard's Interacting Cognitive Subsystems (ICS) theory to provide a framework for understanding how the mind might transform suffering. ICS recognizes two kinds of meaning, one explicit and specific (expressed in a simple proposition such as 'the cat sat on the mat'), the other implicit and holistic (felt in the language of the poet or storyteller).

Teasdale and Chaskelson show how suffering can be seen in psychological terms as a response to 'particular patterns of information' (for example, patterns that convey certain 'affectively-charged' meanings). If 'working memory' can hold separate pieces of information and then integrate them into wider patterns, then suffering can be transformed by changing the very patterns of information that produce it: 'Working memory provides a place where these patterns can be held and integrated with other patterns to create new patterns that do not produce suffering'. In ICS terms, mindfulness is a way of creating such new patterns of implicit, holistic meanings. For readers who are already familiar with the ICS model, this re-statement of it will be a welcome contribution. For readers who do not already know it, this article will provide a wonderful gateway into it.

Marrying Buddhist teaching and contemporary mindfulness practice

The next group of papers explores the challenges inherent in bringing to life the deep and lasting truths and practices of the dharma within the secular context of day to day clinical work with people, examining how one mindfulness-based intervention (mindfulness-based cognitive therapy [MBCT]) combines on the one hand the need to be faithful to recent scientific discoveries about depression with, on the other, faithfulness to the broad foundational tradition of Buddhist meditative practices and understanding.

Melanie Fennell and Zindel Segal point out that, on the face of it, MBCT is an unlikely marriage. What happens when one partner to a marriage is mindfulness meditation, rooted in Buddhist thought and practice, and the other partner comes from a western tradition of cognitive and clinical science? As MBCT/mindfulness teachers whose original professional training was in cognitive therapy and cognitive science, these authors are well-placed to see the possible strains inherent in the marriage and to map them out with precision and clarity. The authors examine points of congruence and divergence between the two traditions. Particularly helpful is their brief and authoritative summary of the origins and current practice of Cognitive Therapy (CT), its key underpinnings, and the way it interfaces with the world of psychotherapy. Their discussion reminds us that the development of a mindfulness-based intervention for depression which incorporates and extends the success of CT in bringing about lasting relief of recurrent suffering needs to keep in mind and respect those insights and successes in their own right and on their own terms, and not make throwaway comments about whole fields of psychotherapy (such as CT) simply because it has taken a different tack than mindfulness-based approaches. Fennell and Segal's article reminds us that CT is a complex and valid approach in its own right, sharing common features with mindfulness. They characterize MBCT as a marriage between equal partners and suggest that, despite some appearances, it is a marriage that may well endure.

Kuyken and Feldman zero in on one particular aspect of mindfulness-based interventions: compassion. What is compassion? It is, in their words, both an 'orientation of mind' and a 'capacity to respond'. In compassion, the mind is both oriented to recognize pain in human experience and cultivates an ability to meet it with kindness, empathy, equanimity and patience. While Fennell and Segal provide the evidence on the efficacy of MBCT in reducing risk of depression in general, Kuyken and Feldman now build on this foundation by showing, from clinical work with those who come for help for their depression, how it is through the cultivation of compassion that people can learn to change their perspective on and gain some freedom from long-lasting conditions that have previously been utterly disabling. Interestingly, there is now evidence that, even where a mindfulness-based intervention does not include specific lovingkindness or compassion practices, the instructors' own embodiment of these qualities in all aspects of their teaching of the curriculum and in their interactions—from the initial welcome to class, to the guiding of formal practices and the enquiry following it—enables participants to cultivate a compassionate response to their own suffering. Research has shown that the extent to which participants are able to cultivate such a compassionate response, where before there was self-denigration, underlies the effectiveness of the mindfulness programme in reducing risk of future depression (Kuyken et al. 2010).

Martine Batchelor's article places the recent developments in the clinical application of mindfulness in the context of her own experiences as a Korean Zen nun. She studied Zen Buddhism under the late Master Kusan Sunim and became his interpreter and translator. After his death she began to write extensively about what is core in Buddhist thought and practice. Her article tells how, in 1992, as part of her research for a book on women and Buddhism (*Walking on lotus flowers*, 1996 — re-issued as *Women on the Buddhist path*, 2001) in which she interviewed women from different Buddhist traditions (Asians and Westerners, nuns and laywomen) she discovered that 'the techniques of meditation they used did not seem to matter as much as their dedicated sincerity as practitioners of the Dharma'. She suggests that that no matter which Buddhist tradition we follow, the practice of samatha (calmness and stability) and vipassanā (insight) will lead to the cultivation of mindfulness.

She then builds on this analysis to make an even more radical suggestion: that examination of the 'four great efforts' described in the Mahasatipatthana Sutta extends the overarching umbrella of common intentions and discoveries within different Buddhist traditions to include the therapeutic approaches embodied within MBCT and MBSR, and even including traditional cognitive behavioural therapy. Each, she says, 'share a pragmatic, self-reliant approach to life that recognizes the great value of acceptance and compassion'.

Edel Maex gives himself a similar task in his article, but from the other end, so to speak. He came to Zen as a practising psychiatrist coping with the burdens of a busy clinic, and then, wishing to offer his patients something of the same insights and practices he had found so liberating, came upon the writings of Jon Kabat-Zinn. In Jon's book, Full Catastrophe Living (Kabat-Zinn 1990), he found something that, as his endearing down-to-earth language expresses it, would save him 10 years of work! Maex points out the dangers of taking mindfulness out of the Buddhist context: it runs the risk that instead of allowing patients to appreciate the power of the dharma experientially, it might become just another technique, stripped of all the very depth and wisdom that he feels carries the healing power inherent in mindfulness. What, then, was it that he noticed in this modern writing that he found authentic, both as a Zen practitioner and as a busy clinician?

He calls his article an exercise in 'back translating' some 'clinical' mindfulness concepts back to basic Buddhist concepts. His intention was to write for contemporary mindfulness teachers to help 'reconnect with some treasures that are present in our roots' and for his Zen friends and colleagues to reassure them that contemporary approaches have not thrown out the Dharma in a rush to be relevant. As he concludes: 'As the history of Buddhism shows, it is in a process of continual reformulation in accordance with the present needs of those in front of us'.

Sharon Salzberg contributes to the renewing of our intentions by reminding us in her article how mindfulness and lovingkindness are intrinsically cultivated together. Mindfulness is not just 'knowing what is happening', such as hearing a sound, but knowing it in a certain way — free of grasping, aversion and delusion. It is this freedom that provides the platform for more sustained transformation and insight. Mindfulness, she says, 'helps us break through the legends, the myths, the habits, the biases and the lies that can be woven around our lives. We can clear away the persistence of those distortions, and their familiarity, and come to much more clearly see for ourselves what is true. When we can see what is true, we can form our lives in a different way'. The refining and expanding of lovingkindness follows because deepening of insight includes seeing how all of our lives are inextricably interconnected, thus allowing an inclusiveness of caring. Sharon Salzberg does not just assert this—her paper embodies it, with a gentleness and humour in her stories and examples that invite us to respond.

Mindfulness in education and medicine: the challenge of institutional change

We started this Introduction by indicating how mindfulness has become popular very rapidly. A central catalyst to this growth has been the willingness to take teachings that had been handed down in monasteries in Asia over centuries, and then taught in retreat centres over several decades, into contexts such as hospitals and clinics that had not explicitly asked for them, or for that matter, knew of their existence. As we have seen from the contributions so far, bringing mindfulness to the world outside the monastery or retreat centre requires a constant translation and back-translation. This work is never finished, for systems and institutions and people change; different language, images and metaphors need to be sculpted, tried, refined, used and then discarded (at least for a while) when they lose their power to communicate.

This point is no better illustrated than by Miribai Bush who, in her article, draws on insights gathered from 13 years of leading the Center for Contemplative Mind in Society and its pioneering programme that encourages and supports the innovative integration of contemplative practices into novel courses and curricula across a wide range of settings in higher education. She describes courses integrating contemplative practices and perspectives across a diverse range of disciplines—from architecture to physics, from economics to poetry. Some are taught by Buddhist scholars; others by authorities within their own disciplines, each of whom has a personal meditation practice. Contemplative practices include various forms of meditation, yoga, and visualization as well as unique practices that have emerged from the disciplines themselves: in behavioural economics, for example, self-awareness practices reveal the unconscious emotions governing economic choices; in architecture, meditation encourages design of the built environment that harmonizes with the natural environment.

She discusses how the centre developed and still supports this movement, showing what questions this experience of contemplative education raises about its future impact on the academy. The article culminates in a wonderful summary of the 'languaging' of mindfulness in the classroom: how teachers have explored images and metaphors from the history or philosophy of their own discipline (for example, a science teacher teaching mindfulness of sound, talking of an 'acoustic ecology'). She shows how, in this way, the skilful and creative teacher can define and introduce practices in an accessible way that still resonate with the deep wisdom of the traditions from which they are drawn.

One institution of higher learning where mindfulness seemed, from the outside at least, to be securely established was the University of Massachusetts Medical Center, the institution where MBSR was originally developed. For this reason alone, the story that Saki Santorelli recounts in his article is extraordinary. In 1998, the University of Massachusetts Hospital, home of the Stress Reduction Clinic from its beginning in 1979, merged with another hospital. Several years later, due to severe budget constraints, the Stress Reduction Clinic was in one fell swoop eliminated from the clinical system. All of a sudden, the clinic that had, through the vision and hard work of so many people, developed a world-renowned reputation based on extensive clinical research, and that had transformed the lives of hundreds of thousands of people, either directly or indirectly, was threatened with extinction.

Saki Santorelli begins his elegantly told and electrifying story with an e-mail that anyone in a leadership position would dread receiving. It came three months after his assuming the directorship of the Center for Mindfulness. All of a sudden the heart of the entire enterprise, the Stress Reduction Clinic, was threatened, and along with it, everything else and all of the people who worked at the centre and had devoted their lives to the work. How to respond? Santorelli's essay reveals what mindfulness practice might mean—did mean—in such a situation of crisis, and we see in penetrating starkness how leadership is honed not in the good times only, but also when all apparent hope is exhausted, and there seems nothing left to do except to honour 'our innate capacity for residing in the raw, open heart and remembering the true source of wisdom and power.'

How can even a taste of such wisdom be transmitted to participants in a programme of classes lasting only eight weeks? It seems incredible. Yet the evidence, published in scientific journals around the world, suggests that participants, taught by instructors who themselves have learned to embody some of those qualities of which Saki Santorelli speaks, can and do experience transformation that they never imagined. Perhaps it is this that partly explains its enormous popularity and its increasing impact in the world.

Can we define, research, and measure mindfulness without denaturing it?

As already noted, the introduction of an ancient Buddhist meditation practice into mainstream medicine and other disciplines is perforce associated with a particular set of challenging circumstances related to the major cultural and epistemological shifts it inevitably engenders. Buddhist scholars, in particular, may feel that the essential meaning of mindfulness may have been exploited, or distorted, or abstracted from its essential ecological niche in ways that may threaten its deep meaning, its integrity, and its potential value. This may or may not be an inevitable cost of developing and operationalizing new and secular Dharma-based portals such as MBSR and MBCT, aimed at individuals whose lives might be transformed in some ways by authentic practice but who would never come to it if offered in a more traditional Buddhist framework or vocabulary. This theme emerged from Miribai Bush's description of the different languages in which scholars from different disciplines are teaching the relevance of mindfulness practice to their students, and it is a topic that is revisited again in Jon Kabat-Zinn's closing article.

Once mindfulness was introduced into clinical settings and into other disciplines such as higher education, and once it began to be evaluated scientifically, it was virtually inevitable that the very rules for gathering empirical evidence through scientific enquiry would require that new bridges be built between domains that previously may have had no prior communication or intellectual discourse. For instance, in psychology, there are rules about qualitative methods that govern what can and cannot be done when interviewing participants, and about what can be inferred from a transcript of such interviews. There are also rules about how to set up a trial to test quantitatively the claims of efficacy of a mindfulness programme. Building such bridges with an open mind can be a painful process for all concerned on both sides of any epistemological divide.

Paul Grossman and Nicholas Van Dam present an eloquent call for caution in this regard. They are particularly concerned that the rush to define mindfulness within Western psychology may wind up denaturing it in fundamental ways that may not even be guessed at by those who make use of the term in clinical and laboratory settings, that is, unless they are themselves deeply grounded in first person experience of the dharma through their own personal practice, study, and exploration. Their article first considers how many psychologists are currently characterizing mindfulness. They then explore the question of whether these characterizations are at all compatible with the original Buddhist teachings on mindfulness. They then consider whether scientific characterizations of mindfulness meet the empirical standards of contemporary scientific methodology. Their conclusion is that there is a great deal of fundamental work to be done in this area, that a fresh look at how we name the self-report questionnaires and their subscales that claim to measure the construct of 'mindfulness' might be in order, and that caution and patience are needed 'lest we reify and trivialize concepts that may have a richness of which we cannot yet be fully aware'.

Ruth Baer's paper presents a cogent and empirically powerful alternative perspective. She articulates the fundamental challenge presented to us by evidence-based medicine and psychology: that we need to see if it is possible to work out why something that appears to bring about change is doing so, and therefore to explore by whatever valid methods we have at our disposal what processes may underlie it. This is important because most therapies have some beneficial effects that have little to do with what the clinician actually believes is the critical ingredient. It is the oft-maligned and underappreciated placebo effect. The placebo effect is one of the most powerful effects in medicine. In general, teachers and therapists are reluctant to acknowledge its potential influence, because we'd all prefer that it was the teaching and therapy we offered that was life-transforming to our patients. Research into what is actually the case can be very sobering.

So Baer asks: how is this investigation to be done and what is actually learned if we do not take up the challenge of actually attempting to assess a person's understanding or depth of mindfulness practice (at least as it is taught in a clinical mindfulness-based programme or intervention), and then evaluate whether training leads to change in these qualities and in the general tendency to respond mindfully to the experiences of daily life? If this could be done, might we also see whether any such changes are correlated with the improvements in mental health that are often observed? Her paper elegantly summarizes the quest for and development of reliable and valid mindfulness questionnaires, and the research to date on how useful they may or may not be, and the on-going challenges of their interpretation.

Traditional teaching and contemporary application revisited

The last two articles bring us full circle to the connection between traditional teachings and contemporary applications.

Rupert Gethin revisits some traditional Buddhist sources to see how they understand mindfulness, exploring how their understanding fits—or does not—with some of the ways mindfulness is now presented in the context of mindfulness-based interventions. Starting with well-known sources such as the Satipaṭṭhānasutta, he moves on to pay more attention to some of the details of the understanding of mindfulness in later Buddhist systematic thought. These details, though less well known, provide important clues about traditional Buddhist approaches to the cultivation of mindfulness. In particular, he explores the notion of mindfulness as 'non-judgmental'. He very cogently maps out the full range of the territory and potential issues at the interface of the converging epistemological streams:

> How one views the adaptation of Buddhist mindfulness practice to a modern clinical context for the treatment of stress and depression will depend on one's particular perspective. From one sort of Buddhist perspective, the abstraction of mindfulness from its context within a broad range of Buddhist meditative practices might seem like an appropriation and distortion of traditional Buddhism that loses sight of the Buddhist goal of rooting out greed, hatred and delusion. From a different Buddhist perspective, it might seem to be an example of 'skill in means' (upāya-kauśalya): it provides a way of giving beings the opportunity to make a first and important initial step on the path that leads to the cessation of suffering. From yet another perhaps still Buddhist perspective that might be characterized as 'modernist', it strips Buddhism of some of its unnecessary historical and cultural baggage, focusing on what is essential and useful. A non-Buddhist perspective might regard the removal of the unnecessary historical and cultural baggage as finally revealing

the useful essence that had hitherto been obscured by the Buddhist religion. Finally we might regard the coming together of practices derived from Buddhism with the methods of modern western cognitive science as affording a true advance that supersedes and renders redundant the traditional Buddhist practices. As observers of social history, we might also see it as an example of a change from a cultural situation where we turn to religion to heal our souls to one where we turn to medicine and science.

Jon Kabat-Zinn's concluding essay recounts some strands of the history of how MBSR came into being from his own personal perspective, and emphasizes his view of the opportunities and dangers associated with attempts to bring the Dharma in its most universal expression into the mainstream culture and its institutions in ways that have the potential to catalyse profound learning, growing, healing and transformation. From the beginning, the aim was to contribute to a shifting of the bell curve of the society toward greater levels of sanity, well-being, and kindness, engendering what he terms elsewhere (Kabat-Zinn 2005) an 'orthogonal rotation in consciousness' in both individuals and institutions, both locally and globally. He touches on a theme that Miribai Bush also brings up in her paper, namely the question of the very language we use when we speak about mindfulness. Terminology and emphasis have always changed over time as the Dharma entered new cultures, and this is happening once again in our era. One question that arises is how we consciously use language in teaching mindfulness, including the implicational dimensions so elegantly evoked and described in the second paper by Teasdale and Chaskelson. How might we expand the meaning of a term such as 'mindfulness' in the English language so that it may sometimes carry the meaning of 'the Dharma' in its entirety, as Kabat-Zinn suggests? Is it possible to do so authentically, without falling into delusion or ignorance? Can it be a skilful approach for catalysing a more universal and hopefully still authentic and liberative understanding of the mind and its potential for wisdom, compassion, and freedom? Can such an approach be effective in both recognizing and mobilizing our individual capacities as human beings to realize the full dimensionality of our being, what some call our true nature, in this lifetime?

This, of course, was the intended purpose in introducing the term mindfulness into mainstream medicine in the first place. One risk is that some may have surmised that 'mindfulness' was being decontextualized, and promulgated as the only important element in Buddhist practice. Kabat-Zinn directly addresses this issue in his paper, and suggests that rather than a decontextualizion of the Dharma, MBSR is an attempt to recontextualize it in its essential fullness. Had MBSR employed traditional Buddhist language, or insisted that medical patients referred by their doctors to the Stress Reduction Clinic because of their suffering be introduced to the practice of mindfulness through the explicit framework of the Four Noble Truths, the Eightfold Noble Path, and the Four Foundations of Mindfulness, for example, it may very well have prevented MBSR and other interventions in medicine and psychology from taking root in the first place.

Such a perspective may have some relevance to the debates and differing views expressed in this special issue. Now that there is widespread interest and activity in mindfulness and its potential applications in secular life, the kind of close examination and potential clarification of the various traditional dimensions, attributes, virtues, and implications of the various elements of mindfulness that are being articulated and discussed in this forum, a first of its kind, become important, in fact, absolutely necessary, for the deepening and flourishing of the field as a whole.

Concluding remarks

Mindfulness, as it is taught in mindfulness-based interventions, has always been associated with the elements of what are technically known as clear comprehension and discernment. It is not merely bare attention, although bare attending is an intimate part of it. Nor is it merely conceptual, cognitive, or thought-based. Indeed, in essence, it is awareness itself, an entirely different and one might say, larger capacity than thought, since any and all thought and emotion can be held in awareness. Both are powerful dimensions of the human experience. While we get a great deal of training in our education systems in thinking of all kinds, we have almost no exposure to the cultivation of intimacy with that other innate capacity of ours that we call awareness. Awareness is virtually transparent to us. We tend to be unaware of our awareness. We so easily take it for granted. It rarely occurs to us that it is possible to systematically explore and refine our relationship to awareness itself, or that it can be 'inhabited.' This is a profound area for both first person and third person investigation and debate.

In the cultivation of mindfulness in secular settings, a spirit of self-inquiry and self-understanding is central. This is one reason why we take pleasure in the coming together of Buddhist scholars, scientists, educators and clinicians in this format and are optimistic about its value. Our hope is that this kind of scholarly inquiry and cross-discipline dialogue will continue and will yield new fruit, and nourish our ongoing understanding and practice of the meditative disciplines that rest firmly on a foundation of respect for the traditional understandings of dharma and value remaining faithful to those understandings in new and appropriate ways.

The enormous interest in mindfulness theory and practice within western science, medicine, healthcare and education will continually bring new challenges and also new opportunities. Ancient and modern, Eastern and Western modes of inquiry and investigation are now in conversation and cross-fertilizing each other as never before. Indeed, we could say the field of mindfulness-based applications is in its infancy and there is great promise that it will continue to yield new insights and avenues for research as it develops in multiple directions. For example, there are western psychologists who are using new methodologies to show how the mind and body generate both delusion and clarity. Consider the phenomenon of change blindness. Studies show that, when someone's view of a person is occluded for a second or two, he or she may not realize that a new person has taken the place of the original one, even as the conversation continues (Simons and Levine 1998). Or consider experiments showing that if you are induced to inadvertently nod your head when listening to a view being expressed, you are more likely to endorse that view later without knowing that your opinion was experimentally manipulated (Briñol and Petty 2003; Wells and Petty 1980); or the recent findings showing that conceptual processing can have extraordinarily maladaptive consequences, such as making someone with an eating disorder feel that they are heavier than they really are (Rawal, Park, and Williams 2011).

All these studies are compelling demonstrations of the mind's capacity to delude itself. None needs an explicitly dharma-based interpretation; yet all are consistent with a dharma-based perspective, and provide important examples and potential insights into the ways of one's own mind for people who will never read a Buddhist text. In their own way, these lines of research speak to the importance of paying attention without forgetfulness and with compassion to the mind's capacity to fool us moment by moment.

The essays in this book bear witness to the need for constant inquiry, translation, renewal, and dialogue. We might say that the teachings are actually kept alive by our continual willingness to test them out. If they become dogma, they may give false comfort for a while to some, but they are likely to ossify, creating needless disputes and losing their enlivening and liberative potential. A dried flower can be very beautiful, but it is no use to a bee.

As co-editors, our role in this Introduction has been to introduce the original aim of this book and give you a taste of its contents from a diverse and passionate group of contributors. Our aim has been equally to preview a few of the creative tensions inherent in an enterprise of this scope and magnitude and make them explicit. For it is precisely from within the 'tension' between the Buddhadharma, with all its highly developed and diverse traditions and lineages, and what we might call a 'lived universal dharma' in an everyday idiom, that the potential for insight, healing, and transformation emerges—a transformation that can be seen, day after day, in those who come to mindfulness-based clinical programmes seeking help with their suffering, and who, through their cultivation of mindfulness and their implicit exposure to the Dharma, even if they have never heard the word, experience profound changes that continue to astonish and humble all involved.

NOTE

1 This meeting was organized, with the support of the Fetzer Institute, by Richard Davidson, Zindel Segal and Amishi Jha.

REFERENCES

BRIÑOL, P., and R. E. PETTY. 2003. Overt head movements and persuasion: A self-validation analysis. *Journal of Personality and Social Psychology* 84: 1123-39.

KABAT-ZINN, J. 1990. *Full catastrophe living: Using the wisdom of your body and mind to face stress, pain and illness.* New York: Dell, (15th anniversary ed., 2005.).

KABAT-ZINN, J., and DAVIDSON, R. J., eds. 2011. *The mind's own physician: A scientific dialogue with the Dalai Lama on the healing power of meditation.* Oakland, CA: New Harbinger.

KUYKEN, W., E. R. WATKINS, E. R. HOLDEN, K. WHITE, R. S. TAYLOR, S. BYFORD, A. EVANS, S. RADFORD, J. D. TEASDALE, and T. DALGLEISH. 2010. How does mindfulness-based cognitive therapy work? *Behaviour Research and Therapy* 48: 1105-12.

LUTZ, A., J.-P. LACHAUX, J. MARTINERIE, and F. J. VARELA. 2002. Guiding the study of brain dynamics by using first-person data: Synchrony patterns correlate with ongoing conscious states during a simple visual task. *Proceedings of the National Academy of Sciences USA* 99: 1586-91.

LUTZ, A., J. P. DUNNE, and R. J. DAVIDSON. 2007. Meditation and the neuroscience of consciousness: An introduction. In *Cambridge handbook of consciousness*, edited by P. Zelazo, M. Moscovitch, and E. Thompson. New York: Cambridge University Press.

RAWAL, A., R. PARK, and J. M. G. WILLIAMS. 2011. Effects of analytical and experiential self-focus on stress-induced cognitive reactivity in eating disorder psychopathology. *Behaviour Research and Therapy* 49(10), 635-45

SIMONS, DANIEL J., and DANIEL T. LEVIN. 1998. Failure to detect changes to people during a real-world interaction. *Psychonomic Bulletin and Review* 5: 644-9.

THOMPSON, E. 2007. *Mind in life: Biology, phenomenology, and the sciences of mind.* Cambridge, MA: Harvard University Press.

VARELA, F. J., E. THOMPSON, and E. ROACH. 1991. *The embodied mind: Cognitive science and the human experience.* Cambridge, MA: MIT Press.

VARELA, F. J., and J. SHEAR. 1999. First-person accounts: Why, what, and how. In *The view from within: First-person approaches to the study of consciousness,* ed. F. J. Varela and J. Shear. Thorverton, UK: Imprint Academic.

WELLS, G. L., and R. E. PETTY. 1980. The effects of overt head movement on persuasion: Compatibility and incompatibility of responses. *Basic and Applied Social Psychology* 1: 219-30.

WHAT DOES MINDFULNESS REALLY MEAN? A CANONICAL PERSPECTIVE

Bhikkhu Bodhi

The purpose of this paper is to determine the meaning and function of mindfulness meditation using as the source of inquiry the Pāli Canon, the oldest complete collection of Buddhist texts to survive intact. Mindfulness is the chief factor in the practice of satipaṭṭhāna, the best known system of Buddhist meditation. In descriptions of satipaṭṭhāna two terms constantly recur: mindfulness (sati) and clear comprehension (sampajañña). An understanding of these terms based on the canonical texts is important not only from a philological angle but because such understanding has major bearings on the actual practice of meditation. The word sati originally meant 'memory,' but the Buddha ascribed to this old term a new meaning determined by the aims of his teaching. This meaning, the author holds, might best be characterized as 'lucid awareness.' He questions the common explanation of mindfulness as 'bare attention,' pointing out problems that lurk behind both words in this expression. He also briefly discusses the role of clear comprehension (sampajañña) and shows that it serves as a bridge between the observational function of mindfulness and the development of insight. Finally, he takes up the question whether mindfulness can legitimately be extracted from its traditional context and employed for secular purposes. He maintains that such non-traditional applications of mindfulness are acceptable and even admirable on the ground that they help alleviate human suffering, but he also cautions against a reductionist understanding of mindfulness and urges that investigators respect the religious tradition in which it is rooted.

1. Mindfulness in the Buddhist path

The entry of systematic mindfulness practice into the fields of stress reduction and psychotherapy has dramatically altered modern medicine's perspectives on our capacity to regulate and overcome our human vulnerabilities. Mindfulness made its debut as a therapeutic discipline in 1979, when Jon Kabat-Zinn introduced his programme of 'Mindfulness-Based Stress Reduction' at the University of Massachusetts Medical Center. Since then its use to reduce pain and stress has been adopted by hundreds of medical centers, hospitals, and clinics around the world. The application of mindfulness in clinical settings has spread beyond stress reduction to psychotherapy, where it has proven a potent tool for helping patients deal with conditions such as depression, anxiety, and obsessive-compulsive disorders.

While the use of mindfulness for medical purposes may initially seem to be a modern innovation, its roots actually go back 25 centuries to the teaching of the Buddha, who lived and taught in northeast India in the fifth century BC. The Buddha offered his teaching, called the *Dhamma* (Sanskrit *Dharma*), not as a set of doctrines demanding belief but as a body of principles and practices that sustain human beings in their quest for happiness and spiritual freedom. At its heart lies a system of training that leads to insight and the overcoming of suffering. This training spread throughout Asia along with Buddhism itself, and as Buddhism sent down roots in different lands, various lines of meditation flourished in the countries where its teachings were embraced. Many of these lineages have continued down to the present day, preserved in monasteries and hermitages by monks and nuns dedicated to the contemplative life.

In the late 1960s and 1970s, cheaper jet travel facilitated a cultural exchange that would have far-reaching consequences. Asian teachers of Buddhism, yoga, and other spiritual disciplines came to the US and attracted followings of young people disenchanted with materialism, militarism, and the flatlands of modernity. Young westerners also travelled to Asia and studied meditation with Buddhist masters, and then on returning to their home countries began to share what they had learned with their fellow countrymen. As meditation gained in popularity, it caught the attention of medical professionals, neuroscientists, and psychotherapists, setting off an exciting conversation between practitioners of eastern spirituality and western science.

At the heart of all classical systems of Buddhist meditation is a particular discipline that has come to be known as mindfulness. The Buddha himself gave particular prominence to mindfulness by including it in the noble eightfold path, the fourth of the Four Noble Truths into which he compressed his teaching: suffering, its origin, its cessation, and the way leading to its cessation. Right mindfulness (*sammā sati*) is the seventh factor of the path where, wedged between right effort and right concentration, it connects the energetic application of the mind to its stilling and unification.

The Buddha's discourses, as preserved in the Pāli Nikāyas, the early collections, employ a mnemonically terse formulaic style. We thus find right mindfulness consistently defined by a fixed formula that runs as follows:

> And what, monks, is right mindfulness? Here, a monk dwells contemplating the body in the body, ardent, clearly comprehending, mindful, having removed covetousness and displeasure in regard to the world. He dwells contemplating feelings in feelings ... contemplating mind in mind ... contemplating phenomena in phenomena, ardent, clearly comprehending, mindful, having removed covetousness and displeasure in regard to the world. This is called right mindfulness.[1]

The most influential text in the Pāli Canon on the systematic practice of mindfulness, the *Satipaṭṭhāna Sutta*, the 'Discourse on the Establishment of Mindfulness,' opens with a proclamation highlighting both the purpose of this training and its methodology:

> Monks, this is the one-way path for the purification of beings, for the overcoming of sorrow and lamentation, for the passing away of pain and displeasure, for the achievement of the method, for the realization of *nibbāna*, that is, the four establishments of mindfulness. What four? Here, a monk dwells contemplating the body in the body ... feelings in feelings ... mind in mind ... phenomena in phenomena, ardent, clearly comprehending, mindful, having removed covetousness and displeasure in regard to the world. This, monks, is the one-way path for the purification of beings ... for the realization of *nibbāna*, that is, the four establishments of mindfulness.[2]

In this statement, the Buddha indicates the *goal* of the practice to be the extinction of suffering and the attainment of *nibbāna* (Sanskrit *nirvāṇa*), a state of transcendent bliss and peace. The *method* is the four *satipaṭṭhānas*, the four establishments of mindfulness. From the formula for right mindfulness, we can deduce two important facts about the practice, one pertaining to its objective side, the other to its subjective side. On the objective side, we see that right mindfulness involves the reflexive contemplation of one's own experience, subsumed under the four objective domains of the body, feelings, states of mind, and experiential phenomena. The last of these is, in Pāli, called *dhammā*, a word which we can understand to designate experiential phenomena as organized into certain groups determined by the objectives of the Buddha's teaching, '*the* Dhamma' in the broadest sense.

On the subjective side, the formula shows that the 'establishment of mindfulness' involves not only mindfulness but a constellation of mental factors that work in unison. Mindfulness, in the context of *satipaṭṭhāna* practice, always occurs as part of an *anupassanā*, a word that further clarifies its role. We usually translate *anupassanā* as 'contemplation,' but it might also be illuminating to understand it more literally as an act of 'observation.' The word is made up of the prefix *anu,* which suggests repetition or closeness, and the base *passanā*, which means 'seeing.' Thus mindfulness is part of a process that involves a close, repetitive observation of the object.

In the '*satipaṭṭhāna* refrain' several mental factors enter into this *anupassanā*, indicated by the phrase 'ardent, clearly comprehending, and mindful' (*ātāpi sampajāno satimā*). Each of these words, according to the classical commentaries, represents a specific mental factor. 'Ardent' (*ātāpī*) implies energy, the strength to engage in the practice. Mindfulness (*sati*) is the element of watchfulness, the lucid awareness of each event that presents itself on the successive occasions of experience. The cognitive factor is indicated by the word *sampajāno*, 'clearly comprehending,' an adjective related to the noun *sampajañña*, 'clear comprehension.'

The two terms, *sato* and *sampajāno*, often occur in proximity, implying a close affinity between their respective nouns, *sati* or mindfulness and *sampajañña* or clear comprehension. To distinguish the two, I would describe mindfulness as lucid awareness of the phenomenal field. This element of lucid awareness prevails in the initial stages of the practice. But with the strengthening of mindfulness, clear comprehension supervenes and adds the cognitive element. In the practice of insight meditation, the meditator clearly comprehends the nature and qualities of arisen phenomena and relates them to the framework defined by the parameters of the Dhamma, the teaching as an organic whole. The expression 'clearly comprehending' thus suggests that the meditator not only observes phenomena but *interprets* the presentational field in a way that sets arisen phenomena in a meaningful context. As the practice advances, clear comprehension takes on an increasingly more important role, eventually evolving into direct insight (*vipassanā*) and wisdom (*paññā*).

2. The meaning of *sati*

A problem in hermeneutics, with intimate bearings on the actual practice of meditation, concerns the exact meaning of the word *sati* both in general and in relation to Buddhist contemplative activity. We take the rendering 'mindfulness' so much for granted that we rarely inquire into the precise nuances of the English term, let alone the meaning of the original Pāli word it represents and the adequacy of the former as a rendering for the latter. The word 'mindfulness' is itself so vague and elastic that it serves almost as a cipher into which we can read virtually anything we want. Hence we seldom recognize that the word was chosen as a rendering for *sati* at a particular point in time, after other terms had been tried and found inadequate.

In Indian psychology apart from Buddhism, the word *smṛti*, the Sanskrit equivalent of Pāli *sati*, normally means memory. Thus Monier-Williams, in his Sanskrit-English Dictionary, defines *smṛti* as 'remembrance, reminiscence, thinking of or upon, calling to mind ... memory.'[3] The Buddha's discourses, too, still preserve this meaning in certain contexts, as we will see. But we should not give this excessive importance. When devising a terminology that could convey the salient points and practices of his own teaching, the Buddha inevitably had to draw on the vocabulary available to him. To designate the practice that became the main pillar of his meditative system, he chose the word *sati*. But here *sati* no longer means memory. Rather, the Buddha assigned the word a new meaning consonant with his own system of psychology and meditation. Thus it would be a fundamental mistake to insist on reading the old meaning of memory into the new context.

It would not be a mistake, however, to try to determine how the word *sati* acquired its new application on the basis of the older meaning. Unfortunately for us, the Nikāyas or early discourse collections do not formally define *sati* in the clear expository manner that we are accustomed to finding in modern textbooks or in scholarly studies of meditation practice. For four centuries, the Buddhist scriptures were preserved and transmitted orally, from one generation of reciters to the next. This method of transmission required that the compilers of the Buddha's discourses compress the main points into simple repetitive formulas that were conducive to easy memorization. Thus when we consult the texts to find out what they mean by *sati*, what we mostly encounter, instead of lucid explanations, are *operational demonstrations* that indicate, in practical terms, how *sati* functions in Buddhist psychology and meditation practice. It is from these that we must tease out the word's implications, testing them against each other and evaluating them by personal reflection and experience.

The first scholar, it seems, to render *sati* as 'mindfulness' was the great British translator T. W. Rhys Davids, founder of the Pali Text Society. His comment in the introduction to his translation of the *Mahāsatipaṭṭhāna Sutta* still shows remarkable acumen:

> Etymologically Sati is Memory. But as happened at the rise of Buddhism to so many other expressions in common use, a new connotation was then attached to the word, a connotation that gave a new meaning to it, and renders 'memory' a most inadequate and misleading translation. It became the memory, recollection, calling-to-mind, being-aware-of, certain specified facts. Of these the most important was the impermanence (the coming to be as the result of a cause, and the passing away again) of all phenomena, bodily and mental. And it included the repeated application of this awareness, to each experience of life, from the ethical point of view.[4]

The Nikāyas employ two recurrent formulas to illustrate the meaning of *sati*. One harkens back to the old meaning of memory; the other refers to its occurrence in relation to the four *satipaṭṭhānas*. We meet the first in SN 48:9, which provides an analysis of the five spiritual faculties: faith, energy, mindfulness, concentration, and wisdom. The *sutta* briefly defines each with a short formula, the 'faculty of mindfulness' (*satindriya*) as follows:

> And what, monks, is the faculty of mindfulness? Here, the noble disciple is mindful, possessing supreme mindfulness and alertness, one who remembers and recollects what was done and said long ago. This is called the faculty of mindfulness.[5]

The operative expression in Pāli here is *saritā anussaritā*, 'one who remembers and recollects.' Both words are agent nouns derived from the verb *sarati*, 'to remember' or 'to be mindful'; the first is simple, the second is prefixed with *anu*. While the two words, taken in isolation, might be interpreted as referring either to remembrance or mindfulness, the phrase 'what was done and said long ago' (*cirakatampi cirabhāsitampi*) favours interpreting *sati* here in terms of memory.

However, in the next *sutta*, SN 48:10, the five faculties are defined again. The faculty of mindfulness is first defined, as in the preceding *sutta*, as the ability to recollect what was done and said long ago. But then, as if admitting that this definition is inadequate, the text adds the stock formula on the four establishments of mindfulness: 'He dwells contemplating the body in the body ... phenomena in phenomena, ardent, clearly comprehending, mindful, having removed covetousness and displeasure in regard to the world. This is called the faculty of mindfulness.'[6] This indicates that the compilers of the texts were not satisfied with the simple definition in terms of memory but felt the need to supplement it with another definition that underscores its connection with meditation practice. The next *sutta*, SN 48:11, raises the question: 'What is the faculty of mindfulness?' and answers: 'The mindfulness that one obtains on the basis of the four establishments of mindfulness: this is called the faculty of mindfulness.'[7] Here, *sati* as memory is not brought in at all. One might suggest that *sati* as mindfulness, in the sense of a lucid awareness of the present, enables *sati* to function as memory. While this may be factually true, the texts themselves make no such suggestion but simply juxtapose the two formulations without explanation.

We find this ambivalence in the meaning of *sati* emerge from two otherwise parallel expositions on the seven factors of enlightenment (*satta bojjhaṅga*). The first enlightenment factor is mindfulness (*satisambojjhaṅga*), which is followed in order by investigation, energy, joy, tranquility, concentration, and equanimity. The earlier *sutta*, SN 46:3, opens with the Buddha praising the benefits of associating with monks fully accomplished in the training, one benefit being that a monk gets to hear the Dhamma from them. Having heard the Dhamma from them, 'the monk recollects that Dhamma and thinks it over. By doing so, on that occasion the monk arouses, develops, and fulfills the enlightenment factor of mindfulness.'[8] In this passage, invisible in the English translation, mindfulness (*sati*) as an enlightenment factor is derived from the act of recollecting and reflecting on the teaching one has heard. The two verbs used are *anussarati* and *anuvitakketi*. The first is an augmented form of *sarati*, 'to remember,' from which the noun *sati* is derived; the second is the basis for the noun *vitakka*, thought or reflection. The discourse continues through the other six factors of enlightenment and ends with the fruits of the practice.

Taken on its own, this text seems to reinforce the interpretation of *sati* as the exercise of memory. However, in another *sutta*, SN 54:13, the Buddha treats each of the four establishments of mindfulness as a springboard to the seven factors of enlightenment. And so, when a monk 'dwells contemplating the body in the body ... phenomena in phenomena, on that occasion the monk arouses, develops, and fulfills the enlightenment factor of mindfulness.'[9] Once mindfulness has arisen, the other factors of enlightenment arise in turn, culminating in 'true knowledge and liberation.' This text has the same scaffolding as the earlier one, but here the enlightenment factor of mindfulness emerges *not* from memory, *not* from recollecting teachings that one has heard, but from direct contemplation of the body, feelings, mind, and experiential phenomena.

There is one Pāli word used by the commentaries to clarify the meaning of *sati* which, I think, testifies to an attempt to underscore the new role being assigned to it. This word is *upaṭṭhāna*. *Upaṭṭhāna* means, firstly, 'setting up, establishing,' which is what one does with mindfulness. Already in the Nikāyas the word is closely connected with *sati*. The compound *satipaṭṭhāna* is itself composed of *sati* and *upaṭṭhāna*. The four *satipaṭṭhānas* are the four *establishments* of mindfulness, a process *of setting up* mindfulness, distinguished as fourfold by way of its objective domains. This analysis indicates that to establish mindfulness is not to set about remembering something that occurred in the past, but to adopt a particular stance towards one's present experience. I characterize this as a stance of *observation* or *watchfulness* towards one's own experience. One might even call the stance of *sati* a 'bending back' of the light of consciousness upon the experiencing subject in its physical, sensory, and psychological dimensions. This act of 'bending back' serves to illuminate the events occurring in these domains, lifting them out from the twilight zone of unawareness into the light of clear cognition.

The sense of 'presence' pertaining to the word *upaṭṭhāna* comes out more explicitly in a canonical exegetical work called the *Paṭisambhidāmagga*, which glosses each of the five faculties with another term through which it is to be 'directly known' (*abhiññeyyaṃ*). Thus the faculty of faith is to be directly known as conviction; the faculty of energy, as exertion; the faculty of mindfulness, as presence (*upaṭṭhānaṭṭhena satindriyaṃ*); the faculty of concentration, as non-distraction; and the faculty of wisdom, as seeing.[10] Here, *sati* is equated with *upaṭṭhāna* not in the sense that the meditator 'establishes mindfulness,' but in the sense that mindfulness is itself an act of establishing presence. Mindfulness establishes the presence of the object and thereby makes it available to scrutiny and discernment.

This interpretation brings out the impact the practice of *sati* has on its objective field. On the one hand, we might say that it brackets the 'objectification' of the object that occurs in our everyday interactions with the world, whereby we treat objects as things 'out there' subservient to our pragmatic purposes. On the other hand, *sati* makes the objective field 'present' to awareness as an expanse of phenomena exhibiting their own distinctive phenomenal characteristics, as well as patterns and structures common to all conditioned phenomena. The net effect is to make the objective field clearly available for inspection. The *Visuddhimagga* supports this hypothesis when it states that *sati* has as its manifestation 'directly facing the objective domain' (*visayābhimukhabhāvapaccupaṭṭhānā*).[11] We might characterize mindfulness in this sense, in the simplest terms, as *lucid awareness*.[12]

I believe it is this aspect of *sati* that provides the connection between its two primary canonical meanings: as memory and as lucid awareness of present happenings. *Sati* makes the apprehended object stand forth vividly and distinctly before the mind. When the object being cognized pertains to the past—when it is apprehended as something that was formerly done, perceived, or spoken—its vivid presentation takes the form of memory. When the object is a bodily process like in-and-out breathing or the act of walking back and forth, or when it is a mental event like a feeling or thought, its vivid presentation takes the form of lucid awareness of the present.

In the Pāli *suttas*, *sati* has still other roles in relation to meditation but these reinforce its characterization in terms of lucid awareness and vivid presentation. For example, the texts include as types of mindfulness recollection of the Buddha (*buddhānussati*), contemplation of the repulsiveness of the body (*asubhasaññā*), and mindfulness of death (*maraṇassati*); for each brings its objective domain vividly before the mind. The *Metta Sutta* even refers to meditation on loving-kindness as a kind of mindfulness.[13] In each of these cases, the object is a conceptual phenomenon—the qualities of the Buddha, the repulsiveness of the body, the inevitability of death, or lovable living beings—yet the mental pose that attends to them is designated mindfulness. What unites them, from the side of the subject, is the lucidity and vivacity of the act of awareness, and from the side of the object, its vivid presentation.

Apart from the meditative context, *sati* enters the noble eightfold path in another role that cannot be overlooked if we are to determine its exact meaning. This is as a guarantor of the correct practice of all the other path factors. MN 117 draws distinctions between the wrong (*micchā*) and right (*sammā*) versions of the first five path factors, from views to livelihood. After making each distinction, it then explains how right view, right effort, and right mindfulness occur in association with each path factor. Taking right intention as an example, the text reads: 'One understands wrong intention as it is and right intention as it is; this is one's right view .... One makes an effort to abandon wrong intention and to acquire right intention: this is one's right effort. Mindfully one abandons wrong intention and mindfully one acquires and dwells in right intention: this is one's right mindfulness.'[14] The same stipulation is laid down with regard to the other factors, including right speech, right action, and right livelihood, thus ensuring that one mindfully embraces the ethical constituents of the path.

This explanation makes problematic the common interpretation of mindfulness as a type of awareness intrinsically devoid of discrimination, evaluation, and judgment. While such a depiction of mindfulness has gained currency in the popular literature on meditation, it does not square well with the canonical texts and may even lead to a distorted view of how mindfulness is to be practiced. There are certainly occasions when the cultivation of mindfulness requires the practitioner to suspend discrimination, evaluation, and judgment, and to adopt instead a stance of simple observation. However, to fulfill its role as an *integral* member of the eightfold path mindfulness has to work in unison with right view and right effort. This means that the practitioner of mindfulness must at times evaluate mental qualities and intended deeds, make judgments about them, and engage in purposeful action. In conjunction with right view, mindfulness enables the practitioner to distinguish wholesome qualities from unwholesome ones, good deeds from bad deeds, beneficial states of mind from harmful states. In conjunction with right effort, it promotes the removal of unwholesome mental qualities and the acquisition of wholesome qualities. It is only in this way that the practice of mindfulness can lay a foundation for correct wisdom to arise and extirpate the roots of suffering.

3. Mindfulness and bare attention

Many commentators who teach and practice in the contemporary vipassana movement have sought to convey the experiential flavour of mindfulness by means of the expression 'bare attention.' With certain reservations (which I will discuss below), I believe this characterization is acceptable if understood as a *procedural directive* for cultivating mindfulness in accordance with certain methods. It helps a novice meditator who has newly embarked on this unfamiliar enterprise get a grip on the appropriate way to observe the phenomenal field. The purpose of the expression would then be seen as pragmatic rather than doctrinal, as pedagogical rather than definitive.

When, however, it is considered in the light of canonical sources, it is hard to see 'bare attention' as a valid *theoretical* description of mindfulness applicable to all its modalities. As I showed earlier, mindfulness is a versatile mental quality that can be developed in a variety of ways. While certain methods emphasize a type of awareness that might be pragmatically described as 'bare attention,' in the full spectrum of Buddhist meditation techniques this is only one among a number of alternative ways to cultivate mindfulness many of which are not shy about utilizing conceptual thought and an explicit scheme of values. We saw above that mindfulness can be developed by attending to the repulsiveness of the body, contemplating death, and pervading beings with loving-kindness. What unites all these—as well as bare attention—is a quality of lucid awareness that allows the object to stand forth with a vivid and distinct presence.

A further problem that arises when the expression 'bare attention' is taken to be more than a pedagogical device is that it involves a crossing of technical terms that in a rigorous deployment of Buddhist terminology should be kept apart. One influential attempt to establish a theoretical equivalency between mindfulness and 'bare attention' is a passage in Ven. Henepola Gunaratana's popular book, *Mindfulness in Plain English,* often cited on the internet. Here we find mindfulness identified with the brief moment of preconceptual awareness that, in Buddhist cognitive theory, precedes the onset of conceptual determination:

> When you first become aware of something, there is a fleeting instant of pure awareness just before you conceptualize the thing, before you identify it. That is a state of awareness. Ordinarily, this state is short-lived. It is that flashing split second just as you focus your eyes on the thing, just as you focus your mind on the thing, just before you objectify it, clamp down on it mentally, and segregate it from the rest of existence. It takes place just before you start thinking about it—before your mind says, 'Oh, it's a dog.' *That flowing, soft-focused moment of pure awareness is mindfulness* . . . . That original moment of mindfulness is rapidly

passed over. It is the purpose of vipassana meditation to train us to prolong that moment of awareness.[15]

A little later, the author emphasizes the non-conceptual, non-discursive quality of mindfulness, which he explicitly identifies with bare attention:

> Mindfulness is nonconceptual awareness. Another English term for *sati* is 'bare attention.' It is not thinking. It does not get involved with thought or concepts .... It is, rather, the direct and immediate experiencing of whatever is happening, without the medium of thought. It comes before thought in the perceptual process.[16]

These passages seem to conflate two mental functions that, in classical Buddhist accounts of cognition, are regarded as distinct. One is the immediate preconceptual apprehension of an object that occurs as soon as the object comes into range of cognition. This act occurs automatically and spontaneously. It is ethically indeterminate, common to the thief and the saint, the toddler and the thinker, the sensualist and the yogi. Mindfulness, in contrast, does not occur automatically but is a quality to be cultivated (*bhāvetabba*). It arises when the cognitive processing of the object is already well underway and, far from being spontaneous, comes into being through a deliberate effort. It also has an ethical function, being part and parcel of the attempt to eliminate the unwholesome and establish the wholesome.

Since mindfulness plays the key role in such meditations as recollection of the Buddha, the perception of the body's repulsiveness, and mindfulness of death, it is also hard to see how mindfulness can be essentially non-conceptual and non-discursive. In certain types of mindfulness practice, conceptualization and discursive thought may be suspended in favour of non-conceptual observation, but there is little evidence in the Pāli Canon and its commentaries that mindfulness *by its very nature* is devoid of conceptualization. In some types of mindfulness practice emphasis falls on simple observation of what is occurring in the present, in others less so.

Even in the simple observational stance, there is a dichotomy in how mindfulness is applied. Mindfulness may be focused on a single point of observation, as in mindfulness of breathing, especially when developed for the purpose of attaining concentration (*samādhi*). But mindfulness may also be open and undirected, accessing whatever phenomena appear, especially when applied for the purpose of developing insight (*vipassanā*). Still other types of mindfulness practice make extensive use of conceptualization and discursive thought, but apply them in a different way than in ordinary thinking. Instead of allowing thought to drift at random, governed by defiled emotions, habit patterns, and practical survival needs, the meditator deliberately uses thought and concepts to keep the object before the mind.

To my knowledge, the first person to use the expression 'bare attention' to characterize mindfulness was the elder German monk, Ven. Nyanaponika Thera, my own spiritual teacher with whom I lived for 12 years at his hermitage in Sri Lanka. Nyanaponika was also probably the first Western writer on Buddhism to explore the practice of mindfulness at length, which he did both in his influential book, *The Heart of Buddhist Meditation*, and in his tract, *The Power of Mindfulness*. Nyanaponika did not intend 'bare attention' to be a translation of *sati* (he used the established rendering 'mindfulness'), but coined the term to highlight the initial stage in the practice of *satipaṭṭhāna*. To distinguish the two components of the practice, *sati* and *sampajañña*, he wrote that 'mindfulness (*sati*) applies preeminently to the attitude and practice of bare attention in a purely receptive state of mind [while] clear comprehension (*sampajañña*) comes into operation when any kind of action is required, including active reflective thoughts on things observed.'[17] I will have more to say about clear comprehension below. For now I am concerned with bare attention.

Nyanaponika defines bare attention quite succinctly thus:

> Bare attention is the clear and single-minded awareness of what actually happens to us and in us, at the successive moments of perception. It is called 'bare' because it attends just to the bare facts of a perception as presented either through the five physical senses or through the mind ... When attending to that sixfold sense impression, attention or mindfulness is kept to a bare registering of the facts observed, without reacting to them by deed, speech, or by mental comment, which may be one of self-reference (like, dislike, etc.), judgement or reflection.[18]

Contrary to some contemporary vipassana teachers, Nyanaponika did not regard 'bare attention' as non-conceptual and non-verbal. The Mahasi Sayadaw system of insight meditation, which he had practiced, stresses the importance of precisely labeling the constituents of one's experience, and Nyanaponika developed this methodology in his own way informed by keen psychological acumen. Although he highlights the open, receptive, and non-judgmental attitude inherent in bare attention, he also held that precise verbal designation plays a critical role in the three tasks of knowing, shaping, and purifying the mind.

In *The Power of Mindfulness* Nyanaponika calls this process 'tidying up the mental household.'[19] He writes that this work requires us to examine the mind's 'dark, untidy corners,' which are 'the hideouts of our most dangerous enemies,' the mental defilements of greed, hate and delusion. Such examination is the work of mindfulness as bare attention, which involves calling things by their true names:

> The calmly observant glance of mindfulness discovers the demons in their hiding-places. The practice of calling them by their names drives them out into the open, into the daylight of consciousness. There they will feel embarrassed and obliged to justify themselves, although at this stage of bare attention they have not yet even been subjected to any closer questioning except about their names, their identity. If forced into the open while still in an incipient stage, they will be incapable of withstanding scrutiny and will just dwindle away. Thus a first victory over them may be won, even at an early stage of the practice.[20]

Although I see significant differences between Nyanaponika's interpretation of mindfulness and interpretations in popular presentations of meditation, I still believe it was a mistake for him to use the expression 'bare attention' to describe this preliminary stage of mindfulness. I make this claim for two reasons, one pertaining to the word 'attention,' the other to the word 'bare.'

My reservation regarding 'attention' derives from the use of this word as the standard rendering for another technical term in the Buddhist analysis of mind, *manasikāra*, which designates a mental function whose role is quite different from that of mindfulness. The principal role of *manasikāra* is to turn the mind to an object. It is a spontaneous and automatic function exercised whenever an object impinges on a sense faculty or arises at the 'mind door.' It is translated 'attention' in the sense that it is the turning of attention to an object, the mind's 'advertence to the object.'[21] This, however, is not the role of *sati*. By explaining *sati*, even in its rudimentary stage, as 'bare attention,' Nyanaponika merged its meaning with that of *manasikāra*. But whereas *manasikāra* generally predominates at the inception of a cognitive process, *sati* supervenes at a later stage, sustaining attention on the object and making it appear vividly to lucid cognition.

Nyanaponika was a keen scholar of the Buddhist psychological system known as Abhidhamma and thus his choice of 'attention' to characterize *sati* could not have been due to carelessness. I suspect that the underlying reason for his choice was a melding of words in the two European languages in which he wrote, German and English. In his earliest works, written in German, he had rendered *sati* as *achtsamkeit*, which means 'attentiveness, heedfulness, ... mindfulness, care.'[22] Thus, whereas 'mindfulness' might be regarded as synonymous with 'attentiveness' in the sense of sustained attention, when it is glossed as 'bare attention' this risks confounding *sati* and *manasikāra*, deliberate mindfulness and the automatic act of advertence. I think it was this conflation of the two technical terms that led Gunaratana, in the passage cited above, to identify mindfulness with the brief moment of non-conceptual awareness that precedes the arising of concepts and discursive thought.

My reservation about using the word 'bare' to qualify this type of attention rests on more philosophical grounds. I think the expression 'bare attention' can be pragmatically useful to guide a beginning practitioner in the method of setting up mindfulness, and this is presumably what Nyanaponika had in mind when he wrote that bare attention 'is kept to a bare registering of the facts observed, without reacting to them by deed, speech, or by mental comment.' However, from a theoretical perspective it is questionable whether any act of attention, or any other mental act, can literally be 'bare.' As I see it, virtually any intentional act is necessarily subject to a vast set of determinants, internal and external, that governs the way it functions. It occurs *embodied* in a particular person with a unique biography and personality, and it occurs *embedded* in a particular context—historical, social, and cultural—that gives it a specific orientation on which its very identity depends.

We can, for example, distinguish contextual orientations depending on whether the practice is taken up by a traditional Buddhist who subscribes to the classical Buddhist worldview or by a contemporary westerner who takes up meditation against the background of a holistic secular perspective. The difference is neatly summarized by Gil Fronsdal:

> Rather than stressing world-renunciation, they [Western lay teachers] stress engagement with, and freedom *within* the world. Rather than rejecting the body, these Western teachers embrace the body as part of the wholistic [sic] field of practice. Rather than stressing ultimate spiritual goals such as full enlightenment, ending the cycles of rebirth, or attaining the various stages of sainthood, many Western teachers tend to stress the immediate benefits of mindfulness and untroubled, equanimous presence in the midst of life's vicissitudes.[23]

Surely these differences in orientation are going to flow over and shape the experience of mindfulness. One might argue that awareness of the breath is awareness of the breath no matter who is breathing. While I certainly could not dispute this, I also think it likely that once a meditator goes beyond this preliminary stage, presuppositions and expectations will inevitably come into play.

Instead of thinking of mindfulness as being exclusively 'bare,' I prefer to think of it as spread out along a spectrum, with varying layers of conceptual content ranging from 'heavy' to 'light' to 'zero,' depending on the particular style of mindfulness being practiced. Even the *satipaṭṭhāna* system itself shows such variation. In certain *satipaṭṭhāna* exercises, the determining context and orientation might be 'heavy,' in others 'light.' For example, in contemplation of the repulsiveness of the body, attention to the four elements, or the charnel ground meditations, the orientation towards disenchantment and dispassion is heavily loaded from the start. From the outset, mindfulness works in close association with thought and examination (*vitakka* and *vicāra*), which requires a sophisticated deployment of conceptual activity. The style of insight meditation taught by Mahasi Sayadaw makes much lighter use of conceptualization. A meditator begins by merely noting the expansion and contraction of the abdomen, and then gradually extends the act of noting to anything that impinges on awareness.[24] In a system that aims at the attainment of the *jhānas*, the conceptual content will be much thinner and effectively vanish with the actual attainment of *jhāna*, even while mindfulness becomes purer and clearer.

But in all cases, if mindfulness is to qualify as the 'right mindfulness' (*sammā sati*) of the noble eightfold path, it will have to be connected to a web of factors that give it direction and purpose. As a component of the path, it must be guided by right view, the first path factor, which links the practice to understanding. It must be directed by right intention, the second factor, the aspiration for dispassion, benevolence, and harmlessness. It should be grounded in the three ethical factors of right speech, right action, and right livelihood. And it should be conjoined with right effort (*sammā vāyāma*), the endeavour to eliminate unwholesome mental qualities and to awaken and fulfill wholesome qualities.

In short, the expression 'bare attention' seems faulty in two respects: first, because it conflates the two distinct mental factors of *sati* and *manasikāra*; and second, because no act of cognition is ever entirely devoid of factors imparting to it orientation and meaning. In relation to *satipaṭṭhāna* practice, one might perhaps speak of different degrees of colouring, different 'weights' of a determining context. However, I do not believe one can ever leave behind all determinants and achieve a state of absolute openness, vacuity, and indeterminacy.

4. What the *suttas* say

Nevertheless, despite my reservations about the use of 'bare attention' as an alternative expression for *sati*, if we consider *how* mindfulness is to be practiced in the system laid down in the *Satipaṭṭhāna Sutta*, we can find considerable support for the idea that the initial task of *sati* is to 'keep to a bare registering of the facts observed' as free as possible from *distorting* conceptual elaborations. The problem, as I see it, is not with conceptualization itself, but with conceptualization that ascribes erroneous attributes to the objects and the experiential act itself. An experiential event can be viewed as a field distributed between two poles, the objective datum and the subjective act that cognizes it. Ordinarily, on account of the spontaneous functioning of unenlightened consciousness, this polarity is reified into a sharp duality of subject and object. The subjective pole seems to coalesce into a substantially existent 'I,' an ego-self that hovers in the background as an autonomous and independent entity. The objective pole presents itself as an object that is there 'for me,' ready to serve or oppose my purposes; thus it becomes a potential object of craving or aversion. This process is what the *suttas* refer to as 'I-making' and 'mine-making' (*ahaṃkāra mamaṃkāra*). It is the task of meditation to dismantle this structure by penetrating the selfless nature of all phenomena, whether pertaining to the objective or subjective poles of the experience.

While it is only *paññā* or wisdom that can eradicate the cognitive distortions, *sati* helps to keep them in check. By bringing into focus the experiential field, *sati* illuminates objects without the usual overlay of distorted conceptual elaborations that obscure their real nature. The initial instruction on mindfulness of breathing, the first exercise in contemplation of the body, exemplifies this well. The meditator sits down, holds his body erect, and establishes mindfulness in front of him. Then, 'just mindful he breathes in, mindful he breathes out' (*sato va assasati, sato passasati*). The expression *sato va* is emphatic: *just* mindful, *only* mindful, *simply* mindful. Here, contrary to its original sense, *sati* could not mean 'remembering.' The only thing the meditator should be remembering is to keep the breath in mind. The breath is something occurring in the present, not in the past, which means that in this context *sati* is attentiveness to a present event, not recollection of the past.

The instruction continues: 'When a monk breathes in long, he knows, "I breathe in long"; and when he breathes out long, he knows, "I breathe out long."' The same is said with regard to short breaths. The key word here is *pajānāti*, 'one knows.' The verb is the source of the noun *paññā*, usually translated 'wisdom,' but it is clear that at this point *paññā* as wisdom has not yet arisen. What occurs, rather, is just a simple, even minimal, discernment of the quality of the breath. We might see two phases to be involved in this process. First, mindfulness, as the quality of *upaṭṭhāna* or lucid awareness, illuminates the presence of the breath. Then, almost simultaneously, a simple cognition, indicated by *pajānāti*, steps in and registers the breath as coming in or going out, as long or short. We can see this as a rudimentary act of *sampajañña*, clear comprehension.

The same method of description is found in the sections on feelings and states of mind. When the meditator experiences a particular feeling—pleasant, painful, or neutral—he knows what he feels. When a particular state of mind has arisen—a mind with lust, hatred, or delusion, or a mind without lust, hatred, or delusion—in each case he knows that state of mind just as it is. As I see it, in such contemplation, the role of *sati* or mindfulness is to lay open the contents of the experiential field; the role of *sampajañña*, clear comprehension, is to determine and define the contents for what they are. *Sampajañña* advances and begins to turn into *paññā* in the section on contemplating the arising and vanishing of each type of object. This act explicitly relates them to the broad scheme set up by the teachings.

With the fourth contemplation, contemplation of phenomena (*dhammā-nupassanā*), the situation becomes more complex and thus clear comprehension gains prominence. The first division of this section deals with the five hindrances: sensual desire, ill will, drowsiness, restlessness, and doubt. Once again mindfulness lays open the experiential field and clear comprehension recognizes the presence or absence of a particular hindrance. When mindfulness and clear comprehension have jointly exercised this preparatory function, *paññā*, in the sense of wisdom, enters and subsumes the hindrance under the principle of conditionality. The meditator must understand how the hindrance arises, how it is abandoned, and how it can be prevented from arising again in the future.

A similar sequence is found in the following exercises on the five aggregates, the six inner and outer sense bases, the seven enlightenment factors, and the Four Noble Truths. In each case, considerably more is involved than 'bare attention' to the flux of immediate experience. Rather, investigation is needed in order to understand how certain factors arise, how they are eliminated or strengthened, and in the case of the positive factors, how they are brought to fulfillment. As a matter of necessity, one adopts certain conceptual schemes as matrices through which to view the vortex of experience, schemes that plot phenomena against the guidelines mandated by the Dhamma and steer the practice towards its intended goal, the realization of *nibbāna*. At this point the direction, context, and orientation of the practice, far from being dispensable, have a decisive impact on the way mindfulness operates.

5. Clear comprehension

While I said just above that clear comprehension plays a more prominent role in the contemplation of experiential phenomena, the refrain on right mindfulness shows that clear comprehension has been present to some degree all along. The formula describes clear comprehension as a constant entering each exercise virtually from the start. Whether contemplating the body, feelings, states of mind, or experiential phenomena, the meditator dwells 'ardent, clearly comprehending, and mindful.'

In the Nikāyas, there are two stock passages that describe the practice of clear comprehension. The more frequent passage occurs as a separate section in the *Satipaṭṭhāna Sutta*, comprised under contemplation of the body:

> And how, monks, does a monk exercise clear comprehension? Here, a monk acts with clear comprehension when going forward and returning; when looking ahead and looking aside; when drawing in and extending the limbs; when wearing his robes and carrying his outer robe and bowl; when eating, drinking, chewing his food, and tasting; when defecating and urinating; when walking, standing, sitting, falling asleep, waking up, speaking, and keeping silent. It is in such a way that a monk exercises clear comprehension.[25]

Taken in isolation, this account might give the impression that clear comprehension refers solely to the deliberative performance of one's daily tasks. However, a pair of *suttas* addressed to sick monks in the infirmary shows that mindfulness and clear comprehension jointly lead to insight and liberation. On two separate occasions the Buddha visits the infirmary and enjoins the monks to be mindful and clearly comprehend things. He explains the former by way of the stock formula on the four *satipaṭṭhānas* and the latter by the above formula on clear comprehension. He then states that a monk who is mindful and clearly comprehends things will understand the dependent origination of feelings, contemplate their impermanence, and abandon lust, aversion, and ignorance, whereby he attains *nibbāna*.[26]

The other passage on clear comprehension has a different emphasis. It describes clear comprehension, not as discernment of one's day-to-day activities, but as a reflexive cognition of mental events:

> And how does a monk exercise clear comprehension? Here, for a monk feelings are understood as they arise, as they remain present, as they pass away. Thoughts are understood as they arise, as they remain present, as they pass away. Perceptions are understood as they arise, as they remain present, as they pass away. It is in this way that a monk exercises clear comprehension.[27]

This stage of contemplation evidently marks a turning point where *sampajañña* is maturing into *paññā*, where clear comprehension becomes insight into impermanence, direct knowledge of the arising and passing of phenomena.

The Pāli commentaries consistently explain clear comprehension to have a fourfold application: (1) as comprehending the purpose of one's actions; (2) as prudence in the choice of means; (3) as engagement with the meditation subject; and (4) as discernment of things in their true nature. We might correlate the first two applications with clear comprehension in one's daily tasks, as described in the first formula. The third might be interpreted as the clear comprehension referred to by the word *sampajāno* in the *satipaṭṭhāna* refrain. And the fourth obviously marks the stage where clear comprehension turns into actual insight.[28]

6. Expanding into new frontiers

Mindfulness has travelled a long way from its homeland in northeast India. It has journeyed to the island of Sri Lanka, the river basins of southeast Asia, the mountain monasteries of China, Korea, and Japan, and the hermitages of the Himalayan kingdoms. But the last lap of its journey is without parallel. Today, Buddhist meditation has been lifted from its traditional setting in Buddhist doctrine and faith and transplanted in a secularized culture bent on pragmatic results. Here it is finding new accommodations in urban meditation centres and even in busy hospitals, pain clinics, and treatment centres. Its teachers and practitioners are more likely to wear street clothing or white coats than ochre robes; they are more likely to hold degrees in medicine and psychology than in Buddhist philosophy and scripture. Meditation is being taught to help people obtain release, not from the cycle of birth and death, but from the strains of financial pressures, psychological disorders, and stressful relationships.

As stress-reduction specialists and psychotherapists seek new methods to help their patients deal with physical pain, grief, and distress, the ancient system of mindfulness meditation offers fresh promise. But the response from the Buddhist side has not been exclusively enthusiastic. Confirmed adherents of Buddhism have given the secular adaptation of Buddhist meditation mixed reviews. While some applaud the application of mindfulness to an array of new fields, from medical centres to high schools to maximum security prisons, others have reacted with skepticism if not with shrill denunciations. Many sincere Buddhists, still undecided, struggle with questions to which the canonical texts provide no clear answers: 'Is the pure Dhamma being diluted for secular ends, reduced to a mere therapy? Won't the outcome be to make *saṃsāra* more pleasant rather than to liberate people from the cycle of rebirths? Did anyone ever attain enlightenment in a medical clinic?'

It is my personal belief that we need to strike a balance between caution and appreciation. There is a real danger that scientists who investigate traditional eastern contemplative practices might be swayed by materialistic premises to explain their efficacy reductively, on the exclusive basis of neurophysiology. There is a real danger that the contemplative challenge might be reduced to a matter of gaining skill in certain techniques, dispensing with such qualities as faith, aspiration, devotion, and self-surrender, all integral to the act of 'going for refuge.' However, I do not think we need be alarmed about the adaptation of Buddhist practices for secular ends. I call to mind a statement the Buddha made in the weeks before his death: 'The Tathāgata has no closed fist of a teacher with respect to teachings.'[29] By this he meant that he had taught everything important without holding back any esoteric doctrines, but I like to interpret his words to mean that we can let anyone take from the Dhamma whatever they find useful even if it is for secular purposes.

I feel that if psychotherapists can draw upon Buddhist mindfulness practice to help people overcome anxiety and distress, their work is most commendable. If clinicians find that mindfulness helps patients accept pain and illness, that is wonderful—and having a chronic pain condition myself, I give extra kudos to their work. If peace activists find the meditation on loving-kindness helps them be more peaceful in their advocacy of peace, again, that is splendid. And if a businessman finds his Zen practice makes him more considerate of his clients, again this should merit our approval.

It is inevitable that mindfulness and other practices adopted from Buddhism will find new applications in the modern West, where worldviews and lifestyles are so different from those of southern and eastern Asia. If such practices benefit those who do not accept the full framework of Buddhist teaching, I see no reason to grudge them the right to take what they need. To the contrary, I feel that those who adapt the Dhamma to these new purposes are to be admired for their pioneering courage and insight. As long as they act with prudence and a compassionate intent, let them make use of the Dhamma in any way they can to help others.

At the same time, I also believe that it is our responsibility, as heirs of the Dhamma, to remind such experimenters that they have entered a sanctuary deemed sacred by Buddhists. Thus, respectful towards their sources, they should pursue their investigations with humility and gratitude. They should recognize that while the Dhamma bids everyone come and take what they need, they are drawing from an ancient well of sacred wisdom that has nourished countless spirits through the centuries and whose waters still retain their potency for those who drink from them today.

NOTES

1. DN 22.21 (II 313; LDB 348-49). MN 141.30 (III 252; MLDB 1100-1101). SN 45:8 (V 9-10; CDB 1529). See also Appendix.
2. DN 22.1 (II 290; LDB 335). MN 10.1 (I 55; MLDB 145).
3. Monier-Williams (2005, 1272).
4. Rhys Davids (1910). Cited from unpaginated online version.
5. SN V 197 (CDB 1671). The formula also occurs at AN 5:14 and AN 7:4 as a definition of the 'power of mindfulness.' Interestingly, the Chinese parallels to SN 48:9 (SĀ 646 at T II 182b19) and AN 5:14 (SĀ 675 at T II 185c12) define the faculty and power of mindfulness, respectively, by way of the four bases of mindfulness. This might have resulted from standardization made at a time when the old meaning of memory had faded even further into the background.
6. SN V 198 (CDB 1672).
7. SN V 200 (CDB 1673).

8. SN V 67 (CDB 1571).
9. SN V 329-33 (CDB 1780-85).
10. Paṭis I 20. Though included in the Pāli Canon, the *Paṭisambhidāmagga* obviously dates from a period later than the old Nikāyas, which contain the Buddha's discourses. The work was a major influence on the *Visuddhimagga*, which often quotes from it.
11. *Vism* 464. See Ñāṇamoli (1991, 14.141).
12. I hesitate to use the word 'awareness' without qualification as a rendering of *sati*, for this word has been chosen to represent a number of Pāli technical terms ranging from *viññāṇa* (consciousness) and *citta* (mind) to *sati, sampajañña*, and *vijjā* (penetrative knowledge).
13. Recollection of the Buddha is at AN 6:10, AN 6:25, etc. Contemplation of the body's repulsiveness is at DN 22.5 (LDB 337) and MN 10.10 (MLDB 147) and elsewhere. Mindfulness of death is at AN 6:19 and AN 6:20. Sn v. 151 says about meditation on loving-kindness: *etaṃ satiṃ adhiṭṭheyya*, 'one should resolve on this mindfulness.'
14. MN 117.10-15 (III 72-73; MLDB 935-36).
15. Gunaratana (2002, 138, italics mine).
16. Gunaratana (2002, 140).
17. Nyanaponika (1962, 29). Here and below I take the liberty of lower casing the first letters of Buddhist technical terms that Nyanaponika, following German custom, capitalized.
18. Nyanaponika (1962, 30). An almost identical definition is found in Nyanaponika (1968, vii).
19. Nyanaponika (1968, 1).
20. Nyanaponika (1968, 8).
21. *Manasikāra* also occurs in another context, when it is prefixed either by *ayoniso* or *yoniso*. *Ayoniso manasikāra* is 'careless reflection,' attending to an object in a way that causes unarisen defilements to arise and arisen defilements to increase. *Yoniso manasikāra* is the opposite: careful reflection on an object that prevents unarisen defilements from arising and removes arisen defilements.
22. http://en.bab.la/dictionary/german-english/achtsamkeit.
23. Fronsdal (1995).
24. See Mahasi Sayadaw (1971, 3–12).
25. DN 22.4 (II 292; LDB 337). MN 10.8 (I 57; MLDB 147). The same passage occurs in many discourses on the 'progressive training.' See, for example, DN 2.65 (I 70-71; LDB 100); MN 27.16 (I 181; MLDB 274); AN 4:198 (II 210).
26. SN 36.7, 36.8 (IV 210-14; CDB 1266-69).
27. SN 47:35 (V 180-81; CDB 1657). See, too, AN 4:41 (II 45), which calls this the development of concentration that leads to mindfulness and clear comprehension.
28. The four types of clear comprehension are discussed at length in Nyanaponika (1962, 45–55). I have translated the commentarial explanation in Bodhi (2008, 94–130).
29. DN 16.2.25 (II 100; LDB 245).

REFERENCES

BODHI, BHIKKHU, trans. 2000. *The connected discourses of the Buddha: A translation of the Saṃyutta Nikāya.* Boston, MA: Wisdom Publications.

BODHI, BHIKKHU, trans. 1989, reprint 2008. *The fruits of recluseship: The Sāmaññaphala Sutta and its commentaries.* Sri Lanka: Buddhist Publication Society.

FRONSDAL, GIL. 1995. Treasures of the Theravada: Recovering the riches of our tradition. *Inquiring Mind* 12 (1). http://www.insightmeditationcenter.org/books-articles/ articles/the-treasures-of-the-theravada/.

GUNARATANA, HENEPOLA. 2002. *Mindfulness in plain English.* Boston, MA: Wisdom Publications.

MAHASI SAYADAW. 1971, reprint 2006. *Practical insight meditation.* Kandy, Sri Lanka: Buddhist Publication Society . http://books.google.com/ (page references are to the online version).

MONIER-WILLIAMS, MONIER. reprint. 2005. *Sanskrit-English dictionary.* Delhi: Motilal Banarsidass.

ÑĀNAMOLI, BHIKKHU, and BHIKKHU BODHI, trans. 1995. *The middle length discourses of the Buddha: A translation of the Majjhima Nikāya.* Boston, MA: Wisdom Publications.

ÑĀNAMOLI, BHIKKHU, trans. 1964. *The path of purification (Visuddhimagga).* Reprint 1991, Kandy, Sri Lanka: Buddhist Publication Society.

NYANAPONIKA THERA. 1962. *The heart of Buddhist meditation.* London: Riders. (Reprint 1992, Kandy, Sri Lanka, Buddhist Publication Society).

NYANAPONIKA THERA. 1968. *The power of mindfulness.* Kandy, Sri Lanka: Buddhist Publication Society. http://www.buddhanet.net/pdf_file/powermindfulness.pdf (page references are to the online version).

RHYS DAVIDS, T. W., and C. A. F. trans. 1910. *Dialogues of the Buddha.* London: Pali Text Society. http://www.levityisland.com/buddhadust/www.buddhadust.org/ TheSatipatthana/SettingUpMindfulness.htm.

WALSHE, MAURICE, trans. 1995. *The long discourses of the Buddha: A translation of the Dīgha Nikāya.* Boston, MA: Wisdom Publication.

Appendix

Key to abbreviations

All references to Pāli texts are to the editions published by the Pali Text Society. Canonical references are to *sutta* number, followed by volume and page of the PTS Pāli edition, followed by title and page number of the Wisdom Publications 'Teachings of the Buddha' series. My translation of the Aṅguttara Nikāya is still in progress and thus has not been referenced.

AN   Aṅguttara Nikāya
CDB   *Connected Discourses of the Buddha* (Bodhi 2000)
DN   Dīgha Nikāya
LDB   *Long Discourses of the Buddha* (Walshe 1995)
MLDB *Middle Length Discourses of the Buddha* (Ñāṇamoli and Bodhi 1995)
MN   Majjhima Nikāya
Paṭis   Paṭisambhidāmagga
SĀ   Saṃyuktāgama
SN   Saṃyutta Nikāya
Sn   Suttanipāta
T   Taisho Chinese Tripiṭaka (CBETA edition)
Vism   Visuddhimagga

IS MINDFULNESS PRESENT-CENTRED AND NON-JUDGMENTAL? A DISCUSSION OF THE COGNITIVE DIMENSIONS OF MINDFULNESS

Georges Dreyfus

This essay critiques the standard characterization of mindfulness as present-centred non-judgmental awareness, arguing that this account misses some of the central features of mindfulness as described by classical Buddhist accounts, which present mindfulness as being relevant to the past as well as to the present. I show that for these sources the central feature of mindfulness is not its present focus but its capacity to hold its object and thus allow for sustained attention, regardless of whether the object is present or not. I further show that for these sources mindfulness can be explicitly evaluative, thus demonstrating the degree to which classical Buddhist accounts differ from the modern description of mindfulness as non-judgmental. I conclude that although this modern description may be useful as an operational definition intended for practical instruction, it does not provide an adequate basis for a theoretical analysis of mindfulness, for it fails to emphasize its retentive nature to privilege its alleged nonconceptuality.

It is only a few years ago that I discovered the extent to which the concept of mindfulness had become common within the field of psychology. I was at first pleasantly surprised that a concept so central to Buddhist practice could be used with great effectiveness as a therapeutic tool, but quickly my enthusiasm gave way to a certain unease at the ways in which psychologists treated this topic, taking it as more or less self-evident or discussing it through cursory definitions based on the work of Jon Kabat-Zinn (1990). I was struck by the extent to which these psychological discussions proceeded without any serious reference to the original Buddhist sources from which they were supposed to derive. As a Buddhist scholar I felt that these discussions often missed important points and presented a view of mindfulness that I had trouble recognizing at times. The first temptation for me was to view these presentations as simply inauthentic, failing to be true to the ideas found in the original texts. This did not disqualify them, for I thought that there is nothing wrong with a thorough reinterpretation of old ideas to adapt them to the modern context. I understood the therapeutic use of mindfulness as an invention of tradition that provided tools and concepts useful within the context of therapeutic interventions, but I thought everybody would be better served by just dropping the reference to Buddhism and the pretense to represent authentically its ideas and practices.

Further reflections have changed my opinion without, however, completely assuaging my discomfort. This change has come as a result of my increased awareness of the great multiplicity of religious traditions. As a scholar of religious studies, I understand that the pretension to provide 'the Buddhist view of mindfulness' should be resisted as an attempt to privilege certain parts of the tradition at the expense of often less well-known aspects. Buddhism is a plural tradition that has evolved over centuries to include a large variety of views about mindfulness. Hence, there is no one single view that can ever hope to qualify as 'the Buddhist view of mindfulness.' What is often presented as 'the Buddhist view of mindfulness' is often derived from scholastic traditions, particularly from the multiple versions of the Abhidharma. These presentations are certainly of great importance to understand some of the central Buddhist ideas but they cannot be taken to provide the normative reference point, in relation to which other presentations can be judged as inauthentic. In fact, I believe that the use of the rhetoric of authenticity should be viewed with great suspicion. It is more often than not an attempt to claim authority and disqualify other views within the tradition, views that may have been marginal but are not necessarily illegitimate. Thus, I realize that some of my earlier reactions to the mindfulness movement may have reflected some of my discomfort at seeing my own claims to authority go unrecognized and my expertise bypassed. And yet, as mentioned above, this realization has not fully appeased my uneasiness.

In the following pages, I reflect on some of the reasons for this discomfort and examine the problems that I see in some of the current analyses of mindfulness based on my understanding of the Buddhist sources, which I am familiar with as a textual scholar who is interested in meditative practices and in relating Buddhist ideas to contemporary scientific discussions. It should be clear that my discussion of mindfulness is not claiming to provide a definitive or authoritative account of the Buddhist conception of mindfulness since I do not believe that such an account is feasible. It should also be clear that I am not attempting here to provide a critical evaluation of the therapeutic practices concerning mindfulness, something completely outside of my competences. Rather, I am offering a reflection on the problems that I see in the way mindfulness is conceptualized in the psychological literature and ask: does mindfulness need to be present-centred and non-judgmental, as seems to be assumed in the psychological literature? To answer this question I start by examining a standard definition of mindfulness in the literature, which presents it as a non-elaborative and non-judgmental present-centred awareness. I show how this definition reflects practical instructions given in training and argue that it does not provide the basis for a good theoretical account, for it misses the central feature of mindfulness, which is to hold its object and thus allow for sustained attention regardless of whether the object of attention is present or not. In arguing that mindfulness is best understood as retentive, I emphasize its cognitive contribution rather than its nonconceptuality. I further argue that this retentive ability plays a central role in many cognitive processes, reminding us not to lose sight of the mnemonic aspect of mindfulness and not to confuse practical instructions and operational definitions with theoretical analysis. I conclude by showing the consequences of the failure to give due place to the cognitive importance of mindfulness.

A standard definition of mindfulness

In examining what I find problematic in many of the contemporary views of mindfulness in the psychological literature, I obviously can not do justice to all the accounts. Nevertheless, I believe that there is something close to a consensus in the professional literature concerning the characterization of mindfulness. Such an account can be found in the works of, for example, S. Bishop, who has provided what has become by now a well-accepted definition. Bishop offers this definition:

> Broadly conceptualized, mindfulness has been described as a kind of nonelaborative, non-judgmental, present-centered awareness in which each thought, feeling, or sensation that arises in the attentional field is acknowledged and accepted as it is. (Bishop *et al.* 2004, 232)

This definition, which reflects the point of view of the therapist engaged in practical interventions, stresses two features of mindfulness. First, it emphasizes the non-judgmental nature of mindfulness as a state of awareness that allows for an observation of mental states without over-identifying with them so as to create an attitude of acceptance that can lead to greater curiosity and better self-understanding. This provides a way to disengage from the habitual patterns of discursive and affective reactivity so as to allow a more reflective response to the difficult circumstances of one's life rather than remain prisoner of one's own habits and compulsions.

Second, there is a strong emphasis on the present-centred nature of mindfulness, which is seen as focusing on what is happening in the present moment. The basic idea is that to free ourselves we need to quiet the mind and disengage it from its compulsive tendencies to conceptualize our experiences in terms of what we like and dislike. This de-automatization of our habitual judgmental tendencies is brought about by limiting the scope of our attention to what is happening in the moment. Instead of constantly evaluating our experiences in term of past memories and future expectations, we need just to take note of what is taking place in the moment, observing the experience and our reactions rather than elaborating on their content. In this way, we will be able to develop a state of non-reactive equanimity that enables us to see things as they are and act in accordance with reality rather than remain prisoner of our usual patterns of evaluative reactivity.

At the outset, I should say that there is a great deal to be commended in this characterization of mindfulness. The de-automatization of habitual patterns of reactivity and weakening of pre-potent responses is certainly an important part of Buddhist practice, which seeks to free the mind from the internal compulsions that lead to suffering. It is also clear that the emphasis on the present-centred character of mindfulness is helpful, especially at the beginning of one's practice when the mind is prisoner of its unbridled discursivity. This is not to say that mindfulness is necessarily present centred (as we will see shortly) nor that it is necessarily non-judgmental, but there is no doubt that the discipline of being able to keep the mind to stick to the present moment and refrain from its usual chatter is an important stage in the education of attention, which is the basis of meditative practice.

Let me make it clear that my point here is not to critique the practice of therapists and Buddhist teachers who have attempted to adapt classical Buddhist concepts to the modern context. Such an adaptation is necessary and not in question. What I wish to critique is the theoretical model that seems to be assumed by these practitioners so as to provide a better theoretical understanding of the cognitive mechanisms involved in the practice of mindfulness. To do this I examine the treatment of mindfulness in some of the classical Buddhist sources. I focus mostly, but not only, on the clear treatments of the question found in the scholastic commentarial tradition, particularly the presentations of various Abhidharmas (the part of the Buddhist canon that analyses the realm of sentient experience and the world given in such experience into its basic elements [*dharma*], listing and grouping them into the appropriate categories so as to undermine the postulation of an enduring unified subject). A cursory look at these sources reveals that the classical definitions of mindfulness do not correspond to the characterization of mindfulness as present-centred non-judgmental aware-ness. Although such description is not alien to the tradition, it does not occupy the central place that many modern mindfulness practitioners assume. We may then wonder how does the classical scholastic Buddhist tradition understand mindfulness if it is not defined as present-centred non-judgmental awareness, and, perhaps more importantly, what can we learn from the classical sources about mindfulness that may help to bring out some of the features that have been missed by the standard account delineated above? But before we can do this, we should be clear about the terms of the inquiry and understand the semantic range of the words used in this discussion.

Mindfulness, *sati* and retention

The English *mindfulness* is an old word that indicates the quality of being aware and paying attention. Interestingly for our discussion, it also had the connotation of remembering and having a purpose in mind, though these usages seem to have faded away. This word has been used to translate various Buddhist terms, mostly the Sanskrit *smṛti* (Pāli *sati*, Tibetan *dran pa*). These terms are widely used within the Buddhist tradition where they are understood to be central to the practice of meditation. There is nothing wrong with their translation as *mindfulness* as long as one keeps track of the semantic range of these terms. When we do this, however, we realize that the understanding of mindfulness/*sati* as present-centred non-evaluative awareness is problematic for it reflects only some of the ways in which these original terms are deployed.

The word *smṛti* (Pāli *sati*) comes from the Sanskrit root *smṛ*, which means to remember and keep in mind. The word itself can refer to the act of remembering and keeping in mind, as well as to what is kept in mind. Thus, the Hindu tradition calls some of its lesser sacred texts *smṛti*, that which is remembered, in opposition to the Vedas, which are *śruti*, that is which have been directly heard. Within the Buddhist context, this word has usually a related but more restrained meaning and refers to the quality of the mind when it is recollecting or keeping in mind an object. The great scholiast Buddhaghosa gives this definition of *sati* within the context of the classical Theravāda tradition:

> By means of it, they [i.e. other mental processes] remember (*saranti*), or it itself remembers, or it is simply just remembering (*sarana*). Thus it is *mindfulness (sati)*. Its characteristic is not wobbling; its function is not to forget. It is manifested as guarding or the state of being face to face with an object. (Nyānamoli Bhikkhu 1976, XIV 141).

This characterization of *sati* is worth noticing for at least three reasons. First, one cannot but be struck by the obscurity of the text, which proceeds by glossing the word *sati* as 'not wobbling.' What does this mean? Second, the various connotations provided by Buddhaghosa such as 'not wobbling' and 'remembering' do not seem to fit comfortably within a single concept. Hence, we cannot but wonder why they are described by the same term? Third, this gloss of *sati* does not look at all like the understanding of mindfulness as present-centred awareness. It is clearly at odds with this understanding of mindfulness since *sati* includes the act of remembering the past and hence is not necessarily present-centred.

Turning to other classical texts suggests views of mindfulness that are even further apart from the contemporary understanding. *The Questions of King Milinda*, for example, gives us a description of mindfulness as being explicitly evaluative. Responding to the questions of Greek King Milinda, the monk Nāgasena provides a long gloss of mindfulness as 'not drifting' and 'taking up'. While explaining the former, he emphasizes the ethical dimensions of mindfulness, pointing out that the function of mindfulness is not just to keep in touch with whatever is present in the ken of attention but also includes the not drifting away from the wholesome and unwholesome mental states. This ethical emphasis confirmed by the gloss of mindfulness as the taking up, which is explained as the examination of the beneficial or detrimental nature of various mental states (Mendis 1993, 37–8) This understanding of mindfulness is quite far from the idea of mindfulness as non-judgmental awareness, for if mindfulness is to distinguish wholesome from unwholesome mental states, it must be explicitly cognitive and evaluative, in contrast with the idea of mindfulness as non-judgmental acceptance of whatever arises within the stream of consciousness.

It should be clear that the purpose of my discussion is not just to play a game of scholarly 'got you' by pointing out the contrast between the understanding of mindfulness as present-centred non-judgmental awareness and the ways classical sources deploy this concept. Rather, what I seek here is a better conceptualization of mindfulness so as to retrieve its cognitive implications, which are in danger of being lost in the rush to equate mindfulness with present-centred non-judgmental awareness. To do so, I believe that it may be useful to reflect on the ways in which classical sources deploy the concept of mindfulness/*sati*. How come that this term has very different connotations ('not wobbling,' 'remembering,' 'being face to face with the object,' 'taking up and examining' etc.)? What do these connotations have in common? It should be clear that the idea of present-centred non-judgmental awareness is not going to be of much help here since *sati* can concern recollection of the past as well as attention to the present. Hence, rather than rest satisfied with this depiction of mindfulness, I believe that we should examine the ways in which it functions cognitively, particularly the ways in which it retains information rather than merely attends to its object.

The idea of mindfulness as a retention of information may come as a surprise given the almost universal acceptance of the definition of mindfulness as present-centred non-judgmental awareness. And yet the idea of mindfulness as a holding rather than a merely passive attending fits quite well with the classical Buddhist descriptions found in the Abhidharma, which all concur in presenting mindfulness as the ability of the mind to remain present to the object without floating away. I would like to argue that it is this retentive ability of the mind that should be taken as defining mindfulness, not its alleged present-centred nonconceptuality. It is this retentive ability that allows the mind to hold the object in the ken of the attention as well as remember it later. Hence, it should come as less of a surprise when mindfulness is presented as being relevant both to the present holding of an object and its future recollection. Both are ways of holding information and hence described as forms of mindfulness/*sati*. I would also argue that this retentive ability is central to account for how mindfulness operates cognitively and goes a long way to explain the cognitive transformations brought about by this practice.

I would further argue that this retentive ability of mindfulness is crucially connected to working memory, the ability of the mind to retain and make sense of received information. When we see an object, we are not just presented with discrete time slices of the object. Rather we integrate them within a temporal flow so that they are given as making sense. I do not see a person moving through various positions in space but rather see her as smoothly moving from one place toward another. Thus, consciousness involves the ability to put in resonance various cognitive processes so that the information they deliver makes sense and produces coherent patterns, which may not be fully accurate representations of external objects but are good enough to guide our actions. This making sense is crucially connected to working memory, the capacity of the mind to maintain and manipulate relevant information so as to be able to engage in purposeful activities.

The idea here is not to equate the retentive ability of consciousness, working memory and mindfulness, but to argue that there is a significant overlap that helps us to understand what Buddhaghosa has in mind when he characterizes mindfulness as 'not wobbling.' Mindfulness is the mind's ability to keep the object in the ken of attention without losing it. Such an ability cannot be understood simply as a bottom-up process in which our mind remains open to whatever arises but should be seen as involving the top-down ability of the mind to retain and bind information so that the present moment of experience can be integrated within the temporal flow of experience. This holding ability of mindfulness is a natural ability that the mind has, ability that can be strengthened by practice but which exists naturally in every person, at least to a certain extent. It is this top-down capacity to hold information that is strengthened by the practice of meditation and that accounts for the development of sustained modes of attention when the mind is not carried away by the fleeting stream of data but is able to attend to objects in sustained ways.

Mindfulness is then not the present-centred non-judgmental awareness of an object but the paying close attention to an object, leading to the retention of the data so as to make sense of the information delivered by our cognitive apparatus. Thus, far from being limited to the present and to a mere refraining from passing judgment, mindfulness is a cognitive activity closely connected to memory, particularly to working memory, the ability to keep relevant information active so that it can be integrated within meaningful patterns and used for goal directed activities (Jha *et al.* 2010). By paying close attention, practitioners of mindfulness strengthen their cognitive control because they increase their ability to retain information and thus see their true significance rather than being carried away by their reactions. What is well attended to can be maintained by working memory and thus become available for appropriate evaluation.

This connection between mindfulness, working memory and proper evaluation comes through quite clearly when one looks at the Buddha's foundational teaching on mindfulness, the *Satipaṭṭhāna Sutta*. This complex text, which purports to be the Buddha's own words (in oppositon to the Abhidharma, which is a systematization of the words of the founder), presents a complex practice to develop mindfulness around four topics: mindfulness of the body, feelings, consciousness and mental factors (the four applications of mindfulness, *satipaṭṭhāna*). For each of the four applications, the discourse explains how mindfulness has to be practiced. In relation to the body, the text lays out several contemplations pertaining to the activities of the body, its breathing, postures and anatomical composition. In dealing with postures, for example, the text explains the development of mindfulness as based on the awareness of the posture. The text says: '...when walking, he knows "I am walking," when standing,...'

(Anālayo 2003, 5). Similarly, when dealing with the activities of the body, breathing, feelings and other objects of contemplation, the discourse emphasizes the development of the presence of mind to what is being contemplated so that one is wide awake to the experience one is undergoing. Hence, it is quite clear that for the *Satipaṭṭhāna Sutta*, mindfulness is not just present-centred non-judgmental awareness but involves the mind's ability to attend to and retain whatever experience one is engaged in so as to develop a clear understanding of the experience and the ability to recollect such experience in the future. This evaluative aspect of the practice of mindfulness comes through even more clearly in the passage of *The Questions of King Milinda* discussed above where it is presented as the capacity to discriminate between positive and negative qualities. To understand further the place and role of this form of evaluative mindfulness, it may be helpful to widen the scope of our investigation and include, however briefly, a description of the ways in which the Abhidharma presents the full spectrum of the various forms of attention.

A phenomenology of attention

The Abhidharma offers a rich analysis of the various aspects of the mind, presenting it as composed of a series of momentary mental states. Each mental state comes to be in dependence of various conditions (such as preceding moments of awareness, object, sensory basis). Having arisen, it performs its function and dissolves, giving rise to the next mental state, thus forming a stream of consciousness or continuum not unlike James' stream of thought. Each state is understood as being a moment of awareness (*citta, sems*) endowed with various characteristics, the mental factors (*caitasika, sems byung*). Awareness, which is also described as consciousness (*vijñāna, rnam shes*), is primary in that it is aware of the object, whereas mental factors qualify this awareness and determine it as being pleasant or unpleasant, focused or unfocused, calm or agitated, positive or negative, etc. Some of the mental factors are omni-present or universal in that they are necessarily present in all mental states, whereas other factors are only present in some mental states.

These mental factors belong to various aspects of the mental. Some (feeling) pertain to the affective domain whereas others (intention) are conative or cognitive (discernment) in nature. To greatly simplify, we can say that the Abhidharma understands these various aspects to operate simultaneously and to be simply the qualities that characterize moments of awareness. Among these qualities, several pertain to the domain of attention, an important aspect of the mental processes analysed by the Abhidharma. For the Abhidharma, attention starts at an early stage with orienting (*manasikāra*, often translated as *attention*). This is the pre-attentive and automatic ability of the mind to turn toward the object and select it. Bhikkhu Bodhi explains: 'Attention (i.e. orienting) is the mental factor responsible for the mind's advertence to the object, by virtue of which the object is made present to consciousness. Its characteristic is the conducting of the associated mental states to the object. Its function is to yoke the associated mental states to the object.' (Bodhi 2000, 81) Every mental state, inasmuch as it is conscious, has at least a minimal amount of focus on its object. Hence, orienting is an omnipresent factor, that is, any mental state contains some degree of it. It accounts for the pre-attentive noticing that takes place when an object draws our attention before being selected for closer scrutiny.

The attentive process continues with mindfulness and concentration (*samādhi*). The former is described, as argued above, as the retention of information so that the mind is not carried away from the object. Vasubandhu describes it as universal whereas Asaṅga limits it to the operative states of mind, arguing that it is absent in subliminal states of consciousness. Nevertheless, both agree that it is a fundamental aspect of the mind's ability to pay close attention by not wobbling away from the object. Orienting turns the mind toward the object whereas mindfulness retains the object and keeps the mind from losing the object. Concentration completes this analysis of the Abhidharma treatment of attention. It is the ability of the mind to remain focused and unified on its object. Hence, Asaṅga describes it as the unificatory focus of the mind on its object (Rahula 1980, 8). Although this faculty is greatly enhanced by the practice of meditation, it exists naturally in the mind, for it is simply the ability of consciousness to fixate an object. Vasubandhu describes it as a universal factor whereas Asaṅga excludes it from subliminal states. Still, both agree on its centrality in the attentional process.

These two factors (mindfulness and concentration) work in cooperation, strengthening and enhancing features of attention. Both correspond to the stage at which we purposefully notice an object and bring it into the ken of full-blown attention, the mind's ability to focus on the object and retain it. But these two factors work also in different ways. Concentration enhances the selective ability of pre-attentive orienting. It stabilizes the mind on the chosen object but tends to restrict the purview of what is being considered. Left on its own, it leads to a greater but narrower focus. Mindfulness on the other hand expands the scope of attention so that one becomes aware of the characteristics of experience (Anālayo 2003, 63–4). Thus, for the Abhidharma, attention is not just as a way of selecting particular sensory stimuli and focusing on it, but is also understood as having the cognitive function of bringing together the various aspects of the objects we encounter so as to make sense of them. Attention is the cognitive glue that holds together elementary features and transform them into identifiable forms and objects so that our experiences make sense. I take it that this cognitive ability to hold together various aspects of the perceptual process is a central aspect of mindfulness as understood by classical authors such as Buddhaghosa.

Still, this understanding of mindfulness as retentive focus does not cover all the possible meanings of mindfulness. We recall, for example, the mention by *The Questions of King Milinda* of an explicitly evaluative mindfulness, whose role seems to go beyond that of merely retaining the object. To understand this form of mindfulness, we need to consider the role of another aspect of its practice, the development of clear comprehension (*samprajñāna, sampajañña*). This is not a separate mental factor but a form of discrimination (*prajñā, paññā*) closely connected to mindfulness that enables the mind to observe, comprehend and evaluate what needs to be evaluated. It is seen as a central element of the practice of mindfulness for it provides the comprehension deriving from paying close attention to experience. Hence, it can be described as a form of attention, a wise attention or mindfulness that derives from the cultivation of this faculty. This *wise mindfulness* is to be distinguished from what we can now call *mindfulness proper*, the more basic ability of mind to retain its object. Mindfulness proper is the cognitive basis of the more explicitly cognitive wise mindfulness, which is central to the practice of mindfulness as understood by the Buddhist tradition whose goal is not to attain higher states of consciousness through the practice of concentration but to develop a clear understanding of one's bodily and mental states as impermanent, suffering, and no-self so as to undo our suffering-inducing habits. It is mindfulness proper that leads to this understanding by paying close attention to the rise and fall of mental and bodily states. The real goal of the practice of mindfulness is the development of such an understanding, the bare observation of mental states as they arise without over-identifying with them being just a means to such an end.

Although various Buddhist traditions concur in emphasizing the centrality of clear comprehension in mindfulness practice, they present it in different ways. The Theravāda tradition does not seem to stress the introspective nature of clear comprehension, which is described simply as the knowing of what happens. This knowing can concern one's mind, body, breath, as well as other objects (Wallace and Bodhi 2006, 10). The Sanskrit tradition as expressed, for example, by Shantideva, seems to stress more its introspective nature. Clear comprehension becomes then the reflective knowledge of one's mental and bodily states. Shantideva describes it as 'the repeated examination of one's body and mind' (Batchelor 1979, V.108, 59). Similarly, Tibetan thinkers such as Tsongkhapa present clear comprehension (*shes bzhin*) as being especially focused on the observation of the workings of one's mind during the practice of meditation (Tsongkhapa 2002, 57–71). The metaphor given is that of a watchman, who does not look continuously but is ready at all times to notice events as soon as they happen. By developing mindfulness we become much more skilled at this kind of observation. Whereas at first we were slow to detect when the mind was off target in meditation, the development of mindfulness leads to a shortening of the time necessary to detect the rise of distractions and other obstacles in the mind. When we become proficient, we gain the ability to notice such obstacles almost as soon as they arise. Understood in this way, clear comprehension is the meta-attentive ability to monitor one's mental states. It is an essential part of the practice of developing attention, practice that is not just based on the ability to focus on an object (video game players can do this quite well) but involves the ability to modulate one's attention, correcting the mind when it wanders and bringing it back to the object. The Tibetan tradition captures this type of skillful or wise mindfulness with the term *dran shes*, the combination of the retentive ability of mindfulness proper (*dran pa*) with the ability to use clear comprehension (*shes bzhin*) to understand what is happening in one's mind. It is this kind of wise mindfulness that eventually leads the practitioner to a deeper insight into the rise and fall of mental states. It is only by including this form of mindfulness that one can understand the full scope of mindfulness and realize its cognitive implications.

Conclusion: Consequences of ignoring the cognitive nature of mindfulness

We have now hopefully gained a richer understanding of the scope and semantic range of the scholastic Buddhist concept of mindfulness. We understand that mindfulness at its most basic level (mindfulness proper) is the ability of the mind to retain its object and not float away from it. This ability to retain the object is what allows the mind to bring this object into focus so that we are able to recollect it later. It is also what leads to the development of clear comprehension, a decisive aspect of the practice of mindfulness that allows the practitioner to evaluate the various aspects of his or her experience and to distinguish, for example, between wholesome and unwholesome mental factors, as stressed by *The Questions of King Milinda*. This form of wise mindfulness differs from mindfulness proper in that it explicitly includes the comprehension and discrimination of the object. Mindfulness proper is limited to the retentive aspect, which provides the basis for clear comprehension. Wise mindfulness is broader, including more explicitly evaluative and often introspective dimensions, whereas mindfulness proper is limited to the retentive aspect, so as to allow evaluation.

The practice of retentive focus (mindfulness proper) is not the goal but a means to a more explicitly cognitive end. Its main point is not to obtain a calm and focused state, however helpful such a state may be, but to use this state to gain a deeper understanding of the changing nature of one's bodily and mental states so as to free our mind from the habits and tendencies that bind us to suffering. In classical Buddhist scholastic terms, this means that mindfulness and concentration are developed for the sake of gaining insight (*vipaśyanā, vipassanā*) into the impermanent, suffering, and no-self nature of our bodily and mental aggregates so as to free our mind from defilements. This understanding of the body mind complex is provided at an early stage by clear comprehension, which is conceptual. But to be really effective, this insight needs to take place at the non-conceptual level. This is where mindfulness plays a decisive role. When we are able to remain carefully in touch with our experiences and to comprehend them as being impermanent, we are able to change their meaningfulness so as to see them in a different light. We then gain a direct insight into their impermanent nature, insight that is brought about by close attention and clear comprehension but goes beyond this conceptual understanding. In this way, we come to see experientially bodily and mental states as impermanent and later as suffering and no-self, thereby lessening the mesmerizing character of our experiences so that pleasant events are seen as fleeting rather than permanently satisfactory, and unpleasant encounters are seen as temporary setbacks rather than deeply upsetting defeats. This cognitive shift is based on the development of mindfulness, the retentive ability on the basis of which we are able to make sense of our experience. This leads to clear comprehension, which operates at the conceptual level and leads to the deeper non-conceptual insight through which a decisive transformation is brought about. Thus, changes in the focus of attention lead to changes in cognitive content, something entirely obvious that seems, however, to be lost in the rush to identify mindfulness with present-centred non-judgmental awareness.

We can now see that the modern understanding of mindfulness as present-centred non-judgmental awareness although not completely mistaken reflects only a partial understanding. It is only in certain contexts, particularly but not only at the beginning of one's practice, that mindfulness can be assimilated to the bare noticing of whatever arises in the present moment. Such present-centred non-judgmental attention is only one of the modalities of mindfulness, which is much broader in its scope, including explicit recollective abilities to remember the past and cognitive abilities to evaluate mental and bodily states. We also realize that the identification of mindfulness with present-centred non-judgmental awareness ignores or, at least, underestimates the cognitive implications of mindfulness, its ability to bring together various aspects of experience so as to lead to the clear comprehension of the nature of mental and bodily states. By over-emphasizing the non-judgmental nature of mindfulness and arguing that our problems stem from conceptuality, contemporary authors are in danger of leading to a one-sided understanding of mindfulness as a form of therapeutically helpful spacious quietness. I think that it is important not to lose sight that mindfulness is not just a therapeutic technique but is a natural capacity that plays a central role in the cognitive process. It is this aspect that seems to be ignored when mindfulness is reduced to a form of non-judgmental present-centred awareness of one's experiences.

I often get the feeling that the problem with such presentations of mindfulness stems from the failure to distinguish between operational definitions intended for practical instructions and adequate theoretical descriptions. There is no problem in instructing practitioners to remain aware of their mental and bodily states as they arise in the present moment while abstaining from judgments and evaluations. As mentioned above, this is a helpful way to develop mindfulness, for to do so we need to disengage from the usual patterns of discursivity and reactivity through which we usually function. But to believe that these practical instructions provide adequate theoretical models of how mindfulness works strikes me as a serious confusion. Mindfulness should not be conceptualized as being only the bare noticing of whatever arises in consciousness, for it involves essential cognitive abilities. Mindfulness is central to Buddhist practice not because it provides the degree of self-acceptance necessary to mental health but because it leads to liberative cognitive transformations. From this perspective, it becomes important to distinguish the mature understanding provided by mindfulness from the reactive evaluative patterns that dominate our minds prior to its transformation by practice. These reactive patterns are harmful not because they are evaluative but because they are reactive, being the product of our habituation to clinging to pleasant experiences and rejecting unpleasant ones. Ordinarily, most of our judgments are dominated by this unbalanced pattern. We adopt ideas, attitudes and objects not out of mature consideration of their advantages but because we like them. The practice of non-judgmental awareness is then a useful discipline to lessen this reactivity and create the space in which we can become able to form mature judgments. Hence, it is important not to lose sight of the proper role of the nonevaluative form of mindfulness. It is not an end in itself but a skillful means that allows the weakening of pre-potent responses so as to allow more adequate attitudes.

I believe that the consequences of the misleading presentation of mindfulness as present-centred non-judgmental awareness can be seen clearly in the cognitive scientific literature. There, mindfulness is almost invariably introduced as a therapy, similar to a relaxation technique or a psychological method of self-acceptance. It is almost never presented as having important cognitive functions. Its absence is glaring in the considerable literature concerning the awareness of intentions, their role in action and the degree to which they play causal roles. I am deeply struck by the fact that I have never seen the idea of mindfulness mentioned in this context or heard about its use in relevant experiments. And yet, I would think that mindfulness practitioners would be ideal subjects for such experiments and discussions, since they are supposed to have the ability to pay close attention to their bodily and mental states. Hence, they should be able to distinguish more carefully their own intentions and the degree to which those precede their actions or fail to do so. This is at least what one would expect, and verifying or falsifying such a hypothesis through experiments would seem an obvious thing to do. And yet, very little has been done in this direction. I believe that the neglect of mindfulness by cognitive scientists is due for the most part to the ways in which this concept has been theorized in the psychological literature, where its non-judgmental aspects are over-emphasized at the expense of its cognitive dimension. I think we need to correct this situation so that the true importance of the Buddhist concept of mindfulness can come through and be part of the cross-disciplinary conversation that is likely to lead to a better understanding of the mind and its abilities.

REFERENCES

ANĀLAYO. 2003. *Satipaṭṭhāna: The direct path to realization*. Birmingham: Windhorse.
BATCHELOR, S. 1977. *A guide to the Bodhisattva's way of life*. Dharamsala: Library of Tibetan Works and Archives.

BISHOP, S., M. LAU, S. SHAPIRO, L. CARLSON, N. ANDERSON, J. CARMODY, Z. SEGAL, S. ABBEY, M. SPECA, D. VELTING, and G. DEVINS. 2004. Mindfulness: A Proposed Definition. *Clinical Psychology: Science and Practice* 11: 230–41.

BODHI, BHIKKHU, ed. 2000. *A comprehensive manual of Abhidhamma*. Seattle: BPS Pariyatti Editions.

GETHIN, R. 2001. *The Buddhist path to awakening*. Oxford: Oneworld Publications.

JHA, A., E. STANLEY, and M. BAIME. 2010. Examining the protective effects of mindfulness training on working memory capacity and affective experience. *Emotion* 10 (1): 54–64.

KABAT-ZINN, J. 1990. *Full catastrophe living*. New York: Dell.

MENDIS, N. K. G. 1993. *The questions of King Milianda: An abridgment of the Milindapañha*. Kandy, Sri Lanka: Buddhist Publication Society.

NYĀNAMOLI BHIKKHU, trans. 1976. *The path of purification (Visuddhimagga)*. Boston, MA: Shambala.

PALMER, S. 1999. *Vision science*. Cambridge: MIT.

POUSSIN, L. DE LA VALLÉE. 1971. *L'Abhidharmakosha*. Bruxelles: Institut Belge des Hautes Etudes Chinoises.

RAHULA, W. 1980. *Le compendium de la super-doctrine d'Asaṅga*. Paris: Ecole Francaise d'Extreme Orient.

TSONGKHAPA. 2002. *The great treatise on the stages of the path to enlightment*. Ithaca: Snow Lion.

WALLACE, A., and BHIKKHU BODHI. 2006. The nature of mindfulness and its role in Buddhist meditation. A correspondence between B. Alan Wallace and Bhikkhu Bodhi. Not published.

THE CONSTRUCTION OF MINDFULNESS

Andrew Olendzki

Mindfulness is examined using the Abhidhamma system of classification of phenomena (dharmas) as found in the Pali work Abhidhammattha-saṅgaha. In this model the mental factors constituting the aggregate of formations (saṅkhāra) are grouped so as to describe a layered approach to the practice of mental development. Thus all mental states involve a certain set of mental factors, while others are added as the training of the mind takes place. Both unwholesome and wholesome configurations also occur, and mindfulness turns out to be a rather advanced state of wholesome constructed experience. Wisdom, the prime transformative factor in Buddhist thought and practice, arises only under special conditions. This system is then contrasted with the different parsing of phenomena presented in the Sanskrit Abhidharmakośa, where both mindfulness and wisdom are counted among the universal factors, which provides a basis for an innatist model of development; this is then critiqued from a constructivist perspective.

One of the most compelling aspects of the expansive and enduring Buddhist tradition is the sophisticated model of mind and body presented in the *Nikāyas* of the Pali Canon and systematized in both the Pali Abhidhamma literature of South Asia and the Sanskrit Abhidharma literature of Northwest India and beyond. The historical Buddha is surely the source of most of these ideas, though they were significantly developed by many others as time went by and the lore was taken up by new communities. The comprehensive analysis and description of experience offered in these teachings is of particular interest to modern thinkers, both because of its empirical underpinnings and its remarkable affinity with post-modern thought. Rooted in ancient yogic meditative practices and articulated with great intellectual precision, they offer a dynamic, process-oriented view of experience as a series of interdependent cognitive events arising and passing away each moment as the senses encounter incoming environmental data and the mind builds a world of meaning to interpret this information and respond to it both emotionally and behaviourally. Moreover, this system of thought goes beyond mere description to offer practical guidance for optimizing wellbeing, which is accomplished by overcoming the habitual compulsions deriving from the pleasure/pain reflex and by developing a greater working understanding of the nature of human experience.

This ancient knowledge about how the mind and body constructs experience and how a person can use this knowledge to attain greater health and happiness rests at the heart of the early Buddhist tradition, but was soon bypassed and relegated to a scholarly and meditative backwater as Buddhism turned in more popular, devotional, and culturally syncretic directions. It is gradually being rediscovered by the current generation of scholars and teachers, and is of special concern to those in contemporary fields who study human experience and who have an interest in augmenting human wellbeing. Among these are cognitive scientists and psychologists, and the many others who overlap with these disciplines. Early Buddhist thought employs a crisply defined technical vocabulary that can be useful in identifying and untangling the thickets of subjective experience. It also offers a detailed examination of the mechanisms of attention, which may help in working towards a better definition of mindfulness and related mental states, and may even suggest a way of measuring levels of greater or lesser attention. Of particular value to the therapeutic agenda is the basic orientation of these teachings toward transformation and the alleviation of suffering, insofar as they track progress along a scale of change from a state of affliction toward one of profound wellbeing under any circumstances.

What most characterizes the model of mind and body expressed in early Buddhist literature is the breaking down of experience into its constituent phenomenological bytes, called *dharmas*, and then the organization and classification of these *dharmas* in various ways to clarify their definition and delineate their function as part of a complex interdependent system. Just as the natural world presents itself one way at a certain level of scale and another upon closer examination, so too Buddhist thought identifies the manner in which lived experience at the level of macro-construction differs significantly from its constituent processes as they are revealed under the close investigation of a concentrated mind. For example, it can be relatively easily shown, both experientially and neurologically, that what appears as an uninterrupted flow of continuous and coherent experience is actually a series of discreet sensory and mental events that arise and pass away in rapid succession, while the sense of continuity and narrative coherence is something supplied by higher level imaginative capabilities. At the heart of the Buddha's insight is the discrepancy between what appears to be the case, which is characterized as misapprehension or even delusion, and what is actually the case, which is called wisdom.

A central feature of this model that is seldom part of corresponding Western psychological models is the evaluative characterization of various *dharmas* as either wholesome or unwholesome. The word for this quality (*kusala/akusala* in Pali) might better be translated as healthy or unhealthy, insofar as it delineates not a moral standard or a normative definition of right and wrong as much as a description of what factors contribute to or detract from the result of wellbeing, the reduction of suffering and the capacity for understanding. The word also has the sense of skillful and unskillful, which means that the Buddhist practice of integrity (*sīla*) is regarded as a skill that can be learned, while even the most atrocious misbehaviour is evidence not of an evil nature but of a lack of understanding. The centrality of this ethical evaluation reveals the extent to which this entire system, both in its *Nikāya* origins and in its *Abhidhamma* extension, is meant as a tool for effecting personal psychological transformation rather than as an intellectual exercise of building doctrine.

Another important constituent of this system is the distinction made between the object of consciousness on one hand and the attitude or emotional involvement with that object on the other. *What* is cognized with consciousness is one thing; *how* it is cognized, that is to say with what quality of mind it is cognized, is something else. Thus many of the *dharmas* enumerated in the Abhidhamma system correspond to what we might in another context call emotional attitudes, and this becomes important for understanding how meditation is regarded in early Buddhist thought. Part of meditation training has to do with learning to focus the mind on a particular object or on a series of emerging objects, but most of the training has more to do with cultivating particular qualities of mind by means of which the object is regarded. The technology of awareness is a matter of how the aggregate of consciousness (*viññāṇa*) interacts with the aggregate of material form (*rūpa*) as it manifests in the sense organs of the body and the sense objects of the environment; but the development of mindfulness and insight is rather a matter of how the aggregate of formations (*saṅkhāra*) co-arises with the other aggregates. This should become more clear as we examine the details of how experience is constructed.

The construction of experience

Consciousness arises and passes away each moment because it is a process or an event that occurs rather than something that exists in any stable and identifiable way. It is characterized just by 'knowing' and thus can only arise in relationship with an object that is known and an organ by means of which the object is known. Six classes or modalities of consciousness are enumerated, which correspond to the five sense organs (eye, ear, nose, tongue, and body) and the mind as sixth, as well to the five sense objects (forms, sounds, smells, tastes, and touches) with thoughts as the sixth. The starting point or foundation of all experience is thus an episode of cognition in one or another of these six modes, which occurs again and again in a temporal series we generally refer to as the stream of consciousness. Since consciousness manifests in dependence upon organs and objects that are constantly changing, consciousness itself it always 'moving and tottering, impermanent, changing, and becoming otherwise' as one passage puts it.[1] Moreover, consciousness does not carry any characteristics other than the mere knowing or cognizing of an object, so all the textures and qualities of experience are supplied by other mental functions arising in various combinations. A detailed account of any given moment of experience thus consists of identifying first, which of the six modes of consciousness is manifesting (i.e. in dependence on which pair of organs and objects) and second, what associated *dharmas* or constituent factors are co-arising with consciousness to shape the overall experience. The method for describing mental states in this way is outlined in the *Nikāyas* and greatly refined in the *Abhidhamma* literature.

Rather than undertake a systematic review of this method, which would lead very far afield, let us focus on one particular aspect of this mapping of the *dharmas*, one that may prove helpful in understanding the definition and function of mindfulness. It has to do with the grouping of *dharmas* into several categories, delineating those that arise and pass away together in any given moment of consciousness. According to the Abhidhamma analysis summarized in the *Abhidhammatthasaṅgaha*,[2] seven mental factors arise together in all states of consciousness and are thus called *universals;* six other mental factors may or may not be present in any particular moment and are called *occasionals.* In addition to these two groupings, 39 other mental factors are classified as either *unwholesome* or *wholesome,* but factors from each group will never arise together with those of the other group—the two are mutually exclusive. Finally, these 39 states are further broken down into four *unwholesome universals,* 10 *unwholesome occasionals,* 19 *wholesome universals* and six *wholesome occasionals.* We are thus left, generally speaking, with six different groupings of the mental factors that co-arise with consciousness to help give shape and texture to the attitude or emotion with which an object is cognized by consciousness. The whole range of individual configurations are a good deal more complex than this, but these six basic groupings yield a model that layers mental experience, so to speak, into six general levels of mental functioning, and it is these six levels that can help us understand how experience can be viewed as building upon itself to delineate a scale from lesser to greater degrees of conscious awareness.

1. The universals

The simplest manifestation of mind is characterized by the universal mental factors inherent in all moments of consciousness. It is not possible, according to the Abhidhamma, for consciousness to manifest with anything less than seven mental factors, but it may arise and pass away with only these seven and no more. Thus even in its most austere forms consciousness includes the mental functions of: *contact* between consciousness, an object and organ; a *feeling* tone that may be pleasant, unpleasant or neither; a *perception* of that object as something categorized symbolically according to prior experience; a *volition* or intentional response to the object that produces karma; a degree of *one-pointedness* or focus upon only one object at a time; a cohesive quality of *mental vitality* sustaining and supporting the interdependent functioning of the seven universal mental factors; and a function of *attention* that directs the associated factors toward the object as a rudder might steer a ship. The fact that these dharmas are always present means that they must describe even the most unreflective states of mind. We are thus always paying attention, for example, even if we are not aware we are doing so or even if we are paying attention to an object different than the one to which we would like to be attending. Similarly, the mind is always focused upon a single object, even in entirely untrained mind moments, though the object upon which it is unified might change moment to moment. If we were not capable of such baseline focus and attention, coherent mental experience would presumably not be possible.

2. The occasionals

In addition to these seven universal mental factors, six other factors are listed that may or may not arise either individually or as a whole. These include: *applied thought*, by means of which one deliberately place attention on a chosen object; *sustained thought*, the mental factor that enables one to hold the attention upon the object over multiple mind moments; *decision*, a state of confident and committed engagement with the object; *energy*, a factor that upholds and supports the others by bringing additional interest to bear; *joy*, a quality of uplifting enthusiasm; and *impulse-to-act*, a desire to act that is not rooted in greed or attachment but nonetheless impels the mind to initiate appropriate action. These are the factors called upon when we train the mind in meditation, since such training involves consciously directing attention to be placed upon and then held steadily upon a chosen object such as the breath. The steadiness of focus induces decision, requires energy, and often can result in joy, and impulse allows the meditator to shift attention from one part of the body to another, or toward the wellbeing of all creatures above, below, and all around, without doing so in ways that engage desire or compulsion. These factors may not always manifest from the moment one sits down to meditate until the bell rings an hour later, just as a baseball player is in the game even when sitting in the dugout between innings or standing around in the outfield, but to the extent deliberate mental training is ever successful, even for a moment, some combination of these factors come in to play.

3. The universal unwholesomes

The thing about the occasional factors just mentioned is that they are ethically variable, meaning they may be operative in wholesome or unwholesome mind states. All unwholesome mind moments will add four more factors: *delusion*, defined as not understanding some basic truths about experience, such as its impermanence, selflessness, and the causes of suffering; *restlessness*, a state of agitation that ruffles the mind like wind upon water; *suspension of conscience*, rendering momentarily inoperative the innate sense of self-respect that prevents us from serious wrongdoing; *suspension of respect*, turning off the innate sense of respect for the rights and opinions of others that also restrains our behaviour to stay within socially defined norms. This is the minimal set of mental factors that will be arising in the mind during any moment's misbehaviour, along of course with the seven universals. In the case of universals, it is all or nothing—when delusion is present the other three necessarily will be present as well. One interesting point about this analysis is that restlessness will always be unwholesome, suggesting that any practice that encourages one to relax and calm down is inherently healthy. It is a helpful and transformative practice in itself to reduce restlessness in the mind, since this will lead naturally to the elimination of its co-arising factor delusion, and will thus purge the moment of its most dangerous toxins and nudge it out of its unwholesomeness. Another point of some interest is the suggestion that conscience and respect function naturally as a sort of innate ethical immune system, protecting individuals and society from egregious wrongdoing, but that this is suppressed at those moments when one misbehaves.

4. The unwholesome occasionals

While delusion can manifest in such a simple form as to involve only the four universal unwholesome factors, more often than not delusion is joined by either *greed* or *hatred*, the other two components of the three toxins. Yet greed and hatred are really opposite expressions of the same impulse, namely desire. Greed is the desire to want or like or remain attached to that which is pleasing or gratifying, while hatred is the desire to not want, not like, or otherwise ignore or destroy that which is displeasing or identified with pain. As such, greed and hatred are mutually exclusive and cannot arise together in the same mind moment. One can be deluded and greedy, deluded and hateful, or just plain deluded, but one will never be both greedy and hateful in the same instant. When this appears to be the case, the Abhidhamma models asserts, the two are simply alternating one after another in rapid succession, with the illusion of simultaneity being constructed at higher levels of mental organization. Other unwholesome factors that may arise with delusion and the other universals include *wrong view, conceit, envy, avarice, worry, sloth, torpor* and *doubt*. One way of looking at these unwholesomes is as unique shades of colour mixed from the three primary colours of greed, hatred and delusion.

From the point of view of meditation practice, there is not much difference between the two groups of universal and occasional unwholesome factors—they are both serving as obstacles to mental serenity and clarity. They include, for example, the classical list of five hindrances (sense desire, ill-will, restlessness and remorse, sloth and torpor, doubt), mental factors that must be temporarily abandoned in order for the mind to reach entry level concentration and begin the process of consciousness attenuation known as the absorptions (*jhāna*). For our present purposes it suffices to say that little progress toward transformation can occur while any unwholesome state is arising in experience, and learning how to abandon such states is a fundamental part of the path. For example, while it is important to be able to notice the arising and passing away of all mental states, noticing annoyance (a mild form of hatred—not liking what is happening) with an attitude of annoyance will only reinforce the quality of annoyance. Similarly, avoiding, repressing, or otherwise pushing away the annoyance will only ensure that it comes back again later with greater urgency or intensity. The middle way between accepting and rejecting the experience of annoyance is to notice it, see it for the unwholesome factor that it is, and gently release one's hold upon it. All unwholesome states need to be similarly neutralized, and will just proliferate if met with other unwholesome states.

5. The wholesome universals

Altogether there are 19 mental factors that arise together in every wholesome mind moment, and these comprise a remarkable list. *Mindfulness* is one of them, which is regarded as a particular attitude or emotional stance toward the object of awareness. One cognizes an object with a quality of attention shaped by mindfulness, that is to say with presence of mind, non-forgetfulness, and a certain stability of focus. As a universal wholesome factor, mindfulness is exclusive of restlessness, delusion and all the other unwholesome states, and cannot co-arise with these in the same moment. It is also a mental state that arises over and above basic levels of attention, intention and one-pointedness, and that arises over and above factors that help train the mind, such as applying and sustaining attention on a consciously chosen object of awareness and generating energy or joy. The factors that co-arise with mindfulness under all circumstances also help define it and refine how it functions in the mind. *Non-greed* and *non-hatred* help clarify that mindful attention neither favours nor opposes the object, but rather it expresses an attitude of *equanimity*. This is where modern definitions of mindfulness get the sense of not judging the object but of accepting it just as it is. Also arising with mindfulness are the twin guardians of *conscience* and *respect*, which were suspended in all unwholesome states, as well as *confidence* or faith, construed as a basic trust that comes from the dispersal of the toxins. These six factors arising with mindfulness are joined by six others that can be taken in a two-fold sense of applying to both consciousness itself and to the associated mental factors: *tranquility, lightness, malleability, wieldiness, proficiency,* and *rectitude*. These can be seen as qualities of mindfulness, further shaping the attitude with which an object will be cognized by consciousness when it becomes an object of mindful awareness, rather than just an object of awareness. All 19 of these wholesome universal factors will arise and pass away as a group, not only when one practices insight meditation formally but at any time one has a wholesome thought, performs a wholesome action, or speaks a wholesome word. As such, mindfulness is a non-extraordinary mind state which may come up frequently, though mindfulness meditation involves its deliberate cultivation in a continuous series of mind moments.

6. The wholesome occasionals

The final set of factors to consider are those that build upon the universal wholesome factors. There are six of these, which can only arise if the previous 19 are present but which may or may not arise together with one another. Three of these are elements of the eightfold path, namely *right speech*, *right action* and *right livelihood*. It is a bit hard to gather how these act as mental factors, since they seem to be descriptive of behavioural patterns rather than psychological states, but they are described as being present in the mind in any moment when one deliberately abstains from misbehaving in one of the three modes. The next two are *compassion* and *appreciative joy*, two of the four *brahma-vihāras* or illimitable mind states (the other two being loving kindness and equanimity, both on the list of wholesome universals). This means that one can be simply mindful, a state which includes a benevolent and even-minded attitude toward an object, or one can also be mindful with compassion or with appreciative joy, which adds something to mindfulness. Compassion adds an empathic response to suffering, while appreciative joy adds an empathic response to good fortune or happiness. And finally one can also add *wisdom* as a wholesome occasional factor. Wisdom in Buddhist thought is a quality of understanding the nature of experience, of seeing clearly the impermanence, interdependence, and impersonality of it all, as well as seeing the origin and cessation of suffering as it manifests moment to moment in experience. It is only when the wisdom factor arises that insight meditation really occurs, for while mindfulness can regard an object with balanced objectivity, it is understanding that is ultimately transformative. As the matter is expressed in one metaphor, just as a reaper will grasp a handful of barley in one hand and a sickle in the other, one takes hold of the mind with attention and cuts off its defilements with wisdom.[3]

A model of layered attention

With the data on the table we may now step back and see what pattern emerges from this analysis of experience. Whatever the number of possible combinations of mental factors mapped out by this model, it seems helpful to make use of the six groupings outlined above and postulate that five (if we conflate the unwholesome factors into a single group) levels or layers of experience can be identified. Each of these represents a general type of mental functioning whose particular details might be almost infinitely variable. Every moment of consciousness is going to arise in correspondence with one or another of the six pairs of organs and objects (eye and forms; ear and sounds, etc.), but then each will be additionally augmented by some combination of mental factors following along the lines of these groupings. Depending on what mental factors arise in conjunction with consciousness, awareness of the object will be directed, shaped and otherwise characterized each moment by the particular combination of mental factors.

In its most basic configuration, the mind has enough support from the seven universal mental factors to be capable of cognizing any object (utilizing *contact*, *attention*, and *mental vitality*), holding the attention steadily upon it (with *volition* and *one-pointedness*), and understanding its features (*perception*) and textures (*feeling*) sufficiently to yield coherent experience. As long as one is not dead, in a coma, or in deep sleep, at least this much mind is functioning at all times. Thus even when daydreaming, multitasking, or otherwise thinking in an entirely unstructured way, these factors always cooperate to help guide and support consciousness as it cognizes an object by means of an organ. Each moment the process arises, passes away, and arises again, with all seven factors working together to construct meaning around the incoming torrent of stimuli. As moments string together into a stream of consciousness, it can feel like we are deliberately choosing to shift attention from one object to another and thus are directing awareness, but in fact most of the time what comes next in the series is conditioned by causes that lie entirely outside the scope of conscious awareness. In any given string of free association, for example, one image suggests another in ways that are habitually conditioned, and we can do all sorts of actions and behaviours of which we are entirely unaware. Paradoxically, even though consciousness is always occurring, we may well be entirely not conscious that this is the case.

At a second level of experience, built upon the foundation of the first, functions we identify with conscious awareness begin to come into play. When the mind is deliberately placed upon a particular object (using *applied thought*) rather than allowed to drift there 'on its own,' or held deliberately upon a chosen object (using *sustained thought*) even though it may be inclined to wander elsewhere, we are imposing some control on the process and it is no longer entirely conditioned by unconscious forces. As factors such as *decision, energy, joy,* and *impulse-to-act* are added, the sense of conscious engagement becomes amplified. It is at this level of mental function that mental training takes place, and the heightened concentration that comes from applying and sustaining attention in particular ways is useful to learning all sorts of skills, both wholesome and unwholesome. Training at this level of mind is where most meditation, especially for recent initiates to the practice, takes place. Instead of allowing the mind to wander wherever it will, one attempts to bring and then hold attention on the physical sensations associated with the breath, for example, or upon a phrase of loving kindness. Or, one may sanction the free and easy wandering of the mind among various different objects, but try to bring heightened awareness by applying attention with enhanced energy to following its series of manifestations. Because it takes effort to direct the mind in particular ways, this sort of mental training can feel like hard work much of the time.

The third and fourth level of mental function might best be viewed as two aspects of the same process, insofar as both deal with the arising and passing away of unwholesome states. Whether it manifests as pure *delusion*, such as what occurs when one is confused or dazed, or whether it includes the primal driving forces of *greed* and *hatred*, unwholesome mind states are worked with in Buddhist practice in similar ways. When they are strong we are swept away by their force and act out their emotions in behaviour that is harmful to ourselves and others. Much of the time we are not even consciously aware that we are in their grasp, in which case the universal factors are co-arising with the unwholesome factors without the participation of the occasional factors. Other times the occasional factors are present and we are acting in harmful ways even though we know they are harmful. One of the effects of the three poisons in such states is that we do not really care that we may be acting badly and are even enthralled by the power and gratification of such emotion. On still other occasions we might bring attention to bear upon the unwholesome states by exercising applied and sustained thought, but these are now in the service of the unwholesome state and are co-opted by delusion. One can thus be consciously aware of hatred, for example, but such awareness is not going to be transformative and may only serve to perpetuate the hatred.

It is at the next level that the transformative power of mindfulness comes to bear upon experience. As mentioned above, mindfulness and its associated factors shape the awareness of an object in very different ways than mere attention. Mindfulness is not just heightened attention, but is attention that has become confident, benevolent, balanced, and fundamentally wholesome. As such it builds not only upon the seven universal mental factors, as do all mind states, but it also builds upon the occasional factors. Basic attention (included among the universals) is augmented by deliberate conscious attention (brought in by the occasionals), and is then further refined and enhanced by mindful attention, which is always a wholesome universal. For example, one breathes all the time and may or may not be aware of the fact because of a range of various conditions. When distracted by something else we lose track of the breath; when unable to breathe or when winded we attend naturally to the breath; but in these cases our attention is 'stumbling upon' the breath as if by chance (though according to Buddhist thought there is always a cause for attention going where it does, whether one knows it or not). With meditation training, one may deliberately direct attention to the breath, but the quality of this attention may still be quite ordinary, especially when it phases in and out as the mind wanders all over the field of experience. Such directed attention may also be present in unwholesome mind states, such as when one breaths heavily in a rage or in the process of committing a terrible crime. But when the wholesome form of attention manifests, namely mindfulness, the breath is viewed in a different light, is held with a different touch, is cognized with a different quality of mind. Now the emotional tone, the intentional stance, the attitude with which one beholds the object is rooted in non-greed, non-hatred, and non-delusion, which functionally excludes from the mind their opposites, the three poisons, and even though the object of awareness is something as ordinary as the sensations of breathing, the moment is profoundly transformative. Shifting from the breath to a more challenging topic, in the case where someone who is angry is able to bring attention to the anger, and then further is able to bring mindfulness to the anger, then the anger has become a mental object, an echo from the preceding mind moments, and is no longer functioning as the attitude driving the mind. One cannot be angry and mindful at the same moment, so at whatever point true mindfulness arises the actual anger is already banished and it is only a relic of that angry state that is acting as the object of consciousness. If the wholesome attention can be sustained moment after moment, the entire stream of consciousness becomes purified of its naturally-arising toxins and wholesome dispositions are reinforced while their unwholesome counterparts atrophy. Mindfulness of unwholesome states is transformative precisely because the unwholesome quality of awareness has been replaced with a wholesome attitude.

The final grouping to consider is the wholesome occasional factors, which arise building upon the foundation of the wholesome universals. Here we meet with wisdom, which according to this model does not arise automatically with mindfulness. It is possible, in other words, to experience purification of the mind stream through mindful meditation without necessarily understanding with wisdom the nature of experience. Mindfulness practice ripens into insight meditation when one sees directly such things as impermanence, suffering and selflessness in the arising and passing away of the objects of awareness. Once again, it does not matter what the object is; it is the way of understanding the object that is important here. Wisdom in this model is itself as impermanent and tenuous as every other element of the mind and body. It arises under certain conditions, and cannot be sustained if those conditions change even slightly. One tends to experience wisdom in brief glimpses, therefore, which may be repeated more often as one's skills increase.

Meditation as process

What this model provides is a layered way of understanding what happens when one sits down to practice meditation. Much of the time there is only a rudimentary form of attention manifesting, as the mind registers changes in the environment, such as sounds, or moves from one association to another in a natural and ordinary way. The mind is constantly shifting its attention from one object to another, and one can guide this process somewhat by exercising volition and attention to encourage engaging the mind with one thing rather than another. Most forms of popular self-development strategies work at this basic level of *changing the mind* (1) by guiding attention from one thing to another. What Buddhists would call *training the mind* (2) begins as the commitment to cultivating attention in a more directed and deliberate way. One becomes gradually more adept at placing the attention on a chosen object and maintaining it upon that object for some period of time. If one is practicing concentration meditation the attention might even remain steady upon an object for a considerable length of time, or might be capable of focusing well on a long series of changing objects. While doing any of this, it is natural that unwholesome mind states will arise and pass away in experience, both deluded states with greed and hatred and states that are merely deluded. One will try to abandon these as they are noticed, either right away or after a long ride on a train of thought that carries one well down the track. Abandoning such toxic mind states after they have arisen and guarding the mind from the arising of such toxic states are important Buddhist practices for *purifying the mind* (3). At other moments, when these toxins do not manifest, mindfulness may arise with its host of associated factors, and this too will either pass away quickly or be sustainable for multiple mind moments. Mindfulness practice serves the function of *transforming the mind* (4) by simultaneously blocking all unwholesome states and developing and strengthening wholesome states. And when mindfulness does become steady enough, the conditions ripen for wisdom also to arise and greatly magnify the transformative effect of mindfulness, although it may collapse just as rapidly as it arose. Wisdom has the function of *liberating the mind* (5), both in the short-term, as the unconscious effects of delusion are neutralized, and in the long-term, as the latent disposition toward greed, hatred and delusion are expunged from the mind altogether and are no longer capable of arising.

In this way of looking at things, the mind is intrinsically neither polluted nor pristine. It is capable of functioning at a basic level of awareness that includes the six internal and six external sense bases, the six corresponding modalities of consciousness, and all five of the aggregates. Over and above this, it can add either wholesome or unwholesome mental factors (both of which are volition formations or *saṅkhāras*) in various combinations, which will serve to clarify or pollute the resulting quality of awareness. Mental training in general, and the development of mindfulness and wisdom in particular, will optimize the functioning of the mind, and will culminate in its transformation such that unwholesome states can no longer occur at all and the mind will become entirely liberated from its suffering. The process unfolds something like the classical image of the lotus, whose roots are in the mud, growing through the water and ultimately opening its petals to the sky.

Abhidhamma and Abhidharma

All that has been said so far is from the perspective of the Pali Abhidhamma, those texts that emerged and stabilized in the Southern Buddhist schools of South and Southeast Asia. These texts include such works as the seven books of the *Abhidhamma-piṭaka* and such later manuals as the *Abhidhammatthasaṅgaha*. There is also a parallel Sanskrit *Abhidharma* tradition, expressed in texts that developed in Northern Buddhist schools of North West India and elsewhere. Here too we find seven (somewhat different) books of an *Abhidharma-piṭaka* and later compilations such as the *Abhidharmakośa*. For the most part there is a great deal of similarity and agreement between these two textual, meditational, and philosophical traditions, which can clearly be seen as two parallel strands of development from a more or less common source. On the matter at hand, however, namely the classification of the *dharmas* into groupings of universal and occasional wholesome and unwholesome factors, there is a very interesting divergence between the two traditions. This discrepancy is not trivial, and speaks to the very core of the different models of practice and liberation the two approaches take.

In the *Abhidharmakośa*, the mental factors of *mindfulness* and *wisdom* are considered among the universal mental factors, and thus arise and pass away in every single mind moment.[4] They are presumably eclipsed or over-ridden by unwholesome factors, but nevertheless underlie such mental states. This model is thus in line with the later Buddhist view of the mind as already awakened, inherently wise, but with its wisdom habitually occluded by greed, hatred and delusion. The practice becomes one of uncovering the originally pure nature of mind rather than of building up wisdom upon the prepared ground of mindfulness.

The implications of this distinction are huge, and clearly go beyond the scope of what can be said here. Suffice it to say that including mindfulness and wisdom among the universal factors provides a rationale for the so-call 'innatist' model of later Buddhist tradition, as contrasted to the 'constructivist' model favoured by the earlier tradition (see Dunne 2011). A natural historical question to emerge is whether the philosophical changes of the Abhidharma system preceded or postdated the emergence of the innatist model of awakening. And the doctrinal question that naturally arises is whether a new approach to practice led to revisions of the Abhidharma system, or whether the patterns laid down by the Abhidharma paved the way for a different orientation toward practice. Again, these questions need to be pursued elsewhere, though it might not be surprising if it turned out these two had a chicken and egg relationship. Let us conclude here with a brief reflection upon the innatist approach from the perspective of the constructivist model outlined above.

A constructivist critique of non-duality

From the earlier constructionist perspective of the Nikayas and the Abhidhamma, the whole issue of dual or nondual experience is somewhat puzzling. The *Nikāyas* tell us that every cognitive event depends not upon a duality between subject and object, but upon a trinity of sense organ, sense object and consciousness.[5] The coming together of these three constitutes contact (*phassa/sparśa*), the starting point of any episode of knowing. If there is indeed a duality in early Buddhist thought, it is not one of subject and object but of organ and object. The events cognized by cognition are the collisions between the inner and outer world, the interaction of stimuli such as light and sound waves (etc.) upon the sensitive matter of retina and inner ear (etc.) that translate these modulations into the neuronal activity we call consciousness. The knowing of an object by means of an organ is not the same as the subject-object relation. Consciousness is not a subject, but an activity, a process, an event recurring moment after moment. It is a relationship between organs of sensation and thought on one hand, and objects of sensation and thought on the other. It is a natural interface between the sensitive matter of the body's sense receptors (which would include the brain) and the data contained in the surrounding (and internal) environment that is mediated by mental states of knowing. This mentality is likely an emergent property of materiality, but the virtual world constructed of this mental activity presents as a robust phenomenology of experience.

The experience of arising and passing phenomena do indeed involve the arising and passing away of moments of consciousness, but these do not in themselves qualify as a subject. The subject is constructed elsewhere in the model, at the point where desire is generated toward the objects of experience. By liking or not liking the object, a subject who likes or does not like the object is created. It is craving, manifesting as clinging, that leads to the becoming of a self (*atta-bhāva*), and it is only when one has become a self, a subject, there can then also be suffering. The one who craves becomes the one who suffers, as pointed out in the Second Noble Truth. And as the Third Noble Truth indicates, the cessation of craving will lead to the cessation of suffering by means of the cessation of the making of a self (*ahaṃ-kāra*). The duality to which non-dual Buddhist thought seems to be pointing, therefore, is the duality between the object and the subject who likes or does not like it, rather than between the object and the knowing of the object. That knowing, the mere functioning of consciousness, is an impersonal event; the liking or disliking of it is a personal construction. From earliest times, in this way of looking at it, the Buddha was always directing his students toward non-dual experience, but this had nothing to do with the relationship between consciousness and the object cognized by it. It was only about the object and the illusory sense of being a person who stands in relation to it. It is then entirely perplexing to discover that the solution to this 'problem' in later tradition is to de-couple consciousness from its object and aspire to an experience of consciousness that takes no object. This seems to preserve the subject at the expense of the object, while the entire point of the early teaching is to understand the fundamentally illusory nature of the subject and thus allow the object to be known with consciousness as it really is (*yathā-bhūta*).

If the non-dual experience has to do with the dissolution of the subject-object relation, then according to Abhidhamma analysis it must refer to the elimination of the mistaken view of self (*sakkāyadiṭṭhi*).[6] This eliminates one dichotomy, between phenomena as they really are and the illusory sense of there being a separate person to whom the experience of the phenomena belongs. But it leaves intact the dichotomy between the organs and objects of experience, because each only exists as an interaction with the other and each therefore requires the other by definition. Cognition thus remains, even after the person who experiences the cognition is vanquished, as the mere view it really is.

It seems as if somewhere along the line a conflation occurred between consciousness and the view of self, insofar as consciousness is identified as the subject in a subject-object relation. I think the entire concept of subject-object duality is an issue inherited by Buddhist thinkers from non-Buddhist schools of Indian philosophy, where the issue is simplified by the real existence of a soul. In

Hindu thought, consciousness (*cit*) is inextricably bound up with real existence (*sat*), so it is taken for granted that where there is something known (*grāhya*) there must be a knower of it (*grāhaka*). But the Buddha sought to purge his language of all agent nouns, and would likely regard any reference to a 'knower of the known' to be fundamentally deluded.[7] A soul in relation to anything constitutes a duality, and the liberation of the soul from anything results in a non-dual state. In this binary environment of self and other it is natural to explore the subject-object distinction philosophically, and it seems Buddhist thinkers were drawn in to this discourse. But in the non-binary world of the non-orthodox Indic teachings, such as Buddhism, where consciousness is seen to be a multiply-conditioned natural phenomenon, the situation is more complex. The interdependent arising and cessation of consciousness (along with its corresponding organs and objects and the other four aggregates) unfolding each moment is one thing, while the construction of an illusory sense of being the person to which it is all happening is something else again.

So I would entirely agree that Buddhist insight has to do with experiencing non-duality of subject and object, but would suggest that this is accomplished when the sense of self is lost, either briefly, as in the short-term loss of self occurring in any peak experience, or unshakeably, as with the awakening of a Buddha. This sort of non-dual understanding is hardly an innovation of the fourth century, however, and has been an intrinsic part of the Buddhist message from its earliest times.

NOTES

1. *Saṃyutta Nikāya* 35:93.
2. Bodhi (1993). In what follows the impulse to list each of the following technical terms along with their Pali and Sanskrit names is replaced with a simple English rendering. See Bodhi (1993) for the Pali and Pruden (1991) for the Sanskrit. See also Olendzki (2010, 163ff).
3. *Milindapañho* 2:1.8.
4. *Abhidharmakośa* 2:24 (Pruden, 1991, 189–90). The universals are here called *mahābhūmikas*.
5. See, for example, the *Mahāhatthipadopama Sutta*, *Majjhima Nikāya* 28.
6. *Majjhima Nikāya* 48: 'This is the way leading to the origination of personality: One regards [all experience] thus: "This is mine, this I am, this is my self." This is the way leading to the cessation of personality: One regards [all experience] thus: "This is not mine, this I am not, this is not my self." Notice the functioning of consciousness remains unchanged.
7. *Saṃyutta Nikāya* 12:12: 'Venerable sir, who makes contact...who feels...who craves...?' "Not a valid question. I do not say "One makes contact...one feels...one craves..." If one should ask me, "Venerable sir, with what as condition does contact come to be...with what as condition does feeling come

to be ... with what as condition does craving come to be?" —this would be a valid question.' See also, e.g., *Visuddhimagga* 16:90: *kāriko na ... vijjati; gamako na vijjati* ... etc. (a do-er is not found; a go-er is not found).

REFERENCES

BODHI, BHIKKHU. 1993. *A comprehensive manual of Abhidhamma*. Pariyatti: Seattle.

DUNNE, J. 2011. Toward an understanding of non-dual mindfulness. *Contemporary Buddhism* 12: 71–88.

OLENDZKI, A. 2010. *Unlimiting mind: The radically experiential psychology of Buddhism.* Boston, MA: Wisdom.

PRUDEN, L. 1991. *Abhidharmakośabhāṣyam*. English translation by Louis de La Vallée Pussin. Berkeley, CA: Asian Humanities Press.

TOWARD AN UNDERSTANDING OF NON-DUAL MINDFULNESS

John Dunne

The aim of this article is to explore an approach to 'mindfulness' that lies outside of the usual Buddhist mainstream. This approach adopts a 'non-dual' stance to meditation practice, and based on my limited experience and training in Mindfulness Based Stress Reduction, this non-dual notion of 'mindfulness' seems an especially appropriate point of comparison between Mindfulness Based Stress Reduction and Buddhism. That comparison itself will not be the focus here—given my own inexpertise and lack of clinical experience, it would be best to leave the comparison to others! Instead, the aim here will be to explore some features of 'mindfulness' in the context of non-dual styles of Buddhist practice. To begin, we will assess some difficulties that emerge when one attempts to speak of 'mindfulness' in Buddhism. Next, we will turn to the somewhat radical notion of 'non-dual' practice in relation to the more mainstream descriptions found in the Buddhist Abhidharma literature. We will then examine some crucial features of Buddhist non-dualism, including attitudes and theories about thoughts and judgments. A brief foray into specific practice instructions will help us to understand the role of 'mindfulness' in a specific non-dual tradition called, 'Mahāmudrā' (the 'Great Seal'). Finally, after some reflection on 'mindfulness' in the non-dual practice of Mahāmudrā, I will conclude by considering a crucial issue: the context of practice.

This mind itself, bound by its knots—if one lets go, There is no doubt: it will be free. (Saraha)

1. Authority and the problem of one Buddhism

As other authors here have affirmed, the Buddhist tradition is not monolithic: Buddhism exhibits great diversity in its philosophies, meditation techniques, institutional structures, political roles, cultural expressions and numerous other features. Some scholars have even suggested that, in contemporary academic contexts, it is highly misleading to use the single term 'Buddhism' to describe these diverse manifestations in cultures as divergent as India, Sri Lanka, Vietnam, Nepal, Tibet, Korea, China, Japan, North America and so on. The well substantiated claim here is that any attempt to speak in the singular of 'Buddhism' necessarily obscures actual diversity in philosophy and practice by masking it with our own, particular notion of what 'Buddhism' in the singular might be. Clearly, if we are to avoid simply projecting our own assumptions and desires, we must explore the diversity of Buddhisms and see how some strands might object to the understanding of 'mindfulness' in Mindfulness Based Stress Reduction (MBSR), while other strands might endorse it readily.[1]

In moving beyond a monolithic notion of a singular Buddhism, however, we face two difficult challenges that emerge from Buddhist traditions themselves. One is simply the problem of finding the right term(s) to interpret as 'mindfulness.' The same problem of diversity applies here, except that even within single strands of Buddhism, conflicting opinions appear. Let us mark this problem by dropping the awkward quotation marks and capitalizing Mindfulness so as to remind ourselves that this singular term can easily mask great diversity within Buddhism and in contemporary usage.

Setting aside for the moment the problem of Mindfulness's diversity, we encounter another, perhaps more difficult issue: the various Buddhist traditions and teachers themselves often insist that, in the final analysis, Buddhism is indeed singular and monolithic. This does not necessarily mean that a tradition or teacher will claim that the one true Buddhism is the one found in that tradition's philosophy and practice. Certainly, such claims are made, but another approach is to demonstrate that one's tradition fits into an overarching, unitary vision of Buddhism, and to do so, one must reconcile the current features of one's tradition with earlier practices and texts that, at least on the surface, may appear to be quite different from one's tradition. This approach appears especially in Buddhist commentarial literature—precisely the texts that one would consult for a detailed analysis of Mindfulness. Each Buddhist tradition takes a set of older texts as in some way authoritative, and even if these texts appear to contradict the practice or philosophy of one's tradition, a skilful commentator can find a way to reconcile these older materials with the contemporary tradition.

When commentators reconcile their own traditions with earlier materials, they implicitly (or sometimes, explicitly) argue for the overall unity of Buddhism. But the unity of Buddhism is not what is actually at stake. Instead, if commentators cannot connect their particular tradition to earlier, authoritative texts written by great, authoritative figures, then that tradition's followers and its critics may all doubt whether the tradition itself is authoritative. In other words, the drive toward One Buddhism in traditional scholarship is largely driven by the need to justify the authenticity of the commentator's tradition. This problem becomes especially acute when a tradition develops new practices and philosophical perspectives. Critics (especially those in competing Buddhist traditions) can claim that these new practices and philosophies are inauthentic, and followers may develop similar doubts that will block the effectiveness of practice techniques. For these reasons, Buddhist traditions usually resist any claim to novelty: in some sense, each tradition claims that it embodies just what the Buddha taught (even if it was taught only implicitly).[2]

In India and Tibet, the need to justify the authenticity of one's tradition required Buddhists to demonstrate how their traditions connected to a number of older Buddhist texts of various kinds, but for our purposes, the most important body of texts is the *Abhidharma*. For later Mahāyāna thinkers in India and Tibet, two texts in particular were touchstones: the *Abhidharmakośa* of Vasubandhu and the *Abhidharmasamuccaya* of Asaṅga. These texts themselves harkened back to earlier materials, and in the end, they are generally understood to be rooted in the 'speech of the Buddha' *(buddhavacana)* itself. These *Abhidharma* texts are especially relevant here because in them we find technical discussions of meditative practices and terminology, including notions of Mindfulness. Thus, if later Mahāyāna Buddhists in India and Tibet wrote about their meditation theories and practices, they were obliged to demonstrate that it was possible to use these *Abhidharma* theories, terms and categories to explicate their traditions' practices. It is crucial to note, however, that the theories, terms and categories in these *Abhidharma* texts were formulated no later than the fourth century (C.E.), and none of their major theories, terms or categories has been revised since. This would pose no problem if theories and practices of meditation in later India and Tibet remained completely static, or at least did not change in a way that is difficult to reconcile with the *Abhidharma*. But theory and practice did indeed change in that way. In particular, and of special relevance here, is the emergence of styles of practice that are best called 'non-dual,' especially the one we will consider below: Mahāmudrā.[3]

2. The non-dual and the *Abhidharma*

Notions of non-duality (Skt., *advaya*) occur early in Indian Buddhism. Certainly, the ultimate non-duality of *saṃsāra* and *nirvāṇa* is one example that is critical to the emergence of Mahāyāna Buddhism around the first century (C.E.). In speaking of Mahāmudrā as a non-dual style of practice, however, I am referring specifically to a form of non-duality that finds its first expression no earlier than the third century (C.E.), and that undergoes further development around the seventh century. This form of non-duality is concerned specifically with the duality of knowing subject vs. known object *(grāhyagrāhakadvaya)*. From an historical perspective, two developments within Indian Buddhism allow this style of practice to develop. First, Yogācāra philosophy (starting around the second or third century) maintains that ignorance *(avidyā)* occurs in its subtlest form as the seemingly real appearance of an ultimately false distinction between object and subject in experience. In other words, for Yogācāra thought, ignorance in its subtlest form manifests as the sense that there is a subjectivity that stands distinct and separate from the objects it apprehends. Since one central goal of all Mahāyāna practice is to eliminate ignorance by experiencing reality as it truly is *(yathābhūtadarśana)*, for Yogācāra thinkers a truly liberative meditative state must not be caught in the false distinction between subject and object. In other words, the state must be *non-dual*, in that the experience is not structured by the duality of object and subject. It is, instead, 'non-dual wisdom' *(Skt., advayajñāna)*.

For practitioners to experience a non-dual state, however, there must be some form of knowing or experiencing that is not structured by subject–object duality. This form of knowing is 'reflexive awareness' (Skt. *svasaṃvitti*, Tib., *rang rig*), and it does not receive a robust theoretical treatment until the works of Dharmakīrti and his major commentators (seventh to ninth centuries). Once a clear account of reflexive awareness is in place, Buddhist authors now have the tools to speak of truly non-dual meditative states, namely, those in which the meditator experiences consciousness in its true form as utterly devoid of subject–object structuring. And this is precisely the type of practice that emerges historically as Mahāmudrā in India by the end of the first millennium (C.E.).[4]

Below, we will examine some features of Mahāmudrā theory and practice, especially in terms of Mindfulness, but let us first point to an immediate problem that Mahāyāna commentators face when they wish to speak of Mahāmudrā in technical terms. The technical tools and vocabulary that they use must be drawn from the *Abhidharma* works mentioned above, since these are taken to be the authoritative sources for such purposes. But according to those works, *all* liberative meditative states necessarily have an object; that is, any meditation that a Buddhist would use to eliminate ignorance would have to be structured by subject–object duality. Simply put, the *Abhidharmasamuccaya* or *Abhidharma-kośa* do not articulate any theory about a meditative state that eliminates ignorance and is devoid of subject–object duality. Indeed, except for some unusual cases that are not considered useful on the path, the *Abhidharma* as a whole assumes that a state that one would cultivate on the path is necessarily a state that is oriented toward some object that one meditates upon.

Clearly, it is not easy to formulate an *Abhidharma* account of 'non-dual wisdom'—a form of knowing that is radically unstructured by object and subject. And since the *Abhidharma* account of Mindfulness likewise assumes that meditative states are structured by subject–object duality, it seems obvious that we should not attempt to map *Abhidharma* categories directly onto non-dual practices such as Mahāmudrā. Indeed, it seems highly problematic to use any Buddhist sources prior to the seventh century (C.E.) to explicate the cognitive details of non-dual practices, inasmuch as these sources lack the theoretical tools and terminology to address non-dual meditations, including their features such as non-dual Mindfulness.

One can object, however, that members of the non-dual Mahāmudrā tradition in Tibet certainly did use *Abhidharma* categories and terminology just for this purpose. In other words, as the Mahāmudrā tradition moved from India to Tibet, it also developed in ways that led to more systematic explications of the practice, and while many new terms were coined or adopted, much of the *Abhidharma*'s technical vocabulary was also adapted (in ways that are sometimes quite confusing) for the purpose of analysing Mahāmudrā practice. For example, the *Abhidharma* term *śamatha* (Tib., *zhi gnas*) occurs frequently in later Tibetan accounts of Mahāmudrā, even though the *Abhidharma* use of the term always assumes that there is an object of meditation, whereas in Mahāmudrā *śamatha* is clearly set in a context where the goal is to move beyond focus on an object.

Why do later Tibetan scholars of Mahāmudrā employ *Abhidharma* terminology, even though the fit is at times quite loose? One reason may simply be that *Abhidharma* terms were the best available ones, and without engaging in some laborious update of the entire *Abhidharma*, it was best to adapt and update a few select terms that were especially useful for understanding Mahāmudrā practice. Another reason, one coming from a contemporary academic perspective, is that to maintain the authenticity of Mahāmudrā practices, Tibetan commentators *had to* connect those practices with the *Abhidharma*. If the practice could not be explicated in *Abhidharma* terms, it was not authentic. Thus, no matter how difficult the fit might be at times, there was no choice but to use *Abhidharma* terms to explain Mahāmudrā, at least in certain contexts.[5]

In the contemporary context, it certainly remains legitimate to employ *Abhidharma* tools to understand practices that emerge long after the *Abhidharma*, but it is probably important to ask some questions. If we are examining a non-dual style of practice, have we updated the *Abhidharma* terms so that they fit better? And if we are examining a non-dual style, why not examine non-dual texts themselves, rather than the *Abhidharma*? Is our motivation to use the *Abhidharma* as a means to argue about authenticity and authority? In other words, in the face of the obvious diversity within Buddhism, do we prefer to argue for one authentic version of Mindfulness? If so, then why?

3. Key features of non-dual styles of practice

By now it is perhaps obvious that, in comparing Mindfulness in MBSR to Buddhist practice, I do not see the *Abhidharma* itself as providing the best tools. Based on my experience in MBSR training, my research on the topic, and my many conversations with MBSR practitioners, it seems clear to me that MBSR is overall adopting a non-dual approach to practice.[6] The appropriate point of comparison must be found within non-dual Buddhist traditions, and with that in mind, I will now turn to some relevant key features of non-dual practice styles.

These features connect to an overall concern that fundamentally distinguishes non-dual Buddhist traditions from other approaches: to put it simply, what is the continuity between an ordinary mind and the mind of a Buddha? In other words, to what extent are the qualities of buddhahood or awakening *(bodhi)* present in an ordinary person? In answering this crucial question, Buddhist traditions fall along a spectrum. At one end of the spectrum, *all* the qualities of awakening are already present in an ordinary person's mind; at the other end of the spectrum, only some very minimal qualities are present, just enough to make it possible for an ordinary person to develop the other qualities. Each of these options has its philosophical and practical challenges. If one maintains that all the qualities of awakening are already innate in any sentient being's mind, it would seem that we all should already be buddhas. The answer is that, yes, in a sense we are essentially already awakened, but our minds are occluded by other features that prevent our natural buddhahood from manifesting spontaneously. For the other position, those who say that the qualities of buddhahood must be acquired or constructed, the problem is explaining how we can even begin, if we are cluelessly mired in our ignorance. Here, the answer is that, given the cognitive qualities we do have, the proper training and instruction can move us beyond that ignorant state, if we apply sufficient effort.

The two endpoints of this spectrum are often referred to as 'Sudden' (Tib., *cig car ba*) and 'Gradual' (Tib., *rim bzhin pa*) approaches to Buddhahood, but since these terms can be confusing, I will refer to these endpoints as 'Innateism' and 'Constructivism.' For the Innateist, progress along the path mostly involves eliminating the obscurations that prevent our innate buddhahood from emerging. For the Constructivist, the path involves eliminating obstructions, but it also requires carefully acquiring or constructing the qualities that eventually result in buddhahood. Again, it is important to see that these two positions fall at the ends of a spectrum, and various Buddhist traditions can be located at one or another point along that scale. And here is the crucial point: non-dual approaches always tend toward the Innateist approach, while the classical *Abhidharma* perspective is far more Constructivist.[7]

For the non-dual Innateist, a central task is to eliminate the obstructions that mask one's innate Buddhahood, but here the obvious question is: just what are these obstructions? As Buddhism historically develops increasingly sophisticated accounts of experience, this question raises the possibility that many qualities of ordinary experience itself are obscuring Buddhahood. For a host of reasons that cannot be explained here, the Mahāmudrā adepts of India generally took a fairly radical Innateist stance: they conclude that most or even *all* the structures of ordinary cognition are part of the problem. In other words, the ordinary structures of cognition—including time, space, identity and many others—are the main obstacle to the spontaneous emergence of one's innate Buddhahood. These structures, subsumed under the Sanskrit term *prapañca* (Tib., *spros pa*), are the subtlest manifestation of ignorance, and the goal of both philosophy and meditation practice must be to eliminate them.

Buddhist Constructivists, on the other hand, maintain that it is more the content of these structures, rather than the structures themselves, that are the problem. Certainly, some of the structures of one's ordinary cognition must change, but most of the basic structures such as time, space, and subject–object orientation are not taken to be problematic in themselves. Indeed, they are essential to progress along the path because without them, one cannot create one's own future Buddhahood, which must be constructed piece by piece over time. For the Constructivists, it is more some specific content, such as an automatic belief in one's own fixed identity, that must be eliminated, and other qualities, such as compassion, that must be cultivated. This process of elimination and cultivation (or construction) leads to Buddhahood for the Constructivist.

It is important to recall that the majority of Indian Buddhist scholars would be placed somewhere on the Constructivist end of this spectrum, and when the Innateist position arises, it does so in response to Constructivism. In part this means that the Innateist approach in India was *contrarian*: it stood outside the Buddhist mainstream and critiqued it. Thus, Saraha (fl. c. 975?), one of the great Innateist authors of India, even mocks the mainstream, scholastic approach with its highly technical accounts of meditation. And Maitripa (fl. c. 1035?), who was more willing to use some of the mainstream philosophical tools, nevertheless argues radically that proper meditation involves *asmṛti* ('non-mindfulness') and *amanasikāra* ('non-attention').[8]

In speaking of 'non-mindfulness' and 'non-attention,' Maitripa directly invokes the *Abhidharma* account of meditation, whereby *smṛti* ('mindfulness') and *manasikāra* ('attention') are considered essential to proper meditation practice. In the classical *Abhidharma* account, these two facets of awareness must be present in order for an object to be held with stability in a meditative state. And it is precisely for this reason that Maitripa insists that in proper *non-dual* meditation, these two facets must be inverted or negated. From the non-dual Innateist perspective, if one is cultivating *smṛti* (Pāli, *sati*) and *manasikāra,* then one is cultivating ignorance because one is only strengthening the subject–object structures of awareness— the very structures that are the subtlest manifestation of ignorance itself.

Below we will examine some specific practice instructions that emerge much later from this radical inversion of the Buddhist mainstream, but let us first explore some further implications of the non-dual Innateist approach. Maitripa's coinage of 'non-mindfulness' and 'non-attention' already point to a central theme: whatever techniques are employed in meditation, they must be aimed at eliminating *prapañca,* the structures of ordinary cognition that occlude one's innate Buddhahood. At the more advanced levels of practice, contemplative practice targets the structures that involve 'dualistic cognition' (Tib., *gnyis 'dzin gyi blo*), but since those structures are understood to be quite subtle, beginners (and even fairly advanced practitioners) cannot aim to allow them to dissipate from the start. Instead, grosser structures that depend on dualistic cognition are the starting point of practice, and these include especially the structures that permit judgments (discursive thoughts) to arise.

To understand the nature of thoughts and judgments in this context, it is useful to turn to the Buddhist epistemological tradition descending from Dharmakīrti (fl. seventh century C.E.) and his commentators, since their works seem to be an important source for the Innateist styles of practice that eventually arise in India.[9] Their theories point to three features of thoughts and judgments that are especially relevant to a novice's practice. The first is that judgments involve what cognitive scientists call 'time travelling,' that is, the projection of oneself as the thinking subject into the past or the future. According to the relevant Buddhist theory of concept formation, all concepts necessarily involve this feature. Hence, to eliminate entrapment in the structures of thoughts or judgments, an obvious starting place is to cultivate present-centred awareness, as will be evident from the practice instructions below.

There is a second key feature of the Buddhist theory about thoughts: even though judgments or discursive thoughts are only representations and not real in themselves, they nevertheless present themselves as real. In other words, the thought of an 'apple' is not an actual apple; it cannot be eaten. Nevertheless, we have an innate tendency to construe our thoughts as real. Thus, in a way that is similar to the notion of 'cognitive fusion' in Acceptance and Commitment Therapy, we 'fuse' or meld our representations of reality with reality itself.[10] As a result of seeming to be real in this way, thoughts often seem highly relevant to one, and they thus draw one into a whole series of thoughts. In practice, then, one cultivates the capacity to break this cognitive fusion and not become caught in a chain of thoughts.

A third key aspect of this Buddhist view of judgments or thoughts is that they necessarily involve 'cognitive effort' (ābhoga, Tib., rtsol ba).[11] Further research on this notion in the Buddhist epistemological tradition is necessary, but it clearly rests on some kind of distinction between perception as a more receptive process and thought or judgment as a more active, constructive process. This does not mean that thoughts or judgments arise only when one makes a conscious effort, but rather that the process of forming thoughts requires additional, mental conditions beyond those which are necessary for sheer perception. The formation of thoughts or judgment could thus be well below one's usual level of awareness, but it is nevertheless driven by factors such as interest, goal-orientation, desires and dislikes, and so on. All these together constitute a kind of 'cognitive effort,' and this seems to be one factor in the emphasis on 'effortlessness' as a means to release the structures that allow thoughts to arise. This may explain why one of the major themes of Innateist practice such as Mahāmudrā is the 'letting go' (Tib., lhod kyis glod) of thinking itself.

Finally, building on these three features of judgments or thoughts, the Mahāmudrā practice texts suggest another important aspect: the more value-laden the thought, the more likely it is to have strong 'cognitive fusion' and thus pull one into a chain of thoughts. The implicit theory here seems to be that thoughts seem especially relevant to oneself when they are highly charged or value-laden—this includes thoughts about the good and the bad, the ethical and the unethical, the pleasant and the unpleasant, and so on. As a result of seeming to have great relevance, these thoughts ensnare us all the more easily. Hence, the practice instructions discussed below will show that an additional feature of practice, especially for the beginner, is not to become caught in value judgments during meditation, including especially judgments about the meditation itself.

In the next section we will briefly examine some actual practice instructions that illustrate the points made above, but first, let us note some problems with applying an Abhidharma analysis to non-dual Mahāmudrā practice. Given the features discussed above, it should already be clear that non-dual Mindfulness must eventually move beyond ethical judgment, recollection of the past (including recalling one's vows), or prospection (thoughts about the future). However, as Georges Dreyfus points out in his article elsewhere in this issue (Dreyfus, 2011), ethical judgment, recollection and prospection are crucial to the Abhidharma model of Mindfulness. Dreyfus correctly notes, for example, that the interpretation of Mindfulness as 'present-centred nonevaluative awareness is problematic, for it reflects only some of the ways in which these original terms are deployed.' He points to the interpretation of *sati* (Skt., *smṛti*) as Mindfulness, and remarks that it must 'distinguish wholesome from unwholesome mental states.' Thus, Mindfulness 'must be explicitly cognitive and evaluative.' This means that Mindfulness involves 'retention of information' and also prospection with regard to future spiritual goals. In short, based on his reading of the *Abhidharma* approach, he rejects the interpretation of Mindfulness as primarily being 'present-centred non-judgmental awareness.' Indeed, for the Constructivist approach of the *Abhidharma*, an emphasis on present-centred, non-judgmental awareness would seem to lose the moral or ethical framework of Buddhist practice. At the end of this article, I will return to the way that non-dual Innateist traditions respond to this issue.

In any case, Dreyfus's analysis is an excellent presentation of a 'classical' *Abhidharma* approach to Mindfulness, but it may not be a good fit for the non-dual Innateist approaches to Mindfulness. The features discussed above already indicate the importance of allowing the mind to settle in a non-judgmental, present-centred state, and it likewise indicates how non-dual traditions, striking a stance deliberately contrary to *Abhidharma* scholasticism, remain highly skeptical about the utility of evaluative thought in practice. Instead, one must become released from the very structures of such thoughts, since they are a manifestation of ignorance itself. All this will become more salient when we explore some instructions for Mahāmudrā practice and examine the role of Mindfulness therein.

4. Examples from practice instructions

Let us turn briefly now to some instructions from a well known meditation manual in the Mahāmudrā tradition, the *Ocean of Definitive Meaning* by Karma Wangchûg Dorjé, the ninth Karmapa (1556–1603). The text, composed by a central figure in the Tibetan Mahāmudrā lineages, is one of the most complete compendia of practice instructions available. Along with another, more polemical compendium by Dakpo Tashi Namgyel (1512–1587),[12] the *Ocean* often serves as a reference not only for practice instructions, but also for the sequence of training in Mahāmudrā practice. Innateist traditions such as the Mahāmudrā often avoid systematic presentations, in part because they do not adequately account for the need to adjust practices to suit the propensities and capacities of particular individuals. Certainly, the early Indian Mahāmudrā adepts completely eschewed any attempt to give a systematic account of their practice. Karma Wangchûg Dorjé explicitly recognizes the importance of individualization, and he too seems suspicious of systematization. But perhaps moved by a need to clarify or preserve lesser known elements of his lineage, he carefully lays out the sequence of practice through a wide range of techniques based on numerous sources, including the oral lineage. His text thus becomes a remarkable source not only for a relatively systematic version of practical instructions, but also for an historical inquiry into a broad range of Mahāmudrā practice. At the same time, in comparison to Dakpo

Tashi Namgyel, Karma Wangchûg Dorjé is much less intent on responding to critics of Mahāmudrā by harmonizing it with more Constructivist approaches; instead, he focuses on practical instructions.

Ocean is divided into short segments that address a particular stage of practice, and for present purposes, the most relevant sections concern the general instructions that a beginner would receive at the outset of formal meditation practice. This point in the practice has already been preceded by important preliminaries, which set the type of context that will be discussed at the end of this article. With those preliminaries in place, the beginner will now start to develop the mental stability necessary for Mahāmudrā, and the term used to refer to this stage of training is *śamatha* ('Calm Abiding'), a term that distinguishes this phase from the next, when *vipaśyanā* ('Insight') arises. It is with the arisal of *vipaśyanā* that one gains liberative insight into the nature of reality itself.

Before turning to the actual instructions, the meaning of *śamatha* and *vipaśyanā* as phases of meditation training must be clarified. These terms are drawn from the *Abhidharma*, and in that context they are understood to be strictly structured by subject–object duality. In Mahāmudrā training, however, one eventually must move beyond such structures, and even the earliest methods of training proceed quickly from a focus on a visual object, to focus on the breath, and on to a state without explicit focus. Thus, it would be a mistake to construe *śamatha* in the Mahāmudrā tradition as simply equivalent to the cultivation of mental stability on an object, as it is understood in *Abhidharma* contexts.

What then, at the very outset of formal practice, does Karma Wangchûg Dorjé recommend for the beginner? The initial, overall instructions are simple (*Ocean* 78):

> Do not pursue the past. Do not usher in the future. Rest evenly within present awareness, clear and nonconceptual.

These general instructions, while remarkably simple, are difficult to follow because they require that the beginner not be caught by the features of thought noted above. First, one does not 'pursue' *(rjes bcad)* the past nor 'usher in' *(sngun bsu)* or anticipate the future. As Karma Wangchûg Dorjé notes, 'The past has ceased and ended; it is gone. Hence, there is nothing to think about. And the future has not yet come; it is not real, nor can it exist as an object.' When thoughts arise, they necessarily involve both 'time travelling' and the sense that the thought itself is somehow 'fused' with some real thing that it allegedly represents. The simple instruction here is to realize that thoughts about past and future cannot be about real things because neither the past nor the future truly exist except in our thoughts. This breaks the fusion and allows one to drop the time-travelling thoughts so as to 'rest within present awareness.' Thoughts about the present can arise also, however, and so Karma Wangchûg Dorjé adds that even these thoughts are caught up in fusion, which he refers to as 'cognitive grasping' *(mtshan 'dzin)*. Again showing that thoughts cannot actually be what they seem to represent, he adds that one must drop all notions of 'is' or 'is not'; 'existent' or 'non-existent'; 'good' or 'bad'; and so on. He notes that 'interrupting the stream of thoughts about the three times [i.e., past, present and future]' is essential for the beginner to advance in practice (*Ocean* 78).

Much more could be said here, and Karma Wangchûg Dorjé unpacks these general instructions at length. The gist, however, remains the same, even up to the most advanced levels of practice: drop thoughts of past, present and future and release the mind into its natural state of clear, non-conceptual awareness. These core instructions hearken back to some famed advice from the Indian Mahāmudrā master, Tilopa (988–1069). Karma Wangchûg Dorjé repeats that advice (*Ocean* 83):

> Not pondering.
> Not thinking.
> Not wondering.
> Not meditating.
> Not analyzing.
> Just place the mind in its natural state.

Citing the great Tibetan adept Ogyenpa (1230–1309), Karma Wangchûg Dorjé interprets the first three lines as referring to past, present and future, and this echoes the instructions given just above. But one is further advised that one should not strive to 'meditate' by becoming absorbed in some blank thoughtless absorption in nothingness. Nor should one 'analyze' what is arising, since this too will perpetuate the structures of cognitive grasping. Both of these—'meditating' and 'analyzing' relate to the role that 'cognitive effort' plays in producing thought. Releasing that effort, one is advised again to simply release the mind into clear, non-conceptual awareness, which is its natural state.

Tilopa's famed advice is only one passage from a long section in which Karma Wangchûg Dorjé uses various citations, stories and analogies that again and again return to the basic theme of his original instructions. My aim here is not to convey these instructions—a task that I am not qualified to do. Instead, I aim to show that they clearly target the features of thought that ensnare the beginner: time travelling, cognitive fusion and cognitive effort. In addition, Karma Wangchûg Dorjé also writes passages that underscore the Mahāmudrā tradition's additional insight into the way thoughts ensnare the mind: they seem especially relevant to oneself, and with a sense of urgency, they carry us away in a chain of judgments, evaluations, hopes and fears. He tells a somewhat amusing story to highlight the role of anticipation and evaluation (*Ocean* 84–5):

> For example, suppose a man comes to a place and is told, 'The official says not to send you anywhere else, so stay here today.' So, even though he came with an interest in staying there, the situation gets him to thinking, 'He is going to order me to do all kinds of hard work—what else could this be about? Maybe it would be better to steer clear of all this.' And thus he gets to the point of running away. But if the official had not said anything, the man could easily have stayed for however long he was to stay. Therefore, don't give the mind work. Instead, relax and release it, do not meditate on anything. Relaxed, free and easy, release the

mind into mere non-distraction. Within a state free of hopes and fears, devoid of evaluation or judgment, be carefree and open. And within that state, do not purse the past; do not usher in the future; place [awareness] within the present, without adjustment, without hopes or fears. Cutting all conceptual structures about the external, do not allow phenomenal appearances to surge outward. You might think, 'Meditation has arisen! Great!' or 'It has not arisen. What a shame.' But even if just that much happens, it causes the profusion of thoughts, so within a state free of anything to meditate upon or any action of meditation, clearly and directly release the mind. And thus, from that point forward, the mind naturally abides [with stability]. As Saraha said, 'If one lets go of this very mind, bound by its knots, there is no doubt: it will be free.' So without contrivance or adjustment, one releases it, having cut the structures of the three times [past, present and future]. This is the best way to seek mental stability.

This passage covers all the elements discussed above: time travelling, fusion, and cognitive effort. But it also notes the role that expectation and evaluation play in distracting one from actual practice. Here too we see the additional instruction, one repeated many times, that one need not 'adjust' or 'contrive' *(bcos)* the state. Attempts to tinker with the mind in this way reflect not only the disturbance of cognitive effort, but they are also motivated by evaluations and judgments about what meditation is supposed to be. For the practitioner, notions about 'what meditation should be' present themselves with special relevance. After all, if one is fully committed to meditation practice, what could be of more importance than proper meditation? Since such thoughts seem so important and relevant to practice, they easily ensnare the practitioner. Hence, even these evaluations and judgments about 'meditation' itself must be suspended if one is to release the mind into its natural state, unadjusted and uncontrived.

Overall, the gist of these instructions is unambiguous and indisputably clear, and as with the instructions cited earlier, they strongly suggest that, at least when engaged in actual practice or *mnyam bzhag*, even the beginner should not be recollecting anything explicit, nor somehow retaining awareness of spiritual goals or 'hopes and fears' (Tib., *re dogs*). Instead, without evaluation, one should simply release attempts at 'meditating' and instead rest in present-centred awareness. In light of these instructions, it seems difficult to construe Mindfulness in the non-dual, Mahāmudrā context as being 'explicitly cognitive and evaluative' or 'retaining information,' to cite again Dreyfus's account of the *Abhidharma* model (Dreyfus, 2011). Such attitudes seem quite contrary to the above instructions. Instead, something like 'present-centred non-judgmental awareness' would seem to be a better fit. Is this, then, Mindfulness?

5. Non-dual Mindfulness?

What is non-dual Mindfulness? This is not an easy question, and I would not dare to attempt a complete answer. Not only is my own research still ongoing, but the Mahāmudrā authors themselves disagree on how best to construe Mindfulness. We can appreciate the difficulties they face when we consider this apparent paradox: to properly practice Mahāmudrā, even as a beginner, it would seem that one must remain within the present without evaluation or judgment, yet clearly, to do so requires that one recollect the instructions: 'Do not pursue the past. Do not usher in the future. Rest evenly within present awareness, clear and nonconceptual.' Not only must one remember these instructions, but to implement them, surely one must evaluate one's present state to confirm that the instructions have been followed. And the tradition would not disagree: meditation here (which, in the end is 'non-meditation') is not a matter of simply entering a blank, unconscious state, nor is it a matter of randomly suppressing thoughts. There is a targeted outcome, which is the cultivation of an objectless, reflexive awareness of the mind's true nature. To this end, the instructions are to be followed, and for authors such as Karma Wangchûg Dorjé, there is a clear distinction between proper and improper practice.

These issues point to the need for some kind of monitoring—a capacity to examine one's practice as it is occurring, especially for the beginner. And this monitoring connects to one aspect of Mindfulness for Karma Wangchûg Dorjé. Although the contemporary concept of Mindfulness may well extend beyond any single Buddhist term, it clearly must involve *dran pa* in Tibetan (Skt, *smṛti;* Pāli, *sati*). Employing this term, Karma Wangchûg Dorjé speaks of a kind of monitoring as the 'Spy of Mindfulness' *(dran pa'i so pa)*. He mentions the 'Spy' at several points connected especially to the early phases of practice. At one such phase, for example, one turns to focusing on the breath as an object, following the principle that 'In dependence on [practicing with] a focal object, the objectless [practice] emerges' (94; *dmigs pa la ni brten nas su / mi dmigs pa nyid rab tu skye*). As is common with beginners, a deluge of thoughts may flow when one attempts to focus in this way, and Karma Wangchûg Dorjé recommends that one not attempt to suppress the thoughts, but that one can nevertheless remain aware 'like someone threading a needle.' He notes (*Ocean* 95):

> In such contexts, cultivate the motivating notion ('*phen pa'i 'du shes*), 'I will apprehend the mind.' Then, during the actual session, set up the Spy of Mindfulness*(dran pa, Skt., smṛti)* and carefully examine one's mental continuum, thinking, 'Is my mind stable, or not? Is it agitated or dull?' Doing so, when one sees that the mind is abiding naturally; release it without leaving that state [of natural abiding]. If it is not abiding stably, then whether there are the faults of agitation or dullness, strive to apply the specific remedies for removing each.

Here, the 'Spy' of Mindfulness is clearly a term for a kind of monitoring function that, in accounts from more Constructivist traditions, is usually referred to as 'discriminating alertness' or 'clear comprehension' (*samprajanya;* Tib., *shes bzhin*). Clearly, this Spy cannot occur when one has released the mind into its clear, non-conceptual nature because the Spy requires thought and effort. Yet, since it draws on the capacity of awareness to be aware of itself, it is appropriate to use the same term as the Mindfulness present in the mind's natural state, namely, the 'Mindfulness of mere non-distraction' *(ma yengs tsam gyi dran pa)*.

The term 'non-distraction' is crucially important in Mahāmudrā literature, and it is even equated with meditation itself. Karma Wangchûg Dorjé himself repeatedly uses it (including in one of the passages cited earlier) to refer to the type of continual, uninterrupted awareness that, without any effort, is fully aware without any adjustment or contrivance. The Mindfulness of mere non-distraction is a feature that is always present when one successfully releases the mind into the clear, non-conceptual, natural state that is the point of even the basic instructions discussed above. One implication here is that this 'Mindfulness of mere non-distraction' is somehow essential to the natural continuity of awareness itself, and the 'Spy' is a gross, conceptual manifestation of this fundamental capacity of consciousness. Thus, the same term, 'mindfulness' *(dran pa;* Skt. *smṛti)* can be applied both to the 'Spy' and to the more fundamental capacity that is mere non-distraction. A further implication, one suited to an Innateist tradition, is that even the beginner is not cultivating a capacity that is not already present in awareness, but rather, even when invoking the 'Spy,' a practitioner is drawing on the fundamental, innate capacity of awareness to know itself that manifests in its uncontrived form as mere non-distraction.

Far more could be said here about Mindfulness, or more specifically, the use of the term *dran pa* (Skt., *smṛti)* to describe these aspects of awareness in practice. One might profitably turn to a parallel description given by Dakpo Tashi Namgyel who, in a manner similar to the rhetoric of the 'Spy' and 'mere non-distraction,' discusses the distinction between 'Effortful Mindfulness' *(rtsol bcas kyi dran pa)* and 'Effortless Mindfulness' *(rtsol med kyi dran pa),* which itself amounts to 'mere non-distraction.'[13] In any case, it would seem that effortless Mindfulness of mere non-distraction lies at the core Mahāmudrā practice. And, in comparison to more dualistic approaches drawn from the *Abhidharma,* this Mahāmudrā approach to Mindfulness seems a much better candidate for comparison with many contemporary approaches for cultivating mindfulness such as those found in MBSR.

6. Conclusion: The role of context

The question of how the non-dual Mindfulness of Mahāmudrā might relate to contemporary versions is one that I will leave to other, far more qualified authors. My hypothesis is that the comparison will be very fruitful, largely because the styles of practice and rhetoric appear to overlap in significant ways. If, however, a non-dual style of Mindfulness is indeed a much more apt point of comparison for contemporary approaches, another issue immediately surfaces: the context of practice.

In some ways, the manner I have presented the instructions on practice and Mindfulness in Mahāmudrā is misleading because even a casual glance at Karma Wangchûg Dorjé's text reveals much more. Many highly conceptual and effortful practices are included even in the section that presents the general instructions for the formal practice aimed at 'resting in present awareness, clear and nonconceptual.' And when Karma Wangchûg Dorjé moves on to more specific instructions for the beginner, one encounters visualizations, exhortations to consider the meaning of practice, and ethical appeals. These passages seem to move far beyond the simple cultivation of present-centred, non-evaluative awareness. In short, it is clear that even the formal practice itself is framed by a carefully developed and delivered conceptual framework of instructions. And even more important are the preliminary practices that are considered essential for the practitioner who seeks to live in the utter absence of distraction that lies at the core of Mahāmudrā practice.

What role do these preliminaries play? They establish, first, a test for the practitioner, since no one can receive formal instruction without long and intense practice of the preliminaries. They include contemplations on, for example, the inevitably of death and the essentially dissatisfactory nature of one's confused life. They thus provide an intense motivation fuelled by the realization that one could die at any moment. And they cultivate the urge to move beyond dissatisfaction toward genuine flourishing and lasting happiness. Through the intense cultivation of devotion in the preliminaries, practitioners are made uniquely receptive to the challenging instructions of the main practice, but they are also provided with a clear spiritual goal, embodied by the living, human teacher who inspires such devotion. And through an understanding of how the present mind is karmically conditioned, practitioners encounter a context to interpret the difficulties of practice, including the anxieties, intense ecstasies and moments of depersonalization that are side effects of the practice. Clearly, these and other features of the preliminary practices require one to work with highly evaluative and complex thoughts that are themselves built on time travelling, cognitive fusion, and cognitive effort. Hence, even if evaluative judgments and value-laden thoughts are suspended in actual practice, they play a crucial role in the success of that practice.[14]

Far more could be said about the context created by the preliminaries, including especially their psychological function. But in a broader sense, this strong emphasis on preliminary practices locates the Mahāmudrā lineages squarely within the world shared by all Tibetan traditions: an ethics based in non-harm and compassion; an orientation toward the spiritual goal of eliminating all suffering; the centrality of wisdom embodied by a long lineage of realized persons—these and many more elements were shared. Yet the traditions also disagreed at times, and Mahāmudrā was certainly the target of searing critiques. In response, authors such as Dakpo Tashi Namgyel vigorously defended Mahāmudrā practice by interpreting it in classical *Abhidharma* terms. One easy explanation for his efforts is that he sought to authenticate Mahāmudrā by appealing to the unquestionable authority of the *Abhidharma*, and to a great extent, that motivation makes sense, given the social and political upheaval that threatened his Mahāmudrā tradition during his lifetime. This explanation is plausible and relevant, but it sidesteps precisely the issue just raised: the importance of context. In India, Maitripa, Saraha, Tilopa and other influential proponents of a non-dual Innateist approach located themselves in deliberate opposition to the Buddhist mainstream. One might argue that, as long as that mainstream was present, there was little danger of losing the context of ethical values and spiritual goals that are expressed in the preliminary practices discussed above. What happens, however, when a non-dual style becomes mainstream? Perhaps Tibetan authors such as Dakpo Tashi Namgyel were not simply apologists for the non-dual approach; perhaps they were also pointing to the danger of having no mainstream against which to be contrary. In short, as Mahāmudrā practice became institutionalized in Tibet, it could no longer rely on the mainstream to provide a framework of goals, ethics, aesthetics and so on. There was no mainstream to turn to because, at least for many great monastic institutions of Tibet, Mahāmudrā had become the mainstream. In other words, the tradition could no longer rely on the mainstream to provide a context for a contrarian practice, because that contrarian practice had become an institutionalized mainstream.

With this in mind, we might ask whether contemporary mindfulness—in MBSR or in contemporary Buddhist practice—might also be emerging as its own mainstream. Certainly, it may stand in opposition to many features of mainstream culture in the United States, for example. Yet mindfulness (in the largely non-dual sense) is now widespread in the therapeutic community, and perhaps a deliberate engagement with questions of context is inevitable. Lacking clinical experience, I cannot answer this question, but perhaps it is worth posing. Or perhaps, in the spirit of the most radical non-dual approaches, all the context we need is already present, fully innate.

NOTES

1. For the issue of diversity within Buddhism, see, for example, Hallisey and Reynolds (1989) and Lopez (2005).
2. For more on this and other features of commentaries, see the introduction to Ganeri (2007).
3. Georges Dreyfus' article in this special issue of *Contemporary Buddhism* is an excellent source for the *Abhidharma* interpretation as applied to contemporary practice (Dreyfus, 2011). Others include Wallace (2006). For the *Abhidharma-samuccaya*, the translation of Rāhula's French translation (Asaṅga, 2001) is the best English source for the *Abhidharmasamuccaya*, while the translation of de la Vallée Poussin's French translation (Vasubandhu, 1990) is the only available English translation of the *Abhidharmakośa*. See also the relevant summaries in Potter (2002) for other scholarly resources.
4. In addition to 'reflexive awareness,' other English translations of *svasaṃvitti* include 'self-awareness' and 'self-knowing.' For more on Dharmakīrti, see Dreyfus (1997) and Dunne (2004).

5. An important parallel here is the role played by the works of the Indian author Candrakīrti in justifying Tibetan interpretations of Madhyamaka thought, even though his works were not easy to reconcile with many Tibetan interpretations. See Vose (2009).
6. My exposure to MBSR comes through formal training in the week-long 'MBSR in Mind-Body Medicine' and through the works of Jon Kabat-Zinn, who has also graciously clarified the notion of Mindfulness in MBSR over the course of numerous conversations and email correspondence.
7. For a scholarly treatment of the Innateist (or 'Sudden') and Constructivist (or 'Gradual') debate in the context of Tibetan Buddhism, see Ruegg (1989).
8. See Higgins (2008) and Mathes (2008) for more on the dates of these figures and the notion of *amanasikāra*. And see especially Jackson (2004, 2005) for an excellent overview of Mahāmudrā and translations from Saraha's poetic works.
9. One commentator of particular note is Śākyabuddhi (fl. Seventh to eighth centuries, C.E.), who states explicitly that the state of meditative absorption consists of the non-dual, reflexive awareness of mind itself (Dunne, 2004, 406, n.15). For more on the relevant Buddhist theories of concept formation, see Dunne (Forthcoming).
10. For 'cognitive fusion,' see chapter 3 of Hayes *et al.*, (2003).
11. See Dharmakīrti's Pramāṇavārttika (3.6), translated in Dunne (2004, 394).
12. Dakpo Tashi Namgyel's text is the famed *Phyag chen zla zer* (see references).
13. *Phyag chen zla zer* 244b-247a. Note here Dakpo Tashi Wangyel's attempts to reconcile *Abhidharma* notions of mindfulness with non-dual practice.
14. See Gyatso (1999) for the issue of the role of context in Tibetan contemplative experience.

REFERENCES

ASAṄGA. 2001. *The compendium of the higher teaching*. Translated by W. Rāhula and translated from French by S. Boin-Webb. Fremont, CA: Asian Humanities Press.

DREYFUS, GEORGES. 1997. *Recognizing reality: Dharmakīrti's philosophy and its Tibetan interpretations*. Albany: State University of New York Press.

DREYFUS, GEORGES. 2011. Is mindfulness present-centred and non-judgmental? A discussion of the cognitive dimensions of mindfulness. *Contemporary Buddhism* 12: 41–54.

DUNNE, JOHN. 2004. *Foundations of Dharmakīrti's philosophy*. Boston: Wisdom Publications.

Dvags po Bkra shis Rnam rgyal [Dakpo Tashi Namgyel], 1997. *Nges don phyag rgya chen po'i sgom rim gsal bar byed pa'i legs bshad zla ba'i 'od zer*. In *Nges don phyag rgya chen po'i khrid mdzod*, Vol. 8. Edited by Zhva dmar Rinpoche. TBRC No. W23447, Vol. 1898. New Delhi: [=*Phyag chen zla zer*].

DUNNE, JOHN D. Forthcoming. Key features of Dharmakīrti's Apoha theory. In *Apoha*, ed. M. Siderits, T. Tillemans, and A. Chakrabarti. New York: Columbia University Press.

GANERI, JONARDON. 2007. *The concealed art of the soul: Theories of self and practices of truth in Indian ethics and epistemology.* New York: Oxford University Press.

GYATSO, JANET. 1999. Healing burns with fire: The facilitations of experience in Tibetan Buddhism. *Journal of the American Academy of Religion* 67 (1): 113–47.

HALLISEY, CHARLES, and FRANK E. REYNOLDS. 1989. Buddhist religion, culture and civilization. In *Buddhism and Asian history*, ed. Jospeh M. Kitagawa, and Mark D. Cummings, 4–28. New York: Macmillan Pub. Co.

HAYES, STEVEN C., KIRK D. STROSAHL, and KELLY G. WILSON. 2003. *Acceptance and commitment therapy: An experiential approach to behavior change.* New York: The Guilford Press.

HIGGINS, DAVID. 2008. On the development of the non-mentation (*amanasikāra*) doctrine in Indo-Tibetan Buddhism. *Journal of the International Association of Buddhist Studies* 29 (2): 255–303.

JACKSON, ROGER. 2004. *Tantric treasures three collections of mystical verse from Buddhist India.* New York: Oxford University Press.

Karma Dbang Phyug Rdo Rje [Karma Wangchûg Dorjé]. 2006. *Lhan cig skyes sbyor gyi zab khrid nges don rgya mtsho'i snying po phrin las 'od 'phro.* In *Phyag chen rgyas pa nges don rgya mtsho, 'bring pa ma rig mun sel, bsdus pa chos sku mdzub tshugs bcas so.* Varanasi. India: Vajra Vidya Institute Library. [=*Ocean*].

LOPEZ, DONALD. 2005. *The story of Buddhism: A concise guide to its history and teachings.* New York: Harper San Francisco.

MATHES, KLAUS-DIETER. 2008. *A direct path to the Buddha within: Gö Lotsāwa's Mahāmudrā interpretation of the Ratnagotravibhāga.* Boston, MA: Wisdom Publications.

POTTER, KARL H. 2002. *The encyclopedia of Indian philosophies: Vol. VIII, Buddhist philosophy from 100 to 350 A.D.* New Delhi: Motilal Banarsidass.

RUEGG, DAVID. 1989. *Buddha nature, mind and the problem of gradualism in a comparative perspective: On the transmission and reception of Buddhism in India and Tibet.* London: School of Oriental and African Studies, University of London.

VASUBANDHU. 1990. *Abhidharmakośabhāṣyam.* Translated by L. de la Vallée Poussin and translated from French by L. Pruden. Berkeley, CA: Asian Humanities.

VOSE, KEVIN. 2009. *Resurrecting Candrakīrti: Disputes in the Tibetan creation of Prāsaṅgika.* Boston, MA: Wisdom Publications.

WALLACE, B. 2006. *The attention revolution: Unlocking the power of the focused mind.* Boston, MA: Wisdom Publications.

HOW DOES MINDFULNESS TRANSFORM SUFFERING? I: THE NATURE AND ORIGINS OF *DUKKHA*

John D. Teasdale and Michael Chaskalson (Kulananda)

This, the first of two linked papers, presents the Buddha's analysis of the nature and origins of dukkha *(suffering) as a basis for understanding the ways in which mindfulness can transform suffering. The First and Second of the Buddha's Four Noble Truths are presented in a way that has proved helpful to teachers of mindfulness-based applications. These Truths offer a framework of understanding that can guide the application of mindfulness to stress and emotional disorders, while stressing the continuity and inevitability of the experience of* dukkha *in clients, teachers, and those primarily seeking a new way of being. The crucial involvement of self-view and identification with experience are emphasized.*

This is the first of two linked papers discussing mindfulness and the transformation of suffering. This first paper focuses on presenting the Buddha's analysis of the nature and origins of suffering in a way that has proved useful to those who teach mindfulness-based applications (such as MBSR, MBCT). It is based on a talk on the Buddha's First and Second Noble Truths given by John Teasdale to a retreat specifically for instructors of MBSR/MBCT at Spirit Rock Meditation Center in December 2009.

The Four Noble Truths

When we look at the first major teaching that the Buddha gave after his awakening, we find that what he offered, what he saw as most important to tell others about first of all, was actually a conceptual framework, a framework of understanding. This was the teaching of the Four Noble Truths (*Saṃyutta Nikāya* 56:11).

In these truths, the Buddha encapsulated in four key insights the understanding that would allow others to awaken, to find the greater freedom and lasting peace and happiness that he had found.

These truths were presented very much as guides to action, something to be explored, tested, and checked out in our own experience, rather than to be believed in as articles of blind faith (Batchelor 1997). It is for this reason that many people prefer to call them the Four Ennobling Truths—truths which will ennoble our being if we act upon them.

The Buddha was on an existential, or spiritual, quest. As the story is told, he was profoundly dissatisfied with the life of pleasure he had been leading, and set off to find a more ultimately satisfying way of being. And, as an act of compassion, he offered the Four Noble Truths as a guide for others who also feel 'there must be more to life than this.'

But what of the clients and patients who come to our Mindfulness-based Stress Reduction (MBSR) and Mindfulness-based Cognitive Therapy (MBCT) classes? Mostly, they are primarily looking for relief from stress, or from recurrent depression, rather than the resolution of some existential dis-ease. How are the Four Noble Truths relevant to their concerns?

Part of the Buddha's genius, and why his teachings are so relevant to our patients and clients, is that he saw that the patterns of mind that keep people trapped in emotional suffering are, fundamentally, the same patterns of mind that stand between all of us and the flowering of our potential for a more deeply satisfying way of being. Whether we are working to free ourselves from emotional distress, or to awaken to a new way of being, we are dealing with fundamentally the same patterns of mind.

The key concept here is *dukkha*, a Pali word with no real adequate English translation. (Pali is one of the ancient Indian languages in which the Buddha's teachings were first recorded.) *Dukkha* is often translated as suffering, but this translation can be quite misleading. For that reason, many people prefer not to translate *dukkha*, and stick to the Pali term, not because they are enamoured of the trappings of Buddhism, but to avoid the limitations of translation.

Dukkha is the central focus of the Four Noble Truths. This first paper focuses primarily on the first two truths, which concern the nature and origins of *dukkha*. The second paper touches on the third and fourth truths which focus on the cessation of *dukkha*, and how, practically, we bring that about.

The First Noble Truth

The First Noble Truth identifies the problem. Sumedho (1992) expresses this Truth very simply: 'There is *dukkha*'.

Dukkha covers a wide range of experience—from the intense anguish we can suffer from physical or emotional pain, through to the subtlest sense of world weariness or existential unease—the kind of thing that drove the Buddha himself to abandon his life of pleasure and to search for another way of being.

All forms of *dukkha* share a sense of unsatisfactoriness, of incompleteness, a sense that in some way we are missing out on life's full potential. So long as we do not have a sense of complete peace, contentment, ease and wholeness, then we can be fairly sure that *dukkha* is present.

Sumedho's wording of the First Truth—There *is dukkha*—reminds us that *all* unawakened human beings share this experience.

We can often feel that we, alone of all beings, have been unable to get our lives sorted and discover the secret of lasting happiness, whereas everyone else has got this worked out. We can then see this as our own private failure or problem. And that identification, of course, just makes the sense of unsatisfactoriness worse.

The Buddha cut through this personalization of *dukkha* when he asserted quite simply 'There *is dukkha*'—this is just how it is for all of us. We do not need to take it personally—it's not me, it's not my fault but the normal unawakened human condition.

In fact, as we shall see, the inevitability of *dukkha* is pretty much built into the way our minds are structured at the current state of our evolution of consciousness. Once we realize that, it can be curiously comforting—so long, of course, as we know there is some possibility of freedom from *dukkha*.

We also do not need to feel so alone. We are all in this same boat together, whoever we are—whether teachers, patients, clients, or the person we pass in the street. All of us share in common two things—*dukkha*, and the simple wish to be happy. This realization can help us feel a greater sense of connection and compassion to all human beings.

The Buddha helpfully distinguished three domains or bases of *dukkha* (*Saṃyutta Nikāya* 38:14).

The first domain of *dukkha* is unsatisfactoriness related to situations of 'ordinary' obvious suffering: physical pain, emotional pain, having to endure situations we find unpleasant, not getting what we want, or being separated from that which we love.

These are all situations in which we experience clearly unpleasant feelings. The Buddha saw that unpleasant or uncomfortable physical sensations or emotional feelings are inherent in life. In themselves, they are not the problem. Rather, *dukkha* is the suffering we add to unpleasant feelings by the way we relate to them. Most often, it is this suffering, rather than the unpleasant feelings themselves, that is the main source of our unhappiness.

The Buddha put it this way:

When an untaught worldling is touched by a painful (bodily) feeling, he worries and grieves, he laments, beats his breast, weeps and is distraught. He thus experiences two kinds of feelings, a bodily and a mental feeling. It is as if a man were pierced by an arrow and, following the first piercing, he is hit by a second arrow. So that person will experience feelings caused by two arrows.

But in the case of a well-taught noble disciple, when he is touched by a painful feeling, he will not worry nor grieve and lament, he will not beat his breast and weep, nor will he be distraught. It is *one* kind of feeling he experiences, a bodily one, but not a mental feeling. It is as if a man were pierced by an arrow, but was not hit by a second arrow following the first one. So this person experiences feelings caused by a single arrow only. (*Sallatha Sutta*)

The crucial message of this teaching is this: whereas unpleasant and uncomfortable feelings are unavoidable, *dukkha* in the sense of suffering is optional. And it is optional because we are the ones that actually fire that second arrow at ourselves!

So, for example, in depression, the first arrow of a simple feeling of sadness is transformed into a more intense and persistent state of depression when we add the second arrow of ruminative thinking.

Awakened beings still feel unpleasant feelings and sensations—the first arrow—but because they have learned a more skilful relationship to them they do not experience suffering—the second arrow.

Learning how not to shoot that second arrow at ourselves, how to relate more skilfully to unpleasant feelings so that we do not create *dukkha*, is a major focus of our practice and of what we teach in MBSR and MBCT classes.

The second domain of *dukkha* is unsatisfactoriness related to Change.

We would like our experiences of happiness and joy to continue indefinitely, but they do not. We would like our new clothes, our new car to be always just like they were on the day we bought them, but they get old, out of date, shabby and worn. We would like our loving relationships to always be as close and warm as the day we first fell in love but they inevitably have their ups and downs, and, eventually, our loved ones die. All such change is a further basis for *dukkha*.

Change, in and of itself, is not necessarily a problem. It only becomes a problem, a basis for suffering, when we do not want it to happen, as we shall see when we discuss the Second Noble Truth.

The third domain of *dukkha* is the unsatisfactoriness related to Conditionality.

The world and our experience are essentially unreliable and conditional. What this means is that what happens in our inner and outer worlds depends on a host of enormously complex, mutually interacting shifting conditions, many of which we are not even aware of, and most of which we cannot control. It follows that there is a basic unreliability to our experience; because we can never know or control all the conditions that affect whether or not something happens, however much we may try, we simply cannot rely 100% on anything working out in a particular way.

For example, on retreat, we might have the experience of a beautiful blissful meditation in our first sitting of the day. We sit down to the second session and, as far as we can tell, set things up in exactly the same way as we did in the first sitting. But now we find that the mind is all over the place. And the reason is simply that, for one reason or another, a different set of conditions is operating, not least of which is the subtle, perhaps almost unconscious, expectation or wish that this sitting be just like the first.

Again, in itself, this basic unreliability and conditionality of experience does not have to be a problem. It becomes a source of suffering because our minds just do not want to see things that way.

Our minds are concerned with getting us what we want, which means establishing some sense of control and predictability over our inner and outer worlds. To do that, parts of our minds reduce the enormous complexity of the conditional world to seeing it, not in terms of complex, dynamically shifting patterns of conditions, but in terms of independently existing 'things,' categories, or selves with reliable, enduring, fixed characteristics and properties.

For example, rather than seeing the state of a meditation session in terms of the effects of many interacting conditions, our minds tend to see it in terms of simple categories such as 'good meditator' versus 'bad meditator.'

Our minds work in this way because, in some areas, it does, indeed, offer us a greater sense of security and manageability. But the reality of basic unreliability and conditionality means that there are severe limits on the extent to which we can predict and control either the world or our experience.

This fundamental mismatch between the way our minds want to see things and the true nature of reality is an aspect of what is called 'ignorance' in Buddhism, and it is a very deeply rooted and all pervasive source of *dukkha*. It is what we had in mind when we said that *dukkha* is inevitable, given the way our minds are currently structured.

One of the most damaging aspects of ignorance is our tendency to identify with the varying and passing aspects of our experience, our moods, our feelings, our thoughts, the kind of meditation session we are having, as things that belong to or are parts of some underlying independently existing enduring self—me—these are *my* thoughts, *my* feelings, etc, the state of *my* meditation reflects who *I* am.

We will look more closely at the way this identification fuels *dukkha* when we consider the Second Noble Truth.

As we mentioned, the Four Truths are intended as very practical guidelines for us to find liberation and awakening. For this reason, each of the Truths is accompanied by a specific instruction or guideline for action. For the First Noble Truth this is: '*Dukkha* should be fully understood'. Here, in the original Pali, the word translated as 'understanding' (*pariññeyyaṃ*) has the sense of 'knowing comprehensively or completely—from all around'—not just getting to know *about* suffering intellectually or conceptually, but getting to know it by acquaintance, directly, from the inside, from experience.

We can only do that if we are prepared to open to the suffering and sense of unsatisfactoriness we experience—to have the courage to move in close to *dukkha*, to let it be while we investigate and understand its nature, and how we create and sustain it. The theme of moving in close to difficult experiences is of course central to MBSR and related approaches. Here, in the First Noble Truth, is where it came from originally.

Now, moving in close to suffering to understand it fully is, of course, very different from our habitual response, which is to want to get rid of suffering as soon as possible. So, if we are to follow this recommendation of the First Noble Truth, we need to consciously and deliberately set and reset our intention to approach suffering with an open, courageous, and curious awareness, over and over again.

The First Noble Truth suggests that suffering, if we can hold it skilfully, is actually the way in to our quest for greater freedom and happiness rather than an obstacle to it. From the courageous investigation of our experience of suffering and unsatisfactoriness, we can discover the origins of *dukkha*, which are the focus of the Second Noble Truth.

The Second Noble Truth

The key insight of the Second Noble Truth is that the immediate cause of *dukkha* is *taṇhā*—a Pali word usually translated as craving or attachment to desire. But translations such as desire bring their own difficulties. So, again, as with *dukkha*, there is a case for not translating *taṇhā*, and sticking with the Pali—not in our secular mindfulness classes, of course, but as part of a framework for our own understanding.

The crucial essence of *taṇhā* is captured by the notion of unquenchable thirst—a thirst which can never be fully satisfied or quenched but which, tragically, we, nonetheless, feel compelled to keep trying to satisfy. It is this fatal combination of the unquenchability of the desire, coupled with our unwillingness to simply let go of it that creates suffering.

Attachment to desire has a compulsive quality—a subtle, or not so subtle, sense that we *need* things to be one way or another. This compulsion is reflected in our felt experience and inner language which are dominated by a sense of *must, should, ought, have to, need to, if only*.

The key message of the Second Noble Truth is this: Experience itself is not the problem—the problem is our relationship to it—our need to have it be a particular way.

As an idea, this message of the Second Truth is not too difficult to grasp or remember. But for this truth to be actually liberating, we have to embody that understanding experientially right in the moment that we encounter unpleasant feelings. And that can be really difficult. When we are confronted with the reality of searing pain in the knee, or great tiredness, or deep sadness, it is just so easy to see the unpleasant experience itself as the problem. We then put all our efforts into trying to get rid of the feelings, rather than exploring our relationship to them. And, from the perspective of the Second Noble Truth, it is that very reaction of needing to get rid of the unpleasant that actually creates the suffering.

The challenge at times of unpleasant experience is to embody experientially there and then, in the lens through which we view experience and in the way we relate to it, the understanding that will allow us to be with the unpleasant feelings without getting locked into struggle and suffering. And conceptual under-standing, while not liberating in itself, has a key role to play here. Why else would the Buddha have gone to the trouble to teach the Four Ennobling Truths in the way he did?

Some time ago, one of us (JDT) had an experience that underlined very clearly the relationship between understanding the Second Noble Truth intellectually and actually embodying that understanding experientially in liberating insight:

> I was in the middle of preparing a talk on this Second Noble Truth and I had been thinking a lot about it, to the point where, in the early hours one morning, I found myself lying in bed with thoughts floating through my mind about the cause of *dukkha* being our relationship to the difficult, rather than the difficult itself.
>
> And then I realised, with mild annoyance, that I had become quite awake. And, guess what, my mind's immediate reaction was 'Oh no, I don't want to be lying here awake for hours, I *have* to find a way to get back to sleep'. So, even though my thinking had just been focused on the idea that the problem is not experience itself, but our relationship to it, my immediate reaction was to try to work out how to be rid of this unwanted wakefulness, rather than to look at how I was relating to it.
>
> But crucially, the fact that the idea was around meant that it was not long before it dawned on me 'Oh, this is aversion – the problem here is my need not to be awake rather than the wakefulness itself.'
>
> And so, guided by the memory of that teaching, I then looked more closely at my actual experience, and I could sense very clearly in the moment that it was my irritation with being awake, and the somewhat driven quality of my need to get back to sleep that was the source of my annoyance and, ironically, the main thing keeping me awake. And from that clear seeing, there flowed very naturally a letting go of the irritation and of the need to sort out the wakefulness. I consciously befriended my wakefulness, and within a minute or two I was back asleep. (Teasdale)

As this little story illustrates, conceptual understanding of the origins of *dukkha*, is not, by itself, liberating. But if that conceptual understanding can be kept fresh and alive in the mind so that it is available to mould and shape the lens through which we actually see and are aware of difficult experiences, then it can be a vital ingredient of the liberating mix. One of the reasons these teachings repeat the same basic messages over and over again is to keep the conceptual understanding alive in that way. Eventually, after enough experiences in which conceptual knowledge is there as a support to guide the experiential lens, we establish a new experiential view which can continue its liberating work unaided.

The central problem with *taṇhā* is that we cannot let go—we cannot let go of our desire, our need for things to be a particular way, even though that very need is what is creating our suffering.

Why is it so difficult to let go of our attachment to desire? To answer that question, let us look more closely at the kinds of desires to which we get attached and suffer in consequence.

The Buddha identified three—desire for sense pleasures, desire for being, desire for not being (*Dīgha Nikāya* 22).

We get attached to the desire for pleasant sense experiences—pleasant tastes, smells, body sensations, sights, sounds, thoughts and feelings (in Buddhist psychology the mind is seen as a sixth sense).

At one level, such desire is rooted in our biology and has ensured our evolutionary survival. But that cannot be the whole story—in non-humans, these desires are quenchable—hunger and thirst and sexual appetite can be satisfied.

The essence of *taṇhā* is unquenchable thirst—as humans, we look to sense pleasures as a way to give me, this self, not just passing pleasant feelings, but lasting happiness—to make me the happy person I long to be.

But our biological make-up actually guarantees that sense pleasures never last—for example, our first bite of chocolate cake might give us great pleasure, our second and third bites a little less, our second and third slices even less, and if we continue eating the whole cake we discover that what was initially a source of pleasant experiences can quite quickly become a source of displeasure. And if we repeated this experience on a daily basis we would find that even that first bite progressively loses its appeal. For this reason, sense pleasure simply can never deliver the lasting happiness we seek—this thirst is unquenchable by this means.

It is the subtle involvement of self view here that makes it so difficult to let go. The centrality of self in craving becomes even clearer as we turn to the remaining two types of *taṇhā*—the craving to be and the craving to not be.

Attachment to the desire to be or to become has two aspects. The most basic is attachment to the desire to exist at all, to be alive, to continue to exist as this thing we call a self.

There is also attachment to the desire to be or become particular selves—either at the very general level, such as the need to be or become a self that is loved, a self that is respected, a self that is kind, a self that does things well, a self that is a good meditator, a self that is successful, or to be or become particular selves that are related to these more general selves at a specific level—a self that has a calm meditation in this sitting; a self that has crossed off all items from the to-do list, a self that gives a talk that is well received.

This is the realm of attainment, achievement and ambition.

The third area of craving is attachment to the desire to not be, or to not be or become a self that has particular experiences. In contrast to the first two forms of *taṇhā*, this is a negative craving—a need to find peace or relief from suffering by not being.

As with the positive craving to be, the negative craving to not be takes both general and more specific forms.

At the general level, there is attachment to the desire to not exist, to disappear—to be out of it, to put the head under the blankets and stay there, in the extreme, suicide. More commonly, at the specific level, there is attachment to the desire not to be or become a particular self—not to be a self that has certain experiences—for example, not to be a self that lies awake in bed in the middle of the night, not to be a self that feels sad, fearful, or angry, not to be a self that screws up, not to be the self that has these pains in my knees and back, not to be the self that has this mind that wanders incessantly when I am trying to meditate, not to be a self that still has 10 things left on my to-do list, not to be the kind of person who has these experiences.

You will have noticed that, as with the craving to be, over and over again, we have included the phrase 'not to be a self that' and this is because, as far as the creation of *dukkha* is concerned, there is a subtle but absolutely crucial difference between the simple desire not to have a certain experience and the desire not to be a self that has that experience. It is this involvement of self that makes it so difficult to let go. We can explain what we mean here by going back to the example of having a meditation session in which the mind is all over the place.

If we can focus on this as an experience, and remember the fundamental conditionality of all experience, then we would recognize that how a particular meditation session on a retreat unfolds is going to be determined by a whole host of factors such as how tired we are, how much pain the body is giving us, what was on the mind as we started the session, what day of the retreat this is, how much we are comparing our experience this session with another session or with an idea of how it should be, how kind we are with ourselves, and so on and so on.

If we can recognize the conditionality of our experience in this way, we may feel a little disappointed if the mind is all over the place, but we will not feel a great need not to have things be that way and we will not become preoccupied with thinking about what is wrong with us and our meditation.

The situation would be quite different if we were attached to the desire not to be the kind of self that has meditation sessions where the mind is all over the place. Once self view becomes involved, then, having such a session on one particular occasion is no longer seen simply in terms of the patterns of conditions that happened to prevail on that occasion, but in terms of more enduring and general aspects of the self.

The implications are then much wider and stretch longer into the future, and will depend on how the particular self view related to being all over the place in meditation is nested in a wider structure of self-views and self-models. One possibility might be something like this: *That was a bad meditation session. Perhaps I'm the kind of person who will never really get on top of this meditation thing. But I cannot be that, because then I shouldn't be teaching others to meditate, should I? Perhaps I'm just not the kind of person who's cut out for teaching MBSR after all. But I mustn't be that because then I would feel a useless kind of person. I cannot let myself be that kind of person because then I could never be happy in any lasting, real, kind of way* .... And so on, and so on.

We have described this as a thought stream in the mind, but we might very well not be aware of these implications at the conscious level; the mind can derive them quite implicitly, and they will still affect us.

In this situation, having the mind wander in one meditation session is not seen as just an isolated experience, arising from a particular constellation of conditions. Rather, once the self becomes involved, one's whole future happiness and sense of meaning in life can seem to be on the line. So it is no wonder that we might feel such a compulsive need not to be the kind of self that has such experiences.

We could run through a similar analysis for the person who has been recurrently depressed in the past, who is attached to not being a self who gets sad because, on the basis of past experience, being that kind of self implies being a self who goes on to get severely depressed. For such a person, any sense of sadness is potentially threatening and to be avoided.

We can get some sense of the centrality and deep-rootedness of our attachment to not being certain kinds of self if we look at the fear of public speaking. A survey of the US population (Bruskin Associates 1973) found that fear of speaking before a group was the most commonly reported of all the fears surveyed, being reported more than twice as often as the fear of death. Such fear of public speaking reflects a need not to be a self that might be criticized or humiliated in some way. It seems that the possibility that our view of our self might be damaged ('I might look stupid', 'I might make a fool of myself') is more commonly experienced as threatening than the possibility that our bodies might die. And this is not just because we live in a relatively safe and healthy culture where the immediate risk of death is low—quite extraordinarily, the Buddha himself listed fear of public speaking as one of the five fears left behind by a person endowed with the four powers of wisdom, energy, an unblemished life, and beneficience, two and a half thousand years ago in Northern India (Aṅguttara Nikāya 9:5; the Five Fears are: fear for livelihood, fear of disrepute, fear of embarrassment in assemblies, fear of death, and fear of an unhappy future destiny).

It is the identification of experience with a sense of an enduring self that leads to our projecting our present suffering into the future: *I'm tired, I'm tired, again, it feels like I'm always tired, I'm just a tired kind of person who's never going to enjoy life to the full.* As another example, it can sometimes feel as though, unless I do something about it, the pain in my knee will continue until my leg actually drops off. Again, this reflects our 'being a self in pain' rather than simply having the experience 'pain is here.'

Once we are attached to the desire not to be the kind of self that has particular experiences, then the need to avoid those experiences, the anxiety that we might not be able to do so, and the distress if we cannot, all increase enormously. But, of course, the nature of reality means that it is simply impossible never to have the feared experiences, never to have the mind wander throughout a session, never to feel sad, never to give a talk that is criticized. The thirst of *taṇhā* is unquenchable—however hard we try we will never completely satisfy the need not to be the self that has these experiences.

But it is actually even worse than that—the compulsive need to avoid being a certain kind of self creates a great busyness in the mind aimed at preventing that dreaded outcome occurring, or limiting the damage if it does. This 'fixing' busyness just serves to reinforce further the sense of self—'me'—and to bring to the fore yet more self-views that need to be avoided or attained. And that stronger sense of 'me' means that it becomes even more pressing that I be or not be those kinds of self, which adds a further twist to the vicious spiral. This whole process has been called 'selfing' by contemporary teachers (Olendzki, A. 2005), or, more traditionally, 'becoming' (*kammabhava*) (see *Saṃyutta Nikāya* 12).

It is as if we not only had an unquenchable thirst that cannot be permanently satisfied, however much water we might drink, but that we are actually drinking salt water which just increases our thirst with every drink.

We can see such a process at work in many of the aversive patterns of mind that underpin emotional disorders. Self-focused rumination in depression can transform what might be just a passing sadness into a more persistent and intense state of depression. Self-focused worry can transform otherwise transient feelings of fear into persistent anxiety.

So what are we to do?

Well, given that the Second Noble Truth identifies the origin of *dukkha* as attachment to desire, it then goes on, reasonably enough, to the instruction that: 'Attachment to desire should be let go of.' Similarly, the essence of the Buddha's teaching can be summarized as: 'Nothing whatever should be grasped at or clung to as "me" or "mine"' (Buddhadāsa 1989, 138). In other words: 'Do not take anything personally.'

Unfortunately, this is easier said than done. But it is at this point that the conditionality of experience actually comes to our rescue.

The Buddha had the simple but actually quite brilliant insight that if *dukkha* and craving arise as a result of one set of conditions, then they will cease if those conditions can be changed and we deliberately arrange a different set of conditions.

And the wonderful thing about the Buddha was that he then went on to translate this theoretical understanding into action in his own life. What he discovered empirically in that way is summarized in the Third and Fourth Noble Truths.

The Third Noble Truth tells us that the cessation of *dukkha* is possible, and it is to be realized through the cessation of craving.

The Fourth Noble Truth describes an integrated training programme, known as The Noble Eightfold Path that enables us to do that. It consists of eight elements, each of which synergizes and reinforces all the other elements. One element is wise mindfulness. But the path also includes elements related to understanding and intention, ethical behaviour, and to two further aspects of meditation.

The ultimate goal of this Noble Eightfold Path is the complete and final cessation of *dukkha*, in other words nibbana/nirvana. But, fortunately for ourselves and the clients and patients we see in our MBSR and MBCT classes, we do not need to wait until we are at that point before we can experience the benefits of releasing our attachment to desires. As the Thai teacher Ajahn Chah puts it: 'If you let go a little, you will have a little peace. If you let go a lot, you will have a lot of peace. If you let go completely, you will have complete peace' (Chah, Kornfield, and Breiter 2004). In other words, whether we are primarily interested in relieving obvious suffering right now, or whether our ultimate goal is also to eliminate *dukkha* once and for all, letting go of craving and aversion is the path to peace. In the second of these two linked papers we will look more closely at the way mindfulness assists the transformation of suffering in this way.

To conclude this paper, we will briefly consider the relevance to teachers of MBSR and MBCT of the conceptual framework we have described.

Why should teachers of MBSR and MBCT know about the First and Second Noble Truths?

What added benefit is there for teachers of mindfulness-based applications to know and understand the particular conceptual framework we have presented?

There are two aspects to this question: (1) What benefit is there in having *any* conceptual framework to guide the teaching of MBSR, MBCT, etc.? (2) What benefit is there in having the *particular* conceptual framework offered by the Buddha in the Four Noble Truths?

Without any framework of understanding to guide it, the application of mindfulness practices to problems of stress, emotional disorder and the like reduces to teaching and learning a series of techniques. This would offer students an opportunity to learn how to control aspects of their attention, which would enable them to gather and settle the mind. They would then primarily acquire skills of concentration, similar to those taught in other concentration practices, such as transcendental meditation. These are of benefit in calming and relaxing the mind.

However, without an understanding of the nature of the suffering they are experiencing, or of how mindfulness has its range of effects in reducing that suffering (which we will discuss in detail in Paper II), neither students nor teachers would be able to focus the application of mindfulness more specifically and effectively to transform the processes that create and sustain suffering. In this way, patients and clients would be exposed to only a narrow range of the total therapeutic resources potentially available to them. For that reason, the beneficial impact of mindfulness programmes are likely to be less than they might otherwise be.

A further limitation of working without a framework of understanding of how suffering arises and how mindfulness can heal that suffering is that when difficulties or obstacles are encountered, there is no 'road map' to consult to find an alternative way forward—all one can do is to attempt to apply the same techniques more vigorously to 'drive through' the road block. Further, without some underlying understanding to guide and motivate them, it is difficult for either students or teachers to commit to some of the more challenging aspects of mindfulness practice—such as 'moving in close' to suffering—which, according to the analysis we have described, are where the greatest potential for long-term therapeutic change lies.

If we accept that it is useful to have some framework of understanding to guide applications of mindfulness, what are the strengths of the framework we have described? We will here describe three.

First, it has great generality; the analysis offered in the Noble Truths is meant to be equally applicable to the full range of suffering from the slightest sense of existential unease through to the problems of recurrent major depression and panic disorder. This wide generality means: (1) although teachers and clients or patients may be experiencing different intensities of suffering, the underlying mechanisms are the same, so that teachers can share a sense of fellowship and compassion with their students, and can draw on their own experience to enrich their teaching of mindfulness; (2) students can acquire skills and understanding in working with lower intensities of 'everyday' suffering that are directly relevant to working with the more intense problems that led them to seek help; and (3) their experience of practicing mindfulness as part of a 'therapeutic' programme may open a doorway for clients and patients to become interested in exploring the relevance of mindfulness to their lives more generally.

Second, the view that *dukkha* is universal and unavoidable, given the way our minds work, can help reduce the personal identification with suffering, which, as we have seen, is a central aspect of the creation of suffering, according to the Buddha's analysis. If this analysis is correct, it also means that the seductive quest for *any* 'quick fix' solution to the problem of suffering ('if only I had the right car, house, partner, career, looks, knowledge, community, etc. etc., I would be happy') is doomed to failure. If this is the case, it would be good to know it.

Third, this framework of understanding was the one that originally led to the integration and development of mindfulness practices as a central component of an integrated programme to reduce and eliminate suffering. Two and a half millenia of experience in the application of mindfulness in this context have provided an invaluable basis for refining and developing the use of mindfulness to heal suffering. Anecdotal evidence within this tradition also provides innumerable examples showing that, when guided by the framework of understanding of the Four Noble truths, mindfulness 'works'. Most of the recent, more systematic evidence that mindfulness, in the shape of MBSR and MBCT, 'works' has also come from studies in which the instructors have worked within an understanding of mindfulness related, in one way or another, to the framework the Buddha proposed.

REFERENCES

Aṅguttara Nikāya: NYANAPONIKA THERA, and BHIKKHU BODHI, trans. 2007. *Anguttara Nikaya Anthology: An anthology of discourses from the Anguttara Nikaya.* Kandy, Sri Lanka: Buddhist Publication Society.

BATCHELOR, S. 1997. *Buddhism without beliefs: A contemporary guide to awakening.* New York: Riverhead Books.

Bruskin Associates. 1973. In *Spectra* 9 (6): 4.

BUDDHADĀSA, B. 1989. *Me and mine, selected essays of Bhikkhu Buddhadāsa.* Edited and with an Introduction by Donald K. Swearer. Albany: State University of New York Press.

CHAH, A., J. KORNFIELD, and P. BREITER. 2004. *A still forest pool: The insight meditation of Achaan Chah.* Wheaton, IL: Quest Books.

Dīgha Nikāya: WALSHE M, 1987. *The long discourses of the Buddha: A translation of the Digha Nikaya.* Boston, MA: Wisdom Publications.

OLENDZKI, A. 2005. Self as verb: Unraveling the Buddha's teachings on how we construct ourselves. *Tricycle: the Buddhist Review, Summer* 14 (4).

Sallatha Sutta: Saṃyutta Nikāya 36:6. Translated by Nyanaponika Thera. http://www.accesstoinsight.org/tipitaka/sn/sn36/sn36.006.nypo.html

Saṃyutta Nikāya: BODHI, B. 2000. *The connected discourses of the Buddha: A new translation of the Samyutta Nikaya.* Boston, MA: Wisdom Publications.

SUMEDHO, A. 1992. *The Four Noble Truths.* www.buddhanet.net

HOW DOES MINDFULNESS TRANSFORM SUFFERING? II: THE TRANSFORMATION OF *DUKKHA*

John D. Teasdale and Michael Chaskalson (Kulananda)

Mindfulness transforms suffering through changes in <u>what</u> *the mind is processing, changes in* <u>how</u> *the mind is processing it, and changes in the* <u>view</u> *of what is being processed. The 'bearing in mind' aspect of mindfulness is important in understanding these changes, and is discussed in terms of working memory. The Interacting Cognitive Subsystems perspective recognizes two kinds of meaning, one explicit and specific, the other implicit and holistic. We suggest that mindfulness is a configuration of mind in which working memory for holistic implicit meanings plays a central role. It is here that the processing and view of experience are transformed by the creation of new patterns of implicit meaning. This analysis is applied to mindfulness practice, mindfulness as a way of being, the training of instructors and the use of mindfulness with respect to different aspirations.*

In the first of two linked papers (Teasdale and Chaskalson 2011), we described the Buddha's analysis of the nature and origins of *dukkha* (suffering). The Buddha also offered a programme of practice, the Noble Eightfold Path, to bring *dukkha* to an end. Mindfulness is a core component of this path to freedom and awakening. Mindfulness is also, of course, the primary focus of contemporary mindfulness-based applications (such as Mindfulness-based Stress Reduction [MBSR] and Mindfulness-based Cognitive Therapy [MBCT]). In this second paper we consider the question: How does mindfulness contribute to the transformation of *dukkha* that occurs when we practice the Noble Eightfold Path or engage with the programmes of mindfulness-based applications?

For the purpose of our discussion we will use the term 'mindfulness' to refer to the practices and processes cultivated in the Buddha's own core teaching on that subject, the *Satipaṭṭhāna Sutta*.

Origins of *dukkha*

As we saw in the first of these two linked papers, the Buddha's analysis of *dukkha*, expressed in the Second Noble Truth, identifies *taṇhā*, craving, as the origin of *dukkha*. The Buddha also offered a more detailed analysis of suffering, known as Dependent Origination, or Dependent Co-arising. This more detailed analysis suggests that *dukkha* arises and is sustained as a result of complex, mutually reinforcing, and self-perpetuating patterns of interaction between many conditions (Thanissaro 2007). We can usefully regard those conditions as particular mental processes and mental contents. Suffering is then seen as the result of particular configurations, or patterns, of mental processes that interact in ways that keep the whole configuration going. These configurations are dynamic— suffering is actively created and re-created, moment by moment. The maintenance of such configurations depends on the re-creation of a particular set of conditions, from one moment to the next, over and over again.

This analysis suggests that we can bring about a temporary cessation of *dukkha* by changing conditions so that these patterns of processing no longer feed off themselves. To bring about a lasting end to all suffering, which is the aim of the Noble Eightfold Path, we have to change conditions so that configurations that perpetuate *dukkha* no longer even arise. Mindfulness offers us ways to change conditions in both these ways.

We can distinguish three broad routes through which mindfulness can have its effects. Although distinct, these strategies are inter-related. We will describe them briefly, and then explore selected aspects of them in greater depth.

As a way to anchor our theoretical discussion we will illustrate the points we make in relation to a concrete example: imagine that a work colleague phones at 9.30 pm in the evening, intruding into your personal time for rest and relaxation. He wants to talk about some figures you had been working on. His tone seems accusatory—hectoring. You have a rule that *you* do not contact work colleagues after 7 pm—so why does *he* keep doing it? You are angry that your privacy has been invaded. After the call, you find yourself upset and irritable, dwelling on thoughts about the call and your colleague that force their way into your mind.

Participants in mindfulness-based programmes often report a reduction in rumination and distress following such upsetting events. In the present example, they might describe noticing, with some surprise and delight, that as a result of practicing mindfulness such a 'difficult' phone call that previously could have upset them for hours, now only leads to disturbance and dwelling on the experience for a matter of minutes, or even seconds. We will consider some possible explanations for such transformation of suffering.

Three strategies for change

The first, and simplest, strategy for altering the conditions which sustain or create suffering is to change the *content* the mind is processing. We can do this by intentionally redirecting the focus of attention to aspects of experience less likely to support the arising and continuation of configurations that create suffering. So, in the case of the phone call, we can intentionally focus and sustain our attention on the bodily sensations as the breath moves in and out; this relatively neutral focus will provide less 'fuel' for the maintenance of problematic configurations than emotion-laden thoughts related to the call.

A second approach is to leave the 'input' to the mind the same, but to change the configuration of processes, or 'shape' of the mind, through which that material is processed. Whereas the first strategy changes *what* is processed, this alternative strategy changes *how* material is processed. This might mean, for example, intentionally allowing and attending *to* the unpleasant feelings created by the upsetting phone call with interest and curiosity, as objects of experience, rather than being 'lost' *within* them in the automatic reaction of aversion.

The third strategy is to change the *view* that we have of the material being processed. In the Buddha's analysis, the configurations that keep us stuck in suffering are rooted in our fundamental ignorance, the basic misperception in which we see the impermanent as permanent, the unreliable as reliable, what is 'not-self' as 'self', and in which we do not see clearly the nature and origins of *dukkha*, nor the way to end it. If we can see things clearly as they are, if we can let go of our tendency to identify personally with experience, then we remove a basic condition for the arising of the configurations that support *dukkha*. With the upsetting phone call, this might involve a change from the perception 'that person has really hurt me by the way he spoke' to the perception 'unpleasant thoughts, feelings and body sensations are here in this moment.'

Each of these three strategies requires us to be aware; if we are to make intentional changes to what is processed, how it is processed, or the view we have of it, we need to know what is going on in the moment. The practice of mindfulness cultivates meta-awareness—our capacity to know, directly, intuitively, our experience as it arises in each moment. At this fundamental level, mindfulness makes a crucial contribution to each of the three strategies we have identified. We now look more closely at the first of those strategies.

Strategy one: Change the input (the 'what' of processing)

In general, what we pay attention to, whether externally or internally, is dictated, not by our conscious choice, but by relatively automatic, habitual biases to attend one way rather than another. In this situation, our attention is reactive; our minds may focus on aspects of experience that feed suffering, and we have little sense of freedom or control. For example, in the context of upsetting situations, such as the phone call, we may have learned to selectively attend to memories and thoughts related to the origins of the upset ('what did I do wrong?', 'whose fault is this?' etc.). Such selective retrieval from memory is one of the bases of ruminative thought patterns (Watkins 2008) that can perpetuate depressed or angry emotions.

We can free ourselves from the effects of these automatic, unconscious priorities for attention by conscious, intentional, allocation of attention to particular objects or classes of objects. For example, we can switch from the habitual disposition to attend to memories and thoughts related to a distressing event and, instead, intentionally attend to relatively neutral sensory stimuli, such as the sensations of the breath, or sound. In that way, we change the content processed by the mind so that it is less likely to create further suffering.

The initial mindfulness practices taught in both mindfulness-based applications and many forms of Buddhist insight meditation ask the practitioner to maintain a focus of attention on the sensations in the body and of the movements of the breath, to recognize when the mind has wandered away from this focus, and then to release the attention and refocus it back on the body or breath. Even in a relatively brief eight-week MBSR or MBCT programme, practicing formal meditation 45 minutes a day, participants will rehearse this sequence hundreds or thousands of times.

In this way, participants have extensive practice in cultivating the skills of detecting when the mind is lost in thought and then intentionally redirecting attention to a chosen focus. Participants in MBSR and MBCT are explicitly encouraged to use these attention switching skills to release themselves from thought patterns which might create emotional suffering. Systematic studies (Allen et al. 2009) show that many patients report the development of these skills as one of the main benefits of MBCT, offering them a simple coping response that enables them to recognize and interrupt ruminative thought patterns that might otherwise lead on to depressive relapse.

It is, of course, important that these skills are taught in a way that fully acknowledges the presence of unhelpful thoughts or feelings before intentionally refocusing attention as a positively motivated act, rather than as a way to avoid or get rid of unpleasant experiences. The latter would simply reinforce the experiential avoidance which is a core feature of many of the configurations of conditions that maintain emotional distress (Hayes et al. 1996).

Learning to intentionally control attention can also have more indirect long-term effects, such as an increase in the sense of agency and self-efficacy in relation to unpleasant thoughts and emotions (Allen et al. 2009). These more persisting effects can lead to long-term reductions in suffering.

The effects of mindfulness training in reducing suffering through this first strategy of changing *what* the mind processes are not hard to understand, and could be shared by other approaches that involve training in the control of attention. On the other hand, the ways in which mindfulness has its effects through the second strategy of changing *how* the mind processes the content it selects, and through the third strategy of changing the *view* of that content are less obvious. These strategies are also more specifically characteristic of mindfulness-based approaches than of other approaches to training attention. In order to understand these routes to change, we need first to look more closely at certain aspects of the ways in which the mind and heart operate.

Working memory

Dreyfus (2011) has suggested that the concept of working memory helps us appreciate an aspect of mindfulness that has received relatively little attention in contemporary discussions; the view of mindfulness as 'the retentive ability on the basis of which we are able to make sense of our experience.' This aspect of mindfulness is particularly relevant to understanding the cognitive mechanisms through which mindfulness changes the way the mind processes and views experience ('cognitive' here, and elsewhere in this paper, refers to information processing in general, including the processing of feeling and sensations, not just to 'thinking').

Working memory is a limited capacity workspace within our mental architecture, in which different pieces of information can be temporarily held and processed. For example, separate pieces of information held in working memory can be integrated into wider patterns that can then shape new understanding and action. The words of this sentence, processed individually, in isolation from each other, convey very limited information. But if they are all held in working memory, and viewed together, then a wider pattern of information is available that can convey much richer information. In the same way, if the meanings of all the sentences in this paragraph are held in working memory, then the overall pattern of information offered conveys an even richer order of meaning than can be conveyed by single sentences.

Working memory and mindfulness

How is this ability of working memory to hold separate pieces of information and integrate them into wider patterns relevant to the transformation of suffering by mindfulness? A cognitive perspective (using 'cognitive' here in its widest sense) suggests that suffering is a response to particular patterns of information (for example, patterns that convey certain emotive meanings). This perspective suggests that we can prevent or reduce suffering by transforming the patterns of information that produce it. *Working memory provides a place where these patterns can be held and integrated with other patterns to create new patterns that do not produce suffering.* So, as a very simple example, a pattern of information related to a person walking right into us, that might ordinarily evoke an angry response, is less likely to do so if it can be integrated into a wider pattern that also includes a pattern of information reflecting the fact that the person is wearing spectacles with very thick lenses, suggesting that they may not be able to see well.

For this integration to occur, the separate pieces of information have to be present together at the same time in working memory. How can we arrange this or know that it is the case? This is where mindfulness enters the picture; psychologists have repeatedly suggested an association between working memory and conscious awareness (Baddeley 2000; Baars and Franklin 2003). This suggests that mindful awareness of an experience is a marker that related information is being 'held' in working memory, and is available for processing. We might go further and suggest that the actual process of being mindful of an object brings related information into working memory and holds it there. In the present example, awareness of the person bumping into us and of the presence of the thick lenses tells us that patterns of information related to both these experiences are present in working memory and are available to be integrated in ways that may reduce suffering. Mindfully attending to these two aspects of experience is one way to get this information into working memory and to hold it there.

Different working memories

At this point, we need to add a further refinement that reflects both the facts of personal experience and the requirements of cognitive theory. This is that we can be conscious of the 'same' experience in different ways, depending on how we attend to it. Consider, for example, the person who bumped into us. We could be aware of them, at a purely sensory-perceptual, visual level, as simply a pattern of shapes and colours. Alternatively, at the level of 'factual' information, we could be aware of the 'fact' that a person has made physical contact with us. And, at a richer level of meaning reflecting the implications derived from this and other facts, we could be aware of an intuitive sense of them as 'a thoughtless, selfish person with no regard for anyone else's comfort or safety' (although, necessarily, expressed in words here, the conscious experience of this kind of implicit, derived meaning is not actually of verbalised thoughts, but, rather, of a felt 'sense' of the person in this way). (These three aspects are meant to be illustrative rather than exhaustive; there are further aspects of this 'same' experience that we could also be aware of.)

Given the suggested link between working memory and consciousness, the fact that we can be conscious of different aspects of experience suggests that there may also be different kinds of working memory, each related to a different aspect of conscious experience. Psychological research has in fact found that there is not just a single, unitary working memory that deals with all kinds of information, but, rather, several different working memories, each specialized for handling a particular kind of information (Baddeley 2000).

This multiplicity of working memories might seem to make working memory less attractive as an idea to help us understand mindfulness and the ways in which it transforms suffering. In fact, approached from the particular theoretical framework we will describe, awareness of this multiplicity actually assists this task by forcing us to confront the questions: (1) Which working memory holds and integrates the kind of information that is most directly linked to the creation and alleviation of suffering? (2) Is this a working memory that is particularly associated with mindfulness compared to lack of mindfulness?

Cognitive models of emotion suggest that the emotional response to an experience is related to the meaning we give the experience. Given that we can recognize more than one type of meaning (literal, metaphorical, etc.), the crucial question is: which of these different aspects of meaning is most directly related to emotion? After considering this question at length, Teasdale (1993) concluded that implicit holistic meanings, derived intuitively from experience, are the most closely involved both in creating and in healing unhelpful emotion. So, with the person who bumped into us, the implicit derived meaning 'thoughtless selfish person with no regard for anyone else's comfort or safety' would be seen as most directly linked to our anger. This level of meaning (which we will describe more fully later) reflects implications derived from whole constellations of more specific conceptual meanings and associated patterns of sensory-perceptual information. We experience these meanings in consciousness as felt 'senses,' as, for example, in a sense that someone is trustworthy, or unreliable, a sense of confidence, or a sense of apprehension.

If elements of the information related to the implicit meaning 'thoughtless selfish person with no regard for anyone else's comfort or safety' are to be integrated with other information, such as the implicit realization 'he is visually impaired and cannot see where he is going' (derived intuitively from the presence of the thick spectacles), then all the relevant information must be held in the working memory that is specialized for dealing with implicit holistic meanings. This would allow the creation of a new pattern reflecting the implicit theme 'innocent of harmful intent' which would reduce the intensity of the irritation, or even transform it into compassion.

Following this line of reasoning, we can suggest that mindfulness, compared to lack of mindfulness, is a configuration of mind in which working memory for the kind of information that conveys implicit holistic meanings (the level of meaning which is most directly involved in the creation and transformation of suffering) plays a particularly important role. We can express these ideas more formally as hypotheses: *mindfulness is characterized by configurations of cognitive processing in which working memory for implicit, intuitive meanings plays a central role; when mindfulness transforms suffering by changing the way experience is processed or viewed, the integration of information into new patterns within this working memory plays a central role.*

We will use these hypotheses to guide our exploration of the ways in which mindfulness transforms suffering through the second and third routes: changes in how experience is processed, and how it is viewed. First, though, we must look more closely at the notion of implicit holistic meanings, an idea that is both central to the account we will explore, and, at the same time, also subtle and not necessarily easy to grasp. We will draw on the Interacting Cognitive Subsystems (ICS) framework (Barnard and Teasdale 1991; Teasdale 1993; Teasdale and Barnard 1993), in which these meanings are seen as playing a central role in emotion production. This framework has been applied previously to understanding the therapeutic effects of mindfulness (Teasdale 1999; Teasdale, Segal and Williams 1995). (ICS actually uses the concept of 'memory buffer' or 'image record' rather than 'working memory' but, for our purposes, we can use these terms equivalently.)

Two kinds of meaning

The poem 'La Belle Dame Sans Merci' by John Keats begins with these four lines:

> Oh what can ail thee, knight-at-arms,
>   Alone and palely loitering?
> The sedge has withered from the lake,
>   And no birds sing.

For most people, reading these lines communicates a direct intuitive sense of melancholy and abandonment. The effect is very different from that of the factual meaning conveyed by a simple sentence: 'The man felt sad and alone.' The effect is also very different from the sum of the same sequence of literal meanings expressed in 'non-poetic' language: *'What is the matter, armed old-fashioned soldier, standing by yourself and doing nothing with a pallid expression? The reed-like plants have decomposed by the lake, and there are not any birds singing'* (Teasdale and Barnard 1993, 73).

ICS suggests that the intuitive sense of melancholy and abandonment conveyed by the poem is the subjective, conscious, correlate of the communication of an implicit holistic meaning related to those themes. That implicit meaning cannot be reduced to the kind of explicit factual, conceptual meaning that is normally conveyed by a single sentence. You can check that meaning is in fact being conveyed if, having read the poem again and 'sensed' the feeling engendered, you ask yourself the question 'would he be fun to meet at a party?' Most likely, you will know, directly, immediately, and non-conceptually, in other words, without having to 'think' about it, that the answer is an emphatic 'no.' This is another kind of knowing, one that lies at the heart of mindful processing.

ICS distinguishes between specific *Propositional meaning* and more generic *Implicational meaning*. Propositional meaning corresponds to the kind of straightforward explicit, factual, conceptual, or literal meaning conveyed by a single sentence. The associated subjective experience is of 'knowing that' something is or is not the case. By contrast, *Implicational meaning communicates a meaning that is implicit and holistic, that cannot be reduced to the meaning of a single sentence, or to the sum of the specific conceptual meanings conveyed by a sequence of sentences.* To the extent that we can communicate these kinds of meaning by language, it is by poetry, metaphor, story, and parable.

Implicational meanings capture the 'deep structure' of experience; underlying similarities that recur across a range of life situations which, although superficially different, share certain underlying common themes. These prototypical patterns include the common themes within recurring patterns of conceptual meanings, together with the common elements of any recurring patterns of sensory information that typically occur with them. For example, Implicational meanings might capture recurring patterns of meaning (such as 'there is no way for me to get what I want') extracted from 'hopeless' situations, together with information reflecting patterns of body sensations that recur in such situations, such as the physical sense of being 'burdened'. Reflecting these two aspects of Implicational meaning, the meaning conveyed by a poem also depends on the combination of carefully chosen patterns of conceptual meanings, together with the actual sounds of the words, their rhythms, and the visual imagery they evoke.

In contrast to the intellectual 'knowing with the head' or 'knowing that' of Propositional meanings, consciously processing Implicational meanings is associated with a more experiential quality. These meanings are 'felt' or 'sensed' and often have an embodied quality: 'knowing with the heart,' 'gut-level knowing,' and so forth. The lines of the poem we considered convey an actual sense of the *experience* of melancholy and abandonment, albeit in a muted or limited form, rather than telling us *about* melancholy and abandonment, as in a prose passage on the subject.

Two kinds of meaning and the transformation of suffering

Consistent with our earlier discussion, the ICS theoretical framework makes the very strong assertion that only holistic Implicational meanings are directly linked to emotion and suffering. By contrast, Propositional meanings affect emotion only indirectly, through their contribution to Implicational meanings. It follows that the transformation of suffering has to occur primarily in the working memory specialised for Implicational meaning. We can see mindfulness as a way to access and 'work' within Implicational working memory. When we mindfully contemplate experience we 'hold' related elements of Implicational meaning in that workspace in ways that allow them to be integrated into new patterns, or processed within a wider perspective, so that they no longer evoke suffering. We might say that mindfulness allows the poetry of moment by moment experience to rewrite itself, to gracefully change its theme from one of suffering to one of ease and peace. This is one reason why the judicial use of poetry in mindfulness-based interventions can be so effective—it is evocative of a feeling that carries deep meaning beyond the words, into the space of silence during a class session.

By contrast with Implicational working memory, where 'work' on elements of Implicational meaning can heal suffering, Propositional working memory figures prominently in configurations that create suffering (as well, of course, in many configurations that do not) (Teasdale 1999). This is where the mind compares its ideas of where it is with its ideas of where it thinks it should be, and, if it cannot resolve the gap, dwells on the gulf between them in ways that can fuel suffering. Segal, Williams and Teasdale (2002, 68) identified this process with a 'discrepancy monitor' and gave it a central role in the rumination which maintains persistent depression. More generally, Propositional working memory derives elements of Implicational meaning reflecting themes of unsatisfatoriness, disappointment, frustration, and the like from discrepancies between concepts of needed and actual states. These Implicational meanings can then create suffering.

With this theoretical background in place, we are now in a position to consider the second and third routes through which mindfulness contributes to the transformation of suffering: changes in how experiences are processed, and changes in how experiences are viewed.

Strategy two: Change the 'how' of processing

Mindfulness involves a radical shift in the *way* in which we attend to experience. In this second route to the transformation of suffering, mindfulness disrupts configurations maintaining *dukkha* by changing conditions related to *how* information is processed rather than, as in the first route, conditions related to *what* information is processed. Here, the very act of bringing mindful awareness to experience, can, itself, disrupt and transform habitual unhelpful configurations of processing.

How are we to understand this? Some of the changes in processing associated with mindfulness are best understood in terms of mindfulness changing the overall configuration, or 'shape,' of the mind. As we have already noted, processing configurations that create and maintain *dukkha* often prioritize a verbal-conceptual level of information; the angry rumination that fuels the distress following an upsetting phone call involves streams of thinking, often actually experienced internally in verbal form: 'How dare he say that to me!... He's really upset me now.... How can I get on with my evening when I feel like this? ...' Such thinking *about* experience involves the manipulation of concepts related to experience, rather than the direct experience itself, and, from an ICS perspective, reflects an overall processing configuration in which the dominant influence is Propositional working memory rather than Implicational working memory.

On the other hand, mindfulness practice cultivates a more direct, intuitive, experiential way of knowing momentary experience (Farb et al. 2007; Watkins and Teasdale 2004)—*the knowing of the experience is in the very awareness of it*. From the ICS perspective, this kind of knowing reflects an overall processing configuration in which the dominant influence is Implicational working memory rather than Propositional working memory. Mindfully responding to the distress following a phone call involves a shift from ruminatively thinking *about* the call, its effects and consequences, to an awareness of thoughts, feelings and body sensations, known directly, experientially, as aspects of experience in the moment. This shift in mode of knowing, brought about by the intentional deployment of attention in particular ways, reflects a reconfiguration of the mind so that primary influence shifts from Propositional working memory to Implicational working memory. In that way, mindfulness can transform suffering by changing the overall 'shape' of the mind through which experience is processed so that conditions no longer support the continuing creation and recreation from moment to moment of configurations that perpetuate suffering.

Other effects of mindfulness on processing are best understood in terms of changes *within* Implicational working memory. As we noted in the first of these two linked papers (Teasdale and Chaskalson 2011), the Second Noble Truth identifies craving and aversion as crucial conditions for the arising of *dukkha*. Both aversion and craving are rooted in a basic underlying motivation of fear and avoidance. With aversion we need to get rid of unpleasant experiences or states of being, and with craving and clinging the compulsive need to have and hold the object of desire reflects a fear that we may fail to attain it, or that, having attained it, we will lose it. On the other hand, mindfulness cultivates mental processes rooted in approach motivation, and has been shown to shift measures of underlying brain activity from patterns characteristic of avoidance to patterns more characteristic of approach (Davidson et al. 2003).

We can understand these effects of mindfulness in terms of changes within Implicational working memory. It is here that elements of Implicational meaning reflecting the approach themes of curiosity, interest, and engagement, inherent in mindfulness, can be processed alongside patterns of meaning embodying themes of avoidance, aversion and resistance in ways that will transform their capacity to create suffering. In the case of the upsetting telephone call, for example, the very act of deliberately bringing a kindly, curious, interested, mindful awareness to the experience of distress introduces elements of meaning related to such approach themes into Implicational working memory. There, in ways that we will look at more closely below, they can counterbalance the effects of the elements of meaning related to avoidance themes which have been created by the angry ruminative thinking that is perpetuating suffering.

Craving and aversion also reflect a need for experience to be different from how it actually is. Mindfulness intentionally embodies a willingness to allow things to be just as they are. With the upset following the phone call, a mindful response brings a deliberate stance of letting the experiences of the moment, the unpleasant thoughts, feelings and body sensations, be just as they are as we hold them in awareness and come to know them more closely. As we do that, we introduce elements of Implicational meaning related to themes of 'allowing' and 'letting be' into Implicational working memory, where they can be integrated with and transform the Implicational meanings related to wanting to be rid of the unpleasant thoughts, feelings and body sensations, and the person who caused us to experience them. In that way, we change the conditions that support the continuation of the patterns of processing that perpetuate *dukkha* from one moment to the next. Deprived of that support, these patterns dissolve and we are freed from suffering.

In such ways, by integrating Implicational patterns embodying the motivations to approach, rather than avoid, and to allow, rather than get rid of, the wisdom of mindfulness can transform the conditions in which difficult experiences are processed. We can understand the process through which we weave transformative qualities such as patience, trust, non-striving, acceptance and letting go (Kabat-Zinn 1990, 33–5) into mindfulness practice in similar terms.

As these processes are so central to the effectiveness of mindfulness, and distinguish mindfulness from simply paying attention to experience, it will be helpful to look at them more closely.

'Implicational' versus 'propositional' change

Implicational thematic elements are, effectively, distillations of the essence of repeated *experiences* involving approach, allowing, goodwill and so forth, rather than a summary of factual knowledge *about* them. When these elements are incorporated into processing they bring with them an experiential 'flavour' or 'quality' that echoes the 'feel' of the original experiences, just as the four lines of the poem 'La Belle Dame Sans Merci' conveyed something of the 'feel' of melancholy and abandonment. In this way, with ongoing cultivation, mindful awareness can become imbued with a conscious sense of curiosity, interest, kindness, letting go, etc.

In this 'Implicational' approach, our subjective sense can gently guide the process of integrating these thematic elements; we, as it were, 'feel' our way into incorporating the 'spirit' of curiosity, letting be, and the like, as best we can. This 'Implicational' approach is very different from a more goal-focused 'Propositional' approach. This latter might involve, for example, setting conceptually specified targets, such as 'be a kind person,' to be achieved through a list of conceptually described instructions (a 'to-do list'): 'feel kind'; 'act generously'; 'be loving', 'model empathy and compassion,' and so forth. As well as leaving us wondering how exactly we might do this, and engendering a general sense of 'fixing' and 'busyness,' this approach runs the danger of generating yet more suffering; in the discussion of the Second Noble Truth in Paper I, we saw that attachment to a goal such as 'being a self who is kind (curious, accepting, etc.)' is actually the very condition that fuels *dukkha*.

We can illustrate this important distinction between an 'Implicational' approach and a 'Propositional' approach by the alternative ways we might respond to the statement that mindfulness involves 'paying attention non-judgmentally'. An Implicational approach would see this statement as an encouragement to embody the qualities, or spirit, of non-judgmentalness, acceptance, allowing and so on in the attention we bring to experience, to the extent that we can. A Propositional approach would see or use that same statement as an instruction to avoid making judgments. But, of course, we will inevitably find ourselves making judgments. In this situation, the Implicational approach is to receive 'this too' in a spirit of acceptance and allowing, perhaps including the judgments themselves in the scope of mindful awareness. By contrast, the Propositional approach sees the fact that we have made judgments as a failure to achieve the specified goal of not making judgments. This view, of course, is only too likely to lead to more self-devaluative judgments, even as we give ourselves the further instruction not to judge the judging!

How?

How do we bring particular thematic elements into Implicational working memory? How do we incorporate the flavour of kindness and allowing, into mindful awareness? One way is to take advantage of the 'remembering', 'recollective', or 'bearing in mind' aspect of mindfulness, long recognized within the Buddhist tradition and re-emphasized by Georges Dreyfus (2011).

We can illustrate what we have in mind here by returning to the four lines of the poem. Reading the poem evokes a sense of melancholy and abandonment, which, we have suggested, reflects the processing of Implicational patterns related to those themes in Implicational working memory. That sense of melancholy and abandonment soon fades once we stop reading the poem, and are no longer actively processing these Implicational patterns. If, at this point, we were to bring the words 'melancholy and abandonment,' or an image from the poem, to mind, then there is every chance, if we have not left it too long since reading the poem, that we will experience the sense of melancholy again, and to an extent far greater than if we had not read the poem.

We can understand this re-evocation of feeling from the present perspective as follows. Having been processed only recently in Implicational working memory, patterns of Implicational information related to themes of melancholy and abandonment are still relatively 'fresh' and accessible in longer term Implicational memory. They can be brought back from there to Implicational working memory by relevant cues. Processed once more in working memory, these patterns will re-create the sense of melancholy and abandonment, and 'reset the clock' by refreshing the representations of them in longer term memory. By repeating this process over and over again, in other words 'bearing in mind' the sense of melancholy and related cues, it would be possible to keep related patterns of Implicational meaning present and active in working memory. There, they would be accessible for possible integration with information arising from unfolding experience. The process is analogous to the way we can keep a number 'in mind' by repeating it to ourselves over and over again, so keeping it 'fresh' in short-term memory. The process in Implicational working memory is, of course, at a much richer and more complex level of information.

Of course, most of us would not choose to bear themes of melancholy and abandonment in mind, but if the themes related to kindness, curiosity, allowing, and letting go, we can see how useful this might be in the transformation (or even prevention) of any suffering that might arise.

A second way we can keep information related to helpful themes 'alive' in Implicational working memory, is, of course, by actions arising from related motivations. Every time we intentionally act on any naturally arising sense of kindness, or compassion, or generosity, then we extend the time over which thematically related information is present in Implicational working memory. We also, of course, lay down related information in longer term Implicational memory, increasing the chance that such themes will be 'retrieved' later. These are some of the reasons why the Noble Eightfold Path attaches such great importance to wholesome, ethical behaviour and intention, alongside its emphasis on meditation and understanding.

A third way we can introduce particular thematic content into Implicational working memory is indirectly, through the contemplation of related Propositional content. However, as this approach is generally more relevant to the third strategy for transforming suffering that we identified—changing our view of experience—we will return to it when we discuss that topic.

The relevance of these strategies for keeping thematic content alive in working memory goes beyond responding mindfully to particular experiences of suffering. It extends to the more enduring and pervasive effects of mindfulness, to which we now turn.

Mindfulness as a way of being

From what we have said so far, we can understand some of the ways in which intentionally responding mindfully to unpleasant and unwanted experiences, as and when they arise, can reduce suffering. We now consider how mindfulness practice can reduce suffering more generally.

Allen et al. (2009) subtitled their paper on the effects of MBCT with a quotation from one of the patients they studied: 'It changed me in just about every way possible.' Such a comment suggests that this patient learned far more than how to use mindfulness to cope better with particular experiences of unpleasant thoughts and feelings. It is not uncommon for participants in mindfulness-based programmes to report something akin to the opening of a door onto a whole new way of being—a sense of realising a potential for a radically different way of living life which had always been available, but, somehow, had never really been accessed before. In the same way, one of the most intriguing observations in MBSR and MBCT is that patients often report a reduction in upset and rumination following an event such as a difficult phone call, even when they have made no deliberate attempt to respond differently; the quality of their report is more 'this just happened' rather than 'I did this.'

How are we to understand what is going on in such situations? First, of course, we should remember that mindfulness practice is not focused specifically on unpleasant experiences; students of insight meditation, and participants in mindfulness-based applications, are encouraged to be mindful of all experience, the good, the bad, and the indifferent, as much of the time as possible. But the effects we have described seem to go further than simply the sum of many individual 'mindful responses' repeated over time. Rather, they seem more consistent with the cumulative effects of sustained mindfulness producing more lasting changes in the overall 'shape' of the heart and mind. In other words, it is as if mindfulness practice eventually 'tips' the prevailing configuration of mental processes, or what we might call the mode of mind, from a mode which has the potential to create suffering to a mode which has the potential to heal suffering. That new mode of mind, with its different pattern of 'how' experience is processed, then persists for some time until, as a result of some further change in conditions, the mind and heart is 'tipped' back into its more habitual mode.

We have proposed that mindfulness is particularly associated with processing configurations in which Implicational working memory plays a central role. This proposal suggests the hypothesis that the changes in mode of mind we have just described involve a shift from an habitual mode, in which Propositional working memory and conceptual thought have a dominant influence, (a mode which has been called 'doing') to an alternative mode, in which Implicational working memory and experiential knowing have a dominant influence (a mode which has been called 'being' [Kabat-Zinn 1990; Segal, Williams, and Teasdale 2002; Williams et al. 2007]). This shift would explain: (1) the widely generalized effects of sustained mindfulness practice; (2) the way they are experienced as a new way of being; and (3) experiences in which previously upsetting experiences lose their power to evoke distress without the need for any intentional mindful 'coping response'.

The shift in prevailing mode of mind will not be stable, especially in the early stages of mindfulness practice; it will need continuing gentle maintenance to support it from 'tipping' back into the deeply engrained configurations that habitually maintain dukkha. How is this to be achieved?

The 'bearing in mind' aspect of Implicational working memory, which we considered earlier, offers a number of ways to support the alternative mode of mind. It provides a way to embody themes such as approach and allowing, which nurture a mode of Implicationally influenced 'being' rather Propositionally influenced 'doing.' It also, crucially, offers a way to keep alive the intention and motivation to be mindful, itself. But we need to be very sensitive to exactly how we 'bear in mind' that intention. Keeping alive the memory of a Propositional instruction such as 'be mindful' can be useful, but it runs the risk of becoming a nagging voice sitting on our shoulder and 'checking up' on how well we are doing in that respect from moment to moment. That, of course, would be quite counterproductive. The 'Implicational alternative' of keeping alive patterns of Implicational meaning related to the 'spirit' of curiosity, interest, and investigation, from which an unforced mindful awareness may arise more naturally, is likely to be more productive.

We can understand the effectiveness of certain formal practices in which 'choiceless' mindful awareness is sustained over extended periods in terms of such an Implicational approach. Martine Batchelor (2011) decribes how bearing in mind a silent question such as 'what is this?' can keep the whole mindful mode alive: 'When meditating, I would repeatedly ask the question: "What is this?" silently inside myself. I did not do this in order to arrive at an answer but rather to develop a sensation of questioning and then intensify that sensation'. This description bears a striking resemblance to the 'prescription' for maintaining information related to helpful themes in Implicational working memory we described earlier. The question is clearly intended Implicationally, rather than Propositionally (it does not expect a conceptual answer); and it stresses the importance of connecting with the felt 'sense' of the question (which, from the ICS perspective, is the conscious correlate of the processing of themes of curiosity, interest, and investigation in Implicational working memory). In this way the question and the evoked sense can be used to maintain the processing of themes that will support continuing mindful awareness in Implicational working memory. This whole process then 'holds' the mind in a configuration in which Implicational, rather than Propositional, working memory has the prevailing role.

Mindfulness offers the possibility of more skilful modes of mind, or ways of being, in which we can, if we remember, dwell for periods of time. In these states, we experience less suffering and greater ease and peace, and, for that reason, they are of great value in and of themselves. However, they do not bring a lasting end to *dukkha*: like all other states of mind, they are temporary, and when we forget to deliberately practice or nurture them, we are likely to 'tip' back into configurations of conditions that create suffering. For this reason, within the Buddhist tradition, mindfulness is seen, ultimately, as a means, rather than as an end in itself: it offers a path to the development of *insight*, or change of view, the third strategy for change we have identified. Insight offers us the possibility both of reducing our burden of everyday unsatisfactoriness and also of eliminating *dukkha* completely, for good.

Strategy three: Changing the view

Although we have distinguished three strategies through which mind-fulness transforms suffering, it is important to remember that they are inherently inter-related. As we look more closely at this third strategy through the ICS perspective we have outlined, we will see that many situations could be described equally well in terms of changes in view of experience, changes in processing of experience, or changes in relationship to experience.

We make sense of individual experiences within wider views of how things are. These views, schemas, or schematic mental models shape and form the way we see experience, somewhat like a lens. These effects can occur at all levels. At the most basic level, seeing experience in terms of what is internal ('me') and what is external ('the world'), for example, is a function of a very general purpose lens through which we habitually look at all experience. The same could be said of seeing experience in terms of 'subject' and 'object'.

The ignorance that we discussed in Paper I as the foundation of all *dukkha*, involves looking through a lens which: (1) sees experience in terms of independently existing, enduring objects and selves, rather than in terms of dynamically unfolding processes; and (2) leads us to identify personally with experiences as 'me' or 'mine', when in fact they are impersonal phenomena that arise as a function of certain conditions.

In principle, we can transform suffering either by changing the way we apply existing lenses, or by creating new lenses. We can illustrate the first of these strategies by the effects of mindfulness known as 'decentring' (Teasdale, Segal and Williams 1995; Segal, Williams and Teasdale 2002) or 'reperception' (Shapiro et al. 2006).

Decentring and reperception involve a radical shift in the way we use the very basic lens through which we see experience in terms of 'subject' and 'object' so that what we have habitually taken as subject is now taken as object. In mindfulness we attend *to* feelings, thoughts and sensations as mental events in the field of awareness, rather than *from* them as aspects of our sense of subjective self. In the case of the phone call, for example, this would involve making the upset feelings or thoughts the focus of attention as events in the mind, rather than *being* them as 'me' (cf. Kabat-Zinn 1990, 69–70). It has been suggested that this fundamental re-orientation is an important mechanism through which mindfulness can reduce suffering. Half the participants in the study of Allen et al. (2009) reported that MBCT led to 'a new perspective on their depression-related thoughts and feelings that can be summarized as "These thoughts and feelings aren't me."'

In ICS, the lenses through which we look at (and so create) experience are viewed as schematic mental models (Teasdale and Barnard 1993), prototypical patterns of Implicational information that reflect recurring aspects of the 'deep structure' of experience. This perspective suggests that if we wish to change our view of experience by intentionally replacing one lens with another from our 'stock' of existing lenses, or if we wish to create new lenses that remove or attenuate our distorted perceptions, then Implicational working memory is the place where this must happen. This workspace allows us to access existing schematic mental models stored in long term Implicational memory, to integrate and recombine elements of existing Implicational models into new patterns, and to extract new models on the basis of fresh Implicational 'raw data' derived from looking afresh, with clear vision, at more basic aspects of experience.

Given our earlier suggestion that it is the working memory for Implicational information that is particularly associated with mindfulness, the perspective we have just outlined suggests that mindfulness creates optimal conditions for the strategy of intentionally changing view as a way to transform suffering. Mindfulness allows access to the Implicational workspace so enabling us to know the lens through which we are viewing the world, to change that lens, and to create new lenses. We can illustrate these points by revisiting an example we have already considered.

Wakefulness and the Second Noble Truth

In Paper I (page 95) we recounted an anecdote of waking, preoccupied with thinking about the idea that suffering arises from our relationship to experience, rather than from experience itself. Even though the mind was full of thoughts about that idea, this thinking had no effect in reducing the irritation at being awake in the early hours of the morning. From the ICS perspective, this is exactly what we would expect: the subjective experience of 'thinking about' indicated that Propositional working memory, specialized for processing conceptual information, was dominant. Even though this 'thinking about' might produce further ideas about the Second Noble Truth, these, in themselves, would not be liberating, simply because the conceptual level of information is not directly linked to suffering or the transformation of suffering.

On the other hand, contemplation of the Second Noble Truth would have created elements of Implicational information related to the theme that suffering reflects our relationship to experience. But, so long as 'thinking,' with its primary involvement of Propositional working memory, precluded much involvement of Implicational working memory,[1] these patterns of Implicational information *could not be integrated* with other Implicational information, directly linked to suffering, in ways that could transform that suffering. On the other hand, as soon as the focus shifted away from *thinking* about suffering and wakefulness to *mindful investigation* of the actual *experience* of irritation and aversion in the moment, then primary influence swung to Implicational working memory. There, the patterns of Implicational information related to the themes of the Second Noble Truth could be integrated with the patterns related to irritation and aversion to yield the intuitive insight 'this aversion, right now, is what is causing suffering.' And that clear seeing, rather than any attempt to follow a Propositional instruction to 'do' letting go, led very naturally to a release of the attachment to the need to get rid of the experience of wakefulness.

Once the mind sees clearly that it is creating suffering, its inherent wisdom lets go of the processing that creates it, just as we let go of a very hot object as soon as we register the pain it is causing. The new view, or 'lens', that embodies this insight, having once been created and used, could be stored as a new schematic mental model in long term Implicational memory, ready to be accessed when a thematically similar situation arose in the future. In this way, the basis of a more enduring transformation of suffering is established. That is, the next time we are awake in the middle of the night, we will be more likely to 'see' our irritation and attempts to 'fix' our wakefulness as 'aversion' or 'suffering' and we will release ourselves sooner, and, perhaps, eventually, this reaction may not even arise.

'Top down' and 'Bottom up'

The example we just considered involved the development of insight through the integration within Implicational working memory of elements derived 'top down' from contemplation of the Second Noble Truth with elements derived 'bottom up' from the mindful investigation of the experience of the sense of irritation and aversion in the moment. The same combined 'Top down and Bottom up' strategy for the development of insight is evident in the Buddha's own instructions for the practice of mindfulness in the *Satipaṭṭhāna Sutta*.

The practices of mindfulness outlined in that discourse describe a method in which, through mindfulness, new fundamental schematic mental models of experience can be constructed afresh on the basis of direct experiential data, integrated with orienting instructions. We are encouraged to contemplate the body *as* body, feelings *as* feelings, and mind *as* mind, so that we create models in which we see these experiences for what they are—experiences—rather than as aspects of an independently existing self— 'me' or 'mine.' We are instructed to see the arising and passing away of all experiences, and the conditions that relate to those arisings and passings away, so that we create models that embody the theme of transience in relation to shifting conditions, rather than that of continuity of independently existing entities. And we are instructed to contemplate 'internally and externally,' that is, the way in which all aspects of what we experience are also experienced by others, so that we create models of the universal, rather than personal, nature of experience.

The mindful mode of mind, which makes available the workspace of Implicational working memory in which these new models can be created, supports this process. It allows us, ultimately, to create new basic models which see all experience as process, dependent on conditions, rather than as reflections of enduring objects and selfs with stable properties. These new models release the grip of the long-established models embodying ignorance that underpin the configurations that create and sustain suffering. We see the world afresh as if we have awakened from a dream. We are free.

Conclusions and implications

As we conclude by considering some of the implications of our analysis, it is helpful to remember that the ideas we have presented are just that—ideas—hypotheses that can be tested, but that, as yet, await the support of specific empirical data. It follows that any implications we derive from these ideas must also be treated carefully, as possibilities to be investigated further, rather than as statements of established truth.

We have considered three aspects of the way in which mindfulness can transform suffering: changing *what* the mind is processing, changing *how* the mind is processing it, and changing the *view* of what is being processed. We have suggested that whereas the first of these routes to change, based on learning how to intentionally switch the focus of attention, is relatively straightforward, the second and third routes are more subtle. Within the analysis we have presented, this is because these latter routes involve the transformation of implicit holistic (Implicational) meanings.

These distinctions have a number of implications. First, they clarify the ways in which mindfulness involves more than simply learning how to pay attention, intentionally, in the moment. Although we might describe the first route to change in this way, this description cannot do justice to the second and third routes. Within our analysis, the effects of mindfulness through these routes necessarily involves the integration of skilful views, attitudes, and intentions into awareness as a crucial aspect of transformation.

There are also implications for the teaching of mindfulness and the training and selection of instructors. Although teaching skills of attention control may not require extensive training of instructors, the same is not true of teaching mindfulness in a way that capitalizes on the second and third routes to change. In distinguishing 'Propositional change' and 'Implicational change' we suggested that Implicational change involved the integration of the 'spirit' of non-judgmentalness, allowing, affectionate curiosity, kindness, compassion, and the like, rather than compliance with a sequence of conceptual 'do this, do that' instructions. Embodiment of these qualities in the instructor will be one of the most potent vehicles for communicating the 'felt sense' of these qualities to the participants in mindfulness-based interventions. Equally, changing deeply ingrained implicit 'views' or 'schematic models' in participants will be powerfully influenced by the embodied wisdom of the instructor. These are reasons for selecting and training instructors in terms of the qualities of their being and understanding.

Further, an understanding of the relationship between Propositional and Implicational meanings could provide mindfulness instructors with a clearer rationale for the way in which they might gently guide participants' attention—both during formal practices and, perhaps more potently, in the 'enquiry' sessions that usually follow such practices. Consciously using language and conceptual meaning to alert participants to Implicational themes could aid participants: (1) by making helpful themes that arise more explicit in the moment; and (2) by refreshing participants' experience of these from time to time—returning to them later in the session, perhaps, and thus helping participants to keep them alive in Implicational working memory.

The relative importance of the three routes to change is likely to differ in relation to different aspirations. The Buddhist tradition integrates all three routes in its use of mindfulness within the Noble Eightfold Path. This seems necessary when the aim of practice, as in this Path, is the lofty goal of complete and lasting freedom from *dukkha*. It also seems likely that all three routes contribute when patients report discovering a new way of being, or recurrently depressed patients report fundamental shifts in their view of and relationship to depression.

On the other hand, there may be other problem areas where the first route, alone, may be sufficient. For example, this may be enough to give clients and patients the skills to break into relatively circumscribed self-perpetuating mental patterns, such as where thoughts, feelings and body sensations feed off each other in closed loops.

If we can identify the routes to change which are most relevant to particular problems, we may find, for example, problems that would benefit from attention training alone, where relatively simple interventions could be offered. Scarce, highly trained, instructors could then focus on clients and patients who require a more comprehensive approach, transforming suffering through all the routes we have described.

Finally, our distinction between Propositional and Implicational change, and the hypothesis that Implicational change is the more important, reinforces the message of traditional Buddhist teachings: the transformation of suffering arises as a result of changing the conditions that create and support it, rather than 'fixing' 'forcing' or 'making' something happen by an effort of will.

NOTE

1. In the ICS framework only one kind of working memory can be 'dominant' at any one time.

REFERENCES

ALLEN, M., A. BROMLEY, W. KUYKEN, and S. J. SONNENBERG. 2009. Participants' experience of mindfulness-based cognitive therapy: 'It changed me in just about every way possible.' *Behavioural and Cognitive Psychotherapy* 37: 413–30.

BAARS, B. J., and S. FRANKLIN. 2003. How conscious experience and working memory interact. *Trends in Cognitive Sciences* 7: 166–72.

BADDELEY, A. 2000. The episodic memory buffer: A new component of working memory? *Trends in Cognitive Sciences* 4: 417–23.

BARNARD, P. J., and J. D. TEASDALE. 1991. Interacting cognitive subsystems: A systemic approach to cognitive-affective interaction and change. *Cognition and Emotion* 5: 1–39.

BATCHELOR, M. 2011. Meditation and mindfulness. *Contemporary Buddhism* 12: 157–164.

DAVIDSON, R. J., J. KABAT-ZINN, J. SCHUMACHER, M. ROSENKRANZ, D. MULLER, S.F. SANTORELLI, F. URBANOWSKI, A. HARRINGTON, K. BONUS, and J.F. SHERIDAN. 2003. Alterations in brain and immune function produced by mindfulness meditation. *Psychosomatic Medicine* 65: 564–70.

DREYFUS, GEORGES. 2011. Is mindfulness present-centered and non-judgmental? A discussion of the cognitive dimension of mindfulness. *Contemporary Buddhism* 12: 41–54.

FARB, N. A. S., Z. V. SEGAL, H. MAYBERG, J. BEAN, D. MCKEON, Z. FATIMA, and A. K. ANDERSON. 2007. Attending to the present reveals distinct neural modes of self-reference. *Social Cognitive and Affective Neuroscience* 2: 313–22.

HAYES, S. C., K. G. WILSON, K. STROSAHL, E. V. GIFFORD, and V. M. FOLLETTE. 1996. Experiential avoidance and behavioral disorders: A functional dimensional approach to diagnosis and treatment. *Journal of Consulting and Clinical Psychology* 64: 1152–68.

KABAT-ZINN, J. 1990. *Full catastrophe living*. New York: Dell.

SEGAL, Z. V., J. M. G. WILLIAMS, and J. D. TEASDALE. 2002. *Mindfulness-based cognitive therapy for depression: A new approach to preventing relapse*. New York: Guilford Press.

SHAPIRO, S. L., L. E. CARLSON, J. A. ASTIN, and B. FREEDMAN. 2006. Mechanisms of mindfulness. *Journal of Clinical Psychology* 62: 373–86.

TEASDALE, J. D. 1993. Emotion and two kinds of meaning: Cognitive therapy and applied cognitive science. *Behaviour Research and Therapy* 31: 339–54.

TEASDALE, J. D. 1999. Emotional processing, three modes of mind, and the prevention of relapse in depression. *Behaviour Research and Therapy* 37: S53–S77.

TEASDALE, J. D., and P. J. BARNARD. 1993. *Affect, cognition and change*. Hove: Lawrence Erlbaum Associates.

TEASDALE, J. D., and M. CHASKALSON. 2011. How does mindfulness transform suffering? I: The nature and origins of *Dukkha*. *Contemporary Buddhism* 12: 89–102.

TEASDALE, J. D., Z. V. SEGAL, and J. M. G. WILLIAMS. 1995. How does cognitive therapy prevent depressive relapse and why should attention control (mindfulness) training help? *Behaviour Research and Therapy* 33: 25–39.

THANISSARO, B. 2007. *The wings to awakening*. 5th ed. Barre, MA: Dhamma Dana Publications.

WATKINS, E. R. 2008. Constructive and unconstructive repetitive thought. *Psychological Bulletin* 134: 163–206.

WATKINS, E., and J. D. TEASDALE. 2004. Adaptive and maladaptive self-focus in depression. *Journal of Affective Disorders* 82: 1–8.

WILLIAMS, J. M. G., J. D. TEASDALE, Z. V. SEGAL, and J. KABAT-ZINN. 2007. *The mindful way through depression*. New York: Guilford Press.

MINDFULNESS-BASED COGNITIVE THERAPY: CULTURE CLASH OR CREATIVE FUSION?

Melanie Fennell and Zindel Segal

Mindfulness-based cognitive therapy creates an unlikely partnership, between the ancient tradition of mindfulness meditation rooted in Buddhist thought, and the much more recent and essentially western tradition of cognitive and clinical science. This article investigates points of congruence and difference between the two traditions and concludes that, despite first appearances, this is a fruitful partnership which may well endure.

'So where's the cognitive bit?'

In Oxford, we offer experiential eight-week mindfulness-based cognitive therapy (MBCT) courses to professionals working in healthcare and education. Participants' previous experience of mindfulness meditation varies widely, as does their familiarity with cognitive therapy. This inquiry captures the curiosity of a participant with a long established Zen meditation practice, at the end of such a course.

Mindfulness-based cognitive therapy (Segal, Williams and Teasdale 2002) represents a marriage between two very different cultures or traditions: the 2500 year old Buddhist tradition of mindfulness meditation, and the much more recent Western tradition of cognitive and clinical science. Just as in any meeting between different cultures, there is a need to foster mutual appreciation and respect— appreciation of shared perspectives and common humanity, and respect for genuine difference. Yet at times suspicion prevents a sense of shared interests, and differences may seem irreconcilable. Do these unlikely partners have enough in common to ensure continued and growing harmony? Or will the relationship end in divorce?

At first glance, mindfulness meditation and western psychological science might appear to have little in common. How can two cultures, widely separated in time and place, have anything useful to say to each other? Those who have come to MBCT from Buddhism or *vipassanā* meditation express doubts as to the wisdom of the marriage, as do those who have discovered mindfulness from cognitive therapy (CT). These doubts reflect legitimate concerns: that in integrating the two, either might be denatured and something essential lost. In the CT camp, the concern is that the elaborated theoretical foundations of CT, together with its rigorous emphasis on empirical evaluation, will be lost. The scientific community, requiring that clinical interventions be evidence-based, suspects that Buddhism is being introduced into this secular setting by the back door, and may even associate meditation with dubious New Age practices (the fact that respected clinical scientists have developed MBCT has somewhat mitigated this concern). Amongst mindfulness practitioners, the concern is rather than subjecting meditation to radical changes in the service of clinical need, bringing it into a scientific and clinical context and putting it under the cold gaze of the research microscope, will lead to a different kind of loss: loss of the heart and spirit of the approach, its profound spiritual and ethical foundations, and the centrality of acceptance, kindness and compassion. Additionally, both cultures are under-standably (sometimes justifiably) concerned that practitioners without deep understanding of the root traditions will mechanically parrot meditation practices and CT exercises or introduce meaningless innovations, because they fail to appreciate the underlying aims, intentions and conceptual framework of either.

How then was it possible for a Zen practitioner to ask the question in our opening quote? The originators of MBCT, building on the seminal work of Jon Kabat-Zinn (Kabat-Zinn 1990), recognized commonalities between mindfulness and CT, and partnered relatively intensive training in mindfulness meditation with a cognitive-behavioural conceptual framework in order to address the problem of depressive relapse. In this article, we shall explore the relationship between the two partners, identifying points of congruence and differences between them. We write as research clinicians who have approached MBCT from a home base in cognitive and clinical science and invite readers to judge for themselves whether this new marriage is based upon solid foundations, or whether the disparities are such that it must at some point dissolve.

What is mindfulness-based cognitive therapy? A brief reminder

The evolution of MBCT for recurrent depression is economically summarized in the opening chapters of Segal, Williams and Teasdale (2002). It was prompted by a growing recognition that depression is recurrent; the likelihood of future depressions increases with each episode. The authors hypothesized that, with recurrence, links between depressed mood and other symptoms (changes in cognition, behaviour and physical state) become stronger. Eventually even a small 'dose' of normal low mood can activate well-rehearsed thinking patterns which (unless interrupted) spiral into depression of clinical intensity. Depressed mood leads to gloomy, pessimistic ruminations which, in turn, reinforce and deepen it, encouraging withdrawal from others and from everyday activities that might otherwise offer a sense of pleasure or accomplishment. Thus the depressed person becomes trapped in a vicious circle: mood, thinking and behaviour feed into one another.

The central intention of MBCT is to reduce the likelihood of recurrence. Sufferers learn to identify the earliest warning signals of a change in mood and to respond differently, neither taking refuge in avoidance nor becoming entangled in analysis and rumination. The programme, closely based on Jon Kabat-Zinn's mindfulness-based stress reduction (MBSR; Kabat-Zinn 1990), is usually delivered to groups of 10–12 people in eight weekly two hour classes. Independent home practice (mostly meditation practice) is emphasized (up to one hour, six days each week). A day of mostly silent practice may be included, and up to four follow-up sessions may be offered. The course integrates mindfulness meditation with elements drawn from CT for depression (the nature of depression, the role of negative thinking, the impact on mood of nourishing and depleting activities, and relapse prevention). The effectiveness of MBCT for patients (now in recovery) who have experienced three or more episodes of depression, is now supported by controlled outcome trials (Godfrin and van Heeringen 2010; Kuyken et al. 2008; Ma and Teasdale 2004; Teasdale et al. 2000; Segal et al. 2010). These show that it reduces relapse probability in the year following treatment (the period of greatest vulnerability) by about 50% compared to treatment as usual. Contrary to initial expectations, promising preliminary data (as yet to be confirmed by large scale trials) suggest that MBCT may also be helpful to patients who are actively depressed (Barnhofer et al. 2009; Eisendrath et al. 2008; Kenny and Williams 2008).

What is cognitive therapy?

Cognitive elements of MBCT can seem simplistic, even trivial, to practitioners unfamiliar with their theoretical context. However, just as the meditations included in MBCT reflect only a small part of Buddhist practice, so too these exercises are the tip of a larger iceberg, which we shall now explore.

We focus on the CT developed in the mid-twentieth century by Aaron T. Beck (Beck et al. 1979). Beck, a psychoanalyst by training, became intrigued by distressing patterns of thought which were readily evident in therapy sessions within or just below the surface of patients' conscious awareness, and hence accessible to introspection (Beck 1976, 4). These early observations grew into a new, systematic therapeutic approach, initially (like MBCT) developed specifically for depression. Beck saw no discontinuity between the mental processes of people in distress and human beings in general; we all make the best sense we can of our experiences, usually on the basis of incomplete information, and influenced by our immediate context and learning history. Thus CT's underlying theory is not purely a theory of depression, or indeed of pathology, but rather a framework for understanding how human beings function in the broadest sense. Accordingly, it has been possible to adapt CT for depression for a much wider array of conditions, from common mental health problems (anxiety, eating disorders) to longstanding difficulties, severe mental illness, and physical problems including chronic pain and illness.

CT and depression

Beck's cognitive model

The first outcome trial of CT for depression was published in 1977 (Rush et al. 1977). A treatment manual soon followed (Beck et al. 1979). An extensive evidence base now supports CT's effectiveness with moderate-to-severe depression, both post-treatment and in the longer term (Derubeis et al. 2005; Hollon, Stewart and Strunk 2005; Hollon et al. 2005). Thus MBCT, rather than supplanting CT, built on its success in reducing the probability of relapse and recurrence. MBCT was an attempt to capture important elements of CT that might be taught to people when they were well, in order to prevent new episodes of depression.

Beck's model (shown along with an illustrative case example in Figure 1) suggests that, on the basis of early experience, people reach conclusions about themselves, others and the world ('schemas' or 'core beliefs'). Assuming the truth of these, they evolve personal guidelines which encapsulate what they *must do and be* in order to consider themselves worthy human beings, make and keep relationships and succeed in life ('dysfunctional assumptions'). So long as they can fulfil the terms of these, all is well. But if circumstances conspire against them, problems arise. Failing to perform to standard, or please others, or be fully in control—whatever the assumptions require—is seen to reflect inherent shortcomings which will also affect the future. Thus the *meaning* of an event (rather than the event itself) prompts progressive lowering of mood, further negative thinking and increasing changes in thought, emotion, behaviour and body state. The idea of 'cognitive reactivity' (Lau, Segal and Williams 2004; Segal, Gemar and Williams 1999) further suggests that, following repeated depressions, mild normal low mood and other possible symptoms (fatigue, irritability) can trigger this sequence. Instead of being understood as part of the human condition, they become loaded with negative significance.

Beck called the problematic moment-by-moment thinking present in depression 'negative automatic thoughts' (Westbrook, Kennerley and Kirk 2007, 7–8). 'Negative' reflects association with unpleasant emotions, and 'automatic' indicates that these thoughts simply pop into people's heads, rather than being a product of conscious reflection. Beck suggested that depressive thinking was characterized by negative automatic thoughts about the self, the world and the future. These result from processing biases (for example jumping to conclusions, automatic self-blaming) which incline perception, interpretation and memory towards the gloomy and pessimistic. Contrary information is filtered out, ignored, or dismissed. The result is a bleak view which reinforces low mood, saps motivation and energy, and undermines self-esteem—the vicious circle we referred to earlier.

CT for depression

CT is characterized by three essential features: a coherent theoretical framework; a collaborative therapeutic alliance; and an emphasis on empirical investigation. We shall briefly consider each in turn.

Early experience

Parents' high standards for performance

Anything short of perfection criticized

⇩

Beliefs

I am not good enough

Others are demanding and critical

Life is all about doing well

⇩

Assumptions

Unless it's 110%, it's a failure

If someone criticizes me, they're right

⇩

Trigger event

Fail to get anticipated promotion

⇩

Negative automatic thoughts

I'm a failure

No one appreciates me

I'll never get anywhere in life

⇩ ⇧

Other symptoms of depression

Feel miserable and hopeless

Stay home from work and avoid seeing friends

FIGURE 1
Beck's cognitive model of depression

Coherent theoretical framework. The cognitive model forms the core of therapy, and is the framework for individualized case formulations (see Figure 1) which help patients to map the development and persistence of their difficulties, and guide the selection and sequence of interventions. Thorough assessment helps patient and therapist understand what created vulnerability to suffering depression *at some point*, how depression developed *at this point*, and what psychological and environmental factors are *now* preventing recovery. The model indicates how to facilitate recovery and reduce the chances of relapse. Breaking vicious circles that maintain depression is the first priority, not understanding the deep past. In early sessions, moment-by-moment negative thoughts which prevent people from re-engaging with pleasurable and rewarding activities are addressed. Patients keep structured diaries, recording how they spend their time and their satisfaction with what they do, and then using this information to initiate changes—increasing activities that bring enjoyment and a sense of mastery. Through this process, they learn to notice self-defeating thoughts ('There's no point', 'I won't enjoy it'). With the therapist's guidance, they begin to investigate how accurate and helpful these are. As mood lifts, the focus broadens to a wider range of unhelpful thoughts. Through systematic self-observation, again using written records, patients learn to use changes in mood as cues to investigate associated thinking. They learn how to question their thoughts, rather than assuming them to be true, and to find out through direct experience whether they are valid ('behavioural experiments'; Bennett-Levy et al. 2004). As these skills are established, and mood continues to lift, treatment targets the broader attitudes (over-stringent standards, negative beliefs about self, world and future) which create continuing vulnerability to depression. Finally, patients summarize new learning in a 'blueprint for the future', planning how to respond skilfully to warning signs of depression.

The therapeutic alliance. Beck, from the outset, characterized CT as a humanistic therapy and emphasized the centrality of the therapeutic relationship. A therapist who embodies the classic qualities of accurate empathy, unconditional acceptance, warmth and genuineness creates a secure context in which trust develops and change becomes possible. As mindfulness instructors embody acceptance and compassion, so CT therapists model (a cooler word) the stance they encourage patients to adopt towards themselves: non-judgemental interest, curiosity, and open-mindedness. In CT, the alliance is viewed as *necessary but not sufficient* for successful outcome: it facilitates delivery of effective cognitive–behavioural interventions, but is not itself the prime vehicle for transformation.

Central to the relationship is the idea of 'collaboration'. Therapist and patient work as an investigative team, exploring the nature of experience, and searching for new perspectives that are more realistic (free from biases derived from old beliefs and assumptions) and thus more helpful. Therapy is both active and interactive, with a sense of sharing knowledge and expertise, and transparency about theory and about what interventions might be helpful and why. This explicit emphasis on knowledge and skills-transfer reflects therapists' intention to help patients use new learning independently—to make themselves redundant, in other words. This is why treatment includes extensive between-session 'homework' assignments.

Emphasis on empirical investigation. Just as CT has progressed through research, so patients learn not simply through discussion, but through empirical investigations of their own thinking patterns. In the very first session, patients are introduced to the core of the cognitive model (cognition influences emotion, body state and behaviour), and to the treatment rationale (becoming aware of unhelpful thought patterns, as they happen, makes it possible to modify them, and thus change how you feel and what you do). Patients are invited to view their ideas as hypotheses, which can be questioned and tested through experience, rather than as reflections of an objective truth. Therapy then becomes an extended joint investigation of this idea.

CT: The bigger picture

In the last 35 years, CT has expanded radically and is now a psychological treatment of choice for a wide range of mental and physical health problems. Correspondingly, specific cognitive-behavioural models and treatment protocols have been developed, refining understanding of the exact patterns of thought and behaviour that create vulnerability to different conditions and cause them to persist, and demonstrating the clinical power of targeting these with precision. This theoretical and practical specificity is reflected in the focussed intentionality of MBCT for depressive relapse, and implies that CT elements of the treatment protocol described by Segal, Williams and Teasdale (2002) will likely need modification if the approach is to be successfully applied to other psychological difficulties where predominant vulnerabilities and maintaining factors are different from those present in depression.

CT and mindfulness: points of difference

Let us move on to explore differences and congruencies between CT and mindfulness-based interventions (MBIs) in more detail.

Contributions to MBCT

CT and mindfulness meditation make different contributions to MBCT. From MBSR, MBCT draws mindfulness of the breath, of the body in stillness and in movement, of mental activity, of everyday experiences (eating, routine activities, hearing, pleasant and unpleasant experiences), and a spirit of compassion and acceptance. It also includes (sessions 5–7) meditations inviting participants to remain in contact with unpleasant or difficult experiences that arise and, if none are present, to invite one into awareness. Rather than backing off or becoming entangled in 'thinking about' the difficulty, participants practise exploring it in the body, with an attitude of curiosity and compassion. From CT, MBCT draws the conceptual framework described above, experiential elements which (albeit in rather different form) are also part of CT itself (for example, exploring the relationship between thoughts and feelings), and an emphasis on empirical evaluation.

The CT elements in MBCT are often called 'didactic', implying a shift of gear in instructors from mindful embodiment to lecture mode (the same is perhaps true for educational elements of MBSR—the nine dots, stress reaction/response and so forth). Certainly these exercises have an educational function (such as learning how depression works), and whiteboard and pens can be useful in summarizing information gathered from participants, drawing flowcharts, etc. However, in order to encourage ownership by participants, these elements are better taught interactively. That is, key learning points most helpfully emerge from participants' reflections on the exercises, rather than from the mouth of the teacher whose main task is not to tell, but to validate experience, facilitate self-awareness, guide discovery, highlight and summarize. This is also precisely the role of the skilled cognitive therapist.

Individual case formulation

CT is a formulation-based therapy (Butler, Fennell and Hackmann 2008, chapter 3), in which understanding and treatment of an individual patient is shaped by a specific theoretical model of emotional disorder, investigated and tested through experimental and clinical research. Case formulation transforms the deep structure of the cognitive model of depression, applicable to thousands of people, into a unique map of this particular person's experience. Thus, in the hands of skilled therapists, CT reflects standardized models and treatment protocols, but does so without being merely formulaic or mechanical. No two case formulations, and no two treatments, are exactly alike.

Training in CT thus requires understanding of its theoretical and clinical principles, and of existing and emerging evidence bases. This fosters ethical practice, gives therapy coherence, and ensures that treatment is precisely targeted, efficient and directly relevant to patients' problems and valued goals. Without it, therapists may 'drift', seduced by the latest exciting treatment development regardless of its proven utility (Waller 2009). This does not mean that CT is closed to innovation; on the contrary, it would not have survived and evolved without exploring new territories and testing innovative treatment methods—including of course MBCT. However, CT's scientific roots and the imperatives of clinical responsibility demand that creativity be tempered with rigor and careful evaluation of the impact of innovation.

In MBCT, the balance between the idiosyncratic and the generic is different. Pre-class interviews offer opportunities to develop shared understanding of patients' experience, but are rarely as spacious and detailed as the assessment preceding one-to-one CBT. Thereafter, the focus is rightly not so much on what is unique to each person (though this emerges and is explored, session by session, through inquiry), but rather on what participants have in common (for example, the processes of misinterpretation, avoidance and mental elaboration) (Williams 2008). These transdiagnostic (indeed, universal) processes allow us to work effectively with groups of people who have the same diagnosis but different life experiences, or different diagnoses, or no diagnosis at all. The balance between the shared and the unique, however, is more a product of the class format than necessarily inherent in mindfulness-based interventions. A similar balance would likely be evident in group CT, and MBCT offered in individual psychotherapy could (like individual CT) use assessment and formulation as foundations for focused personal work.

Goal-orientation

CT accepts that people seek therapy because they want things to be different, and offers effective ways of achieving this. CT is intentionally designed to 'fix' things, and does it very well. This is perhaps the most difficult transition for cognitive therapists learning MBCT to make: intentionally not 'fixing' can at first feel like doing nothing, rather than doing something equally valid, but different.

CT has an active change agenda. During assessment, problem identification leads into goal definition, through questions such as: 'How do you want that problem to change by the end of treatment?', 'What would mean to you for therapy to "work"? How would we know?' The emphasis on defined objectives means a commensurate emphasis on outcome evaluation—have the goals been reached or not? Has therapy succeeded or failed? This is highlighted, for mindfulness-based interventions as for CT, in research and healthcare contexts where treatment effectiveness and cost-effectiveness are major issues, and service evaluation is routine. The same intention also influences session structure; unlike many other forms of psychotherapy, each CT session opens with therapist and patient agreeing an 'agenda', encapsulating what they wish to address that day. Sessions are structured (barring the unexpected) so that the agenda is covered. A number of standard items are normally included: a mood check; feedback on the last session; a homework review; new homework arising from the work of the session; a learning summary; and feedback on the session just completed. This means that CT usually has a focussed, 'let's roll up our sleeves and get down to business' feel. In the hands of the unskilled this can tip into rush and rigidity. Skilled therapists, however, balance the wish to work productively in an agreed direction with sensitivity, warmth and a willingness to be flexible and responsive. For patients, this offers a sense of being both empowered and contained.

In contrast, mindfulness-based interventions explicitly discourage attachment to particular desired outcomes, and encourage willingness to allow things to unfold in their own time and to tolerate uncertainty and 'don't know mind'. There is however a something of a paradox here. In the field of healthcare at least, people undoubtedly come to classes because they are suffering and hope for relief—and presumably therapists/instructors would not provide classes unless they believed this was possible. Thus it is not entirely accurate to say that mindfulness-based interventions have no goals. Rather instructors engage in what may seem like a paradoxical balancing act: on the one hand, accepting and validating the understandable longing for freedom from suffering—and even setting goals that the client would like to work towards—and on the other hand, encouraging themselves and their participants to let desired outcomes fade into the background and remain open to emerging experience, whatever it is.

'Are we nearly there yet?' thinking is helpful neither to CT nor to MBIs, because it results in constant emotional temperature-taking that makes it difficult, if not impossible, to retain an attitude of open-mindedness, curiosity, and possible friendliness/acceptance towards every experience no matter how unpleasant, and the willingness to experiment necessary for new learning.

Different methodologies

CT utilizes an extensive repertoire of treatment methods designed to help patients to discover that it is in their power to change how they think and act and that, if they do so, emotional transformation and problem resolution will follow. Careful self-observation allows problematic sequences of thoughts, feelings and behaviours to be identified with some precision. Such insights create a foundation for a systematic process of inquiry and exploration, through which patients learn to question their thoughts (rather than taking it for granted that they must be true), and to seek for more realistic and helpful alternatives, and to test them out in everyday life. Thus change in CT arises from close attention to the detail of specific day-to-day experiences, often guided by worksheets which help patients to follow the sequence systematically, rather than becoming mired in distress and confusion. The process is a collaborative enterprise, with therapist and patient working as a team to find a way forward. New skills are established in session, and practised independently between sessions. Over time, repeated practice leads to new general understandings, for example: 'Change is possible', and 'Just because I believe something, it doesn't follow that it's true'. Thus hope is cultivated and a new relationship to old patterns of thought emerges.

In mindfulness-based interventions, intensive mindfulness meditation practice is viewed as the prime vehicle for nurturing insight and a steadier, more spacious perspective. Through a sequence of practices, patients learn to heighten their awareness of thoughts, emotions and body sensations and acquire the capacity to see these clearly without over-engaging with them or attempting to avoid them, and with an attitude of friendly curiosity and acceptance. So although the outcome (a decentred perspective) is at least somewhat similar in both approaches, the route by which it is reached is different.

Different languages

Therapists from other traditions sometimes find the language of CT military in tone. Depression programmes, for example, have titles like 'Beat the blues' and 'Defeat depression'. The implication might be that this psychological state is undesirable and should be eliminated—a 'pest control' approach to psycho-pathology, if you will. And indeed the success of CT is usually measured in terms of improvement in and recovery from problematic states. However this somewhat combative language, while reflecting something of CT's active problem-solving stance, too easily gives rise to a 'cartoon image' of the therapy and misses its warmth and humanity, the sound therapeutic relationship on which it rests, and the atmosphere of exploration and discovery that characterizes it at its best. As we noted above, the cognitive model assumes continuity between healthy and problematic functioning:

> Psychological problems are not necessarily the product of mysterious, impenetrable forces but may result from commonplace processes such as faulty learning, making incorrect inferences on the basis of inadequate or incorrect information, and not distinguishing adequately between imagination and reality. (Beck et al. 1979, 19–20)

CT thus connects easily with everyday life experience. It encourages therapists to recognize the common humanity they share with patients, and allows them to address issues that arise in therapy (including activation of their own unhelpful beliefs and assumptions) using exactly the same conceptual framework and treatment methods.

Nonetheless, the emphasis on change reflected in the language of CT indeed implies a process rather different from mindfully acknowledging and accepting that unpleasant experiences and suffering are a part of the human condition, and that what is necessary is the capacity to witness their presence without grasping or aversion, and with a spirit of compassion.

Different training trajectories

Mindfulness-based interventions usually teach a programme over a time-limited period (8–12 weeks, with up to four follow-up classes over 6–12 months). This means 16–32 taught hours, plus (say) 36 hours of home practice—a drop in the ocean compared to training in meditation in other contexts, which may continue over years. Instructors' experience varies. Some have a long personal practice (including extensive retreat experience) before they begin to teach. Others may have much less, and learn to teach by establishing their own meditation practice, then following a carefully structured supervised pathway with a more experienced instructor or an indepth training programme at a recognized centre, followed in both cases by regular supervision, further training, collegial contact with other teachers, and continued personal practice and retreat attendance.

CT therapists also require formal specialist training, often following achievement of a university-based professional qualification (in psychiatry or clinical psychology). For accreditation to practice by professional bodies, ongoing supervision and continued professional development are also required. However, there is no direct equivalent to lifelong mindfulness meditation practice. Some European countries expect psychotherapists to undergo their own personal therapy as part of their training; for CT, the UK, Canada and USA (for example) do not. Even those therapists whose training includes experiencing CT, or who have needed it for personal reasons, would not be expected to continue sessions forever. This reflects CT's assumption that lasting transformative experiences are possible within a limited time-frame and that, once defined objectives are reached, there is no need for further work.

A question as yet largely unexplored follows: how much knowledge of CT and its underlying theory do MBCT instructors require, who have approached it from other mindfulness-based interventions or psychotherapeutic traditions? There would be a sharp intake of breath in the mindfulness community if a cognitive therapist began teaching MBCT classes on the basis of reading the manual and perhaps attending a one or two day workshop—and rightly so. This is not ethical practice, nor is it consistent with the spirit of the approach. Do the CT elements of MBCT perhaps deserve a similar respect?

Clearly, given that they are not aiming to conduct CT, MBCT instructors do not need to become cognitive therapists. However, what Beck said about becoming a cognitive therapist may also hold true here: 'we do not believe that the therapy can be applied effectively without knowledge of the theory' (Beck et al. 1979, 4). That is, just as MBCT instructors are required to have indepth understanding of the principles and practice of mindfulness meditation, so too they might be most helpful to participants if they had a sound grasp of the psychological processes that CT suggests lead to the development and persistence of distress. Further, just as becoming a mindfulness instructor rests on personal experience of mindfulness meditation, so too learning about CT, rather than being purely verbal/conceptual, might include an experiential element: systematic self-observation, self-reflection, and opportunities to use the approach to explore personal issues and experiment with change. This may be especially important for instructors planning to alter elements of the programme derived from CT theory and research, to adapt the approach for new client populations where psychological vulnerability and maintaining factors may be different, and to train other MBCT teachers. Exactly what knowledge and skills are necessary, how much time this should take, and precisely how it should be done remain issues for investigation and debate.

CT and mindfulness: points of congruence

As we have outlined differences between CT and MBIs, readers might be forgiven for wondering if this marriage is viable. In fact, these unlikely partners have much in common.

A common intention

The fundamental intention of both approaches, despite their different conceptual frameworks and methodologies, is to understand and to relieve suffering. Thus non-judgment, compassion and a movement towards clear seeing are central to both. However, within the Buddhist tradition behind mindfulness meditation this is a part of a much broader intention: liberation, including the experience of joy. In CT, alleviating suffering in a more focussed therapeutic sense is the prime *raison d'être*.

A map of the mind and an investigative tool

From their different perspectives, both approaches offer maps of the human mind-body system, together with sophisticated investigative tools—the practice of mindfulness meditation on the one hand, and systematic self-observation and self-reflection on the other.

How persistent distress is understood

Both approaches, in their different ways, see the roots of persistent human distress in somewhat similar (though by no means identical) terms. Both assign an important role to old habitual patterns, many learned through experience and activated by current circumstances (causes and conditions). Both see automatic, unconscious processing ('thoughtless thinking'; Beck et al. 1979, 5) and identification with thoughts (being lost in subjectivity) as feeding distress. Equally, both highlight the role of mental filters and biases in perception and interpretation, and how these add suffering to inevitable pain and adversity. Both see the difficulties inherent in attachment (in CT, in relation to substance misuse, for example, and more subtly in the way assumptions insist that the person, others or life must be a certain way), and in aversion (from a CT perspective, for instance, adding to pain by demanding it be eliminated, and the avoidance and withdrawal associated with anxiety and depression). Both too give an important role to mental elaboration (papañca in the Buddhist tradition; rumination and worry in CT). Both distinguish between pain (physical or emotional distress) and suffering (a negative evaluation of pain and what caused it, followed by unhelpful reactions such as elaboration or avoidance). Perhaps these commonalities reflect the fact that both are based on close observation of the same human minds.

The essential present moment

Both traditions advocate focusing on what is happening now, rather than on the deep past. Classical CT and newer evidence-based protocols concentrate predominantly on thinking and behaviour that is maintaining old beliefs and assumptions in the present day, asserting that problems are most effectively and efficiently resolved by breaking these vicious circles rather than investigating their origins. In mindfulness-based interventions, the present moment is recognized as the only point where awareness can be cultivated and transformation is possible—the only possibility of being truly alive to experience, rather than lost in mental constructions of past or future.

The learning process

Both approaches view human beings as learning organisms rather than fixed entities. Both cultivate awareness based on close investigation of immediate experience, albeit by different means. Both thus assume that it is both possible and valuable to explore the workings of the mind, and that such awareness enhances the capacity to respond flexibly to experience, even in distress.

Both CT and mindfulness-based interventions offer step-by-step learning, supported by systematic and extensive practice, which is intended to establish new insight, knowledge and skills so firmly that they can be independently maintained. Both approaches may be seen as forms of training—training in focused concentration, in close observation, in responding in accordance with insight into mental phenomena, in acquiring a particular stance in relation to experience (interested, curious and kind), and (in the case of CT) in questioning habitual thinking patterns and testing them out through experience. The evidence on CT's long-term impact on depression suggests that it engenders shifts in perspective which endure (e.g. Paykel et al. 2005), and mindfulness meditation (if people so choose) is for life.

As to the process of learning itself, both approaches are highly experiential. In CT, verbal interventions are important in questioning cognitions but, for emotional transformation to occur, discussion is not enough. It may provide conceptual understanding, but not the 'gut level' learning necessary for profound change. So new perspectives must be translated into changes in actual behaviour in the real world. With the same intention of uniting head and heart, metaphor, imagery, stories, pictures and poems are also an integral part of both approaches (Blenkiron 2010; Hackmann, Bennett-Levy and Holmes 2011; Segal, Williams and Teasdale 2002; Stott et al. 2010).

In MBIs, new learning arises from extensive personal practice of meditation. In CT, it arises from repeatedly approaching painful thoughts and feelings in a different way. The framework of adult learning theory, and in particular the learning process encapsulated in Kolb's (1984) learning circle, has been used to suggest how this may most effectively done (Bennett-Levy et al. 2004). This same sequence can be applied to the process of learning in MBIs (see Figure 2).

Kolb suggested that effective learning and remembering arises from sequence of steps, each building on the one that precedes it, and laying a foundation for the one that follows. For successful learning, direct experience is necessary (in MBIs, meditation practice itself; in CT, testing cognitions through behavioural experiments). However, experience is of little value unless what has been experienced is clearly seen. Equally, lessons derived from specific experiences and observations are unlikely to become part of a new way of being unless reflection follows—placing new observations in context, relating them to pre-existing knowledge, creating meaning. Within mindfulness-based interventions, observation and reflection are facilitated by the inquiry process that follows meditation practices. What may be learned from what emerged within the moment? What did

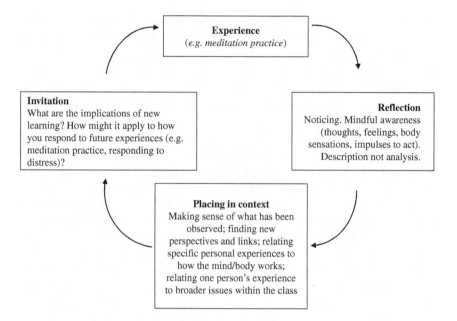

FIGURE 2
The learning process.
Note: Based on Kolb's (1984) learning circle

participants notice? How do these noticings relate to their experience in a more general sense, to the workings of the human mind, to the experience of other participants and—in some contexts—to Buddhist teachings? Within CT, a similar process of guided discovery is facilitated by 'socratic questioning' (Westbrook, Kennerley and Kirk 2007, chapter 3), an exploratory process by which patients are gently guided through observation and meaning-making by open questions interspersed with empathic reflections and capsule summaries. What happened? What thoughts, feelings, body sensations and behaviours did you notice? What do these observations mean? How do they relate to broader assumptions and beliefs? To previous experiences? To the overall case conceptualization? The next step is an invitation to think ahead. How may what has been learned be carried forward? Within mindfulness-based interventions, this might mean preparing for the next practice (for example, preparing to pay particular attention to the feeling tone of some aspect of experience). Within CT, it might mean preparing a new behavioural experiment. And so the cycle begins again.

A common change mechanism?

Teasdale (Teasdale et al. 2002) questioned received wisdom that CT achieved its effects by changing cognitions (for which at that point there was little evidence), and suggested an alternative mechanism: 'metacognitive awareness'.

This means a fundamental change in how people relate to their cognitions, rather than in the cognitions *per se*. By observing the activity of the mind, in the moment, in a spirit of inquiry rather than judgement, and by repeatedly decentring from old mental routines, questioning and testing them, patients learn to *experience* thoughts as events in the mind, rather than 'the truth' or 'me'. The findings of Teasdale and his colleagues suggested that indeed this might be a key mechanism in both CT and MBCT.

This process will be immediately recognizable to mindfulness practitioners. However, whilst mindfulness meditation is attentive to the workings of the mind in the broadest possible sense, within the framework of Buddhist thought, CT has a tighter focus on specific aspects of experience relevant to the particular patient group, and draws on relevant theory and research into the origins and persistence of distress. In working with depression, for example, this means addressing the nature of depressed thinking (Segal, Williams and Teasdale 2002, session 4). In contrast, in chronic fatigue syndrome the emphasis is more on responses to activity and to physical symptoms such as pain and fatigue (Surawy, Roberts and Silver 2005), in eating disorders on eating behaviour and attitudes to weight and shape (see Baer, Fishcher and Huss 2005), and in psychosis on the experience of voices (Chadwick, Newman-Taylor and Abba 2005; Chadwick et al. 2009). In working with mixed groups whose members are experiencing a range of different psychological problems, the narrow spotlight pans out to illuminate more general, transdiagnostic processes such as avoidance and rumination.

Conclusion

We have outlined the theory and practice of CBT, and have highlighted ways in which it is different from mindfulness-based approaches, rooted in Buddhism, and ways in which it is congruent. What then are the prospects for this marriage? Does MBCT represent a real meeting of minds, a creative integration, or does it reflect clashing cultures that will never ultimately be reconciled? Despite authentic differences that deserve to be respected, it would seem that these unlikely partners have enough in common for a productive and peaceful union to evolve and endure.

REFERENCES

BAER, R. A., S. FISCHER, and D. B. HUSS. 2005. MBCT applied to binge eating: A case study. *Cognitive & Behavioural Practice* 12: 351–8.

BARNHOFER, R., C. CRANE, E. HARGUS, M. AMARASINGHE, R. WINDER, and J. M. G. WILLIAMS. 2009. MBCT as a treatment for chronic depression: A preliminary study. *Behaviour Research & Therapy* 47: 366–73.

BECK, A. T. 1976. *Cognitive therapy and the emotional disorders.* New York: International Universities Press.

BECK, A. T., A. J. RUSH, B. F. SHAW, and G. EMERY. 1979. *Cognitive therapy of depression.* New York: Guilford.

BENNETT-LEVY, J., BUTLER, G., FENNELL, M., HACKMANN, A., MUELLER, M., and WESTBROOK, D., eds. 2004. *The Oxford guide to behavioural experiments in cognitive therapy*. Oxford: Oxford University Press.

BLENKIRON, P. 2010. *Stories and analogies in cognitive behaviour therapy*. Chichester, UK: Wiley-Blackwell.

BUTLER, G., M. J. V. FENNELL, and A. HACKMANN. 2008. *Cognitive therapy for anxiety disorders: Mastering clinical challenges*. New York: Guilford.

CHADWICK, P., S. HUGHES, D. RUSSELL, I. RUSSELL, and D. DAGNAN. 2009. Mindfulness groups for distressing voices and paranoia: A replication and randomised feasibility trial. *Behavioural & Cognitive Psychotherapy* 37: 403–30.

CHADWICK, P., K. NEWMAN-TAYLOR, and N. ABBA. 2005. Mindfulness groups for people with psychosis. *Behavioural & Cognitive Psychotherapy* 33: 351–9.

DERUBEIS, R. J., S. D. HOLLON, J. D. AMSTERDAM, R. C. SHELTON, R. C. YOUNG, R. M. SALOMON, J. P. O'REARDON et al. 2005. Cognitive therapy vs. medications in the treatment of moderate to severe depression. *Archives of General Psychiatry* 62: 409–16.

EISENDRATH, S. J., K. DELUCCHI, R. BITNER, P. FENIMORE, M. SMIT, M. MCLANE et al. 2008. MBCT for treatment resistant depression: A pilot study. *Psychotherapy and Psychosomatics* 101: 1–2.

GODFRIN, K. A., and C. VAN HEERINGEN. 2010. The effects of mindfulness-based cognitive therapy on recurrence of depressive episodes, mental health and quality of life: A randomised controlled study. *Behaviour Research & Therapy* 48: 738–46.

HACKMANN, A., J. BENNETT-LEVY, and E. HOLMES. 2011. *The Oxford guide to imagery in cognitive therapy*. Oxford: Oxford University Press.

HOLLON, S. D., M. O. STEWART, and D. STRUNK. 2005. Enduring effects for cognitive behaviour therapy in the treatment of depression and anxiety. *Annual Review of Psychology* 57: 285–315.

HOLLON, S. D., R. J. DERUBEIS, R. C. SHELTON, J. D. AMSTERDAM, R. M. SALOMON, J. P. O'REARDON, M. L. LOVETT et al. 2005. Prevention of relapse following cognitive therapy vs. medications in moderate to severe depression. *Archives of General Psychiatry* 62: 417–22.

KABAT-ZINN, J. 1990. *Full catastrophe living: The program of the stress reduction clinic at the University of Massachusetts Medical Center*. New York: Dell.

KENNY, M. A., and J. M. G. WILLIAMS. 2007. Treatment-resistant depressed patients show a good response to mindfulness-based cognitive therapy. *Behaviour Research & Therapy* 45: 617–25.

KOLB, D. A. 1984. *Experiential learning*. New Jersey: Prentice-Hall.

KUYKEN, W., S. BYFORD, R. S. TAYLOR, E. WATKINS, E. HOLDEN, K. WHITE, B. BARRETT et al. 2008. Mindfulness-based cognitive therapy to prevent relapse in recurrent depression. *Journal of Consulting and Clinical Psychology* 76: 966–78.

LAU, M. A., Z. V. SEGAL, and J. M. G. WILLIAMS. 2004. Teasdale's differential activation hypothesis: Implications for mechanisms of depressive relapse and suicidal behaviour. *Behaviour Research & Therapy* 42: 1001–17.

MA, J., and J. D. TEASDALE. 2004. Mindfulness-based cognitive therapy for depression: Replication and exploration of differential relapse prevention effects. *Journal of Consulting & Clinical Psychology* 72: 31–40.

PAYKEL, E. S., J. SCOTT, P. L. CORNWALL, R. ABBOTT, C. CRANE, M. POPE, and A. L. JOHNSON. 2005. Duration of relapse prevention after cognitive therapy in residual depression: Follow-up of controlled trial. *Psychological Medicine* 35: 59–68.

RUSH, A. J., A. T. BECK, M. KOVACS, and S. HOLLON. 1977. Comparative efficacy of cognitive therapy and pharmacotherapy in the treatment of depressed outpatients. *Cognitive Therapy & Research* 1: 17–37.

SEGAL, Z. V., P. BIELING, T. YOUNG, G. MACQUEEN, R. COOKE, L. MARTIN, R. BLOCH, and R. LEVITAN. 2010. Antidepressant monotherapy versus sequential pharmacotherapy and mindfulness-based cognitive therapy, or placebo, for relapse prophylaxis in recurrent depression. *Archives of General Psychiatry* 67: 1256–64.

SEGAL, Z. V., M. GEMAR, and S. WILLIAMS. 1999. Differential cognitive response to a mood challenge following successful cognitive therapy or pharmacotherapy for unipolar depression. *Journal of Abnormal Psychology* 108: 3–10.

SEGAL, Z. V., J. M. G. WILLIAMS, and J. D. TEASDALE. 2002. *Mindfulness-based cognitive therapy for depression: A new approach to preventing relapse.* New York: Guilford.

STOTT, R., W. MANSELL, P. SALKOVSKIS, A. LAVENDER, and S. CARTWRIGHT-HATTON. 2010. *The Oxford guide to metaphors in CBT: Building cognitive bridges.* Oxford: Oxford University Press.

SURAWY, C., J. ROBERTS, and A. SILVER. 2005. The effect of mindfulness training on mood and measures of fatigue, activity, and quality of life in patients with chronic fatigue syndrome on a hospital waiting list: A series of exploratory studies. *Behavioural & Cognitive Psychotherapy* 33: 103–9.

TEASDALE, J. D., R. G. MOORE, H. HAYHURST, M. POPE, S. WILLIAMS, and Z. V. SEGAL. 2002. Metacognitive awareness and prevention of relapse in depression: Empirical evidence. *Journal of Consulting & Clinical Psychology* 70: 275–87.

TEASDALE, J. D., Z. V. SEGAL, J. M. G. WILLIAMS, V. RIDGEWAY, J. SOULSBY, and M. LAU. 2000. Reducing risk of recurrence of major depression using mindfulness-based cognitive therapy. *Journal of Consulting & Clinical Psychology* 68: 615–23.

WALLER, G. 2009. Evidence based treatment and therapist drift. *Behaviour Research & Therapy* 47: 119–27.

WESTBROOK, D., H. KENNERLEY, and J. KIRK. 2007. *An introduction to cognitive behaviour therapy: Skills and applications.* London: Sage.

WILLIAMS, J. M. G. 2008. Mindfulness, depression and modes of mind. *Cognitive Therapy & Research* 32: 721–33.

COMPASSION IN THE LANDSCAPE OF SUFFERING

Christina Feldman and Willem Kuyken

In this paper we investigate compassion and its place within mindfulness-based approaches. Compassion is an orientation of mind that recognizes pain and the universality of pain in human experience and the capacity to meet that pain with kindness, empathy, equanimity and patience. We outline how learning to meet pain with compassion is part of how people come to live with chronic conditions like recurrent depression. While most mindfulness-based approaches do not explicitly teach compassion, we describe how the structure of the programme and teachers' embodiment enable participants to cultivate compassion in the landscape of suffering. We describe a case example of how this process unfolded for someone through mindfulness-based cognitive therapy.

Dawn had suffered many episodes of depression in her life. Each new episode seemed to have a life of its own and she used the analogy; 'It's like I am being dragged towards and over Niagara Falls.' For her this captured the sense of inevitability, helplessness and horror of each recurrence of depression.

Dawn described a turning point in her recovery.

There was a gradual realization that when I added a layer of judgment to how I was feeling, I suffered more. Instead of answering, 'Why can't I get out of bed?' with 'Because I am a failure,' I came to see that this, my lethargy and negative thinking, were all part and parcel of a depression that would take time to lift. This provided a glimmer of hope that I could begin to cultivate. It was almost okay to be depressed and begin to nourish myself in small ways. Instead of fighting the depression, I started to be gentler with myself. Looking back, these were the first steps out of depression.

Dawn, aged 48.

What is compassion?

In the classical teachings of the Buddhist tradition compassion is defined as the heart that trembles in the face of suffering. At times, compassion is translated as the heart that can tremble in the face of suffering. It is aspired to as the noblest quality of the human heart, the motivation underlying all meditative paths of healing and liberation.

Compassion is a response to suffering, the inevitable adversity all human beings will meet in their lives, whether it is the pain embedded in the fabric of ageing, sickness and death or the psychological and emotional afflictions that debilitate the mind. Compassion is the acknowledgment that not all pain can be 'fixed' or 'solved' but all suffering is made more approachable in a landscape of compassion.

Compassion is a multi-textured response to pain, sorrow and anguish. It includes kindness, empathy, generosity and acceptance. The strands of courage, tolerance, equanimity are equally woven into the cloth of compassion. Above all compassion is the capacity to open to the reality of suffering and to aspire to its healing. The Dalai Lama once said, 'If you want to know what compassion is, look into the eyes of a mother or father as they cradle their sick and fevered child.'

While Buddhist conceptions of compassion have a lineage extending more than 2500 years, psychologists have only more recently started to consider compassion and its role in suffering and resilience. Paul Gilbert sees compassion as an evolved psychological capacity that is part of human beings' care-giving system. Compassion increases our ability to care for our young and is in this sense 'hard-wired' (Gilbert 2009). He defines compassion broadly, and includes dimensions of care, soothing, sympathy, empathy, and non-judgment. Implicit to his understanding is a theory that integrates the biological underpinnings of human behaviour, evolution and human attachment. A recent overview article makes a similar argument that compassion evolved to help social groups protect their weak and those who suffer (Goetz, Keltner and Simon-Thomas 2010). Interestingly, Gilbert's work on compassion grew in part as a response to his earlier work on depression, and the integral role, as he saw it, of self-criticism, shame and powerlessness in depression (Gilbert 1984, 2000).

An alternative definition has been offered by Kirstin Neff in which she articulates three components of self-compassion: self-kindness, common humanity, and mindfulness (Neff 2003a). Her work was motivated by trying to describe a healthy attitude toward the self that moves away from simplistic notions of self-esteem. She describes self kindness as 'being kind and understanding to oneself in instances of pain or failure,' common humanity as 'perceiving one's experience as part of the larger human experience' and mindfulness as 'holding painful thoughts and feelings in balanced awareness' (Neff 2003, 85). She argues that these qualities are intrinsic to a healthy sense of self that taken together enable someone to manage their emotions in the face of difficulties.

We offer the following definition of compassion. Compassion is an orientation of mind that recognizes pain and the universality of pain in human experience and the capacity to meet that pain with kindness, empathy, equanimity and patience. While self-compassion orients to our own experience, compassion extends this orientation to others' experience.

How central is compassion in the healing process?

Compassion allows healing. As human beings we understandably dislike and fear pain. Instinctively we tend to recoil, avoid and become anxious in the face of physical and emotional distress. It is only a small step from these habitual patterns of avoidance into equally habitual patterns of blame, aversion, judgment and agitation. It is the second layer of suffering that is superimposed upon the first. The effect of this layer of reaction is to magnify the actuality of pain and distress but more crucially to trigger further emotional distress in the forms of despair, depression and helplessness. This closed circle of reactivity becomes a self-maintaining loop that locks out any possibility of embracing suffering with courage and compassion.

Our own experience of sorrow and pain, as well as current psychological research, tells us that compassion is as important to our emotional/psychological well being as nutrition is to our bodies (Fredrickson et al. 2008; Gilbert and Procter 2006; Hutcherson, Lutz et al. 2008; Seppala and Gross 2008). In times of greatest distress in our own lives we are touched above all by compassion. Compassion offers a vital alternative to aversion and fear. It is what allows us to turn towards distress and pain rather than fleeing from it. It allows us to surround suffering with kindness and curiosity rather than shame or blame.

Fear and aversion fractures our relationship with all things. Compassion is the beginning of a befriending of what has previously been rejected. Rather than being lost in the extremes of endeavouring to overcome distress or being overcome by it, compassion begins with the discovery of the capacity to 'be with', to be steady and balanced in the face of adversity. It is a relationship of kindness, warmth and connectedness. Healing does not necessarily imply that pain is fixed or disappears, healing is often the softening and dissolving of the resistance and aversion that keeps us stuck in fear and estrangement. Healing has been described by Jon Kabat-Zinn as 'coming to terms with things as they are' (Kabat-Zinn 2005). That is to say, relating to suffering with equanimity and compassion are part of the healing process.

Most emotional disorders are marked by patterns of thinking and behaviour that, while at some level are understandable, at another level exacerbate and maintain the disorder. For example, in depression, negative thinking can be an attempt to make sense of experience and withdrawal an attempt to protect from further aversive experiences (Aldao, Nolen-Hoeksema and Schweizer 2010; Kuyken, Watkins and Beck 2005). In the lead up to her last episode of depression, Dawn was so fearful she pretended to herself it was not happening, working

FIGURE 1
The analogy of Niagara falls with depressive relapse

harder in her job to offset the criticism she feared from her colleagues. The feeling of the impending Niagara Falls was met with denial; '*If I just paddle harder, maybe I can get myself out of this fix*' (see Figure 1). In no time at all, the opportunity and space for a compassionate response or skilful action was diminished.

Now that Dawn is depressed and off work she has the pervasive thoughts, '*I am no good at my job*' and '*my colleagues dislike me.*' She does not return to work

146

to avoid what she feels is an unmanageable situation. There is no space for Dawn to ask herself if these thoughts are based in reality, or whether her reaction is likely to exacerbate her depression or be part of the healing process. In anxiety, fear is strongly associated with thoughts or images of an impending threat. These thoughts and images begin to arise in a whole range of situations creating crippling anxiety that the person tries to manage with a range of behaviours intended to keep them safe. Paradoxically, again these safety behaviours can exacerbate and maintain the anxiety. Dawn's avoidance of social contact is intended to protect her from the feared possibility of criticism and rejection. Instead, it precludes both opportunities for these fears to be disconfirmed and the nourishment of social contact.

Bringing attention and compassion to these feelings, thoughts and behaviours is a first step towards stepping out of reactivity and allowing the possibility of responding more skilfully. When we meet people with a history of depression who have been referred to our mindfulness-based cognitive therapy (MBCT) service, we explain what is involved in the groups using the metaphor of Niagara Falls (Figure 1). Most people with recurrent depression can identify with the helplessness and horror of another episode of depression (being dragged towards Niagara Falls). We explain that learning mindfulness enables people to notice the reactivity of the mind and step out of habitual patterns that inadvertently create more suffering. They can attend to the sound of the distant falls, the churning water, the movement in the air, then anchor in the present moment and choose to respond differently. In small but profound ways, stepping out of reactivity allows the person to chart a course towards the river bank or a tributary. In time, they can even see the whole pattern of reactivity as a fabrication of the mind.

Again, psychological theory and research into compassion in the healing process is at a very early stage. But, while by no means conclusive, every study examining the relationship between compassion and psychological constructs suggests that compassion is positively associated with wellbeing and negatively associated with distress (Fredrickson and Losada 2005; Fredrickson et al. 2008; Gilbert and Irons 2004a; Goetz et al. 2010; Kelly, Zuroff and Shapira 2009; Lutz et al. 2008; Neff 2003a, 2003b). It is too early to say whether it is involved in the healing *process,* but we set out a model below of how compassion is part of healing.

Can compassion be cultivated?

Most people have encountered moments of unhesitating and natural compassion when the heart softens in the face of suffering, pain and helplessness. Images of children suffering in famine, people exposed to terrible injustice, the elderly person struggling to cross a busy road, the toddler that trips in the playground, the woman exhausted by caring for an elderly parent. These can all be moments that evoke a natural wish to reach out to another in the midst of their pain. They are precious moments when the divide between self and other softens, the story of blame and resentment fades and we inhabit, perhaps for a few fleeting moments, a world infused with kindness and compassion. Too often those treasured moments are swept away by the busyness of our minds and we find ourselves once more in the territory of agitation, blame or distraction. The meditative traditions of different spiritual traditions encourage us to cultivate a way of seeing in which these glimpses of compassion are not left to chance.

Many spiritual traditions emphasize that moments of compassion do not have to be fortunate accidents or mysteries. We cannot make ourselves feel compassion yet all the great spiritual traditions confidently assert that we can learn to incline the mind/heart toward compassion. Compassion in these traditions is likened to an art like any other art that is developed though sustained and dedicated practice. It is a re-educating of the heart, learning what it means to be kind and present in the midst of suffering. Researchers examining those who have cultivated self-compassion through meditative traditions have found that there is a forging of new neural pathways that is associated with sustained mindfulness practice (Lutz et al. 2008). It is an undoing of the habits of aversion through returning again and again to the actuality of pain in this moment with kindness. We cannot choose whether or not we will encounter pain and sorrow in our lives, we cannot choose whether or not to participate in the life of our body and mind—we can only choose how we meet those encounters and the way of our participation.

Mindfulness-based approaches to chronic physical health problems and depression cultivate this orientation of mind and heart (Kabat-Zinn 1990; Segal, Williams and Teasdale 2002). In the early stages of the course using the body as the focus for attention, participants learn to develop sustained attention and work with the inevitable attachment and aversion that arise. When they encounter pain, they are encouraged through the mindfulness instructions and enquiry to meet that pain with kindness, empathy, equanimity, acceptance, and patience, to put out the 'welcome mat' for it, so to speak, as best one can. As MBSR and MBCT are group-based, participants see others experiencing similar kinds of pain, judgment and struggle. Realizing that what one thought was unique and personal is also experienced by others can cultivate a strong sense of the universality of pain and that one is not alone in one's suffering. Dawn encountered jaw and neck pain through the body scan, and noted the understandable immediate cycle of aversion and judgment this triggered ('This is making it worse, this pain is intolerable'). Through the first few weeks, Dawn could see that this second layer of suffering led to greater contraction in her body, and that in particular the tensing in her jaw could quickly spread throughout the head and trigger the onset of migraine. It took courage and patience, but in time bringing compassion to the first sensations of pain in the jaw created the conditions for a softening and opening that broke the cycle that led to the second layer of suffering. Later in the course she was able to apply this same attention and compassion to thoughts of self-judgment and feelings of shame and the associated bodily sensations.

Even though the cultivation of self-compassion in mindfulness-based approaches is sometimes not direct—that is, there is no explicit emphasis on loving kindness or compassion via specific meditations that cultivate these qualities, interestingly, the training and orientation of an eight-week mindfulness programme cultivates compassion nonetheless. There is now research showing not only that mindfulness-based interventions cultivate self-compassion, even in the absence of explicit compassion meditations, but that they are effective in alleviating suffering in part *because* they cultivate compassion (Kuyken et al. 2010).

Several other psychological therapies also target the cultivation of compassion either explicitly or implicitly. As already stated, Gilbert has shown that depression is characterized by self-criticism and shame. Preliminary results from a programme in which therapists work with their clients to cultivate self-kindness, self-soothing and acceptance have shown that this approach is both acceptable and effective with at least some clients (Gilbert and Irons 2004b; Gilbert and Procter 2006).

The landscape of suffering

In Buddhist psychology the landscape of suffering, be it the experience of physical or psychological distress, is sometimes described using the simile of the two darts. In this simile it describes the experience of a person being hit by a dart, causing an initial painful experience. It is a pain that would be experienced by anyone in a similar situation. The story goes on to describe the person's *reaction* to the pain, how an 'uninformed, unaware' (that is, not mindful) person would bewail his or her fate, refusing the removal of the dart until it was clear where it came from, who had shot it, what is was made of, and why it had been fired in the first place. As a consequence, the person falls into despair and anguish, resisting the experience altogether, blaming him or herself and everybody else, and ultimately languishing in the pain. Such a reaction to the first dart adds a whole other layer of pain that only compounds the initial experience of suffering. The important point is that this additional layer of pain is optional. The simile is pointing to the fact that in such a reactive mode the person is experiencing two levels of suffering—the initial pain of the first dart, and the emotional suffering of the reaction (the second dart).

Dawn poignantly describes this compounded suffering. Her difficulty getting out of bed, the lethargy brought about by her depression (the first dart) was habitually met by self-judgment and blame (the second dart), which then exacerbated and maintained the depression. She described vividly the fear and aversion that arose in her, both habitual and totally understandable human responses to pain. The reaction ranged from dislike, to resistance, numbness, aggression, judgment and blame. In her depression, the recurrent thought patterns of personal failure, inadequacy and uselessness simply reinforced the aversion. This invariably not only compounded the initial pain, deepening her depression and feelings of failure, but more significantly, paralysed Dawn's

149

capacity to respond with any degree of kindness and creativity to the painful feelings of sadness and bleakness. Then, at some point in the practice, something shifted. Dawn found herself actually befriending the depression, instead of reinforcing its power over her through 'beating it down' with shame and judgment. The glimmer of hope she was beginning to experience was also a first taste of acceptance of her situation with awarenesss and self-compassion.

There is an ancient Greek belief that the only people who deserve compassion are those who do not deserve their suffering. Lack of self-worth combines with habit patterns of aversion and blame to convince many people that suffering is their own fault and a sign of personal failure or inadequacy. Self-judgment and shame inhibit the emergence of compassion and often ensure the continuity and solidifying of psychological and emotional distress. For Dawn, having taken time off work, she was left with a vacuum that her mind filled with self-blame ('*I have failed again, this proves I am no good at my job and I have let down my colleagues*'). These thoughts kept Dawn from answering her phone or getting out of the house, creating fertile ground for rumination, a pattern of poring over her feelings in an endless non-productive attempt at resolution. '*If only I could figure out what went wrong.*' This reified and solidified her experience, closing down the possibility of meeting suffering with compassion. In her Niagara Falls analogy she would hunker down and simply await the inevitable drop into the downward cascade of the Falls (Figure 1).

The cultivation of self-compassion includes a re-examination and investigation of one's core beliefs of unworthiness, unloveability and imperfection that fuel perpetual cycles of inner rejection and condemnation. Self-compassion involves learning to attend to, approach, investigate and unpack negative core belief systems that have been absorbed from others or built upon the foundations of personal experience of failure or rejection. The habit of judging the self harshly only serves to continually reinforce feelings of inadequacy, helplessness and anxiety, undermining the natural capacity for acceptance, generosity and compassion.

Self-compassion is concerned with reframing the personal narrative. Instead of anxiety, depression or obsession being seen as personal failures and inadequacies they are seen simply as suffering, warranting the same compassion that we would extend to anybody else who was suffering. Gradually, we discover that emotional affliction can be embraced with kindness and generosity, forgiveness and acceptance. This profound shift in the relationship with one's own suffering begins in turn to alter the view of inadequacy and failure that underlies the seemingly endless stream of aversive thoughts that constitute depressive rumination. Compassion is not simply a pleasant emotion. It is a radical transformation of our view of suffering and of our view of 'self.'

Dawn speaks of the emotional shift she began to make from blame to acceptance: 'It was almost OK to be depressed and I began to nourish myself in small ways.' The depression, instead of being regarded as an enemy became the landscape in which she could begin to cultivate ways of nurturing her wellbeing. It was a shift from the hopelessness and despair that are part and parcel of depression to a more engaged and confident sense of the possibility of a range of more nourishing responses. The first dart could be explored and investigated. Dawn could see her negative thinking as born of a depressive emotional state. Instead of depression being a personal description of failure, met with blame and aversion, it became an experience that could be met with kindness and curiosity. With mindfulness, she could begin to see thoughts as thoughts, breaking the toxic loop that occurs when depressive thinking is invested with an authority that only reinforces and deepens the depression. The thoughts no longer dictated her actions and reactions.

Gwyneth Lewis wrote of this radical shift in her experience of depression in her autobiographical account of depression, *Sunbathing in the Rain* (Lewis 2002). When she finally stopped trying to escape negative thoughts and feelings (the rain), she was able to appreciate the possibility of being fully present in her experience, whether it was raining or not. This allowed the possibility of turning towards her negative thoughts and feelings with interest, care and curiosity. This apparently subtle shift turned out to be anything but small, enabling her to learn from her depression and make necessary changes in her life.

In the face of suffering, the shift from aversion to welcoming, befriending and accepting is the most radical emotional and psychological shift a person can make. It is a shift, catalysed by mindfulness, from being a helpless victim or sufferer at the mercy of the depression into being a participant in the healing process. Those first steps into understanding the landscape of suffering are also the first steps into the landscape of compassion. Gwyneth Lewis writes of making changes in her life that included not returning to the same job that had been depleting, and pursuing work and interests that were rewarding and nourishing. Reading Gwyneth Lewis' book was helpful to Dawn in seeing that depression could be befriended. Dawn was fortunate to have a supportive boss. She made a gradual return to work, and was able to see for the first time that many of the negative and unkind thoughts she harboured about herself and her colleagues were artefacts of the depression, rather than accurate assessments of reality. Over time, Dawn realized that rather like Niagara Falls, turbulence in her thoughts and feelings needs wise attention. Ignoring times of low mood or negative thoughts and simply 'paddling harder' did little to avoid the apparent inevitability of being dragged towards Niagara Falls. Instead, learning to attend to the sounds of a distant falls, the whirl pools in the water and the mist on her skin enabled Dawn to attend to the situation and respond: *'At those times I need to take care of myself, make sure I continue to exercise and rest—perhaps talk to my boss. I just need to take a few paddle strokes towards a tributary that will take me down a different river, away from what used to seem the inevitable pull towards Niagara Falls.'*

The cultivation of compassion

The building blocks of compassion are woven into mindfulness-based interventions. Intentional attention is cultivated in the first three sessions using a range of core mindfulness practices, the body scan, mindful movement (stretching and walking) and mindfulness of the breath. As well as developing the 'attentional muscle,' it highlights the impulsive and habitual patterns of thinking that are present, and the associated aversion to negative mind states and judgments. With mindfulness, there is a growing ability to withdraw authority from all the self-judgments and blame, which only serves as fuel for depressive thinking, and see what happens when we intentionally step out of habitual patterns of thinking. Clients develop the capacity to be mindful of their breathing and body, cultivating a present moment attentiveness and greater sensory awareness. The pleasant events calendar that patients fill out in the second week reveals a perhaps hidden or unrecognized capacity for appreciation and connectedness with a world not coloured by the bleakness of depression. The continual emphasis upon curiosity, kindness and befriending develops a skill and attitudinal base that can be brought to unpleasant events when they arise, either inwardly or outwardly.

In the second half of the course, mindfulness and compassion are brought to bear on the person's unique signature for depressive relapse so that they can generate skilful responses to the early warning signs of future depressive relapses. Finally, the group enquiry sessions built into mindfulness-based interventions reveal to every participant that depression is not a personal failure, but an affliction that besets many human beings.

In Buddhist psychology it is asserted that 'the mind is the forerunner of all things.' When the mind is shaped by depression, depression becomes the forerunner of all things, including one's self image, perceptions and behaviours. All of the steps in an eight week MBCT prgramme are designed to bring about cognitive shifts, a change in self view and understanding which in turn alters thought processes, habits and behaviour (Segal et al. 2002). Equally in Buddhist psychology it is asserted that the mind exists in a state of potentiality, being shaped and moulded by mental states, intentions, habits, thoughts and by whatever is identified with in the moment (Feldman 1998).

In MBCT programmes clients undertake several steps: learning to be mindful of their mind and its patterns, to instill kindness and an attitude of befriending in the place of judgment and resistance and realize the innate freedom of the mind from the hold of habitual patterns that perpetuate suffering. This gives form to suffering, opens a dialogue with it and offers an alternative way to respond to pain and heal suffering.

Compassion has but one direction which is to heal suffering. Compassion tends to be alien territory to many people with a history of depression. It is a skill that can be learned, and is accompanied by an attitude that can be cultivated at the same time. There are three important cognitive changes that occur as one develops the skills of mindfulness that enable a person to shift from aversion to compassion.

The first change is the cultivation of mindfulness, learning to hold depressive thinking and attitudes with kindness rather than blame, and practicing doing so over and over again. It is being able to ask 'what does this need' rather than 'how do I get rid of it.' It is the beginning of an understanding that depression is an affliction as deserving of compassion as a chronic physical condition or illness. As Dawn discovered on her journey out of depression, what we nourish in our minds and lives is a choice. It is a choice that can only be made when we are mindful within our minds and lives.

The second is the developed capacity to see a thought as a thought, an emotion as an emotion, a habit as a habit and begin to take the 'I' out of the process. Learning that affliction can be tolerated and befriended rather than feared is the root of inner confidence, a quality noticeably absent in depressive thinking. It is a profound shift to be able to see sadness, fear, loneliness, and doubt as impersonal events that are simply unfolding in this moment within the field of awareness rather than as personal statements and making it all about 'me,' as in 'I am sad, lonely and afraid.'

Third, the easing of self preoccupation and identification through mindfulness inevitably nurtures a growing awareness of the universality of human affliction and suffering. During the group conversations in class, people listen to and hear the pain of others, and get to see and feel themselves reflected in the eyes and lives and hearts of the other participants. At the same time, as part of both the meditation practice and the conversations in class, they are inquiring deeply into the nature of their own experience and that of others. Learning how to listen to another without blame, but with tenderness and care is a skill that informs the ways we listen to ourselves. People going through mindfulness classes have commented how this group process was a key aspect of what helped them change (Allen et al. 2009).

In mindfulness practices a range of ways to develop compassion are outlined, rooted in the basic skills of attentive, receptive listening, non identification, empathy and distress tolerance. Compassion equally rests in acknowledging that our wish to be free from pain and affliction is a longing shared by all living beings. Compassion holds no hierarchies, the afflictions of the mind are as worthy as the afflictions of the body, the losses and sorrows part of every human life. All are worthy of compassion.

The role of the mindfulness teacher is instrumental in enabling participants to attend to their suffering and cultivate compassion. The teacher needs first and foremost to have through their own mindfulness practice cultivated compassion in relation to his/her life and experience. This experiential learning is a pre-requisite to teaching others and is experienced by participants as an embodied teacher who 'walks the walk.' This embodiment permeates how mindfulness practices are taught, individual and group enquiry is handled and universality of experience permeates the group (Crane 2009; Crane et al. 2010).

Conclusion

In this paper we have defined compassion as the capacity to meet pain with kindness, empathy, equanimity and patience. Depression is a landscape that is characterized by aversion, negative views and judgment, freezing out compassion. When compassion is cultivated there is thawing that allows healing, responsiveness and an array of nourishing and skilful behaviours that can break up the pattern of depression recurrences and build a person's resilience.

At the end of the mindfulness classes Dawn wrote on her feedback form:

It was as if my mind created an abyss of suffering, rehearsing all the bad things that have happened, worrying about what might happen, not being right in my skin. It was as if my heart provided a way of crossing the abyss.

REFERENCES

ALDAO, A., S. NOLEN-HOEKSEMA, and S. SCHWEIZER. 2010. Emotion-regulation strategies across psychopathology: A meta-analytic review. *Clinical Psychology Review* 30.

ALLEN, M., A. BROMLEY, W. KUYKEN, and S. J. SONNENBERG. 2009. Participants' experiences of mindfulness-based cognitive therapy: 'It changed me in just about every way possible'. *Behavioural and Cognitive Psychotherapy* 37: 413–30.

CRANE, R. 2009. *Mindfulness-based cognitive therapy*. London: Routledge.

CRANE, R., W. KUYKEN, R. P. HASTINGS, N. ROTHWELL, and J. M. G. WILLIAMS. 2010. Training teachers to deliver mindfulness-based interventions: Learning from the UK experience. *Mindfulness* : 74–86.

FELDMAN, C. 1998. *Meditation plain and simple*. London: Harper Collins.

FREDRICKSON, B. L., M. A. COHN, K. A. COFFEY, J. PEK, and S. M. FINKEL. 2008. Open hearts build lives: Positive emotions, induced through loving-kindness meditation, build consequential personal resources. *Journal of Personality and Social Psychology* 95: 1045–62.

FREDRICKSON, B. L., and M. F. LOSADA. 2005. Positive affect and the complex dynamics of human flourishing. *American Psychologist* 60: 678–86.

GILBERT, P. 1984. *Depression: From Psychology to brain state*. London: Lawrence Erlbaum Associates.

GILBERT, P. 2000. The relationship of shame, social anxiety and depression: The role of the evaluation of social rank. *Clinical Psychology & Psychotherapy* 7: 174–89.

GILBERT, P. 2009. *The compassionate mind*. London: Constable.

GILBERT, P., and C. IRONS. 2004a. A pilot exploration of the use of compassionate images in a group of self-critical people. *Memory* 12: 507–16.

GILBERT, P., and C. IRONS. 2004b. A pilot exploration of the use of compassionate images in a group of self-critical people. *Memory* 12: 507–16.

GILBERT, P., and S. PROCTER. 2006. Compassionate mind training for people with high shame and self-criticism: Overview and pilot study of a group therapy approach. *Clinical Psychology & Psychotherapy* 13: 353–79.

GOETZ, J. L., D. KELTNER, and E. SIMON-THOMAS. 2010. Compassion: An evolutionary analysis and empirical review. *Psychological Bulletin* 136: 351–74.

HUTCHERSON, C. A., E. M. SEPPALA, and J. J. GROSS. 2008. Loving-kindness meditation increases social connectedness. *Emotion* 8: 720–4.

KABAT-ZINN, J. 1990. *Full catastrophe living: How to cope with stress, pain and illness using mindfulness meditation*. New York: Delacorte.

KABAT-ZINN, J. 2005. *Coming to our senses: Healing ourselves and the world through mindfulness*. London: Piatkus Books.

KELLY, A. C., D. C. ZUROFF, and L. B. SHAPIRA. 2009. Soothing oneself and resisting self-attacks: The treatment of two intrapersonal deficits in depression vulnerability. *Cognitive Therapy and Research* 33: 301–13.

KUYKEN, W., E. WATKINS, and A. T. BECK. 2005. Cognitive-behavior therapy for mood disorders. In *Psychotherapy in psychiatric disorders*, ed. G. Gabbard, J. S. Beck, and J. Holmes, 113–28. Oxford: Oxford University Press.

KUYKEN, W., E. R. WATKINS, E. R. HOLDEN, K. WHITE, R. S. TAYLOR, S. BYFORD, S. EVANS, A. RADFORD, J. D. TEASDALE, and T. DALGLEISH. 2010. How does mindfulness-based cognitive therapy work? *Behaviour Research and Therapy* 48: 1105–12.

LEWIS, G. 2002. *Sunbathing in the rain: A cheerful book about depression*. London: Flamingo, Harper Collins.

LUTZ, A., J. BREFCZYNSKI-LEWIS, T. JOHNSTONE, and R. J. DAVIDSON. 2008. Regulation of the neural circuitry of emotion by compassion meditation: Effects of meditative expertise. *PLoS ONE* 3: e1897.

NEFF, K. D. 2003a. Self-compassion: An alternative conceptualization of a healthy attitude toward oneself. *Self and Identity* 2: 85–101.

NEFF, K. D. 2003b. The development and validation of a scale to measure self-compassion. *Self and Identity* 2: 223–50.

SEGAL, Z. V., J. M. G. WILLIAMS, and J. D. TEASDALE. 2002. *Mindfulness-based cognitive therapy for depression: A new approach to preventing relapse*. New York: Guilford Press.

MEDITATION AND MINDFULNESS

Martine Batchelor

In this article I share some of my experiences of practising Korean Zen meditation and how, without ever mentioning the word 'mindfulness,' this practice helps us to become mindful. This leads me to suggest that the main ingredients of Buddhist meditation are samatha (which I will translate here as 'concentration') and vipassanā (which I will call 'experiential enquiry'). No matter which Buddhist tradition one follows, the practice of samatha and vipassanā will lead to the cultivation of mindfulness. I also intend to show how the traditional doctrine of the 'four great efforts' is very close to therapeutic methods advocated in MBCT. I will also propose that the Buddha's five methods of dealing with difficult thoughts as presented in the Vitakkhasaṇṭhāna Sutta (Majjhima Nikāya 20) are examples of an early Buddhist cognitive behavioural strategy.

Samatha and *Vipassanā*

I practised as a Zen nun for 10 years in Songgwang Sa Monastery in South Korea. Six months of each year I would practice Zen meditation for 10–12 hours a day. When meditating, I would repeatedly ask the question: 'What is this?' silently inside myself. I did not do this in order to arrive at an answer but rather to develop a sensation of questioning and then intensify that sensation. My teacher Kusan Sunim maintained that this 'mass of questioning' would build up until it would finally burst and an awakening would take place. Leaving aside 'awakening,' by doing this practice I very soon found myself becoming more aware of my thoughts, feelings, sensations and of my relationship with the world and others. Moreover, I started to be more in tune with impermanence, suffering and conditionality, which in turn seemed to have a positive effect in terms of helping me to manifest over time more wisdom and compassion towards myself and others.

These effects were simply the result of asking 'What is this?' while living in a Zen monastery. During my years in Korea, from time to time practitioners from the Theravada tradition would visit the monastery. When we discussed our methods of practising meditation, I realized that we seemed to be talking two different languages. I would talk about 'the sensation of questioning' while they would talk about 'awareness' or 'mindfulness.'

In 1985 I returned to Europe and joined a Buddhist community in Devon, England, where most members practised in the *vipassanā* tradition. I was thus in continuous contact with teachers who taught mindfulness in the context of *vipassanā* meditation. I decided to try this method myself and participated in several retreats. I found that it was very effective.

In 1992, I did research for a book on women and Buddhism, first published as *Walking on Lotus Flowers* (Batchelor 1996). I met and interviewed around 40 women from widely varying Buddhist traditions, both Asians and Westerners, nuns and laywomen. After extensive discussions with them, I became convinced that, in producing results, the techniques of meditation they used did not matter as much as their dedicated sincerity as practitioners of the Dharma. All the women I spoke to appeared to have developed considerable mindfulness and manifested both wisdom and compassion in their lives.

This led me to ask more precisely what we were trying to do in meditation. I wanted to know what were the elements, common to most Buddhist meditation practices that produced such effects. My teacher Zen Master Kusan used to exhort us to cultivate equally *song song jok jok*. This literally means 'bright, bright, calm, calm.' (Nowadays I would translate it as 'aware, aware, calm, calm'). This, of course, was simply *samatha* and *vipassanā* as articulated in the Korean Zen school. In the end I came to believe that for any authentic Buddhist practice, you need to cultivate concentration and experiential enquiry together, while recognizing that they can be cultivated in various ways according to the different traditions.

Let me look first at the Korean Zen way of cultivating concentration and experiential enquiry together. You sit or walk in meditation and ask repeatedly 'What is this?' Concentration (*samatha*) is developed by coming back again and again to the question. You remember repeatedly your intention to ask the question and then return to the question; in order to keep returning, you need the intention but also the awareness that you have become distracted away from your intention. Thus you come back to the question again and again. Experiential enquiry (*vipassanā*) is developed by posing the question with your whole body and mind, which, over time, develops a deep sensation of questioning. You do not just repeat the question like a mantra, but you use it as a means to intensify your enquiry. After a while, I found that this led to a heightened awareness of the central Buddhist ideas of impermanence, suffering and conditionality. This, in turn, seemed to help develop a more creative awareness, or what one might call 'active wise mindfulness.'

Now let's consider the practice of cultivating awareness of the breath (*ānāpānasati*). First, one focuses on the sensations one experiences when one breathes, at the nostrils for example. Concentration is developed by coming back to the breath each time one is distracted, which is possible due to the intention one has to be aware and the awareness that one has become distracted. Likewise, experiential enquiry is developed by being aware, for example, that the air comes into the nostrils cooler and goes out slightly warmer, thus leading to an experiential sense of the changing nature of the breath. At the same time one becomes more aware that thoughts, sensations, feelings as well as background sounds are changing too. This method may give more explicit emphasis to mindfulness than in Zen, but the effect, I feel, is much the same in both cases. This, I think, is due to having cultivated concentration and experiential inquiry together for a sustained period of time within an environment of Buddhist ideas and values.

My understanding of how this works is as follows. Let's imagine we are sitting in meditation. We start by focusing on the breath or a question, then we suddenly find ourselves caught up in planning or daydreaming. When we become aware that we are no longer focused, then we come back, as per the instructions we are following, to the breath or the question. Each time we come back, we do two things. First: we do not feed the planning or daydreaming by getting lost in them again; second: we dissolve the power of the habit to plan or daydream by coming back to focus on the breath or question, where we are no longer actively planning and daydreaming. In this way the disruptive effects of planning and daydreaming are overcome (without, of course, rejecting that both activities can serve useful functions, such as organizing and imagining, in appropriate contexts). It is in this way that meditation helps us dissolve the powers of mental, emotional and physical habits. At the same time, as soon as one is less involved in thinking repetitive thoughts, the mind will be less busy, and thus more calm and spacious.

By posing a question, as in Korean Zen, or being aware directly of impermanence, as in *vipassanā* meditation, we start to dissolve the tendency to fix and solidify experience, such as when we say: 'I am always like this. You always do that. This will never change.' The more we are experientially attuned to impermanence, the less we grasp and fixate, thus leading to our being less encumbered by mental confusion and obsession. It seems to me that it is by cultivating concentration and experiential inquiry together that we develop calmness and brightness of mind, which in turn 'coagulate,' as Kusan Sunim used to say, into a kind of creative awareness or wise active mindfulness.

The Four Great Efforts

And what, monks, is Right Effort? Here, monks, a monk rouses his will, makes an effort, stirs up energy, exerts his mind, and strives to prevent the arising of unarisen, evil, unwholesome mental states. He rouses his will... and strives to overcome evil unwholesome mental states that have arisen. He rouses his will... and strives to produce unarisen, wholesome mental states. He rouses his will, makes an effort, stirs up energy, exerts his mind, and strives to maintain wholesome mental states that have arisen, not to let them fade away, to bring them to greater growth, to the full perfection of development. This is called Right Effort. (Dīgha Nikāya 22)

Thus did the Buddha encourage his followers to cultivate what are sometimes called the 'four great efforts.' I would render them as follows:

1. To cultivate conditions so that negative states that have not arisen do not arise.
2. To let go of negative states once they have arisen.

3. To cultivate the conditions that enable positive states to arise.
4. To sustain positive states once they have arisen.

When I first read *Mindfulness-Based Cognitive Therapy for Depression: A New Approach* by John Teasdale, Mark Williams and Zindel Segal (2001), I was struck by the fact that the eight week course that had been developed by the three authors was in accordance with the four great efforts as taught by the Buddha. During this course the participants seemed to be taught various tools of mindfulness, enquiry and concentration, with particular emphasis on awareness of the body as a means to take the focus and energy away from negative mental ruminations, which, when combined with low moods, could trigger depressive states. People were encouraged to explore, accept and let go of their negative feelings and thoughts, and recognize and build on good feelings, such as their capacity for joy and the ability they have to accomplish something of value and meaning.

The first week of the course is focused on the cultivation of mindfulness. The intention is to make participants aware that they often live their lives on automatic pilot. The danger of living automatically like this is that one will also react automatically and thus be easily caught in destructive emotional and mental patterning. By practising mindfulness, participants become more aware of their experience in each moment and thus can really engage with it, thereby enabling them to start bypassing the grooves of their patterns. This is very similar to the Buddha's first great effort: *To cultivate conditions so that negative states that have not arisen do not arise.*

In the second week, the participants are encouraged to create a calendar of pleasant events. This is designed as an exercise in mindfulness that makes one more aware of what is and can be positive in one's life. It can act as a counterweight to the negative tendency to think that everything in one's life is difficult and unpleasant. This is akin to the third great effort: *To cultivate the conditions that enable positive states to arise.*

During the third week participants are told to focus on the breath as a tool to steady and ground oneself in daily life. This is where the exercise of the 'three-minute breathing space' is taught. I find this exercise interesting in the way it combines three different types of meditation: on questioning, on the breath, and on the body. It involves three steps: 'Awareness,' 'Gathering,' and 'Expanding.' One starts by asking oneself, 'Where I am?' or 'What's going on?' as a way of bringing oneself back to awareness of the present. This has striking similarities with Korean Zen questioning, which likewise brings an immediacy and awareness of one's experience in its multiplicity and helps one to be less caught in abstraction. The second step consists in 'bringing the attention to the breath,' and the third 'expanding attention to include a sense of the breath and the body as a whole.'

In the fourth week, the participant addresses the 'comparing mind' and the 'mind that clings or avoids.' Mindfulness of sounds and thoughts is introduced. One is given a questionnaire that helps one reflect on and note the automatic thoughts that occur repeatedly over the week and colour one's view of reality. This trains one to address the issues in one's life in advance so that one is less likely to be caught in habitual patterns of behaviour. Again this is similar both to the first and third of the great efforts, which I have already discussed. In other words, it is a form of active prevention.

The fifth week focuses on acceptance and on cultivating a different relationship to experience. During a 40 minute meditation session participants are encouraged to let difficulty issues arise in the mind, and then apply instructions to help them become aware of the unpleasant effects that occur in the body and then 'let go of the aversion.' This is very similar to the second great effort: *To let go of negative states once they have arisen.*

By the seventh week, participants start to prepare for what they will do after the eight-week course ends. Now they need to focus on what is positive in their life and what uplifts their moods. In order to do this, they have to become aware of the connection between what they do and how they feel. They are encouraged to write a list of what brings them joy and what shows them that they are good at something. This reminds one of both the third and the fourth of the great efforts. They are also asked to recognize the warning signals of a future relapse: 'irritability, decreasing social participation, change in sleeping or eating habits,' etc. It is then essential for them to map out clearly the actions they can take to prevent the recurrence of a depressive state, which, again, is very much like the first great effort.

Five ways of dealing with disturbing thoughts

Now I would like to look at a *sutta*, that is a Pali discourse attributed to the historical Buddha, which seems to illustrate an early Buddhist cognitive behavioural strategy. This is the *Vitakkasanthāna Sutta* or *Discourse on the Forms of Thought*, the twentieth of the *Middle Length Discourses* in the Pali Canon, in which the Buddha discusses five ways to help one to deal with disturbing thoughts.

The first suggestion the Buddha makes is that *'if some unskilled thoughts associated with desire, aversion or confusion arise and disturb the mind, you should attend instead to another characteristic, which is associated with what is skilled'.* He compares this to *'a skilled carpenter who can knock out a large peg with a small peg'.* The Buddha seems to be saying that in order to dissipate a negative thought you only have to bring up in the mind something positive as a counter-medicine or antidote to it. For example a compassionate thought could replace a hateful one. Instead of thinking that someone you know has done something hurtful, then to aggravate this by telling yourself that this person *always* does bad things, you could deliberately recall occasions where the person has been kind to you and others.

Or if you suddenly have a strong desire to buy something very expensive that you cannot afford, could you instead buy a small object for somebody else and thereby replace greed by generosity? Or if you are waiting for a friend who is late, instead of immediately thinking that the friend has no respect or love for you or she would be on time, you could consider more reflectively that there is probably a perfectly good reason for your friend's delay.

The second method the Buddha gives in the *sutta is 'to scrutinise the peril of these unskilled thoughts by thinking: "these are unskilled thoughts, these are thoughts that have errors, indeed these are thoughts that are of painful results."'* Here the suggestion is to consider carefully the consequences of our thoughts, and realize that certain types of thoughts are indeed liable to produce painful results. For example, on reflecting on a dispute with a friend, one might say to oneself: 'I am going to tell it like it is. This is unfair. I am right, she is wrong.' By continually repeating this, we come to believe more and more that it is true, thus working ourselves up so that by the time we meet the person concerned we are very angry. But as soon as we attack someone verbally, even if we are in the right, the other person will tend to be offended and defensive. Thus not only do we hurt ourselves by working ourselves up in this way, we are likely to hurt others as well. By clearly seeing the pain we are going to cause, we are more likely to let go of such thoughts. The Buddha offers a macabre example. He says it is like *'a woman or a man, young and fond of adornment, who if the carcass of a snake or a dog were hanging around their neck would be revolted and disgusted and throw it away immediately as soon as they notice it.'*

The third suggestion is to *'bring about forgetfulness and lack of attention to those thoughts.'* The Buddha compares this to *'a man who not wanting to see the material shapes that come within his range of vision would close his eyes or look another way.'* At first glance, this method would seem to go against the general teaching of the Buddha to be aware and mindful of whatever arises. But the Buddha was pragmatic and understood the human mind well. When certain thoughts are simply too strong or disturbing to deal with directly, the best way to dissipate them may be simply to think of something else. If one is compulsively ruminating or indulging in unrealistic fantasies, a healthy distraction might be the most skilful thing to do at that time—going for a walk in nature, talking to a friend, reading an absorbing novel or an inspiring book. Doing something different can help one's mind to get out of its rut and thus dissipate the energy and obsessive power of the negative thoughts.

I used to have a tendency to fabricate. A single sentence or image would often be enough to send me into a spiral of negative fabricating thoughts. When I saw what I was doing, I started using the second and the third methods taught in this *sutta*. Either I reflected that these compulsive thoughts would lead to painful results, or, if that failed to work, I would distract myself from them by reading a novel, for example, in order for them to lose their hold over me. The end result was that these kinds of thoughts soon stopped arising. This made me realize that if you do not feed the flames of negativity, the fire will die out by itself. These methods not only help one deal with the situation at hand, over time they help diminish and sometimes dissolve the arising of certain disturbing patterns of thoughts.

The fourth method is to *'attend to the thought function and form of these thoughts.'* To illustrate this, the Buddha says: *'it might occur to a man who is walking quickly: "Now, why do I walk quickly? Suppose I were to walk slowly." It might occur to him as he was walking slowly: "Now, why do I walk slowly? . . . . . . Suppose I were to lie down."'* In this way, 'the man, having abandoned the hardest posture, might take to the easiest posture.' By looking into the root of the thought, we are encouraged to question the form of the thought itself. Why are we thinking what we are thinking? Could we be thinking something else? These questions open up other possibilities. We could enquire even further into what caused us to think what we are thinking. This is not psychoanalytical (looking for explanations in traumatic childhood events, for example) but experiential questioning: what just happened that led me to think in this way?

The Buddha's fifth and final suggestion in this sutta is *'by the mind to subdue, restrain and dominate the mind.'* The comparison is made with a *'strong man, who having taken hold of a weaker man by the head or the shoulders, might subdue, restrain and dominate him.'* This might appear antithetical to certain psychological doctrines that insist that one should never repress anything or forcibly restrain oneself. I like the pragmatism of the Buddha; if everything else fails and you continue to have disturbing and destructive thoughts, then stop them by sheer force of will. Remember that this is just one of five methods, which is only to be applied when necessary. It also points out that one's mind is stronger that any one thought that may preoccupy it. Although we may have the tendency to believe that our thoughts are stronger than us, this is not true. We should not reduce ourselves to just one thought; we are far greater and more resourceful than that.

In the Korean Zen tradition, the *Vitakkasaṇṭhāna Sutta* is neither taught nor even mentioned. When I first heard a *vipassanā* teacher explain this *sutta*, I was particularly struck because it was an exact description of what I had found myself doing after practising Zen meditation for 10 years. This confirmed my impression that Buddhist meditation helps us to develop a creative awareness or an active wise mindfulness that enables us to recognize and deal more effectively with our mental patterns. Then one day, after giving a talk about how meditation can be used to deal with mental patterns, someone in the audience told me that what I was saying sounded just like behavioural cognitive therapy. So I read some books on the subject and indeed found a number of similarities in its approach. Since then I keep on discovering that there are many common points between Buddhist practice and cognitive therapy. They deal and are concerned with the same material: human suffering and ways to relieve suffering. They also share a pragmatic, self-reliant approach to life that recognizes the great value of acceptance and compassion.

Conclusion

Samatha (concentration) stabilizes our attention, while *vipassanā* (experiential inquiry) helps us to see things more clearly. The cultivation of the two together enables us to develop a mindfulness that is characterized by calmness and clarity. As we continue with the meditation, it grants the mindfulness two powerful aspects: acceptance and transformation. For we can only accept something that we can see clearly without rejection or desire. And when we can see both inner states of mind and outer situations with clarity and acceptance, then we may find the strength and capacity to transform them. Whether one is practising Buddhist meditation, mindfulness based stress reduction, or mindfulness based cognitive therapy for depression, it seems that it is such a process that serves as the foundation for effective change.

REFERENCES

BATCHELOR, MARTINE. 1996. *Walking on lotus flowers*. London: Thorsons.

DĪGHA NIKĀYA: *The long discourses of the Buddha*. 1987. Trans. Maurice Walshe. Boston, MA: Wisdom Publications.

MAJJHIMA NIKĀYA: *The middle length discourses of the Buddha: A new translation of the Majjhima Nikāya (Teachings of the Buddha)*. 1995. Trans. Bhikkhu Ñāṇamoli ed. Bhikkhu Bodhi. Boston, MA: Wisdom Publications.

TEASDALE, JOHN, MARK WILLIAMS, and ZINDEL SEGAL. 2001. *Mindfulness-based cognitive therapy for depression: A new approach*. New York: The Guilford Press.

THE BUDDHIST ROOTS OF MINDFULNESS TRAINING: A PRACTITIONERS[1] VIEW

Edel Maex

Jon Kabat-Zinn's Full Catastrophe Living *skilfully succeeded in translating traditional Buddhist concepts in modern everyday language so as to make them accessible to the West. It was a stroke of genius to take mindfulness training out of the Buddhist context, but the risk might be that, instead of opening a door to the Dharma (the Buddhist teaching), it might also close a door leading to the vast richness of that context full of valuable insights and practices. This article aims at back translating some mindfulness concepts to basic Buddhist concepts (in a movement opposite to Jon Kabat-Zinn's first move) to make Buddhist literature more accessible to MBSR/CT teachers that are less familiar with the Buddhist traditions and to allow us reconnect with some treasures that are present in our roots. It freely walks through texts and concepts of different Buddhist traditions when they seem relevant to this enterprise, drawing from the logic of the Pali Canon, the metaphors of the Mahayana sūtras and the paradoxes of Zen koans.*

Years ago, when I was finishing my education as a psychiatrist, I came face to face with one big question: how can I survive the daily confrontation with so much human pain, with sorrow, anxiety, traumas, loss...? I had to find a way to sail safely between two dangerous rocks. On one side there was the risk of being overwhelmed by all the pain and emotion and suffering a burnout myself. On the other side, there was the danger of pushing away my own feelings and becoming emotionless, objective, unavailable, untouched by my patients' pain.

As I was searching for an answer one thing led to another and I found out about Zen meditation. This was the answer to my question. Clearly, meditation was 'my thing.' I have learned an awful lot from it. Not only has it formed me in how I work but also in how I live my daily life.

After about 10 years I began to feel more and more something like: 'This is not fair. I'm keeping the best for myself.' The problem was that I had no idea how to present something like Zen meditation within a psychotherapeutic context. You cannot just start practicing Buddhist meditation in a hospital! And how can you explain to someone who is looking for something to help their pain that you have to sit in silence for a half hour and not expect anything at all from it? The Zen method is not always so accessible.

I began experimenting by weaving into my work some elements of meditation. Then one day someone asked me, 'Don't you know about the work of Jon Kabat-Zinn?' I had never heard of him before but quickly went out and found the book—still unread—in the library of the institute where I was then working. I realized immediately, 'This will save me ten years of work!' Jon Kabat-Zinn had come out of a similar background and, with the same motivations as mine, had created a stress reduction programme. This programme was being used in a hospital and was the subject of thoroughgoing scientific research which was showing it to be an acceptable tool in the medical world. I saw that I did not have to rediscover the wheel myself. I got in touch with Jon Kabat-Zinn and began an eight week training programme based on his work. This was the first of what has now become many.

In the foreword to Jon Kabat-Zinn's *Full Catastrophe Living*[2] Thich Nhat Hanh describes the book as a door from the Dharma to the world as well as from the world to the Dharma.[3] Jon Kabat-Zinn in his book skilfully succeeds in translating traditional Buddhist concepts in modern everyday language so as to make them accessible to the West. Had it not been for Thich Nhat Hanh's foreword the Buddhist origin of them might have gone unnoticed to many readers. Thich Nhat Hanh is one of the foremost Buddhist teachers in the West and his few words certainly attracted many Buddhist practitioners to this book and to the application of mindfulness in clinical practice. This work gave rise to a first generation of MBSR teachers.

Jon Kabat-Zinn not only drew on Buddhist tradition but equally on the scientific tradition he was trained in, thus creating acceptability for his work in the world of science and medicine. This attracted many prominent researchers into the field of mindfulness and exciting results came from that research. What we see now is a second generation of mindfulness teachers, many of whom do not have a background in Buddhism at all, but many of them with a very sincere personal practice. It was a stroke of genius to take mindfulness training out of the Buddhist context, but the risk might be that, instead of opening a door to the Dharma, it might also close a door leading to the vast richness of that context full of valuable insights and practices.

Many questions that arise in mindfulness research today already have a long history in the Buddhist literature as a topic of discussion and experimentation. To give an example: in the *Lotus Sūtra* an eight year old girl, without any meditation experience at all, suddenly attains full awakening.[4] This passage certainly puts on the agenda the question of how much formal practice is necessary (and at that time severely criticized a male chauvinistic monastic attitude). Some of these texts are very precise using philosophical language, such as large parts of the Pali Canon. Other texts, such as the *Lotus Sūtra* or the *Tibetan Book of the Dead*, look very magical and obscure and it is hard to imagine that they contain the roots of mindfulness training.

This article aims at back translating some mindfulness concepts to basic Buddhist concepts (in a movement opposite to Jon Kabat-Zinn's first move) to make Buddhist literature more accessible to MBSR/CT teachers that are less familiar with the Buddhist traditions and to allow us reconnect with some treasures that are present in our roots. I allow myself to freely walk through texts and concepts of different Buddhist traditions when they seem relevant to this enterprise. I have not the slightest pretension to be comprehensive, but I'll be glad to give just a taste of it reminding myself of the Buddha's saying: 'Just as the great ocean contains many treasures, but has only one taste, that of salt, so the teaching contains many treasures but has only one taste, that of liberation.'[5]

Upāya

What Jon Kabat-Zinn did, is in line with a long-standing Buddhist approach called *upāya*, usually translated as 'skilful means'. Buddhism is not dogmatic, it is not a creed. It is a practice to be learned and when we read the oldest texts, closest to the historical Buddha, we see that he was an excellent teacher. The Buddha always addresses the person he is talking to in the language and the frame of reference of that person. This yields an extremely rich literature in which the same message is restated in many different ways. Buddhist teachers after the Buddha have continued that way so you see Chinese Buddhism explained in a very Chinese way and Tibetan Buddhism in a Tibetan style. This accounts for a proliferation of styles, texts and colours.

Jon Kabat-Zinn has done nothing else but continue that tradition and restate the teaching in a way that makes it acceptable to the medical and the scientific world. The development of MBCT again continues the same tradition in reformulating the very same teaching in the language of CBT and adapting it to the sufferings of people with recurrent depression. Further developments will do the same. All this is, very traditionally Buddhist, the product of *upāya*.

Upāya is an important theme in the *Lotus Sūtra*. It tells the story of a rich man, whose children have a lot of toys to play with. At a sudden moment he realizes that the house is on fire and that his children are inside, playing. He calls: 'Fire, fire!', but the children think he is just being playful and continue with their toys. In the end the father says: 'Come outside quickly, I bought you some very exciting new toys.' The children run out and are saved from the fire.[6] This text compares some of the teaching of the Buddha to a toy intended as skilful means (*upāya*) to save us form suffering without any further intrinsic meaning. It criticizes a tendency at that time to become doctrinaire and to lose the real point of the practice.

Research hypotheses are not randomly generated. They always start from an educated guess. For a guess to be educated it can better draw from scientific, clinical and Buddhist resources. This can help us in our research to generate hypotheses that are meaningful and useful and not losing ourselves in studying toys that are intrinsically meaningless.

Four Noble Truths

In the *Kālāma Sutta* in the Pali Canon the Buddha is asked the question: 'There are so many teachers around, who are we to believe?' He answers: 'Do not rely on tradition, scripture, authority or philosophy. Only when you see for yourself that a practice leads to suffering or to wellbeing then you should either reject or accept it.'[7] This text illustrates that suffering is at the core of it all. The Dharma is about suffering and nothing else. No wonder we are drawn to use it in clinical practice!

This is called the *first noble truth*:[8] the observation that there is suffering. It is not a dogma. It doesn't say that all is suffering. It just states the observable fact of suffering. That also explains why it is generic: it is not about chronic pain, not about depression, not about eating disorders but about suffering. So it is meant to be helpful in all conditions that entail suffering. But of course *upāya* teaches us to tailor it to the concrete situation of this concrete suffering individual. Another interesting aspect of this passage in the *Kālāma Sutta* is that the Buddha explicitly presents the Dharma as a testable hypothesis. No wonder many scientists feel attracted to Buddhism.

The *Second Noble Truth* is about the origin of suffering and the *Third* about the ending of suffering due to the ending of its origin. The origin is defined as 'thirst' (Pali *taṇhā*). Thirst in turn originates from feeling (*vedanā*). The link between feeling and thirst is not absolute. Feeling can be prevented from becoming thirst.

To give an example: suppose I fall in love with my neighbour's wife. In a way nothing is wrong with that, until the moment I definitely want to possess her, when I start to see my life as worthless without her, when I am ready to do anything to . . . . That is when feeling becomes thirst and we can be sure that a lot of suffering will follow. It is part of the chain of events that led to many a suicide or murder. The same goes for thoughts, feelings, and actions. The moment I identify with them, the moment I pursue them, suffering follows.

The field of mindfulness in modern medicine and healthcare has some very beautiful language to describe this. We speak of stress reactivity and stress response. Reactivity is when thirst takes over, responding is possible as long as a feeling or a thought remains a feeling or a thought and we can remain aware of that without automatically reacting to it. We also call this 'seeing a thought *as* a thought, a feeling *as* a feeling' metacognitive awareness. Research has shown this to be a key element for mindfulness training to be successful.[9]

How do we learn that? There is a path, a method. The Fourth Noble Truth is the path leading to the cessation of suffering. The path is known as the eightfold path.

The eightfold path

The eight elements of the eightfold path are not just a simple sequence. They are mutually inclusive. They are called 'right' but the Sanskrit term (*sammā/samyak*) derives from music theory and actually means harmonious. They are right in the sense of being attuned to each other to form a scale or chord. Since eight elements are hard to memorize, they are often summarized into three groups: understanding, virtue and meditation.

Understanding (*prajñā*) is the entry into the path. It is my experience that people seeking help in medical and healthcare contexts will not be motivated to engage in MBSR/CT if there is not some understanding and a certain trust as to why they should do this and why it should be helpful.

Virtue (*śīla*) is the element we are probably least at ease with. Isn't science to be value-free? Mindfulness definitely is not. Without kindness, respect and dignity it is not right (*sammā*) mindfulness at all. These virtues are, as well a prerequisite, an element and a consequence of the path. Ethics in Buddhism is completely different from what we are used to in the West in that it is defined in relation to suffering: wholesome is what leads to wellbeing, unwholesome is what leads to suffering. Put in this way even ethics becomes a testable hypothesis. And of course, it is a cornerstone of Western medicine in the Hippocratic Oath and its injunction, *primum non nocere*.

Meditation (*samādhi*) is the third group. Meditation is a lot more popular in the West than it is in the East. We tend to favour it so much that the attuning to the other elements of the path risks getting lost.

Buddhist meditation is an interplay of *śamatha* and *vipaśyanā*. *Śamatha* is stopping, calming. It refers to the act of stopping our habitual activities and to bring our attention to something simple. It is integral to Benson's relaxation response.[10] The next step is *vipaśyanā*: looking, seeing clearly. Such relaxation that occurs during mindfulness training is not an end in itself but it is a step towards looking, toward (metacognitive) awareness. Meditation is the laboratory situation. It is the place where we see our mind at work and learn how to shift from reacting to what presents itself to mindfully holding it and responding appropriately and wholesomely, that is with wisdom and compassion.

Right mindfulness (*sammā-sati*) finds its place here but the meaning of the term mindfulness has expanded in recent years beyond its original meaning.

It is clear that the whole thing does not end on the cushion. From what you discover in meditation grows understanding. From this understanding grows kindness, this in turns motivates and sustains your meditation practice, which leads to a deepening of understanding, which leads to . . . The circle is endless.

Karma

The hot topic of debate at the time of the Buddha was karma. The word karma means intentional action, behaviour. According to the classic texts karma can be generated by way of body, speech, and thought (in a language that sounds surprisingly familiar to a present day cognitive therapist). The discussion at the time was about the consequences of one's behaviour. There was among others a nihilistic faction that denied that behaviour had any consequences at all and that life was more or less random. Others espoused a materialistic view, saying that behaviour only had material consequences and no psychological or ethical consequences at all. The Buddha's statement was very clear: 'I am the owner of my actions (karma), heir to my actions, born of my actions, related through my actions, and have my actions as my arbitrator. Whatever I do, for good or for evil, to that will I fall heir'.[11] The Buddha held a performance view of self. We are what we do.

The Four Noble Truths thus are a theory of karma. They state that there is a problem and that something can be done about it. Our actions do matter. The formula ends with explaining what there is to be done.

For this reason a criterion for participating in MBSR/MBCT is at least some willingness to examine the whole question of control over your behaviour, to explore the possibility that your situation is not solely dependent on outside conditions, that you can take some degree of responsibility for it yourself. Sometimes a patient comes with the expectation that mindfulness will act on them like some kind of drug. In that case I have to say: mindfulness will not do anything for you, but maybe it can teach you how to do something for yourself. For many patients that is exactly what they are looking for and need the most, a way of *participating* in their own health and wellbeing. They are happy to finally find what they can do for themselves instead of helplessly relying on outside conditions, drugs and doctors.

Patients with very severe clinical depression or with psychosis may in that moment not be able to take responsibility for their behaviour and in that case, mindfulness training would be contraindicated. However, even people suffering from psychosis can be helped and can find a way to get some control over disturbing hallucinations, as the work of Chadwick and his colleagues has shown.[12]

Mindfulness training in a clinical context turns out to be a very empowering way of working with people. The focus is not on what is wrong but on what is possible. Through working with mindfulness, I came to realize that, as a clinician, I was trained to underestimate the capacities of people. In reading text like the *Lotus Sūtra* I am touched by the all pervading notion that each of us has the potential to become a Buddha. Starting a new MBSR or MBCT group is not starting with a group of people with more or less severe problems. Rather it is starting with a group of potential Buddha's. At least, that is the way I see it and I know that is true for many people who teach mindfulness-based interventions.

Prajñā-karuṇā

Present day research has shown us the beneficial effects of meditation (*samādhi*). We are acquiring a growing understanding (*prajñā*) of the mechanisms that underlie it. What is least articulated in the field of mindfulness research is *śīla*, virtue. The fact that it is less explicit does not mean that it is not present. It cannot be absent.

In Buddhism the fruit of the practice is often designated as *prajñā-karuṇā* (*karuṇā* meaning compassion). From the early beginnings of Buddhism, the cognitive and the ethical go hand in hand.[13] *Prajñā* and *karuṇā* are not two.

They are one. The cognitive and the ethical element form an inseparable whole. In Zen it is said that understanding and compassion are related to each other as the flame and the heat, one being the function of the other. Compassion naturally flows from understanding. Without compassion no understanding is possible.

How can we explain that in more familiar psychological terms'? Metacognitive awareness is a modern rendering of *prajñā*. But I cannot be metacognitively aware of my feelings of sadness, without bringing a lot of kindness to my feelings and myself. It is impossible to be attentive to everything that presents itself without a big dose of kindness. Being honest with yourself like this is being open to everything. And everything is not always pretty.

It can happen that I sit on my meditation cushion in the evening and suddenly remember something really stupid that I did, a blunder I made, something ridiculous . . . . I was so busy during the day that I totally forgot it. Then in the evening I remember it on the cushion and there is no escape. It would be cruel to become aware of my own stupidity without kindness. We need kindness to make it possible and bearable to have open, receptive attention. I have to let go of judging myself, and reproaching myself for my thoughts and feelings. The act of being cognitively aware is impossible without a compassionate attitude.

In this way awareness needs kindness, but is there also an ethical *consequence* to metacognitive awareness? The ethics of awareness is not at all moralizing. Suppose I am very, very angry, so angry that I might kill someone. My anger narrows my consciousness. In this narrowing lies a great danger. When instead of narrowing I can open up and see my anger and hold it without acting on it impulsively, when I can see my thinking and judging at work without taking it to be reality, what will happen?

There will be a larger awareness of the situation, of the interconnectedness of my own motives, of the perspective of the other, of the causes and consequences of my feelings and my choices, and of the suffering of all involved. Compassion springs from the awareness of suffering, in myself and the other, and of our interconnectedness. The murder will in all likelihood not take place. A greater awareness will probably lead to a more adequate dealing with all the ins and outs of the situation.

I discovered that quite often after an eight week programme, participants realize they became more compassionate towards animals. I have heard of many attempts, sometimes with much humour, of saving spiders that would before thoughtlessly be killed. I was at first surprised to hear these outcomes of mindfulness training, especially since none of the Mahayana rhetoric of 'saving all sentient beings' is found in the programme. But the simple fact of being more aware makes people sensitive to the suffering of even the tiniest animal. I was often touched by that.

It is logical that cognitive researchers approach the field from the cognitive side. It might be wonderful if we also found a way to better conceptualize and investigate the compassionate aspects of mindfulness. The recent work *Compassion Focused Therapy* by Paul Gilbert[14] offers an example in that direction.

Teaching

As with many aspects of the teaching, the different Buddhist traditions have adapted their model of student–teacher relationship to the culture in which it is taught. In MBCT, this relationship enters the world of medicine and psychotherapy. This culture shift gives rise to many pitfalls.

Teaching mindfulness, as in the teaching of any skill, is seen as an interaction between the skill in itself, the skilfulness of the teacher and the skilfulness of the student. The teaching must be skilfully tailored to the abilities of the student. The student him or herself is an equally defining element in the relationship as the teacher.

There is no place where a mindfulness trainer's own practice is more challenged than in the element of inquiry and dialogue. Being a therapist is often an impediment to teaching mindfulness. It is my experience in teaching and supervising mindfulness trainers that therapists and doctors often fall back on their instinct to give advice or be warm and friendly and supportive, sometimes in ways that disempower the person. Mindfulness training instead acknowledges the person's own responsibility for his or her thoughts and feelings, and for his or her practice.

Inquiry during a mindfulness class is only one other technique to teach mindfulness, just like the bodyscan or the three minute breathing space. The common pitfall is to see inquiry as a psychotherapeutic exploration, oriented toward a framing or solution of the problem.

During the process of inquiry the teacher is continuously (although not intentionally) challenged, and it is easy to react instead of to respond. Whether fear comes up or anger or sadness, the teacher attends to it with kindness, without judgment, with an open mind. You accept it as a fact, as the way the trainee experiences his own perspective. You acknowledge the participants perspective as his or her perspective, without having to identify or agree with it.

As trainers, we are called to embody mindfulness. We will notice the tendency of the mind to defend, to console, to agree, to contradict, to react. The group will look at us and wonder: what's he going to say to this? So by responding without reacting to whatever comes, we become a role model in the process of teaching mindfulness. How we respond is guided by the intention to teach the trainee to attend mindfully to his or her own experience. We accept what students present as their perspective on the world and assist in clarifying that experience.

The first place to learn about inquiry is our own meditation practice. To sit or lie down non-judgementally and with kindness, attending to what presents itself, is a powerful training. Exactly the same is what happens in inquiry.

This is why it is very hard to teach someone a skill we have not mastered ourselves to some extent. It all starts from our own practice: 'one teaches out of one's passion for the practice', says Jon Kabat-Zinn. Thich Nhat Hanh, in a conference, told the story of a jealous student who asked him: 'And when will I be ready to be a teacher?'. His quick reply was: 'When you're happy'. A sobering yardstick and a good measure of motivation for anybody wishing to teach mindfulness.

The *Lotus Sūtra* has some touching advice for any teacher: '[the teacher] should enter the room of the Buddha, put on the robes of the Buddha, and sit on the throne of the Buddha.' The *Sūtra* explains: 'Great compassion is the room, kindness and patience are the robes, the emptiness of all Dharmas is the throne'.[15] The first influence of Zen meditation on my clinical practice was that I learned to see my patients not as disturbed but as suffering. For a psychiatrist this is really a paradigm shift. Compassion is the spontaneous healing response towards suffering. Kindness and patience help us to not automatically react to adverse reactions. Like a robe, they can protect us, even when the process of change is difficult. Emptiness refers to the openness we discover and cultivate in our own practice. It refers to insight into the intrinsically insubstantial, empty nature of all things, that they are not permanent and self-existing. It is the point from where it all starts.

Manualizing interventions

In the vast treasure of Buddhist stories the following pearl can be found.

Zen Master Gutei, whenever he was questioned, just stuck up one finger.

At one time he had a young attendant, whom a visitor asked, 'What is the Zen your Master is teaching?' The boy also stuck up one finger. Hearing of this Gutei cut off the boy's finger with a knife. As the boy ran out screaming with pain, Gutei called to him. When the boy turned his head, Gutei stuck up his finger. The boy was suddenly enlightened.[16]

Just to reassure you: this event never really took place. Zen teachers do not walk around carrying knives, let alone cutting off fingers. These kind of didactic stories, called *kōans*, deliberately and with a great sense of humour, challenge our preconceptions.

This story is (among other things) about manualizing interventions. Gutei, in his teaching, seemed to follow a very simple protocol for his intervention: he just stuck up one finger. But when our little 'sorcerer's apprentice' follows his masters protocol he completely fails. The same behaviour, at least so it seems, clearly does not carry the same meaning. Only when the protocol is broken (symbolized by cutting of the finger) does he realize the point.

The behaviour displayed in this *kōan* definitely is not a protocol to be mimicked in mindfulness training! But when we wonder by what behaviour skillful inquiry could be recognized by an observer, this story warns us to not be overly superficial in our understanding of what is actually going on.

Three jewels

At the centre of all Buddhist traditions are what are called the Three Jewels: Buddha, Dharma and Sangha.

Buddha originally stands for the historical person. In later years the meaning shifted from the person to what he stands for. Jon Kabat-Zinn sometimes shows a photograph of a large Buddha statue in his talks and suggests to the audience that this is not so much to be understood as representing a deity, but rather a particular mental state, namely wakefulness.

Dharma is the teaching, and the practice. As the history of Buddhism shows, it is in a process of continual reformulation in accordance with the present needs of those in front of us.

Sangha is the community, originally meaning the community of monastics (monks and nuns) and extending to all involved. There is a strong feeling that this is not an individual thing. The group is important. We support each other when we practice together. That is one reason why it is so powerful to teach mindfulness in groups.

There is also the community of mindfulness teachers and researchers. We are a sangha too. My hope is that this sangha, as it grows and becomes more and more rooted in western science and in clinical practice, will not lose all ties with the richness of its ancient Buddhist roots. There is still a lot to learn from that tradition,

So I want to end this text, as an offering to this sangha, with a beautiful dialogue between the Buddha and Ananda:

> *Ananda said to the Blessed One, 'This is half of the holy life, lord: admirable friendship, admirable companionship, admirable camaraderie.'*
>
> *Don't say that, Ananda. Don't say that. Admirable friendship, admirable companionship, admirable camaraderie is actually the whole of the holy life. When a monk has admirable people as friends, companions, & comrades, he can be expected to develop & pursue the noble eightfold path.'*[17]

NOTES

1. Edel Maex is a practicing psychiatrist and zen student.
2. Kabat-Zinn (1990).
3. Thich Nhat Hanh (1990).
4. *Lotus Sūtra*, chapter 12. There are many English translations of the *Lotus Sūtra* in English, One of the most beautiful is by Reeves (2009).
5. *Udāna* 5.5.
6. *Lotus Sūtra*, chapter 3.
7. *Kālāma Sutta: Aṅguttara Nikāya*, 3.65.
8. *Saṃyutta Nikāya* 56.11.
9. Teasdale et al., (2002).
10. Benson et al., (1974).
11. *Aṅguttara Nikāya*, V.57.
12. Chadwick et al., (2009).
13. Keown (1992/2001).
14. Gilbert (2010).

15. *Lotus Sūtra*, chapter 10.
16. Mumonkan, case 3.
17. *Saṃyutta Nikāya* XLV.2.

REFERENCES

BENSON, H., B. A. ROSNER, B. R. MARZETTA, and H. M. KLEMCHUK. 1974. Decreased blood-pressure in pharmacologically treated hypertensive patients who regularly elicited the relaxation response. *The Lancet* 1 (7852): 289–91.

CHADWICK, P., S. HUGHES, D. RUSSELL, I. RUSSELL, and D. DAGNAN. 2009. Mindfulness groups for distressing voices and paranoia: A replication and randomized feasibility trial. *Behavioural and Cognitive Psychotherapy* 37 (4): 403–12.

GILBERT, PAUL. 2010. *Compassion focused therapy*. London and New York: Routledge.

KABAT-ZINN, J. 1990. *Full castastrophe living: the program of the Stress Reduction Clinic at the University of Massachusetts Medical Center*. New York: Dell Publishing.

KEOWN. 1992/2001. *The nature of Buddhist ethics*. Basingstoke, UK: Macmillan/Palgrave.

REEVES, GENE. trans 2009. *The Lotus Sūtra, a contemporary translation of a Buddhist classic*. Wisdom Publications.

TEASDALE, J. D., R. G. MOORE, H. HAYHURST, M. POPE, S. WILLIAMS, and Z. V. SEGAL. 2002. Metacognitive awareness and prevention of relapse in depression: Empirical evidence. *Journal of Consulting Clinical Psychology* 70 (2): 275–87.

THICH NHAT HANH. 1990. Foreword. In *Full castastrophe living: the program of the stress reduction clinic at the University of Massachusetts medical center*. by J. Kabat-Zinn New York: Dell Publishing.

MINDFULNESS AND LOVING-KINDNESS

Sharon Salzberg

Mindfulness, as the word is commonly used in contemporary meditation teaching, refers to both being aware of our present moment's experience, and relating to that experience without grasping, aversion or delusion. All three habitual tendencies distort our perception of what is happening, and lead us to futile and misguided efforts to deny or control our experience. Loving-kindness is a quality of the heart that recognizes how connected we all are. Loving-kindness is essentially a form of inclusiveness of caring, rather than categorizing others in terms of those whom we care for and those who can be easily excluded, ignored or disdained. Any reduction in our tendency to fall into attachment, aversion or delusion helps refine and expand the force of loving-kindness. A deepening of insight will inevitably include seeing how all of our lives are inextricably interconnected. The diminishing of grasping, aversion and delusion and the increase in insight are both reasons mindfulness naturally leads us to greater loving-kindness.

In contemporary meditation teaching, the word mindfulness is used in several different ways—as meaning the act of recollecting, as being present, and very commonly, as a kind of compound which in Pali, the language of the original Buddhist texts, would be *sati-sampajañña*, or awareness and clear comprehension combined.

One way of seeing this is to say that mindfulness is a relational process—mindfulness is not just knowing what is happening, such as 'In this moment I am hearing a sound.' Being mindful is knowing that we are hearing a sound in a certain way, that is, hearing it free of grasping, aversion and delusion. One of my early meditation teachers, Anagarika Munindra, often emphasized this aspect of mindfulness, saying that it is precisely because of this particular characteristic that we talk about living in a way that is never separated from mindfulness, living in a way that is always connected to mindfulness.

While simply being more aware in the moment that we are hearing a sound, or tasting a flavour, or feeling a sensation, certainly has great and important benefits, it is the fact that mindfulness is free of grasping (greed), aversion (anger), and delusion that means that it provides the platform for more sustained transformation and insight.

We talk about finding a path leading away from greed and anger and delusion because they are forces that distort our perception of what is real and tie us to habits of old even if those habits repeatedly cause us suffering. The path away from those distortions also naturally leads us to greater loving-kindness.

Loving-kindness is a quality of the heart that recognizes how connected we all are. Sometimes it's described as extending friendship to ourselves and others— not in the sense of liking everyone, or dispensing universal approval, but more as an inner knowing that all our lives are inextricably interconnected. When we experience loving-kindness, we acknowledge that every one of us shares the same wish to be happy, and often a similar confusion as to how to achieve that happiness. We also recognize that we share the same vulnerability to change and suffering, which elicits a sense of caring.

Partly mindfulness leads to greater loving-kindness by the diminishing of those painful and habitual reactions like grasping, aversion and delusion in our minds, and partly because that very diminishing becomes the platform for more clearly seeing truths that are always present but may be hidden from our view, such as the interconnected nature of all of life.

Mindfulness is the way out of sheer reflexive reaction to our experience, and so is called the great protector. It works as a protection because it helps us break through the legends, the myths, the habits, the biases and the lies that can be woven around our lives. We can clear away the persistence of those distortions, and their familiarity, and come to much more clearly see for ourselves what is true. When we can see what is true, we can form our lives in a different way.

Let's go back to the moment of mindfully hearing a sound. There are so many ways to hear a sound. That moment of hearing can be an opening into understanding, into insight. Or we can hear a sound and be reactive to it, hear it only in the conventional way.

When I went to Burma to do intensive meditation in 1985, they were doing construction the entire time I was there, building a new dining room about 100 yards away, day after day, hour after hour, metal pounding into metal. It was an unimaginable barrage of noise.

I had gone there with a close friend who was living in the room next to mine. One day, I was out doing walking meditation, moving slowly, noticing the lifting, moving, placing of my leg, in the incredible din of the construction. I glanced up, and she was coming out of her room, with a tin of milk powder in her hand, hoisted behind her shoulder, ready to throw. I looked up, grabbed her arm and told her, 'Don't do it.'

There are so many ways to hear a sound. Do we hear the sound of construction and get filled with delight at the generosity of many donors, even very poor people, who gave to the effort? Do we hear the sound and celebrate the expansion of the monastery? Do we hear the sound and feel irate that the noise is infiltrating our quest for peace? Do we hear the sound and angrily blame the workmen, who are simply working so that they themselves can feed their families (and give to noble projects)?

Mindfulness tells us that there is a distinction between simply hearing the sound and the story we build around it, and when we can find that gap we can take a look at that story and see if we want to further it or not, act motivated by it or not. We can hear the sound and become more and more involved and reactive and upset; we can hear it and look to see what is the nature of this experience, what is actually going on. This doesn't mean that we never try to do something about irritating sounds. It does mean that we look at our reaction to try to understand it more fully, and to understand if in fact the action we are about to take is appropriate. No longer hurling cans at people would be a very good result!

In the Buddhist psychology, it is said every one of our experiences is felt by us to either be pleasant, unpleasant or neutral. Some people fear if they develop a lot of mindfulness, if they become proficient in the practice of meditation, everything will become a gray, neutral blob, and they won't feel anything any more as pleasant or painful. This is not so. This feeling tone is a part of everything we can know—seeing, hearing, touching, tasting, smelling, thinking. What happens after we register the feeling tone of pleasantness, unpleasantness or neutrality is the place where we either relate with mindfulness and emerge into freedom, or we continue to suffer.

There are three main elements or ways of conditioning that we see quite clearly through mindfulness. We see, first of all, that we are conditioned to feel attachment toward pleasant objects—sounds, sights, sensations in the body, pleasant mind states. The quality of attachment in this particular sense is one of holding on, clinging, grasping. To hold on, to grasp, or to cling creates insecurity, dependency since what we are holding on to is fragile because of the constantly changing nature of things, the impermanent nature of all of life.

Winter is coming. What happens if we hold on to autumn? What happens when we hold on to youth? When we hold on to life itself? We can see that people consider it almost a personal humiliation to be sick, grow old, or to die, as if we should be able to determine not to, as though they had made a grave mistake somewhere. Yet, we cannot control it. How can we? The body has its own nature and it is continually changing. The mind has its own nature. If you think how many mind states you have experienced since you've begun reading, which one did not change? Which one was the real you in that sense? People change, outside of our command. How can we get that to stop happening?

Attachment or the greed of wanting things to be a certain way is not somehow bad or wrong, to be judged harshly or condemned. While it may not be useful to see attachment as bad or wrong, it is accurate to it see as the cause of much of the suffering in our lives. To be attached means we are out of harmony with the way things actually are, or out of harmony with the truth, so it is bound to be painful. It is bound to be conflicted somewhere, sometime.

To be attached means we think we should be able to be in control, that things should not change, that they should stay the way we want them to be. Because the happiness we experience while in the state of attachment is transient, fragile, it is going to be shattered again and again. And whatever loving-kindness we might attempt is liable to be overtaken by the demands of attachment.

Loving-kindness is essentially a form of generosity, an offering of the heart, rather than categorizing others in terms of those whom we care for and those who can be easily excluded, ignored or disdained. Loving-kindness may or may not manifest as material generosity, but it is a kind of generosity of the spirit, moving us from our normal self- preoccupation to a completely inclusive attention toward all beings. Attachment will quickly laden loving-kindness with impatience, expectation, an urge to be thanked, a need to see results in someone's changed behaviour or attitude. Any reduction in our tendency to fall into attachment helps refine and expand the force of loving-kindness.

The next habitual conditioning we often see in the mind is aversion. Aversion includes anger, fear, vindictiveness, frustration, impatience, not liking, and corrosive guilt, which is a form of sometimes chronic aversion toward oneself. All of these habits of mind hurt us, they are damaging mental states. They are painful in the moment of experiencing them because there is a kind of burning that accompanies them.

Aversion is the mind state that dislikes the object we know in the moment, it strikes out against it. It is a state that desires separation from what is happening, the creation of distance, non-connection. It's a state that doesn't cling but rather searches for faults. It is a state of repulsion. If it becomes habitual, we tend to find unlikeable, unacceptable experiences everywhere; everywhere we look we see what is wrong. We do not like what that person is wearing, and we do not like who that person is with, and we don't like the wallpaper and so on.

When we react to unpleasant-feeling experiences with aversion, it means we strike out against them, we just do not want to be aware of that unpleasant feeling. We withdraw from the experience, we separate from it, or we are afraid of it, or we are impatient about it. Perhaps we take what is happening in the moment and we project it through time as though it were never going to change in any way. Or we spin out with manufactured associations with what is happening, 'This means I will be alone forever.' 'It is because of this that I will never be happy.'

What mindfulness teaches us is that there can be a big difference between pain and suffering. We can hear a painful sound, see a painful sight, have a painful experience in the body or mind, and we don't need to add to it the suffering of fear, anger, or mental anguish.

There is often a strong factor in aversion of expectations not being met. Expectations about ourselves, about a situation, about another person. It is important to understand that anger does not exist inherent in any painful or disappointing object. Rather, it exists in our relationship to it. In any situation there are many possible responses that run the gamut from anger to compassion and everything in between.

When anger is strong, it functions as a distorting lens so we cannot see clearly what is actually happening. When we feel anger with pain, loss, and change, that means we feel anger toward life itself because these are the inevitable elements of existence. When aversion is repetitive, it becomes habitual and it leads to disharmony, suspiciousness, lack of trust and a lack of joy.

Clearly a mind filled with aversion is not inclining towards loving-kindness. While it is important to not condemn or hate the anger we see arising within us, mindfulness shows us its limiting, binding nature. For example, when was the last time you were very angry with yourself over something indiscreet and foolish you said one day, while you also recalled the 50 good things you had also done that very same day?

Not likely! More likely our sense of who we are and all that we will ever be collapses around that one unskillful comment. Loving-kindness does not insist that that particular comment was brilliant and witty—perhaps it was really foolish and that will have its own consequences—but that indiscreet moment is not the totality of who we are. It could never be. It is a characteristic of anger to foster that collapse, that tunnel vision.

If we do not get lost in the anger we feel, then we do not fall into the trap of concretizing or reifying a trait, a person, a situation, a thought. We do not see impermanence as permanent, or mistake a state that has the potential to change as one forever marking ourselves or others. Mindfulness, which frees us from the grip of aversive feeling, gives us flexibility of attention, buoyancy and spaciousness of attention. This allows us the suppleness to look at our experience from different angles, to see beyond rigid characterizations, like 'I'm so stupid and always will be,' and 'You're so bad, and that's all you'll be forever.' It opens up the door for loving-kindness and compassion to enter.

A third habitual conditioning that dominates our lives is delusion. The word delusion is used in several different ways in Buddhist teaching, as meaning ignorance, as not knowing, and as knowing wrongly. Here I am using delusion as disconnection, numbness, confusion as to what is actually happening right now. Especially when our experience is felt by us to be fairly neutral, not particularly pleasant or unpleasant, we have the tendency to effectively go to sleep by falling into delusion. We are conditioned to not be present, to not be fully awake when something is not striking us as highly pleasant or unpleasant. We space out, we get disconnected, we do not understand what is happening to us because we are not paying full attention.

We tend, by and large, to not be very tuned in to subtlety, and to depend on intensity in order to feel alive. In neutral terrain our attention dulls and slips away. This state of delusion is characterized by anxiety, uncertainty, perplexity, sloth and torpor.

When delusion becomes habitual, it spreads out beyond those times in which our experience is just neutral (which can be problematic enough.) When the mind is filled with delusion or when delusion is strong in us in a particular moment, we do not see grasping or aversion as they are operating. We might barely notice a sense of inner dissatisfaction, or the pain of confusion about what is going on, and to the extent we do notice it, not even care about it. There is complacency about our lives; we just do not care enough to affect change.

Lost in delusion, it is difficult to know what we are feeling, and thus it is harder to sense what others might be feeling, which is an essential foundation for both morality and empathy. If we live more or less in a fog, we tend to be cut off from our own emotional reactions and simply do not recognize how it feels when we are excluded, hurt, lied to, disdained. Without that sensitivity, we are without an important ingredient in the desire to help rather than harm, to include rather than exclude, to be truthful rather than duplicitous.

We also rely on that kind of sensitivity in the deepening of empathy. Recalling what it felt like to be humiliated helps us resonate with the one who seems to be in a humiliating position. Based on that building block, we can find our hearts moved, reach out a helping hand, be in some kind of solidarity with the person, rather looking from on-high distantly, as if our lives had never been touched by such an emotion or situation.

The clearer we are about our emotions and reactions, the more we create a foundation for responsiveness of conscience and caring. The greater our understanding of the nature of life, the more we see of how much we hold in common. We discover a much greater sense of connection to all.

The teachings of mindfulness invite us to be awake and present with balance and serenity and insight, when our experience is pleasant, when it is unpleasant, and when it is neutral. We see, and learn to be free of, the habits of grasping, aversion and delusion through the consistent cultivation of mindfulness. This freedom is the ground out of which much greater loving-kindness for ourselves and others emerges.

MINDFULNESS IN HIGHER EDUCATION

Mirabai Bush

This paper explores the introduction of mindfulness into courses in higher education. Some of these courses are taught by Buddhist scholars; others are taught by scholars within other disciplines who themselves have a meditation practice. Those scholars included here represent a much larger number in diverse settings, including state universities, liberal arts colleges, Ivy League institutions, and historically black colleges. They teach in almost every discipline, including architecture, poetry, chemistry, economics, and law. The courses discussed in this paper are taught by Contemplative Practice Fellows, a programme of the Center for Contemplative Mind in Society. The paper also places this movement into a short history of contemplative education and raises questions about its future impact on the academy.

In this paper, I will explore the introduction of mindfulness into courses in higher education. Some of these courses are taught by Buddhist scholars; others are taught by scholars within other disciplines who themselves have a meditation practice. Those scholars included here represent a much larger number in diverse settings, including state universities, liberal arts colleges, Ivy League institutions, and historically black colleges. They teach in almost every discipline, including architecture, poetry, chemistry, economics, and law. The courses discussed in this paper are taught by Contemplative Practice Fellows, a programme of the Center for Contemplative Mind in Society.

These courses are part of a movement in higher education, inspired by John Dewey and William James to include 'first person' approaches to the study within the disciplines of science, humanities, and the arts as well as in the professional schools. Students are encouraged to engage directly in contemplative techniques, including mindfulness, and then step back and appraise their experience for meaning and significance. These methods are introduced not as a replacement for but as a complement to 'third-person' learning, the critical ability to observe, analyse, record and discuss a subject at a distance.

This movement is happening, not coincidentally, as the scientific research on mindfulness is expanding and producing results relevant to teaching, learning, and knowing. And the classroom context raises interesting questions that may not currently be at the forefront in the health and healing studies about the potential of mindfulness for cognitive transformation. The Buddhist tradition has given us a set of practices for knowing the essential nature of mind. In order to do this, one needs a calm, stabilized mind. Educators are interested in the calming, quieting, focusing qualities of mindfulness that help students reduce stress and become more patient and present in the classroom, but they are also interested in how that calm stability can positively affect cognitive functions like attention, working memory, and long-term memory, and lead eventually toward understanding and wisdom. They honour the power of mindfulness to reduce suffering, but they are also focused on the work of the academy: students need to plan, set goals, set priorities, move back and forth among tasks. They need to think about the meaning of new information and connect it to what they already know. They need to create long-term memories that will be accessible during an exam many hours after acquiring the information (a true relief of suffering!). They need to explore interconnections and to extend their grasp of the verbal and visual dimensions of their work. They need to find meaning in these interconnections. They need to see clearly and cultivate insight. As Arthur Zajonc, Professor of Physics at Amherst College and now Director of the Center, says in *Meditation as Contemplative Inquiry*: 'The true goal of meditation is to achieve a way of directly experiencing the world and ourselves that is not imprisoned or distorted by mental habits or emotional desires. When free of these, we are opened to a richer exploration of reality that presents to us new insights into self and world.'

I first discovered mindfulness in 1970. I had taken a writing year after completing my PhD courses and oral exams in contemporary American literature, and I intended to spend two weeks in India before I began to write. In Delhi, I heard that there was a meditation course being offered to Westerners for the first time in Bodh Gayā. I had studied with some contemplative poet mentors—Robert Creeley, Robert Hass, and others—but I had never meditated, and I had not studied Buddhism. I thought it sounded interesting. The course lasted 10 days, and it affected me so profoundly that I stayed and practiced for two months and then remained in India for two years, meeting and practicing with other teachers as well.

When I co-founded the Center for Contemplative Mind in Society to explore the potential benefits of integrating contemplative practice and perspective into American life, we offered retreats and built programmes in law, business, environmentalism, social justice activism, and journalism. We also considered higher education, but I thought it an unlikely place for systemic societal change to happen, and I thought there would be tremendous resistance to offering practices from the religious traditions to students in secular institutions

As it turned out, there was much less resistance than we imagined, due partly to a partnership we developed with the American Council of Learned Societies, which administered fellowships that we designed called the Contemplative Practice Fellowships. Grantees agreed to develop and teach courses that integrated contemplative practice into their teaching. Over 12 years, 158 fellows were selected from more than 1000 applications. During the first years, many professors simply introduced a few minutes of mindfulness at the beginning and end of class, but over the years, fellows learned from each other and from their students and deepened their own practice. Many courses now have seamlessly combined mindful awareness with the core teachings of the discipline itself, as when an architecture professor asks her students to be mindful of the light through the leaves of a tree as it falls on a building site over 24 hours.

These courses are part of a larger movement in higher education known as contemplative education. Before I describe the courses and the issues they present, I would like to give a short pre-history of contemplative higher education in America—specifically, what led to the Center's programmes and to other courses within the arts, sciences, and humanities that include a mindfulness practice or cultivate a contemplative perspective.

1890: William James publishes *Principles of Psychology*, in which he describes four methods, including introspection, or his study of his own state of mind, and concludes with this quote which is included in every Power Point and website on contemplative education: 'The faculty of voluntarily bringing back a wandering attention, over and over again, is the very root of judgment, character, and will . . . . An education which should improve this faculty would be the education par excellence. But it is easier to define this ideal than to give practical directions for bringing it about.'

1970s: William James Hall, Harvard: After Timothy Leary and Richard Alpert leave the department that was inspired by William James and is housed in William James Hall, interest in expanded consciousness and new ways of knowing continues, encouraged in part by David McClelland, former Chair of the Social Relations Department, whose students then—Daniel Goleman (*Emotional Intelligence*), Richie Davidson (University of Wisconsin, Laboratory for Functional Brain Imaging and Behavior and the Laboratory for Affective Neuroscience), Cliff Saran (Shamatha Project, University of California at Davis), and Mark Epstein (*Thoughts without a Thinker*)—later become important research and thought leaders in the integration of mindfulness practice in the United States. Outside the classroom, David and his artist wife Mary, both Quakers with an interest in Thomas Merton and Eastern religions, host an ongoing conversation in their home about meditative practices and consciousness. A lifelong teacher, David wants to know, how can contemplative practices affect knowing and learning as well as healing, social relationships, and motivation? Among the diverse people who visited the McClelland's big Cambridge house and joined voices with David's students and other of us who lived there for stretches of time were Mexican poet Octavio Paz, author Harvey Cox, Insight Meditation teachers Joseph Goldstein, Jack Kornfield, and Sharon Salzberg, Jon Kabat-Zinn (who was then starting his mindfulness clinic at University of Massachusetts), Zen master Seung Sahn, Kalu Rinpoche, Allen Ginsberg, and Chogyam Trungpa Rinpoche. Richard Alpert, now Ram Dass, was also there.

1974: Chogyam Trungpa Rinpoche founds the Naropa Institute (later Naropa University), based on Buddhist principles of contemplative education, with a summer session in Boulder. He hopes to create an institution where learning is 'infused with the experience of awareness, insight and compassion for oneself and others, honed through the practice of sitting meditation and other contemplative disciplines.' Not well known in the US at that time, Trungpa asks Ram Dass, who has a huge following after publishing *Be Here Now* in 1971, to teach at Naropa in order to attract students. The organizers expect between 300–500 people to take courses at the Institute. Instead, more than 1300 students flock to Boulder:

'Almost overnight, Boulder has become a magnet of learning and excitement and promise... The student body is made up of an astonishing assortment of college students, dropouts, scholars, scientists, artists, therapists, dancers, heads of departments, musicians, housewives, and on and on. The whole first week seems to be filled with a sort of joyous incredulity that Naropa is really happening' (*East West Journal*, September 1974).

Fast Forward to 1995: Charles Halpern, president of the Nathan Cummings Foundation, and Robert Lehman, president of The Fetzer Institute, initiate the Working Group on Contemplative Mind in Society and invite scholars to explore contemplative education in white papers:

Robert Thurman, Columbia: Realistic beliefs, helpful and skillful others, meditations and practices, all these can help by supporting the process of education. But the realistic understanding that liberates is the individual's own process and attainment. Since wisdom is the ultimate cause of awakening, of liberation from ignorance, then these disciplines and practices are educational in the classical sense. One person cannot awaken another. No God can awaken someone. No belief can awaken someone. No meditation can awaken someone. The individual's transformative understanding is their awakening.

Meditation fits in the traditional inner science curriculum at the highest level of the cultivation of wisdom: first learning wisdom, then reflective wisdom, then contemplative wisdom. Therefore, it is virtually indispensable if wisdom is to become fully transformative. The question then for academic, especially liberal arts, institutions, is not a question of adding a desirable frill to their vast smorgasbord of offerings. It is a matter of their effectively fulfilling their duty to provide a liberal, that is, a liberating and empowering, education.

Brian Stock, University of Toronto: We have to teach students what contemplative activity is all about. Among other things, they have to be instructed in reading meditative literature, not as they would read modern poems, plays, or novels, but as contemplatives read them, using texts as a means to an end and not considering them, as is the fashion in contemporary literary practice, as ends in themselves. They would also have to explore types of meditation that are unlike the Judeo-Christian tradition in not requiring the presence of texts, images, or other sensory supports. Beyond that, teachers of the humanities would have to use the renewed interest in the contemplative life to begin an exploration of what we mean by 'the modern identity,' that is, as a means of tracing the various strands of what it means to be a human agent, a person, or a self. This implies broadening the discussion of ethics beyond the traditionally narrow confines of academic speculation and taking up a number of cultural connections: religious history, gender orientation, ecological considerations, etc.

Steven Rockefeller, Middlebury College: Meditation can improve the quality of life of those who choose to practice it under the guidance of competent teachers. When pursued seriously as a discipline, it can add a unique depth to democratic and ecological living. It can help people become free and fully human. By itself meditation does not impel human beings to social action, and it needs to be counterbalanced by a concern with social reconstruction and personal relationship. However, in a democratic ecological society that affirms life in the world and values social action and community, the practice of meditation can help to shape the direction of social action, contributing to an integration of the ethical and the political, the spiritual and the practical. The undergraduate college is one place where these issues should be thoughtfully explored.

1997: The Center for Contemplative Mind in Society is incorporated and partners with the American Council of Learned Societies to offer fellowships to academics who are interested in developing courses with a contemplative component. Advisors to the project include Carolyn Brown from the Library of Congress, Robert Thurman, Sharon Daloz Parks (Kennedy School of Government at Harvard), Francisco Varela (who introduced into neuroscience the concept of 'first person science,' in which observers examine their own conscious experience using scientifically verifiable methods, later key to the research on meditation) and members of the original Cambridge group: Daniel Goleman, Deborah Salter-Klimburg (Director of the Institute for Tibetan Art History at University of Vienna), Joseph Goldstein, and David McClelland. Although the Selection Committee is unsure that they will receive any proposals at all, 136 are submitted. The committee finds many of them extraordinary, creative, and rigorous, and they award the first 16 Contemplative Practice Fellowships to 'create curriculum in diverse disciplines that encompass and encourage the study of contemplation.' By 2010, there are 158 Fellows in more than 100 colleges and universities. Many are using mindfulness practices to enhance learning in the classroom.

The courses discussed below were taught by these fellows. Some were taught by Buddhist scholars and others by professors from other disciplines who were themselves practitioners or who invited local Buddhist teachers to lead practice for their students. Most adopted a definition of mindfulness inspired by Jon Kabat-Zinn: a way of being in which one is highly aware and focused on the reality of the present moment, accepting and acknowledging it, without getting caught up in the thoughts that are about the situation or emotional reactions to the situation. There are other definitions and capacities explored by Georges Dreyfus, John Dunne, and other contributors to this volume, such as the ability of mindfulness to bring together various aspects of experience so as to lead to the clear comprehension of the nature of mental and bodily states. It is clear that the interest of the most experienced of these professors is not only in the spacious non-judging quietness that mindfulness develops but also in its central role in the cognitive process. They report changes that suggest cognitive transformation: increased concentration, greater capacity for synthetic thinking, conceptual flexibility, and an appreciation for a different type of intellectual process, distinct from the linear, analytical and product oriented processes so often valued in contemporary education.

The definitions of mindful learning and teaching are in process. Ellen Langer, part of the Williams James legacy at the Psychology Department at Harvard, addressed 'the power of mindful learning' in 1997. She described it as having three characteristics: the continuous creation of new categories, openness to new information, and an implicit awareness of more than one perspective. She states that the essence of mindfulness is flexible thinking. Dan Siegel, in *The Mindful Brain*, identifies the essential dimensions of mindful learning as openness to novelty, alertness to distinction, context sensitivity, multiple perspectives, and present orientation. He calls reflection the fourth 'R' of education, the skill that embeds self-knowing and empathy in the curriculum. Fellow Mary Rose O'Reilly, in *Radical Presence: Teaching as a Contemplative Practice,* says that it has to do with being awake, being there, being present, listening, creating a space for learning and for developing an inner life by your very attention to the moment.

The question of contemplative epistemology, or meditative knowing, is only beginning to be explored in the academy, but the approach includes a suspension of disbelief (and belief) in an attempt to 'know' reality through direct observation, by being fully present in the moment. It is, like the best of academic methods, an inquiry into the nature of things. Chogyam Trungpa Rinpoche, educated both in Lhasa and at Oxford, said wisdom is 'immediate and nonconceptual insight which provides the basic inspiration for intellectual study.' Having seen clearly one's own mind, one has a natural desire to see how others experience reality.

So, what do these fellows bring to the contemporary classroom? At a meeting of the fellows in arts and architecture at Chautauqua in Boulder, we sat on Stickley wooden chairs, wrapped in quilts to keep warm as snow fell outside, and we asked the questions: What can meditation offer to the arts? How do you describe contemplative practices in arts education to others? What makes me a better contemplative teacher? Simple questions; complex answers. We were reminded of other words of Chogyam Trungpa Rinpoche, who once taught in Boulder: 'Art is based on the idea that first we see our universe very clearly and very precisely and very thoroughly.' Joanna Ziegler, who taught art history at Holy Cross, led us in a mindfulness practice, then projected a painting on the wall, asked us to write briefly what we saw, and read the results. Every one was different. 'What is actually there? What are you bringing to it?' she asked. Look again. And again and again. An hour later, we were still peeling back the onion of our conditioned judgments. Her students do it for 13 weeks.

Amy Cheng, Professor of Studio Art at State University of New York at New Paltz, sees the inherent connection between the arts and mindfulness. 'Our ultimate goal in my course is to find the writing strategies that, like meditation, help us to tap the intuitive creative functions of the right brain: to think in complex images rather than in sequential order, to see the whole as well as the parts, to grasp interconnections, correspondences, resemblances, and nuances rather than the bits and pieces and linear, logical patterns.' Her students looked at three aspects of creativity in a meditative context:

- making something new, original, or unexpected;
- renewing or sustaining what already exists;
- healing and making things whole.

At Syracuse University, Anne Beffel teaches mindfulness within her course on Contemplative Arts and Society. It attracts students who aspire to cultivate creativity, wellbeing, and compassionate connections. They practice what they call paying attention and opening awareness to their connections with their surroundings and each other. They developed the Sitting Still Contemplative Video Project, which includes exercises designed specifically for developing close observation. As part of the Art in Odd Places festival in New York, the City Meditation Crew in white uniforms took their 'hey man, slow down' philosophy to Union Square, where they slowly constructed a giant mandala from discarded gum wrappers (in honour of Gandhi's birthday, October 2).

Performance art like the City Meditation Crew is, in some ways, the perfect Buddhist art form, particularly for this generation: here one moment, gone the next. Did I really see a man walking on a wire between those towers? At a recent summer session at Smith College on developing contemplative courses hosted by the Center for Contemplative Mind, performance artist Akim Funk Buddha presented Hip Hop Tea Ceremony, which he called a 'pray-formance.' Arising one moment, dissolving the next. And although we cannot always eliminate another's suffering (even as we remove causes of pain), we can stimulate imagination and inspire each other to move toward liberation. In a text recommended in Anne Beffel's course, Robert Thurman calls the Buddha's smile 'an original piece of performance art. Like an artist, a Buddha sees beauty in the world. His or her delight naturally flows into an expression that automatically shares that vision and delight with others.' [1]

Because many art and design students are particularly hard on themselves and tend to be perfectionists, Beffel stresses not judging, using Pema Chodren's phrase, being 'unconditionally friendly to oneself.' One student wrote: 'Before this class, I found myself often judging my work while I was creating. I had a hard time staying in the present moment and allowing myself to relax and enjoy the process.

I worried about what others would think about my art. In this course, I realized that I have gotten away from what I believe to be true art: art that completes me as an artist. I wanted to get back to the stage where I didn't notice the judgmental opinions of others and simply did art for myself—connected and accepting.'

Another student wrote, 'I developed a daily practice based on the walking meditation, only with paint. Rather than focusing on the motion of the step of my feet, I focus on the movement of the brush. I paint with water back and forth on a small piece of wood. It allows me to solely focus on the relaxing repetition of painting without judging the outcome.' And others: 'To me, awareness is the feeling of seeing everything as though it were the first time and the last time, at the same time.' 'The acts of slowing down, looking around you, listening to someone, tasting a raisin, all these things are alternatives to violence . . . even though you might not necessarily be thinking 'this is non-violent,' you are acting in that way and it gives you an alternative . . . .'

The most problematic place in the academy to introduce contemplative practices has been religion departments, where the concern has been that a professor who actually practices the religion he or she is teaching would not be sufficiently objective. Teaching such practices to students raises a further concern around proselytizing. These concerns go back to the birth of the modern academy, when enlightened thought and scientific method replaced the earlier monastic institutions. Some professors, however, have found ways based on critical inquiry and 'first person study' to engage students in the practices they are studying in their texts.

Harold Roth, a Taoist scholar, teaches at Brown University, where he has established the Contemplative Studies Initiative, a group of Brown faculty with diverse academic specializations who are united around a common interest in the study of contemplative states of mind, including the underlying philosophy, psychology, and phenomenology of human contemplative experience.

In Introduction to Contemplative Studies, he introduces students to a variety of contemplative experience from the Zen, Taoist, and Vipassanā traditions through both study of the texts and practice in what there is called a 'lab,' but which looks to other eyes like a meditation hall. Early each day, they transform the dance studio while the dancers are still sleeping and do their first-person lab work, meditation. During weeks five and six, they read *Embodied Mind* by Varela, Thompson, and Roach and the *Ānāpānasati Sutta* and practice mindfulness of breath at the tip of the nose and in the diaphragm; in weeks seven and eight, they learn body scan and mindfulness of sensation, feeling, thought, and perception. They discuss their experience in relation to what they read in the text. Those students who choose a concentration in contemplative studies then take a total of 11 more multidisciplinary courses. Brown Medical School now also has a concentration in contemplative studies.

At Mount Holyoke, Professor Lawrence Fine taught Contemplative Practices and Religious Traditions. He covered five traditions, which he thought too many after he taught the course, which also requires contemplative reading and journal writing. His own practices are Jewish and Buddhist. For Buddhist practice, he invited a local Zen priest to teach zazen and a Mount Holyoke alumnus who teaches at Insight Meditation Society to teach Vipassanā. The most exciting aspect of the course for him and for the students was the integration of academic study and contemplative practice. The integration presented him with these questions: How do you naturally and gracefully lead students in contemplative practices in an academic setting? How do you negotiate the different 'presence' you manifest in class, at least during certain moments? How do you move back and forth, wearing 'different hats'? What exactly is the boundary between doing something that feels appropriate experientially, and doing something that feels devotional? How do you invite students to bring their whole selves to the course, and yet judge them by way of evaluation and grading? Those questions turned out to be what made the course challenging yet very rewarding. In a final report, he said, 'For me, perhaps the most rewarding aspect of the course was the permission I gave myself to be more open, more informal, and more personal than I sometimes am as a teacher. '

At Bryn Mawr College, Michelle Francl, Professor of Chemistry, teaches Quantum States of Being: Incorporating Contemplative Practices into the chemistry curriculum. Her intention is to provide nascent scientists with another set of ways to reflect on their work in relation to the larger world. She teaches mindfulness of sound, a practice she calls Listening Out (listening in further and further concentric circles). 'Start with the sounds closest to you—the student at the next desk rustling papers, the pumps chugging at the lab bench, the roar of the fume hoods. Slowly extend your awareness outward . . . .'

In making the case for the importance of mindfulness, she wrote,

It has the potential not to merely produce scientists, but to allow scientists to engage in forming themselves. Science touches nearly everything we touch, the world therefore deserves scientists who do not see themselves solely as masters of nature, able to trick the natural world into doing their will, but as those who can listen attentively enough to the world to hear what needs to be done. The world cries out for reflective scientists, who can intentionally create a space in which to see their work in its full context—scientific, cultural, political and personal. Embedding these practices, then, not just in any course, but in a course that is seen as rigorous and fundamental to the discipline, lets students grow as scientists in a culture that acknowledges that such ways of seeing and relating to the world are useful for their work and not incongruent with what a scientist should be. (Michelle Francl).[2]

Science courses reveal the investigative nature of mindfulness practices. Arthur Zajonc, at Amherst, asks his students to bring their mindfulness to natural and manmade objects. 'First study the physical object carefully: its shape, color, size, structural components, etc. If you have selected a paper clip, observe its shiny surface, the thickness of the wire of which it is made, its peculiar shape, and so on.

Then close your eyes and imagine it before yourself in detail. Can you call to mind the exact shape of the paper clip? If not, go back to the physical object again and make further observations, repeating this until you have a clear mental picture of the whole object . . . .'

At the University of Alberta, Canada, Political Science Professor David Kahane teaches Citizenship for Democracy: Bringing Contemplation and Compassion into Community Service Learning. He used mindfulness (*shamatha*) practice to help students explore habitual modes of engaging with injustice and suffering. Students write about their practice in their journals. The weaving together of mindfulness practice with the service learning context as well as the classroom made meditation 'more richly interesting and instructive, as these contexts really challenged us to remain mindful and to notice how quickly activity, conversation, and complexity could draw us away from awareness of the present moment.' He sees the ability of students to experience their own reactions authentically, without judgment, as the ground for learning. 'This is a profound encouragement for students: to be learning, they don't need to become someone else—smarter, calmer, more confident—but to experience what they are experiencing, with openness and kindness, and then to share what they see with others.'

Al Kaszniak teaches psychology at the University of Arizona. In 2010, he taught The Psychology of Empathy and Compassion: Contemplative and Scientific Perspectives, which integrated breath-focused mindful attention, mindful listening, and reflective journaling into the class. The reflective journaling is actually a mindfulness exercise:

- Before reading, do 10 minutes of breath-focused mindful attention.
- Don't think about the reading—try to stay fully attentive to the breath.
- Allow this mindful attitude to remain as you read.
- After the reading and another breath-focused practice of 10 minutes, write no more than one page describing how the reading relates to your personal experience. Be specific.
- Describe anything you noticed about your experience during the reading.

As he proceeds through the semester, teaching about empathy and compassion from the perspective of both contemplative and scientific traditions, he introduces practices relevant to the session: mindful breathing when he teaches about attention, loving-kindness when he overviews the neuroscience of empathy. The final session met in a contemplative garden, where they practiced mindful attention and discussed how natural and built environments relate to the expression or inhibition of empathy and compassion.

At the American University, Paul Wapner is teaching Practical Environment- alism. He taught mindfulness and other contemplative practices to help students deal with the difficulties of environmental political action, where there are few victories in a battle against immense odds. He introduces mindfulness as a way for his students to reduce stress and be more fully in the classroom, to be aware of their intentions for the course. Mindfulness practice also prepares students to discuss 'the inner experience of political engagement.'

Many educators are concerned about the effects of technology and multitasking on their students. At the University of Washington, David Levy uses contemplative practices as a lens to observe and critique information practices, and in particular to investigate problems of information overload, the fragmentation of attention, and the busyness and speed of everyday life. The basic practice of the course is mindfulness: mindful sitting (attention to the breath) and walking (attention to the feet). Students then mindfully observed an information practice like texting or emailing, documented what they observed, and reflected on what they documented. They discovered, for example, that they tended to check email when they were anxious or bored and that reading email only exacerbated their anxiety.

Their practice became:

1. Observe your own patterns of behaviour, bringing attention to body, breath, emotions, etc.
2. Decide which dimensions of your experience you want to cultivate or minimize (clarity of attention, fatigue, anxiety, etc.).
3. Make conscious choices in order to cultivate some states and minimize others.

Allen Stairs engaged the study of mindfulness as subject matter. He taught a course in Multiple Perspectives on Vipassanā Meditation: Experience, Psychology, and Philosophy at the University of Maryland. He taught mindfulness during class sessions and invited a teacher from Insight Meditation community of Washington DC to teach also. The students read papers on the empirical study of meditation and explored connections between mindfulness and philosophical discussions of the 'so-called problem of personal identity,' including the philosopher Derek Parfit, whose work denies that there is an enduring self. They explored the theme that 'however valuable the perspective recommended by mindfulness, it needs to be enriched by understanding the importance of ways of looking at ourselves that *do not* rest in the here and now.' They also discussed whether our tendency to see ourselves in narrative terms makes a genuine contribution to our flourishing even if the narratives are not 'true' at the deeper level of metaphysics.

Light Carruyo, who teaches Sociology, Women's Studies, and Latin American/Latina Studies at Vassar, introduced mindfulness to explore how it could help students confront difficult issues, which inevitably engage students' experience as social and emotional beings. In teaching the course in the past, she had found that disregarding the personal and focusing on the text was 'infinitely more manageable' but limited the extent of the learning, so she was interested in the effects of mindfulness as part of a 'healing form of critical inquiry.' The mindfulness did increase awareness of emotion, and the discussions led to a dialogue between personal transformation and the transformation of the structures of inequality, a critical dialogue that is also alive and well in the civil society activist community.

The Center held three retreats with Joseph Goldstein for Yale Law School students. Although they were off campus and did not include aspects of law curriculum, they led us to appreciate the many ways in which mindfulness could benefit law education, including the themes of listening, the relationship between internal and external conflict, separation and connection, winning and non-winning. In 1999, Professor Len Riskin, then at the University of Missouri-Columbia Law School, based his course, Understanding Conflict, on these themes, integrating mindfulness, readings, and discussions. They discussed how mindfulness could help lawyers stay present with the suffering of clients, develop compassion and patience, and make better decisions. One student wrote, ' I think the most important thing the practice gives us is deliberation. I find I am less likely to jump to conclusions, the way your law professors try to get you to do. It's harder to push my buttons than it was before I started this practice. I'm cooler-headed and likely to see any issue from more angles, which is the key to solving legal problems.'

More recently, at Roger Williams University School of Law, David Zlotnick taught Trial Advocacy: Integrating Mindfulness Theory and Practice. He introduced mindfulness to help students stay in the moment and let go of the illusion of control, in order to improve their confidence and skills. He also exposed them to deeper practices of compassion and connectedness to teach them that there is a way to be a compassionate trial lawyer without losing effectiveness in the courtroom. One interesting practice was this: Students practiced mindfulness of being present. Then, without advance notice, the students had to redo a direct exam while blindfolded, which required them to put aside their notes and listen to the witness. Students found this exercise liberating and helpful. Later, after doing a mindfulness practice that focused on staying present with discomfort and moving through it, they did a simulated trial during which an attorney tried to frustrate the student with repeated objections (which the judge sustained). When the student lawyer began to get angry, a bell was rung with the instruction to try the mindfulness-of-anger practice. Students reported that the practice allowed them to let go of anger and return to the present moment with a clear mind so they could focus on the facts of the case.

Carolyn Jacobs, Dean of the School of Social Work at Smith, has introduced the first contemplative graduate certificate program for clinical social workers. 'Cultivating awareness,' she says, 'is crucial for clinical practice in a complex, global world. The capacity of the clinical social worker to pay attention to the dynamics of the clinical relationship can be enhanced by continuous self-reflection and contemplative practice.' The students learn mindfulness and mindful listening, in which the words of another person become the object of attention.

In most of these courses, the addition of mindfulness seems to illuminate the relevance of the academic disciplines to life outside the classroom. Here is one last example that seems particularly relevant as I write this in 2010. At Amherst College, Daniel Barbezat teaches a course in behavioural economics in which he uses awareness of thought and emotion to teach larger principles of economics. The course description begins with a quote from Ajahn Chah: ' . . . we see that there is actually nothing worth wanting; there is only arising and passing away, a being born followed by a dying. This is when the mind arrives at letting go, letting everything go according to its own nature. ... And this knowing happiness means that we don't identify it as being ours.'

Barbazet first helps students develop one-pointed awareness and then guides them through meditations in which he evokes emotions like regret. He then asks them to explore the feeling of regret and shows how it is part of even small decisions—will I regret taking an umbrella today if it does not rain? How does that factor into my decision to take it or not? How does it factor into decisions about what I buy, from a chocolate bar (will I regret eating it because of the calories or will I regret not eating it because it is so delicious?) to a house? Being aware of arising thoughts and emotions becomes essential to making good economic decisions at every level, or at least to having more choices.

Economist and former head of the Federal Reserve Alan Greenspan recently said that he had made a mistake that led to the economic collapse of 2008, that he had thought people always act in their own self-interest so their behaviour did not need to be regulated. A lot of suffering was generated in the world through this mis-apprehension. Barbezat demonstrates to his students that we cannot know what our self-interest actually is unless we are mindfully self-aware. As we come to see the nature of desire and aversion, we realize that it can obscure wise self-interest. Some actions benefit us greatly in the short-term but harm us or others in the long-term, as happened to many in the economic collapse. True self-awareness also reveals our interconnection with others, so that we understand how our own self-interest is interdependent with the interest of others.

I hope these few examples, of which there are many more, begin to represent this accelerating movement in higher education, which, like mindfulness itself, has the potential for radical transformation. The Association for Contemplative Mind in Higher Education, a part of the Center, is nourishing the work of its 600 members as they explore this terrain. At the very least, these courses raise many questions for both Dharma teachers and secular educators about the introduction of mindfulness in secular settings and in educational settings. Among these are:

The question of meditation experience for the teacher—how much is enough?

The question of academic value. What value does mindful engagement offer to each discipline, both epistemologically and pedagogically? Does it enhance the creative process, deepen students' engagement with the material, or lead to specific insights that would otherwise be unavailable ?

The question of language. This is an issue for any pedagogy, but it can be especially complex for one rooted in a wisdom tradition where value can be implicit. How do we translate this wisdom into the work of higher education?

Language deserves a paper of its own, but a few examples will begin to identify the issue. In studies of contemplative practices in their historical context, as in a Religious Studies course on Buddhism, use of Pali and Sanskrit terms (*satori, śamatha*) with translations is of course appropriate. But in courses in which mindfulness has been introduced as a secular method for more effectively engaging the subject matter, teachers usually look for more accessible terms to define and to introduce practice, often grounded in the history or philosophy of their discipline. An architecture professor might quote C.S. Lewis, who said that a contemplative (or mindfully designed) building is 'larger on the inside than on the outside.' Or Mies van der Rohe, whose famous aphorisms, 'less is more' and 'God is in the details' make the practice of mindfulness seem like it should be a requirement for a degree in architecture. In art history and appreciation, some teachers refer to contemplative seeing, the mindful study of painting and sculpture, as 'beholding,' a familiar English word with connotations of appreciation and care, a way of being in which the senses are concretely engaged. Joanna Ziegler, who taught at Holy Cross College, traces the roots of beholding to philosophers including Plato and Heidegger, who defines true seeing as 'a reverent paying heed to the unconcealment of what presences.' And she also calls on philosophical anthropologist Josef Pieper, who defines contemplation as 'visual perception prompted by loving acceptance.' Michelle Francl in her Chemistry course at Bryn Mawr, uses the phrase 'finding the bones of a problem' to describe a mindfulness exercise. Several science teachers, in teaching mindfulness of sound, call the practice 'listening out' to notice 'the acoustic ecology.' In his Advanced Trial Advocacy course at the Roger Williams School of Law, David Zlotnick called the mindfulness practice for the Cross Examination unit, 'Balancing Effort and Ease.' The practice for the Opening Statements unit (Finding the Story in the Case) he called 'Finding your Feet, Your Breath, and Your Posture.'

The language of neuroscience has introduced another vocabulary for discussing mindfulness in the classroom. Popular discussions of neuroplasticity, the ability of the human brain to change as a result of one's experience, have educated the general and the academic community about the role of disciplined practice in developing cognitive and emotional capacities. So teachers across disciplines refer to this research when discussing the benefits of mindfulness for deeper understanding of their subject matter.

There is the danger, of course, of reducing the full potential of mindful awareness when using more familiar words and phrases, yet another reason for the continual and deepening practice of those who teach it.

The question of instrumentalism. How do we teach students that cultivating mindfulness is likely to have certain beneficial outcomes while helping them to practice in the spirit of open exploration? There is no attainment and there is no non-attainment. Is it alright to give them a goal of academic attainment to motivate them and trust that it will lead to an understanding that the journey is the goal, that there is no place to go other than right where you are?

May the conversation that engages these questions and others be energetic, surprising, and fruitful!

NOTES

1. Jacquelynn Bass, 2005, xiii.
2. Taken from a report on her Contemplative Practice Fellowship written in 2009.

REFERENCES

BAAS, J. 2005. *Smile of the Buddha: Eastern philosophy and western art*. Berkeley: University of California Press.
EPSTEIN, M. 2004. *Thoughts without a thinker*. New York: Basic Books.
GOLEMAN, D. 1995. *Emotional intelligence*. New York: Bantam Books.
LANGER, E. 1997. *The power of mindful learning*. Cambridge, MA: Da Capo Press.
O'REILLY, M. 1998. *Radical presence: Teaching as a contemplative practice*. Portsmouth, NH: Boynton/Cook.
SIEGEL, D. 2007. *The mindful brain*. New York: Norton.
VARELA, F., E. THOMPSON, and E. ROSCH. 1993. *Embodied mind*. Cambridge, MA: MIT Press.
ZAJONC, A. 2010. *Meditation as contemplative inquiry*. Great Barrington, MA: Lindisfarne Books.

'ENJOY YOUR DEATH': LEADERSHIP LESSONS FORGED IN THE CRUCIBLE OF ORGANIZATIONAL DEATH AND REBIRTH INFUSED WITH MINDFULNESS AND MASTERY

Saki F. Santorelli

Leaders working in diverse spheres of societal influence including medicine, healthcare, public health, legal services, education, and business are increasingly interested in the potential role of mindfulness practice for experiencing, appreciating and living their lives more fully at work and at home. The discipline of mindfulness meditation practice may offer leaders an effective means of actualizing in their lives an enhanced ability to know themselves more directly and, also, to learn how to use, in skillful ways, both the routine and extraordinary work-related demands and challenges they face as a means of cultivating latent yet innate human qualities necessary for effective leadership. Based upon direct experience as a leader facing a significant, protracted crisis, the author details his experience of integrating mindfulness practice into his life and leadership-related decision-making.

A task becomes a duty from the moment you suspect it to be an essential part of that integrity which alone entitles a man to assume responsibility.

(Dag Hammarskjöld)

Prologue

In a very real way, perceived through one set of lenses, the story I am about to relate is history; it passed away a very long time ago. And yet, there is something behind this story that might serve us well by examining in finer relief the lived experience of leadership—leadership individually, collectively and organizationally. Leadership informed by meditation practice, mindfulness, and mastery. Before the telling, here is some background information intended to minimize the potential for confusion because of the array of organizations associated with the unfolding events.

In 1998, 19 years after the founding of the Stress Reduction Clinic and three years after the founding of the Center for Mindfulness in Medicine, Health Care, and Society, the University of Massachusetts Medical Center ceased to exist. As the result of a large merger, in its place two separate entities were formed. One entity, UMass Memorial Health Care (UMMHC) became the home to several hospitals and an extended clinical system and the second, The University of Massachusetts Medical School (UMMS) became the home of three schools: The School of Medicine, the Graduate School of Biomedical Sciences and the Graduate School of Nursing. During the early stages of this merger, the Stress Reduction Clinic—what the Center for Mindfulness was most known for and also the largest source of its revenue—was a part of UMMHC (the hospital and clinical system). All the other aspects of the Center (and far smaller revenue sources) including research, academic medical education, professional education and training, and outreach and public service programmes resided within the Medical School.

One final explanatory comment: throughout this article I have subtitled various sections of the text. In most cases, the topic associated with these subtitles is self-evident. However, in two instances, I have used terms from alchemical writings related to the process of transformation. Latin in origin, they are *solve* (dissolve) and *coagule* (coagulate). For growth to arise, disintegration and dissolution are required—individually and organizationally such dissolution brings with it the death of the old (*solve*). Arising out of this dissolution may occur a new reconstruction and consolidation emerging as vision and as a new capacity for emergent possibility, flexibility, and wise relationship and action (*coagule*). Within each of us and within organizations also, this process is repeated endlessly.

1. Solve

In late October 2000, a little more than three months into my tenure as Executive Director of the Center for Mindfulness in Medicine, Health Care, and Society, I received the following email from the hospital administration:

> *In the next 48 hours, we require you to submit a deficit-free budget for the Stress Reduction Clinic budget totalling not more than $173,000.*

At that time, the Stress Reduction Clinic's annual budget was $283,000. In order to comply, I had to reduce the budget by $110,000. To do so, I cut the clinical budget by $40,000 and because the Stress Reduction Clinic was itself nested within the Center for Mindfulness, I was able to meet the full budget reduction demand by shifting an additional $70,000 of the Stress Reduction Clinic budget into the Center's overall operating budget. In response to these changes, I received the following email:

> *In addition to decreasing your budget to $173,000 you will be*
> *required to generate an additional 100% of your overhead costs.*

This meant that the Stress Reduction Clinic would now be required to generate nearly $350,000 in revenues annually—a virtually impossible task.

The protracted merger and burden of mounting debt may have left the newly formed hospital and clinical system with no choice but to cut a host of clinics and programmes. However, virtually overnight, after 21 years of continuous operation, the Stress Reduction Clinic—the clinic of origin of mindfulness-based stress reduction (MBSR)—was eliminated from the clinical system.

This meant no more formalized physician referral system, no more appointment and reminder system for our patients. No more third party insurance coverage, no more dictation and medical records services, no more billing services through the hospital and no more status as a clinic within the greater hospital and clinical system. Without all this, how could we continue to be an exemplar of possibility for colleagues and nascent MBSR clinics all over the world beginning to introduce mindfulness into their patient care, research and medical education programs?

Within the Center for Mindfulness, this larger institutional tremor was seismic, creating an immediate operating budget shortfall of nearly $300,000. Half the staff had to be cut: some were laid off, a few chose to resign, others found new jobs within the larger institution. Those that were laid off or resigned needed to be respected, protected and paid severance for their years of service and unused vacation time. I had both a moral and fiduciary responsibility to make sure the needed funds were available to them. For the Center for Mindfulness, this meant that either closing our doors or remaining open would require a good deal of capital that we did not have.

My colleagues and I seriously deliberated the merits of closing the doors or attempting to move forward. This analysis and reflection proved to be quite valuable. For my part, I felt like we'd achieved much over the course of two decades. The work of the Center had laid the foundation stones of new fields of inquiry and treatment approaches in medicine and healthcare and, in part, through our efforts a secular form of mindfulness practice was beginning to be known about and experienced directly by a large and growing public and scientific community. I came to see that even if we chose to close the doors, what had been accomplished was substantive. Yet, I also firmly believed that there was far more to be explored and accomplished through the vehicle of the Center and I made the decision to forge ahead and attempt to create a new future within UMass. However, with the loss of a home and operating budget for the Stress Reduction Clinic, a significant budget shortfall, and a staff reduced by 50%, there were many barriers and little space in which to move.

In response to the news about the Center's plight, long-time co-workers, colleagues, and friends nearby and from around the country sent along lots of ideas about how we ought to best respond to the situation. On one extreme, they included quietly closing the doors and writing an open letter in the New York Times announcing this decision and thanking our constituents world wide for their generosity and support. On the other side, there was a call to coalese the goodwill and energy of the 12,000 medical patients (and many additional healthcare professionals) we had worked with since 1979 and mount a massive letter writing and telephone call campaign. In addition, they suggested enlisting journalists at the local and regional papers to get the story out and, as well, organize a culminating event—a several day, around the clock silent 'sit' along all the primary walkways on the main Common of the medical center. While dramatic and intriguing, I judged that embarking on any of the latter strategies would further antagonize senior administrators thereby virtually sealing the deal and foreclosing on any possibility of our existence at Umass.

To remain afloat and simultaneously begin anew, the first thing we needed was a new home for the Center. As everything became tighter, darker, and seemingly more impossible to overcome, a thin sliver of space did open. I received an unexpected email from a senior Medical School officer inviting me to come and talk with him about a possible future for the Center that would locate it fully within the aegis of the University of Massachusetts Medical School. Negotiations were already underway for establishing the terms for vacating the hospital and clinical system. With this invitation, negotiations aimed at establishing the entire Center within the Medical School were initiated. It took four months of intense, painstaking deliberation to complete the process. Some days I met with hospital officials about the terms of vacating; other days I met with Medical School officials about the terms of habitating. My Division Chair, Judith Ockene, PhD, M.Ed, in an act of immense generosity and risk-taking, agreed to underwrite our budget should we fall further into debt and be forced to close shop. In early February 2001, having agreed to the final terms of this transition, the gentleman who had the final determination for our fate turned to me and proclaimed unambiguously the *real* terms:

> Maintain your academic and scholarly work, run your
> operation like a business, float your own boat, or you'll
> be out of here.

Real indeed; the terms were strikingly clear and terribly daunting. There were failures and major losses sustained during the previous four months. Yet, we had made one essential gain; we had a toe hold that offered us the space needed to begin moving forward. Hafiz, the fifteenth century poet and Sufi teacher describes our condition and motivation well:

> Be strong, Hafiz.
> Work here, inside time,
> where we fail, catch hold again
> and climb.[1]

Many of my colleagues who made the decision to stay at the Center had to relinquish significant aspects of their benefits and retirement packages in order to meet the insisted upon terms of the transition. Still, in the face of these unbending terms, we had endured the fire; we were alive.

Whatever had us was not yet done with us...

Eight months later an accounting audit was completed by the larger institution resulting in the reckoning of an additional deficit of $200,000 (originally thought to be an operating account surplus from previous years) requiring payback in full. Thus, in the first 12–14 months of my tenure, five years into its founding and 21 years since the formal introduction of mindfulness into mainstream medicine via the Stress Reduction Clinic and its radical approach to patient care and education, the Center faced a financial deficit of nearly $500,000.

Then, 9/11 burst into fullness. Social chaos ensued; uncertainty and fear took front seats in the collective mind of most Americans, the economy tanked. Clinical referrals dried up; clinic revenue diminished by 50%. The demise and inevitable death of the Center as we had known it for the past 21 years lingered unabated for 36 months. The loss of our organizational 'self' was unmistakable; the reality of inseparability and utter undeniability of a single interdependent reality was experientially validated over and over again *everywhere* to be seen and felt.

While this story is neither exceptional nor unique, it is *real*—shot through with the fundamental characteristics of living, including suffering, impermanence, and non-self. Moments strung together like this one have an awesome, uncompromising way of forcing us to see what appears theoretical or distant as actuality; it all gets close up and evident, vibrantly real and inescapable if we give ourselves over to the *turning towards* rather than away from what is before us.

Ubiquitously permeating this entire unfolding saga was what is sometimes refered to as the 'fourth' characteristic of living—the quality of nowness. *Nowness* in all its palpable, persistent, undeniable wildness played centrally in the unfolding of this story, as there were always multiple and often rivalling perspectives to be ascertained and understood *now* ... branchpoints of possibility turned towards or walked away from *now* ... strong emotions and mind waves felt, seen, and often enough, caught up in or seen through *now* ....decisions affecting the lives and livelihoods of my colleagues, hundreds of medical patients, and thousands of professional colleagues around the world weighed and acted upon *now*.

These were life and death moments; the challenges of leadership were relentless and unremitting. I have chosen to report this story to you in the context of this special issue of *Contemporary Buddhism* because the events as described and those that I will detail more fully raise important and highly relevant issues about mindfulness and its potential role in training the mind and heart as an essential element of the cultivation and development of leaders and leadership.

However, before doing so, I want to make it absolutely clear that while I was the director of both the Stress Reduction Clinic and the Center for Mindfulness and, therefore, the leader and point person for all that I have and will describe, several of my colleagues were also key leaders in this process. Indeed, it was my responsibility to communicate, negotiate and make final decisions. Yet, the leadership was *shared*; it was disbursed among many of us. We were each responsible and fully accountable to ourselves, to one another, and as well, to the larger institutional community in which we were nested. This seems to me to be one of the most salient aspects of leadership infused with mindfulness—the recognition that we are each accountable to ourselves for our own lives and actions ('Be a light unto yourself'). And, equally so, in the spirit of democracy and shared vision, to one another as we attempt to forge a sense of collective organizational ownership, clarity and purpose expressive of our commitment to a universal sense of accountability and responsibility.

Among the Center leaders, my colleague, Larry Horwitz, was particularly invaluable through both the long period of crisis and the gradual transition into a more robust, programmatically rich, and fiscally sound Center for Mindfulness. For a long time, I have likened Larry's role at the Center to *Fudo*—the great protector of the Dharma described as the 'unmoving, immovable, imperturbable guardian.' My trusted colleagues and companions, Florence Meleo-Meyer and Melissa Blacker, were resolute in their commitment to staying the course, creating new programmatic possibilities in the midst of the falling apart and embracing with great understanding and open-hearted acceptance the cascades of mind waves and emotions that visited us as we walked this long journey that, at moments, felt like hell and at other moments like paradise. Similarly, Jean Baril, the Center's business manager, was a strong and much needed pillar while facing, on a daily basis, dismal spreadsheets and the understandable waves of anxiety about the future emminating from the administrative staff she was charged with supervising and supporting.

> Now, back to the story....
> I did not want this to happen on 'my watch'....
> It was happening on my watch.
> I felt like it was all falling apart....
> It was all falling apart.

When the events described first transpired, I felt like I had been ambushed. I got upset, indignant, depressed and then angry. I wrote emails, scheduled meetings with hospital officials, appealed to my staunchest medical center allies and to my Division and Department Chairs. In the end, none of this made a whit of difference in regards to the ultimate outcome. Undone and carried by the sustained gravitational pull of such moments, the Spanish poet, Antonio Machado, recognized our deep seated fear of 'going down.'

As an entity or organization, we were 'going down.' Amidst all the dissolution and dying, I believe to this day that until I saw clearly just how impersonal the entire affair was, I had no real clarity of mind and heart by which to meet this situation fully and attempt to go forward.

In the four months between my stepping into the role of Executive Director and the reception of that first email from the hospital administration about our clinic budget, I had not yet decorated my office. There was just so much to attend to; the learning curve was steep. Quite uncharacteristic of me, I simply didn't make the time to create a comfortable workspace. My colleagues used to laugh about it or in bewilderment shake their heads and say, "Saki, when are you going to move in? Aren't you going to move in?" Soon after the crisis hit, a poem by Rumi made its way into my life; it is entitled, *Ali in Battle*. For me, this was an absolutely fitting poem for the situation. I taped it to the wall I faced every day as I sat at my desk. The only object on my office walls, it remained there for the next 24 months.

Learn from Ali how to fight
without your ego participating.
God's Lion did nothing
that didn't originate
from his deep center.

Once in battle he got the best of a certain knight
and quickly drew his sword. The man,
helpless on the ground, spat,
in Ali's face. Ali dropped his sword,
relaxed, and helped the man to his feet.

'Why have you spared me?
How has lightening contracted back
into its cloud? Speak, my prince,
so that my soul can begin to stir
in me like an embryo.'

Ali was quiet and then finally answered,
'I am God's Lion, not the lion of passion.
The sun is my lord. I have no longing
except for the One.

When a wind of personal reaction comes,
I do not go along with it.
There are many winds full of anger,
and lust, and greed. They move the rubbish
around, but the solid mountains of our true nature
stays where it's always been.

There's nothing now
except the divine qualities.
Come through the opening into me.

Your impudence was better than any reverence,
because in this moment I am you and you are me.
I give you this opened heart as God gives gifts:
The poison of your spit has become
the honey of friendship.'[2]

To me, this is a poem expressing the core of mindfulness, mastery and leadership. It is about stopping in the heat of easily blinding momentum, about refraining from the forces of conditioning, about anchoring oneself in a deep sobriety in the throes of intoxicating circumstances, about making decisions and choosing actions arising out of intrinsic sovereignty and nobility, about fundamental respect for the 'other,' about conciliation and humility, about non-duality and the dissolution of the conventional boundary of self and other and the blossoming of compassion emerging from such seeing, about honouring our innate capacity for residing in the raw, open heart and remembering the true source of wisdom and power.

It was the only office décor that I needed or wanted . . . .

2. Coagulate

In the prolonged battle to keep the doors of the Center open, I needed to remind myself daily, often many times a day, that the decisions that had created this situation were *impersonal* and that they were *workable*. They were not about me and that I did not have any rights of entitlement because of the previous contributions of the Clinic or my past contributions to the medical center. And most importantly, that I had deep internal resources to draw upon in my interactions with everyone. I can tell you this—until I realized this in my heart and mind, body and soul, incontrovertibly, I was caught and therefore, ineffective. When I realized that the situation was completely impersonal, I mean absolutely impersonal, the whole situation became a lot more workable because it was no longer about me; success and failure were no longer at stake. I was free to act.

More so, what was transpiring within me behind all the appearances of the Center 'going down' was the emergence of a deep sense of having been *entrusted* with something precious; something that was well worth expending enormous amounts of energy for. Something that was much larger than me. Something that had a chance of continuing to benefit the world enormously if I attended to it carefully and wisely with my colleagues and our communities of resonance and support locally and all over the planet.

Daily, this vision grows stronger in me. Everyday I pray that I am able to carry, nourish and sustain well what has been entrusted to me. What dawned in me was the realization that the essence of good leadership is dharma—dharma in its essential meaning as *duty*.[3] Perhaps the recognition of universal responsibility *is* the duty of all leaders. Dharma is also a path, a way for human beings to learn to connect with and embody a vaster awareness—a direct, experientially verifiable recognition of reality itself—the boundlessness of the universe animated and made palpable in each one of us. Seen more vastly, it is a means of freeing us from the imprisoning shackles of separation by providing us a means of learning to attune to and seek guidance from the great chain of wise and compassionate beings that have come before us. Tinged with mystery and available to everyone, is this not the reality of the Dharma in all its universality offered to every one of us when, quietly and deliberately, we begin to take responsibility for the whole world each in our own way? None other than the bodhisattva vow made real and compelling because it has arisen out of an intention to courageously meet and positively affect the nitty-gritty affairs of everyday existence.

In the middle of all this dying there was a simultaneous dawning. We were very much alive. We showed up everyday. We laughed. We worked hard and increasingly wisely. We reestablished the Stress Reduction Program in a new location (a little used employee cafeteria) and forged ahead with our research, professional education and medical student programmes. As the first three years of this hard labour wore on, some of my dear and long-standing colleagues who had initially stayed on generously volunteered to leave because they perceived so clearly our financial struggles. Others left because the unwanted yet necessary changes in their job responsibilities were not to their liking. We created a new strategic plan. We asked for help from our patients, professional colleagues and benefactors.

Six months after the first dire audit, the hospital reported to us the discovery of $183,000 of Center funds that had been encumbered during some of the previous fiscal years and not returned to our operating account after we departed the hospital system. Subtracting $183,000 from $480,000 left a deficit of $297,000. Combined with the required lay-offs, the organizational right sizing enacted, and the momentum we had been gathering in tiny increments, climbing out of this pile of debt seemed downright doable. In three years we were free and clear of all debt. More than 80% of the funds required to return to a balanced budget came directly from our programmatic efforts. The remaining came from gifts and donations by friends of the Center. Forged in the crucible of organizational death and rebirth, this accomplishment altered the consciousness of the Center markedly and to this day. We are one example of a vibrant community that arose *in* disaster. [4]

3. The spirit of mastery

In the title of this article I have used the terms 'mindfulness' and 'mastery.' I would like to say something about the latter. Mastery is the deliberate cultivation of inner strength to meet life's continuous challenges. This involves using attainment itself—the objects of attainment and the deliberate renunciation of these objects once attained—as a path of liberation.

Self-discipline, motivation, concentration, patience, endurance, perseverance, will, power, responsibility, and the sense of duty are all cultivated and used in service of learning to *give* rather than take from the world. It is absolutely clear to me that mindfulness and mastery go hand in hand in the cultivation of leadership. Mindfulness meditation is an exquisite technology for cultivating and refining our innate, latent resources for leadership. For most of us living in today's world, it is an inward process completed and made manifest by meeting and mastering the challenges of everyday life.

In all walks of life it will be proved to the seeker after truth that
there is a key to success, a key to happiness, a key to advancement
and evolution in life; and this key is the attainment of mastery...
One must check the wrong impulses, even as small as the thought of eating
something that one likes, the wish to drink something that one wishes, an
impulse to talk back to a person who insults, an impulse to pinch a person by
saying a word, an impulse to hurt a person by
cutting words, an impulse to get into the secrets of others, the impulse
to criticize. All such undesirable impulses can be mastered. And it is
not that one has mastered them, but one has gained control over
oneself.[5]

My own experience suggests that mastery in its more outward and worldly manifestation is not readily spoken about in regards to meditation and mindfulness practice. I have often wondered why this is so. Perhaps it is because mastery seems to be associated with the aggressive exercise of the will—a kind of striving aimed at dominance of mind over body and other forms of repression and subjugation. Rather, in my experience, mastery is about freedom from habit, the subsequent realization of choice and the realization that mindfulness is not confined to specialized situations or circumstances. Additionally, it seems to me that choice always involves control of oneself. Yet, often enough, control seems to be an aversive word in the Dharma community even as control is expressing itself constantly in our lives as refraining, advancing, yielding, as exercising or withholding power, as surrendering, as conciliation, as forthrightness, as goal setting and attainment, as responsibility, and ultimately as the embodiment of intrinsic freedom. It is the place where the proverbial 'rubber meets the road,' none other than meditation in action.

Inwardly speaking, via meditation practice, mastery is cultivated through attending to thoughts, emotions and physical sensations as events in the field of awareness—by allowing these events to arise, be seen, honoured for what they are, and eventually dissipate or dissolve rather than dominating the mind. The process extends and is amplified as we become intimately familiar with our habitual patterns of thinking and acting, and discovering through this familiarization process that we have more choice than we may have previously imagined. It ripens as we recognize that we have our hands on the proverbial tiller and can use all of our interior resources to take our lives into our own hands via the systematic training of the mind and heart. In my experience, this process is enhanced when we begin to turn towards outer circumstances and events with this same inwardly developed approach, perspective, and trained heart-mind. Together, the training of the mind and the cultivation of the heart through meditation and mindfulness coupled with our commitment to meet the outer circumstances of our lives with these same innate qualities and resources (mastery) creates a synergy that may be more powerful than either modality by itself.

My own training has been primarily in the Sufi and Buddhist traditions. I have been a formal student in the western Vipassanā tradition for 27 years and a student of Sufism for 36 years. My primary Sufi teacher, Pir Vilayat Inayat Khan, sent me to my first Buddhist retreat. The Sufi tradition has a deep, extensive and well-developed body of teachings about meditation, mindfulness, and contemplative practice. There are four main orders and from these four have proliferated a wide array of other orders and lineages. Yet, and importantly so in the context of this article, there are no formal monastic orders. Likewise, there is a long and arduous retreat tradition. Yet, relatively permanent withdrawal from the world is not the primary emphasis. In most instances, both teachers and students marry, have children, and establish businesses and professions. Thus, the inward *and* outward cultivation of mindfulness and mastery 'in service of the real' holds a place of critical importance in the life of the Sufi. As a student in this tradition, I have had the good fortune to be exposed to and systematically explore and study these teachings in depth and over an extended period of time. *Mastery Through Accomplishment* (Khan, 1985), written by Pir-O-Murshid Hazrat Inayat Khan in the 1920s (the first Sufi teacher to come to the West), is a beginning primer for this body of teachings.

Mastery is cultivated and nurtured through the friction arising out of inner practice *meeting* the outward circumstances of our lives. It is this meeting point that affords us the possibility of mindfulness being made real and therefore of great and lasting value in our lives, relationships and work in the world. In my experience, accomplishment and attainment are valuable opportunities for making meditation practice useful because the circumstances, issues, and responsibilities we face daily challenge us to consolidate and actualize latent qualities and attributes directly into our lives. It seems to me that the real challenge before us in our current age is to live a life in the world infused by the depth and breadth of the inner life:

> It is not necessary for man to leave all the things of the world and go into retreat. He can attend to his business, to his profession; to his duties in life yet at the same time develop this spirit in himself, which is the spirit of mastery. The spirit of mastery is like a spark; by blowing continually upon it it will grow into a blaze, and out of it a flame will arise. In reality all is within.[6]

4. Leadership

Now, let us turn our attention more directly to the relationship between mindfulness, mastery and leadership. I will begin by posing a question that I posed to myself when I began thinking about the topic for this special issue.

> As a leader facing a significant, protracted crisis, in what ways, if any, was the practice of mindfulness useful in informing and guiding my actions, decisions, and leadership?

The usual list of characteristics found in books about leaders include such attributes as visionary, influencer, role model, powerful, responsible, inspirational, charismatic, dependable, and unselfish. These are worthwhile and valuable attributes of leaders. Yet, for many of the fine leaders that I have met over the years, there is an abiding sense that leaders and leadership are not necessarily the same. Leaders lead; they set goals, make decisions, meet their benchmarks, support, nurture and advance those they lead as well as their organizations. For these same leaders, *leadership* resides in a wider perspective—a view that is global, grounded in the recognition of connectedness and a sense of what they describe as 'universal accountability.' This is heartening and hopefully counters in some small measure our stereotypical view of the concerns and attitudes of corporate leaders.

In the following section, I would like to offer another perspective on the characteristics of leadership by describing qualities that might, in fact, be foundational attributes for many of those referenced above. In this final section, I have attempted to identify five human qualities encouraged by the interior work of mindfulness practice and how they were strengthened and made more solid and available to me in my day-to-day experience of leadership. As you will see, I have paired attributes as a means of effectively identifying both the dissolution (*solve*) and integration (*coagule*) phases of their development and expression. Neither definitive nor exhaustive, I have attempted to describe only what I have lived through.

Falling and intimacy

Learning to fall is a highly underrated skill. When I was a young boy living in Japan I studied Jujitsu. During the entire first year of weekly classes my teacher kept throwing me over his hip, teaching me how to fall. Mostly, this was all that happened.

Through the prolonged crisis I have detailed, I learned over and over again that 'the fear of going down' is far more terrifying than the actuality of 'going down.' The skillfulness by which mindfulness practices teaches us how to be thrown and undone over and over again—and to go along with it voluntarily and purposefully without exerting our conditioned, habitual patterns of control—afforded me the real possibility of being awake in hell as well as a lot of other situations.

In the situation I have recounted, my colleagues and I lost the comfort of history. We lost our status. We lost our place. What could not happen to us actually *did* happen. We disintegrated and dissolved. In the larger community of the medical center, often enough, we were seen as irresponsible or as victims. Even some of our closest colleagues accused us of giving up on or compromising 'the vision' when we altered the original structure of the Clinic as a means of accommodating a range of new financial and operational realities, developing a new strategic plan and initiating a new business model.

Falling gave me a fresh and far deeper appreciation of *intimacy*—intimacy with the texture of failure, the consistency of dissolution, the feel of humiliation, the rough surface of shame and the heat of disintegration. It softened and helped me begin to appreciate and feel more directly the anxiety and uncertainty of my co-workers. This made me a more compassionate leader. I came to see that by allowing myself to closely touch all that was arising within me, I began to develop a deeper appreciation for my own struggles and those of my patients and colleagues. This informed and enhanced my ability to stop, to listen more closely and more fully to my larger institutional colleagues, particularly the ones I came to understand had acted in their own perceived best interests and those of their departments as they attempted to minimize the damage and stave off the looming uncertainty of the merger.

Surrender and sovereignty

In my experience, the capacity to surrender is tremendously powerful. This has nothing to do with resignation, abdication, or giving up. It has everything to do with seeing situations clearly, exactly as they are. It has to do with realizing deep in our bellies and bones that there are moments in our lives when any move is the wrong move, that it is time to *yield* to reality. I know well that allowing the sense of weakness and vulnerability to be present in all its vividness is often a great and hidden source of strength.

> The soft overcomes the hard;
> the gentle overcomes the rigid.
> Everyone knows this is true,
> but few can put it into practice.[7]

Surrendering to the impersonal nature of the events that had transpired, to the perceived sense of hypocrisy or lack of understanding on the part of others about the work of the Clinic and Center that I felt early on in the process, and to the perceived injustice about the situation that I was carrying within me was hard practice. There was a lot of seeing things clearly required and a great deal of letting go asked of me. I had to surrender history and, more so, I had to give up timidity and naïveté. These mind states and attitudes were too safe, too easily taken advantage of and, most importantly, a misrepresentation of what I knew inwardly to be true. As a consequence, I surrendered to having to act: to openly expressing the actuality of my experience, to stating what I saw as so in the presence of people who had the power to exercise their authority in ways that could close our doors. It seemed like everything had to go. I had to surrender all that hindered my giving voice to the lion's roar growing stronger and more uncompromising within me.

Through this process I came to understand more directly and fully the nuanced relationship between surrender and sovereignty. The surrendering I am pointing to is not about surrendering to the will of others in hopes of getting what I wanted. Nor was it a going along with something that fell below my ideals or sense of a clear conscience. By learning to repeatedly surrender my conditioning and small mindedness, I was learning to surrender to the truth, to what was deepest, most functional and indomitable within me. My experience suggests that this larger view of the function of surrender—as a wearing away of the purely personal concerns of self—may be the real source of vision and inspiration, integrity and nobility. As far as I can tell, there seems to be no end to this process. Surrendering and the challenges sometimes associated with this just keep happening over and over again.

Conciliation and wisdom

During the four months of deliberations and negotiations with hospital and medical school officials, my primary aim was to come to an agreement that both parties could live with well. This did not entail giving up principles or positions I believed in or that I deemed best for the Center. It did involve understanding the 'other' far more closely and, in turn, attempting to reside in some broader view of the issues before us that we could agree upon.

One day, deep into the negotiating process, the Center's business administrator and I were scheduled to meet with the man who was ultimately going to decide our fate. The meeting was scheduled to take place in a small conference room next to his office. In private, this administrator strenuously insisted to me that I sit at the head of the table directly opposite this gentleman. I disagreed and instead deliberately sat to his left. I wanted to have to turn towards him, not to 'face off' with him in any way. After the meeting, she was incredibly upset with me. She said that, in her view, my choice of seating had seriously jeopardized the Center's position and hopes of making our way into the medical school. She told me that she knew this man well and that 'He only respected men who challenged him and who he perceived as his equal.' I responded by saying that I had no intention or desire to go 'man to man' with him. As I saw it, something else was called for in our relationship at that moment. I am quite familiar with the value of friction and persistent dialogue and debate around points of difference. However, in this situation I was not going for differences; I was going for understanding and agreement.

Together, he and I looked carefully at documents during this meeting. Seated as we were, we were leaning close to one another, at times our heads were nearly touching; our hands were in close proximity sometimes resting together on the same document. No doubt, on one level there was a clear power differential between us but I was going for agreement, not for defiance. I needed him to understand the potential for the Center to grow and be of benefit to the Medical School, scientifically, programmatically and financially. I remember him stopping at one point while closely examining our proposed business model and forcefully challenging a key yet politically contentious component of our proposal: 'With this new business model, why do you need the Stress Reduction Program any longer?' Being so close, I was able to speak very deliberately and very quietly to him, 'Because it is the heart of our work, the interface of our research and our professional education and training programs.' He responded immediately, 'Oh, it's your laboratory. Okay. I see.' My sense is that this was the turning point of the entire four month process. I am pretty sure that sitting directly opposite from him would not have produced the same result. Of course, one never knows.

In my experience, the quality of conciliation is under-appreciated and, as a consequence, it is not systematically nurtured and cultivated. Yet, looking at my life, I see that it is a foundational source of understanding because it allows me to more thoroughly consider the viewpoints and perspectives, emotions and ideas of others. This does not mean that I have to always agree with or consistently yield to the viewpoints of others but it does help me to meet people where they are and begin to understand them. For me, this process begins at home, in my interior. By learning to meet and befriend myself through mindfulness practice, I am learning to make room within myself for whatever arises, whether I like it or not. This itself is an act of hospitality, an expression of a basic warmth and friendliness that, in turn, begins to flow out into my relationships with others. As such, it is the basis of understanding and therefore the foundation of wisdom. In turn, the increasing sense of understanding of self and others seems to me to be a central wellspring of self-confidence—a requisite quality for all leaders. Increasingly, I notice that it is not possible for me to be conciliatory and defensive—or dismissive of another (even in thought)—at the same time. Because conciliation it is by nature respectful, it helps me get along with people. It makes me humble and allows me to accommodate difference and diversity because I can rest more easily and fully in my interior sense of 'bigness' and capacity to accommodate and consider diverse views more readily.

Standing inside of things and sustained concentration

While there were aspects of this described crisis that required decision making on a daily basis, the capacity to learn how to stand inside of and 'hold' tension for long stretches of time without acting prematurely became one of my greatest allies. This capacity is continually cultivated and sharpened by mindfulness practice and also by working inside a large institution where everything takes time and has to pass through many minds and hands. This aspect of mindfulness practice is not simply learning to 'tolerate'conditions (we have all had a lot of training in this). Rather, it is about recovering or re-learning freshly and then residing for a time in the 'not knowing' and in the willingness to stay put until the right decision or action emerges into awareness.

As I have described above, the negotiation process with the hospital and medical school lasted for four months. However, the final decision about the fate of the Center did not come until very late in the game. For well more than 100 days we had no clear idea about what the final outcome would be. All of this time, we collectively stood inside of uncertainty and not knowing. Still, we came to work everyday, continued many of our planned programmes and activities, watched some of our colleagues depart, faced the webs of our individual and collective minds, and continued to negotiate. Here's what I learned: mental fabrications about the way things used to be (past), how they might be or we wanted them to be (future), are crippling; they drain off enormous amounts of much needed energy and in the process cut off the flow of creativity. More so, in the turbulence of these 'mind waves' the present moment is either unnoticed or, when noticed, nearly intolerable. As I learned to live more lightly in the tension, uncertainty about the future became less paralysing. Likewise, it was no longer an excuse for inaction. As a result, we planned, executed when and where we were able, and developed an enhanced appreciation for the process of emergence.

Nonetheless, the cultivation of patience was and remains a very challenging and difficult practice; it has a lot to do with endurance and the development of a long view with regards to the attainment of a goal or ideal. Described as 'one of the wings to the power of concentration' in the Sufi teachings on mastery (Khan 1962), patience is a critical capacity for leaders who are constantly called upon to develop, direct and sustain unwavering concentration on an object often for long periods of time. The capacity to sustain concentration and remain intently focused is supported and nurtured by patience and is one of the ways that single-mindedness and the capacity for a more focused attention is developed through our everyday affairs.

Emptying of self and innovation

There was something transpiring behind the appearance of dissolution and death. The disintegration of our individual and collective identities was confusing, wrenching, crushing, and ultimately, freeing. There was a time when there was no real direction, no real place to turn and gather advice from. It all stopped us cold. We endured 100 days of not knowing our fate and even after the momentary relief of knowing that we had a place within the medical school, we faced three years of debt and sustained financial uncertainty. All of this forced us to halt, *feel* the situation as fully as possible and the unhinging of the past. We were emptied out. We knew it. Through the dying, my colleagues and I came to life.

We became bold; we began to shape a future that surely had the seeds from the past but that required a new garden in which to nourish the old while planting new seeds and new visions. I discovered that I loved the entrepreneurial spirit required to '*Maintain your academic and scholarly work, run your operation like a business and float our own boat.*' The root meaning of entrepreneur is from the French *entreprende*—to undertake. I loved the feeling of 'undertaking' and shaping something fresh, vital and, hopefully, of greater service to the world. While initially daunting, this mandate was and remains perfectly matched to the innovative and entrepreneurial spirit that has permeated the Clinic and Center for three decades. Being so, it offers my colleagues and I the freedom to be boldly innovative by developing and implementing programmes and initiatives, partnerships, policies and economies that reflected our deepest values. Without hesitation, whether or not I have achieved any success, I can say that I began to discover what Warren Buffet has embodied so fully in his own life:

> You've achieved success in your field when you don't know whether
> what you're doing is work or play.

In summary, my experience strongly suggests that the heat forged in the crucible of this crisis, coupled with my experience of leading the Center for Mindfulness over the last 10 years furthered within me the unfolding of a range of human qualities and attributes generally associated with meditation and mindfulness training. Likewise, it unlocked dormant possibilities that may not have as readily come to the fore and been available within me without the friction and heat arising from these life events. Reflecting upon this, I would have to say that former United Nations Secretary General, Dag Hammarskjold, had a keen insight when he said,

> In our era, the road to holiness necessarily passes through the world of action.

5. Mindfulness practice in contemporary contexts

I have attempted to describe and make more real some small aspect of the interior work of meditation and mindfulness practice and the outer circumstances in which we find ourselves as a fertile ground for the cultivation of leadership. While a topic for another article, likewise, and in parallel, I'd like to suggest that our current conception of practice or Dharma centres might also be in need of a wider view. By example, The Center for Mindfulness in Medicine, Health Care, and Society is a practice centre in the fullest sense of the word. Yet, unlike traditional practice centres, its context bears a very close resemblance to Jonah residing in the belly of the whale. For 31 years, the life and work of the Center as been purposefully *embedded* in a mainstream academic medical centre. Being *inside*, it is subject to all the rules and requirements of medicine and science and patient care, to all the rules, procedural and legal, of a large institution—an institution that is itself nested within a larger University system, that is itself nested within the State of Massachusetts. Therefore, by its very nature and location, the Center stands in two worlds simultaneouly.

Through these years, we have used this unique position as a laboratory—an experimental ground for testing ways to remain absolutely and unequivocally true to the foundational roots of the work while interfacing with and living fully in the world of people not particularly interested in traditional practice centres. Given the state of the world, such 'vehicles' may be well worth contemplating and encouraging. While saddled with their own set of constraints and procedures, working within a large, mainstream institution creates a friction that, if used wisely, can provide an incredibly rich ground in which to realize first-hand the interconnectedness of the world, and to develop a host of approaches and methods that express the potential of the trained mind and cultivated heart. Freed from the cultural constraints, familiar jargon and underlying assumptions of traditional centers for contemplative practice, no matter what their persuasion, such institutional environments force one to skillfully translate, transmit and embody, in a secular manner, the essential reality of interconnectedness, mind-heart training, wholesome ethics and economies and universal responsibility in a manner that is non-alienating and inclusive, welcoming and highly participatory. Given the state of the world, attempts to forge such laboratories should be encouraged, supported and analysed with regards to their accessibility and effectiveness.

As I began one of my earliest long retreats, the parting words of my teacher were, 'Enjoy your death.' He said it with such clear-eyed knowing and genuine care for me. Within the context of that secluded retreat, I discovered the truth of his words. Through the events described, I have lived into the everyday reality of the abiding wisdom in these words *outside* of the practice hall and retreat setting. Of what value might the invitation to *enjoy your death* be for those of us called to lead? What if behind all the doing, decision making and executing, we come to realize in our bellies and bones the power of dissolution and disintegration to reshape in fundamental ways our conditioned ways of perceiving, thinking, and acting? What if we purposefully lent ourselves to these recurring cycles of disintegration and reintegration? What might we learn by allowing our hard held views, opinions and ideas about the way things are to unravel, melt, and dissolve? What might we see and envision freshly? What might happen if, behind all the 'leading,' we reckoned with the possibility that we are being *led*?

Attending to what these questions are pointing to asks much of us. Learning to stop, listening closely, understanding situations and making wise choices and decisions all require us to become increasingly intimate with our interior. Perhaps our real work is to learn to lead from the *inside* out by exploring and understanding, first-hand, our inner terrain and in so doing come to realize that, like any other human capacity, the attributes and qualities needed for effective leadership are innate and, therefore, capable of being called forth and integrated, via the discipline of mindfulness, into everyday life at work and at home.

NOTES

1. Last stanza of 'The Substance You Taste' from *The Hand of Poetry* (Khan, 1993).
2. Coleman and Moyne (1995, Poems in chapter 20).
3. For a more detailed discussion of 'duty is Dharma' see Khan (1962, Vol. I, chap. VII, 'The Purpose of Life', 213–17).
4. For an historical account of community transformation arising *in* disasters see Solnit (2009).
5. Khan (1978, see Chapter 3: 'Man, the Master of His Destiny: Training and Mastery').
6. Khan (1978).
7. Mitchell (1988, chapter 36), translation by Stephen Mitchell.

REFERENCES

BARKS, COLEMAN, with JOHN MOYNE. 1995. *The essential Rumi*. New York: Harper Collins Publishers.

KHAN, HAZRAT INAYAT. 1962. *The sufi message of Hazrat Inayat Khan*. Vol. I and VIII. London: Barrie and Jenkins Khan.

KHAN, HAZRAT INAYAT. 1985. *Mastery through accomplishment*. New York: Omega Press.

KHAN, HAZRAT INAYAT. 1993. *The hand of poetry: Five mystic poets of Persia*. Translation by Cleman Barks New York: Omega Publications.

KHAN, VILAYAT INAYAT. 1978. *The message in our time*. New York: Harper & Row.

MACHADO, ANTONIO. 1983. *Times alone: Selected poems of Antonio Machado*. Translations by Robert Bly. Connecticut: Weslyan University Press.

MITCHELL, STEPHEN. 1988. *Tao Te Ching*. New York: Harper & Row.

SOLNIT, REBECCA. 2009. *A paradise built in hell*. New York: Viking Press.

MINDFULNESS, BY ANY OTHER NAME...: TRIALS AND TRIBULATIONS OF *SATI* IN WESTERN PSYCHOLOGY AND SCIENCE

Paul Grossman and Nicholas T. Van Dam

The Buddhist construct of mindfulness is a central element of mindfulness-based interventions and derives from a systematic phenomenological programme developed over several millennia to investigate subjective experience. Enthusiasm for 'mindfulness' in Western psychological and other science has resulted in proliferation of definitions, operationalizations and self-report inventories that purport to measure mindful awareness as a trait. This paper addresses a number of seemingly intractable issues regarding current attempts to characterize mindfulness and also highlights a number of vulnerabilities in this domain that may lead to denaturing, distortion, dilution or reification of Buddhist constructs related to mindfulness. Enriching positivist Western psychological paradigms with a detailed and complex Buddhist phenomenology of the mind may require greater study and long-term direct practice of insight meditation than is currently common among psychologists and other scientists. Pursuit of such an approach would seem a necessary precondition for attempts to characterize and quantify mindfulness.

Defining mindfulness

Foreground

Mindfulness is the 'heart' of the Buddha's teachings (Hanh 1998) and is the core of, and namesake to, a class of intervention aimed at alleviating common forms of suffering—Mindfulness-Based Interventions (MBI's; originally, Mindfulness-based Stress Reduction [MBSR], Kabat-Zinn 1990; later Mindfulness-Based Cognitive Therapy [MBCT], Segal, Williams and Teasdale 2002; and other related programmes). Among Buddhist scholars and Western scientists, both separately and communally, there is a lack of agreement about the specific definition of mindfulnesss (Baer 2011; Dreyfus 2008; Gethin 1998; Grossman 2008). However, a common basis of understanding exists among Buddhist scholars, although interpretations and descriptions of mindfulness range in emphasis. Some, for example, accentuate aspects of attention, whereas others more explicitly acknowledge the complex and dynamic interplay of numerous factors including the cognitive, emotional, social and ethical.

Mindfulness within Western psychology is generally assumed to reflect the Buddhist construct. However, definitions of the term vary greatly from that of a simple therapeutic or experiential technique (Hayes and Plumb 2007) to a multi-faceted activity, which requires practice and refinement (Grossman 2010). Certainly, a more elaborated definition appears to have greater support from contemplative texts (Dreyfus 2008), modern explanations of consciousness (Thompson 2007), and the functioning of the nervous system (Thompson and Varela 2001; Varela et al. 1991).

When attempts are made to integrate its traditional roots with modern theories of consciousness and psychological function, mindfulness is also promoted in the West as part of a broad set of practices embedded in a transitional path away from ordinary modes of everyday functioning (Grossman 2010; Hanh 1998; Kabat-Zinn 2005). It is within the context of this transitional path, which includes affective, behavioural, cognitive, ethical, social and other dimensions, that mindfulness is believed to contribute to the promotion of wellbeing and amelioration of suffering. Given this contextual complexity, it may be difficult, if not impossible, to separate mindfulness from the other components woven together into the fabric of this transitional path. Conventional scientific methods may not easily lend themselves to a refined exploration of mindfulness. As Christopher and Gilbert (2007) wrote, based on the writings of the Thai monk and teacher Buddhadāsa Bhikkhu (1988) wrote: 'Western psychology mandates that constructs must be explicated and operationalized to be accurately assessed. However, most Buddhist traditions dictate that mindfulness cannot be easily extracted and analyzed in isolation from inherently interrelated concepts.' If this is true, scientists need to embrace new approaches for studying mindfulness, and merely linear, additive models that sum putative markers related to mindfulness will not suffice. Thus, attempts to delineate discrete components of mindfulness (for examples, see the three-factor model of Buchheld, Grossman and Walach 2001; or the five-facet model of Baer et al. 2006) are not likely capture the inherent interrelationships mentioned by Christopher and Gilbert (2007), seen as synergistic and mutually reinforcing.

We examine here current trends in empirical mindfulness research, confining our discussion to a few limited, but, to our minds, crucial questions, namely: (1) how do psychologists and other scientists currently characterize mindfulness; (2) are these characterizations compatible with original Buddhist teachings about mindfulness; and (3) do scientific characterizations of mindfulness meet the empirical standards of contemporary scientific methodology?

Denotations and connotations of mindfulness

'Mindfulness' is the translation of the Pali term *sati*, which also conveys the meaning 'to remember,' possibly as to remember to maintain awareness (Batchelor 1997). The term *sati* is, perhaps, best translated 'to be mindful,' in stark contrast to the use of the word 'mindfulness,' which is, of course, a noun and easily implies a fixed trait. Simple as this distinction may seem, it may have substantial implications for conceptualizations of the term *mindfulness*.

Buddhist texts primarily refer to mindfulness not as a mental function or trait (see early translated texts: Bodhi 2000; Ñāṇamoli and Bodhi 2001), but as a *practice* or process involving at least four distinct phases, as mentioned in the *Satipaṭṭhāna Sutta* (one of the oldest Buddhist discourses on mindfulness), ranging from mindfulness of bodily sensations to awareness of more expansive mental content and processes, such as emotion and altered view of self (Ñāṇamoli and Bodhi 2001). It connotes several features: (1) deliberate, open-hearted awareness of moment-to-moment perceptible experience; (2) a process held and sustained by such qualities as kindness, tolerance, patience and courage (as underpinnings of a stance of nonjudgmentalness and acceptance); (3) a practice of nondiscursive, non-analytic investigation of ongoing experience; (4) an awareness markedly different from everyday modes of attention; and (5) in general, a necessity of systematic practice for its gradual refinement (Bodhi 1994; Hanh 1998; Ireland 1997; Kabat-Zinn 2005; Ñāṇamoli and Bodhi 2000).

The current trend in Western psychology, in contrast, is to define and operationalize mindfulness as a relatively stable trait in a manner that takes little account of the developmental and contextual aspects inherent in the Buddhist formulation (e.g. Mindfulness Attention Awareness Scale [MAAS], Brown and Ryan 2003). The range of definitions of mindfulness varies widely between different questionnaires, from how commonly individuals *think* they experience lapses of attention (Brown and Ryan 2003) to how well they *believe* they can express themselves in words ('Describing' subscale, of the Five-Facet Mindfulness Questionnaire [FFMQ], Baer et al. 2006), but also includes self-attributions of non-judgmental attitudes, openness to experience, attention to the present moment, and personal identification with present experience (Freiburg Mindfulness Inventory [FMI], Buchheld, Grossman and Walach 2001; and FFMQ). As just noted, the trait of mindfulness in psychological research has become defined by, and associated with, people's *descriptions of themselves*, based on very brief paper-and-pencil questionnaire responses. This appears to be problematic, because a substantial body of evidence documents that perceptions of one's own behaviour are often dramatically at odds with documented actions (see Baumeister, Vohs and Funder 2007), perhaps especially in regard to desirable behaviours.

Therefore, definitions of mindfulness in present academic psychology, on the one hand, often rely upon self-description of a supposedly stable trait rather than upon concrete evidence that one is actively engaged in mindfulness practice (see Figure 1). On the other hand, mindfulness is divergently defined and operationalized by different groups of investigators, often dependent upon the specific psychological specializations of the authors (Grossman 2008). Our reading of the literature, furthermore, leads us to believe that developers of mindfulness questionnaires commonly imply that their own questionnaires largely reflect a Buddhist definition of mindfulness, albeit in Western terms (FMI, Buchheld,

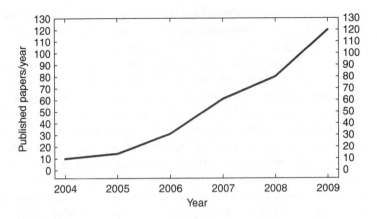

FIGURE 1
Number of published papers with citations per year referring to validation studies of three of the most popular questionnaires purporting to measure 'mindfulness': Kentucky Inventory of Mindfulness Skills (KIMS), and Five Facets of Mindfulness Questionnaire (FFMQ) (Baer et al. 2004, 2006); Mindfulness Attention Awareness Scale (MAAS) (Brown and Ryan 2003). A total of 350 studies during 2009 were found in websites indexing scientific publications (PubMed, eb of Science, Google Scholar)

Grossman and Walach 2001; Kentucky Inventory of Mindfulness Skills [KIMS], Baer et al. 2004; MAAS, Brown and Ryan 2003). We believe that developers of these inventories have insufficiently addressed distinctions between their own characterizations of mindfulness and general Buddhist definitions. Even when certain caveats regarding this theme are stated in publications, they are often only briefly mentioned, which may contribute to their being overlooked by other scientists who later employ the questionnaires.

The state of affairs regarding the measurement of mindfulness also needs to be placed within the general context of current tendencies in psychological research. In recent years, questionnaire data have become extremely popular in contemporary psychological research, perhaps because they are quick to administer and easy to obtain. Baumeister et al. (2007) provide evidence suggesting that up to 80% of current research in social and personality psychology may rely upon such indirect assessments of behaviour. This penchant for indirect measurement is also clearly evident in mindfulness investigations (see Figure 1) and may have serious consequences for the future of mindfulness in psychology. One possibility is a situation in which large numbers of individual researchers— unfamiliar with basic knowledge of Buddhist constructs about mindfulness— employ disparate questionnaires to 'measure' mindfulness, believing their results closely approximate the original Buddhist construct of mindfulness.

Yet another potentially important issue is that some psychologists have promoted a highly restricted interpretation of mindfulness, narrowing in on the cognitive capacities of attention and awareness (Hayes and Plumb 2007). A lone focus upon specific cognitive capacities, of course, limits the scope of what is investigated. From the traditional Buddhist perspective, the notions of attention (from the Pali term *manasikāra*) and awareness (from the Pali term *citta*) have separate originations from that of *sati*, or mindfulness. In the Buddhist interpretation, attention and awareness are part of any discriminative mental state (Dreyfus and Thompson 2007). Minimally, this indicates that attention and awareness are at most *aspects that serve as preconditions*, rather than *equivalents*, of mindfulness.

Attempts to understand and measure mindfulness can, consequently, be hampered by methodological and practical approaches that neglect to take into account the unique composition of multifarious interacting factors involved in the Buddhist construct (see Grossman 2008, 2010; Van Dam, Earleywine and Danoff-Burg 2009; Van Dam et al. 2011). Discussing mindfulness without including other integral aspects of Buddhist practice, the noble Eightfold Path and Four "Immeasurables" (that is *brahmavihāra*; compassion, loving kindness, sympathetic joy and equanimity), may lead to significant denaturing of mindfulness. Although a denatured approach may, nevertheless, yield some health benefits, such a tact is more in line with implementing limited components of a broad, not easily dissected, process, rather than exploring the process as a whole (Gethin 1998).

Developing mindfulness

Buddhist and common psychological approaches

The classic Buddhist method for developing mindfulness is by means of meditation, progressing from a practice of refining attention and awareness to one of deep analytical probing and insight, within the broader context mentioned above (Bodhi 1994). The process of refinement is typically engendered using a type of practice called *samatha* (or calm abiding) meditation (see Bodhi 1994; Hanh 1998), whereas insight and understanding are engendered through *vipassanā* (or insight) meditation (see Rosenberg 1998). According to Buddhist views, only insight (*vipassanā*) can truly generate wisdom, but progress cannot be made without first developing mental focus through *samatha* (Bodhi 1994). Refined attention and developed concentration are considered prerequisites for insight (Gethin 1998), partially explaining why so many contemplative practices start with the seemingly simple (but, in fact, considerably challenging) goal of sustaining attention on the breath.

A brief description of the role that awareness of breathing sometimes plays in mindfulness practice may illustrate how central features of meditation practices are compatible with, and comprehensible within, scientific disciplines like psychology. It may also point to the complexity of the process of mindfulness practice and underline the gradual nature of the acquisition of 'right' concentration, 'right' mindfulness and insight (Gethin 1998).

The breath often serves as a very practical object of, and anchor to, consciousness in meditation. Respiration is the one vital physiological function continuously accessible to sensation and perception during awake states. Although people rarely pay attention to their breathing during ordinary, healthy states, it is both experientially and empirically apparent that (given intact mental capabilities) we are able to turn attention to the breath in all situations and at all times, until respiration is finally extinguished at death. The breath is available to all the core senses—taste, touch, smell, sound, and vision—as well as to other internal perceptual processes tightly bound to conscious experience of the self (interoception, proprioception and kinesthetic experience). Additionally, the lungs represent the largest and most powerful pumping system (and physiological oscillator) in the body. As a consequence, other vital functions (the heartbeat, blood pressure, central nervous system activity) often synchronize with the rhythm of the breath (Grossman 1983). The breath is also exquisitely sensitive to numerous emotional, cognitive and behavioural activities (Grossman and Wientjes 2001). Furthermore, breathing can alternatively function almost entirely under unconscious control or almost completely under conscious control (Phillipson et al. 1978), placing this physiological process precisely at the juncture of conscious and unconscious experience. For all these reasons and more (see Grossman 2010), awareness of the breath can put us in touch with experiences below the threshold of usual conscious experience and may serve as a powerful tool to refine and broaden understanding of one's own thoughts, feelings, and other mental states.

The apparent 'simplicity' of awareness of breathing is contradicted by the actual experience of practicing mindfulness of the breath: the meditator is confronted with the wandering, clutching, aversive and judging mind. A committed engagement with the practice of mindfulness of breathing quickly makes clear that the process is challenging and complex, and that the learning curve is steep and long. The 'simple' breath becomes a microcosm of experience, with constantly changing textures, pleasures and discomforts, allures and aversions, mental presence in one moment and its utter absence in the next. Contrast this *lived experience* of mindfulness of breathing as a practice with a psychological *concept* of 'mindfulness of breathing' that might, for example, be based upon a 10-minute 'mindfulness of breathing' taped exercise aimed at relaxation. By making this comparison, one may gain appreciation of the chasm often occurring between Western academic psychology's understanding of mindfulness and that derived from a more deeply experiential and existential Buddhist orientation (Rosenberg 1998).

Nothing in the above example of mindfulness of breathing—its utility, practical application, complexity, empirical basis, and particularly its very gradual course—should be difficult for scientists and psychologists to understand. However, even cursory examination of the academic literature indicates that current psychological thinking is oriented toward quite short-term interventional approaches. Perhaps that may, at least partially, account for the fact that understanding of mindfulness among psychologists tends not to be explicitly developmental and does not seriously factor in lengthy practice and experience over years. We believe that a greater emphasis upon considering the very gradual nature of cultivation of mindfulness may benefit efforts to define, operationalize and even measure mindfulness. We return to this issue later in another context.

Towards greater value of the subjective

It is worth considering that different understandings of mindfulness in Western science *vs.* Buddhist psychology may reflect deep cultural differences in the extent to which subjective experience is valued as a source of inquiry within traditions. A surgeon in the US or Europe is not necessarily likely to place great value upon the benefit to her surgical skill that may be gained from being the subject of surgical procedures. Neither is she ordinarily systematically trained toward greater sensitivity of her own immediate, inner experience, nor that of her patients. Medical science has historically emphasized intellectual knowledge and concrete experience as surgical qualifications—not investigation of subjective inner life by the physician during consultations or surgery. Behaviourist and other positivist movements in psychology have similarly promoted the value of intellectual knowledge of cognitive and behavioural states, and of the systematic techniques used to alter them, often to the neglect of self-inquiry (Grossman 2010).

An inclination to short-cut the self-experiential foundations of mindfulness practice may, consequently, seem natural to many psychologists who may have known little in the way of self-investigation in their studies. Exploration of one's own subjective experience even tends to play a minor role in the training of many psychotherapists. Therefore, it may, in fact, be difficult for psychologists—when first considering this unfamiliar way of approaching experience—to fathom a type of understanding that does not exclusively or very predominately rely upon the intellectual and conceptual (see Bush 2011). This lack of experience is bound to have serious consequences for the understanding, definition and transmission of mindfulness. Batchelor (1997) points out, 'Experience cannot be accounted for by simply confining it to a conceptual category. Its ultimate ambiguity is that it is simultaneously knowable *and* unknowable. No matter how well we may know something, to witness its intrinsic freedom impels the humble admission: *I don't really know it.*' In other words, phenomenological understanding cannot solely rely upon intellectual knowledge or upon popular contemporary scientific methods of assessment and experimentation and the thinking behind them.

The value placed upon investigation of accessible inner experience may also have consequences for how mindfulness is applied in MBIs. A high value would imply the need for teachers who are, themselves, highly experienced in inner exploration and who are able to embody this experience in their teaching. Within this perspective, the teacher (and perhaps even the therapist and researcher) will be unable to address what he, himself, has not yet explored (Kabat-Zinn 2003; Segal et al. 2002). One can recite passages from books and give prepared responses to questions, but the fundamental shift in experience cannot be simulated (Teasdale et al. 2002).

Another related point, rarely considered in the psychological literature, is whether benefits to wellbeing of MBIs are importantly related to participants learning to *value* aspects integral to the cultivation of mindful awareness, for example appreciation of stillness, attentiveness and patience. Conceivably, such changes in value system may play a far larger role in clinical outcomes than actual mastery of mindfulness during everyday life. This topic seems worthy of investigation.

Measuring mindfulness

Mindfulness is a difficult concept—or perhaps more accurately, percept—to pin down, as should be apparent from the above discussion. Therefore, two questions logically seem to arise: (1) How can we know when someone becomes more mindful; and (2) should we even be asking such this question at such an early phase of scientific inquiry? Some argue that in order to validate MBIs within psychological and basic science, a way must be found to measure the construct and determine that the proposed mechanism of change is responsible for what has changed (for example, Baer 2011).

Those who research mindfulness have, in our opinion, made laudable strides towards identifying features that may be *related to* mindfulness. However, as we hope later to make clear, many quantification efforts confuse discrete psychological characteristics with a definition and quantification of mindfulness. We find this confusion unhelpful to this area of investigation. We believe preliminary self-report questionnaires may lead to oversimplified representations of mindfulness that at times may hardly represent the general idea. This problem is compounded by the fact that widely disparate working definitions of mindfulness are found in the current psychological literature, and there is no external 'gold standard' referent to validate measures. Additionally, some popular questionnaires seem marked by inconsistent psychometric properties. A further issue is that understanding of questionnaire items may also greatly vary between different groups (for example meditators vs. non-meditators), which would make comparisons invalid.

One serious consequence, we see, of the enthusiasm for measurement is that self-report questionnaires may come to define mindfulness in psychology (see Figure 1). The iterative process of refinement and reevaluation within the scientific method, often seen as a self-correcting process, may, in fact, end up not correcting fundamental conceptual misunderstandings about mindfulness, but rather serving to perpetuate and fortify them. The ease and quickness of administration of these scales to large numbers of people, as well as the large number of researchers who may embrace them, could facilitate proliferation of publications about 'mindfulness' in relation to other psychological phenomena. In other words, these scales may take on a life of their own to define and reify mindfulness in the psychological literature. Additionally many scientists with limited or no experience in mindfulness practice may confuse psychological and Buddhist characterizations of mindful awareness. Vested interests (defence of previous studies that used these scales or novel funding possibilities engendered by a popular new approach) are, in turn, likely to exert significant effects upon the direction that the development of such assessment techniques takes. Given these concerns, the rest of this paper will address potential shortcomings of the current attempts to quantify mindfulness by paper-and-pencil questionnaires.

What can mindlessness tell us about mindfulness?

Some have suggested that employment of items assumed to reflect the opposite of mindfulness (operating on 'automatic pilot') can serve as a useful index of mindfulness (employing a little mathematical manipulation, namely, reverse-scoring of items; see Baer 2011; Brown and Ryan 2003). One example is asking people how often they drift off or do not pay attention, and then inverting their responses such that a response of 'My mind doesn't wander off very often' (that is, the low end of the scale) is taken to suggest something like 'My mind stays focused on the task at hand most of the time.' While items employing this reversed scoring procedure are often useful in a questionnaire for identifying participants who are not giving full attention and may be responding carelessly during completion, the majority of items in questionnaires are typically positive formulations that directly assess the idea of interest.

Consider a popular depression inventory that includes four items (out of a total 20) that reflect positive mood instead of depression, and the fact that these positive items may correlate poorly with other items in the scale. Reflecting upon this issue, two prominent psychological statisticians recently emphasized that endorsement of the low end of a trait scale does not imply the strong presence of its opposite, for example low endorsement of depressive symptoms does not necessarily suggest happiness, or endorsing the low end of a scale of physical impairment does not suggest physical fitness (Reise and Waller 2009). This is not to say that such reverse-scored items are never useful, rather that inclusion of such items in questionnaires is a complex process.

An entire scale comprised of reverse-scored items is considerably more problematic. Suppose, in fact, that an individual responded to all items about his current level of physical impairment by endorsing the lowest response (not at all). Could we necessarily label him as physically fit on the basis of his responses? He may not be physically impaired, but that is quite different from being very fit. So what then are we to make of a mindfulness scale that measures perceived inattentiveness? The most commonly administered scale that putatively measures mindfulness (MAAS; Brown and Ryan 2003) relies completely on such negatively formulated items based on self-attributions of inattentiveness (see Grossman, forthcoming, for an indepth discussion). Several investigations, however, suggest that this scale may relate more to propensity to experience lapses of attention than it does to positive qualities possibly associated with mindfulness (Carriere, Cheyne and Smilek 2008; Cheyne, Carriere and Smilek 2006). Additionally, more recent analyses also go in the same direction by suggesting that the MAAS reflects the experience of general inattentiveness, not mindfulness (Van Dam, Earleywine and Borders 2010).

Can we know when we have lapses of attention?

Almost everyone has had the experience of 'awakening' from a daydream or arriving somewhere only to realize they paid no attention to how they got there. Such observations suggest that we all know what lapses of attention feel like. But how good are we, on the whole, at identifying our general disposition towards acting in this fashion? In other words, does our experience or self-attribution of inattentiveness during everyday life accurately reflect just how inattentive we really are? Can we accurately estimate how much time we generally spend in inattentive states or how typical such states are for us, as some mindfulness questionnaires suggest (Brown and Ryan 2003)?

Research suggests that mind-wandering (akin to daydreaming) is often associated with a lack of meta-awareness (or awareness that one is aware; see Schooler 2002). Furthermore, experiments in cognitive neuroscience suggest that individuals process very little of their external environment when their minds wander (Smallwood et al. 2008), creating a lack of reference for states of lapsing attention. Other research has, additionally, shown that expert meditators use fewer cognitive resources to return their attention to the task at hand and are better able to prevent their minds from wandering (Pagnoni et al. 2008). These findings create a conceptual conundrum for the self-report of absent-mindedness: Individual differences in psychological or other characteristics may importantly influence people's accuracy to assess extent of their own inattentiveness. Therefore, it is plausible that the MAAS may not even be a very accurate instrument for assessing actually occurring lapses of attention, much less mindfulness. On the other hand, it may accurately assess how poorly respondents *think* they pay attention in everyday life. A similar argument might also pertain to other self-report measures described as 'mindfulness' questionnaires, which may emphasize abilities other than those of the MAAS (for details, see Grossman, Forthcoming).

Mind the bias

Mindfulness questionnaires avoid arcane language in favour of simple words and statements that *appear to be* equally accessible to everyone (even those without mindfulness training). This simple language, however, is commonly based on the wording involved in the MBIs themselves (MBSR and MBCT).

Accordingly, many phrases used in 'mindfulness' questionnaires (operating on 'automatic pilot,' focusing on the present moment), are more readily accessible after participating in a MBI than before. Mere accessibility does not necessarily mean individuals are more likely to endorse the items, although there is evidence that it may (Mayo, White and Eysenck 1978).

The extent to which the participants value the ideas that the items represent may, additionally, have an impact on the extent to which they endorse an item (Grossman 2008). Someone who has gone through an eight week intervention requiring 45 minute daily meditation practice, or someone else who has spent the last 15 years regularly meditating, is likely to attribute some importance to the values that are part of this practice, especially if he has come to internalize those values. Accordingly, individuals might want to demonstrate (unconsciously or consciously) to themselves or others that they possess, at least to some extent, the qualities that the questionnaire describes. Alternatively, they might just confuse aspirations toward certain attributes with actual achievement. There is a substantial literature related to other questionnaires that supports the likelihood of such biases influencing outcomes.

Baer (2011) suggests that bias is not a problem because participants in MBIs are willing to report home practice times that are less than recommended amounts, potentially painting the participants in a negative light. While, on the surface, this may seem to deal with the issue of bias (participants are in fact willing to be perceived negatively), it is more likely that *unconscious* bias presents a problem, rather than *conscious* bias.

There are numerous factors that contribute to bias in self-report measures (Van Dam et al. 2011), and these biases have been repeatedly observed in the psychological literature. Research evidence, specifically related to mindfulness questionnaires, also suggests that biases may play an important role in self-reports. In a comparison of a small group of meditators to students with no meditation experience, evidence was found that people with comparable overall scores were likely to endorse entirely different response options based on their group membership (Van Dam, Earleywine and Danoff-Burg 2009). Meditators were equally likely to endorse options that suggested mindfulness and absent-mindedness, whereas students were more likely to reject absent-mindedness statements than to endorse items that positively purport to reflect mindfulness. This research indicates that even though a long-term meditator and a college student might have the same total score on a scale of 'mindfulness,' that score might be attained in entirely different ways (see Van Dam, Earleywine and Danoff-Burg 2009). This suggests differential interpretations of the meaning of items between groups.

In response to the above study, Baer et al. (2011) suggest that a recent study of their own, using comparable analyses with a demographically well-matched group of meditators and non-meditators, shows 'very little evidence for differential interpretation of items.' However, the statistical methods Baer et al. (2011) chose to use may unduly favour the position that differential interpretations of items are not a problem, that the threshold for proof of evidence they chose may, itself, preclude finding such differences. We performed alternative statistics on the same data set using conventional levels of probability to evaluate each item, and found that on two subscales of their questionnaire ('Observing' and 'Acting with Awareness'), half of the items in one subscale and three-quarters of the items in the other showed evidence of such problems—exceeding what would be expected by chance. At best, the Baer et al. (2011) study may suggest that using samples well matched for demographic variables (age, gender and education), may modestly reduce these kinds of problems with mindfulness scales, but it also underscores the fact that different groups are likely to interpret the meaning of the same items differently. In some cases, those differences might be due to demographics, and in other cases, to mindfulness training. This is not an optimal state of affairs for a questionnaire aiming to compare different populations. Furthermore, evidence from Baer et al. (2008) indicates that a central aspect of mindfulness ('Observing'; also one of the two subscales showing evidence of differential item functioning) could not be reliably assessed so that meditators and nonmeditators might be validly compared: items in this subscale seem to have had different meanings for each group.

Varying interpretations by nonmeditators and meditators (Baer et al. 2008; Grossman 2008; Van Dam, Earleywine and Danoff-Burg 2009) suggest that ordinary language may not do justice to the complexity of mindfulness, because the words used in the assessment instrument will be understood differently by the different groups. If meditation practice entails a qualitative rotation in subjective experience (Kabat-Zinn 2005), then choice of wording will continue to be problematic when comparing those with *vs.* those without exposure to meditation.

One example indicates that differences between groups in item interpretation can lead to absurd conclusions when mindfulness self-reports are employed (Grossman 2008): FMI[1] scores of binge-drinking and normal college students (Leigh, Bowen and Marlatt 2005) were compared with those of experienced meditators immediately following a multi-day meditation retreat (Buchheld, Grossman and Walach 2001). Figure 2 shows that binge-drinking students scored significantly higher than experienced meditators on 'mindfulness,' with normal healthy students in the middle. Interestingly, Leigh, Bowen and Marlatt (2005) conclude that constructs of mindfulness 'can be measured reliably through self-report and may assist in identifying an important relationship between substance use and mindfulness.' Hence, implications of this study should be clear: excessive alcohol intake is conducive to mindfulness, but mindfulness meditation is not. In a more serious vein, one way in which these paradoxical findings might be explained is that binge-drinking students interpreted the meaning of items (relating to awareness of bodily sensations) very differently than the meditators.

Similar issues, if somewhat less frivolous, have arisen in other research as well. Another study of the MAAS and KIMS across a Thai population (where Buddhist beliefs are predominant) and US sample (where Buddhist beliefs are in

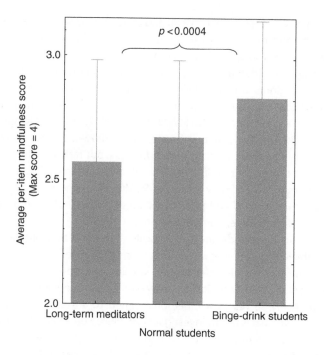

FIGURE 2

Mindfulness scores (Freiburg Mindfulness Inventory [FMI]); means (whiskers, standard deviations) of long-term experienced insight meditators, healthy non-meditating students, and binge-drinking, non-meditating students. Difference between meditators and binger drinkers ($p < 0.0004$); differences between meditators and normal students approached significance ($p < 0.06$)

the minority) found no overall differences on the MAAS (even though rates of meditation in the two groups were substantially different); also the KIMS exhibited inconsistent relationships among its items across the groups (Christopher et al. 2009). Such findings bring into question what psychologists are actually measuring with these questionnaires and whether there is adequate scientific support for their continued use, if characterized as measures of mindfulness.

Diversity of definition in mindfulness scales

There exists no gold standard of reference that can be used to evaluate questionnaires purporting to measure mindfulness. Thus we cannot know whether a questionnaire reliably measures some aspect of mindfulness. Unlike testing mathematical skills, there is no litmus test for mindfulness, no telltale growth or activity in the brain, nor are there any behavioural referents that have been documented as *specific* to mindfulness. This situation opens the door for definitions of mindfulness that are in danger of losing any relationship to the practices and teachings that gave rise to MBSR and MBCT. It may sometimes result in hybrid definitions and operationalizations of mindfulness possibly far afield from the original Dharmic roots of this way of being (Grossman 2008).

We have already provided the example of the MAAS, items of which assess the perception of attentional lapses in daily life. Nevertheless, the authors of this scale clearly assume that they are measuring mindfulness and refer to it as such when MAAS findings are presented. The FFMQ (Baer et al. 2006) directly adopts many items of the MAAS into one of its subscales, Act with Awareness. However, these authors do not label these responses 'mindfulness' but rather, 'acting with awareness,' one of five facets of mindfulness. This alone is a source of significant confusion. Is 'MAAS mindfulness' only a facet of 'FFMQ mindfulness' or merely a measure of experienced lapses of attention, as still other studies indicate (Carriere, Cheyne and Smilek 2008; Cheyne, Carriere and Smilek 2006)?

Baer et al. (2006) also include another subscale that seems to evaluate how well respondents think they can verbally express themselves. Baer (2011) justifies such a subscale by claiming it reflects the labeling, or noting, technique sometimes employed in insight meditation. However, as we understand it, such verbal labelling primarily serves as a mnemonic aimed to sustain moment-to-moment awareness. The goal is not to investigate experience on a verbal level but to employ labelling to aid *seamless* contact with momentary experience, a process often, in fact, characterized as preverbal or nonverbal, but certainly nowhere described as a rich, running monologue of momentary experience. A mental sequence—such as 'in-breath, out-breath, itch, warmth, discomfort, out-breath, thinking, thinking'—is not, itself, the essence of the meditation experience. Also the practice of such verbal labelling during meditation is unlikely to be importantly associated with evaluations of how well one thinks one can generally express oneself. This subscale possibly derives from the authors' own interest and work in dialectical behaviour therapy (DBT; Linehan 1993), because verbal expressiveness is often deficient in the targeted population of DBT, and a technique promoting verbal description has been termed a 'mindfulness' skill in DBT. Thus, its inclusion seems to indicate that this five-subscale inventory provides a hybrid definition of mindfulness, and at least some subscales bears little resemblance to the original Buddhist construct (see first section). The FFMQ contains: (1) one verbal expressiveness subscale that appears to have little to do with a traditional understanding of mindfulness; (2) another subscale that assesses *perceived* lapses of attention; (3) a third scale reflecting how well people *believe* they can observe or pay attention to experience (however, as mentioned earlier, this subscale performs very differently among meditators and nonmeditators); and (4) two additional subscales that assess self-reports of emotional nonreactivity and non-judgmentalness. Thus, two of the five subscales may not reflect mindfulness at all. A third, although aimed at one of the central features of mindfulness (observing/noticing/attending), is not methodologically valid to use across different groups of people (Baer et al. 2008) and is probably highly susceptible to variations in semantic interpretation. Nevertheless, this five-facet scale is quite popular, employed by many psychologists to measure extent of mindfulness.

We do not wish here to single out this scale but use it as an example of the types of problems that arise with self-report questionnaires claiming to measure mindfulness. Virtually all available questionnaires have similar shortcomings, including the FMI, with which the first author has been intimately associated. Also they often correlate poorly—or at best moderately—with each other (Baer et al. 2004, 2006; Grossman 2008, forthcoming), which means that a person might easily be high in 'mindfulness' on one scale and low on another. Without some reliable external criteria to evaluate such claims, it is impossible to say what such findings actually mean.

Is everyone mindful?

Several mindfulness questionnaires have been developed with the sole intent of measuring mindfulness in individuals who have meditation experience (FMI, Buchheld, Grossman and Walach 2001; Developmental Mindfulness Questionnaire (DMS), Solloway and Fisher 2007; Toronto Mindfulness Scale (TMS), Lau et al. 2006), although two have subsequently been adapted by a few of the original authors for use as trait measures (e.g., FMI, Walach et al. 2006; TMS, Davis, Lau and Cairns 2009). Other questionnaires have been developed with the idea that mindfulness is accessible to, and understood by, everyone in the general population, regardless of exposure to meditation (see Baer 2011). Recently, scales have even been developed that purport to measure mindfulness in children. This general approach, therefore, assumes that it is possible and meaningful to measure mindfulness in almost everyone.

Revisiting an earlier discussion, the development of greater mindfulness is understood, from the earliest Buddhist discourses to modern-day teachings, as an extremely gradual developmental process. It is assumed that people unfamiliar with mindfulness practice possess incipient qualities of mindful awareness, characterized as elementary, undeveloped, and immature (in a contemporary vein [Kabat-Zinn 2005]: '... these capacities need to be uncovered, developed, and put to use'). Only slow and gradual cultivation by means of continual mental training is presumed to result in a deepening of mindfulness and its comprehension. Thus in one of the earliest Buddhist treatises (Ireland, translation 1997): 'Just as the great ocean gradually shelves, slopes, and inclines, and there is no sudden precipice, so also in this doctrine and discipline there is a gradual training, a gradual course, a gradual progression, and there is no sudden penetration...' More recently, Rosenberg (1998) wrote: 'Mindfulness is the observing power of the mind, a power that varies with the maturity of the practitioner.'

From this perspective, individuals without meditation experience are almost inevitably going to respond to the word 'mindfulness'—and questionnaire items purporting to measure it—radically differently from people with meditation experience. As one prominent meditation teacher (Khema 1989) wrote about effects of meditation training: 'The difference between the trained and untrained mind is the understood experience.' And even those at varying levels of mental training are likely to have divergent understandings. Definitions and operatio-nalizations of mindfulness that do not take into account the gradual nature of training attention, the gradual progression in terms of greater stability of attention and vividness of experience or the enormous challenges inherent in living more mindfully, are very likely to misconstrue and banalize the construct of mindfulness, which is really not a construct as we traditionally understand it in Western psychology, but at depth, a way of being.

Conclusions on understanding mindfulness

Within a relatively short period of time, notable progress has been made toward integrating strikingly unfamiliar concepts into Western paradigms of psychology. Not long ago, it seemed unimaginable that mainstream psychology might so quickly come to acknowledge the inner world as a legitimate topic of study, even opening itself to investigation of such qualities as compassion, loving-kindness and equanimity. Because this area is in its infancy, caution and patience would, therefore, seem helpful when pursuing these matters at this phase, lest we reify and trivialize concepts that may have a richness of which we cannot yet be fully aware.

What are some of the possible quantitative strategies that might be appropriate to this phase of scientific investigation of mindfulness? We do not presume to have all the answers. However, we can suggest a number of plausible approaches that avoid the various limitations and potential pitfalls of self-administered rating scales discussed above.

1. One might be to evaluate, in similar self-report format as current inventories—not how skilled people think they are in specific qualities or behaviours—but the extent to which they value those characteristics, that is examining whether mindfulness practice is associated with differences or changes in value system. For example, how valuable do different people find the act of just sitting still; noticing what sensations, thoughts and/or emotions arise from moment to moment; or examining momentary experiences whether pleasant, unpleasant or neutral? Such questions would have to be carefully formulated but could provide significant information about *what is important* to people who do and do not practice mindfulness meditation. Additionally, this approach might shed light on how mindfulness practice influences people's perspectives on life's challenges and uplifting experiences. Such scales may remain subject to many of the same biases as other self-report measures, but at least they would be less likely to conflate achievement with aspiration.

2. One viable option for preserving the integrity and richness of the Buddhist understanding of mindfulness might be to call those various qualities now purporting to be mindfulness by names much closer to what they actually represent ('experienced lapses of attention' in the case of Brown and Ryan 2003;

'perceived self-competency of verbal expressiveness' in the case of one subscales of Baer et al. 2006). Names could be fully descriptive of what the individual scales actually assess, and full disclaimers in published studies might state that these scales do not directly assess mindfulness. Relationships between these measures and aspects of mindfulness practice could still be evaluated, but there would be clear distinction between the characteristics measured ('experienced lapses of attention') and mindfulness. Such a careful approach is, indeed, already followed by some researchers ('de-centering', Fresco et al. 2007; meta-cognitive awareness (Hargus et al. 2010; Teasdale et al. 2002). Greater employment might serve to increase insights into psychological mechanisms beyond those gained when investigators globally term their measures 'mindfulness.'

3. Interview approaches (Teasdale et al. 2002; Hargus et al. 2010), although more labour intensive, are likely to provide greater insight into psychological mechanisms and characteristics associated with mindfulness than five minute self-report inventories, especially because semantic complexities and response biases may be better addressed in one-on-one interactions (especially with skilled and knowledgeable interviewers).

4. Because mindfulness practice has been hypothesized to contribute to alleviation of suffering, outcome measures could be emphasized that test specificity of effects, even dimensions based on ancient constructs like the seven factors of awakening (energy, joy, concentration, calmness, interest and equanimity, and mindfulness). Although such qualities may also often be difficult to equate with Western terms, they may offer an approach to measurement that evaluates specific effects of mindfulness interventions, provide a basis for testing Buddhist assumptions about consequences of mindfulness practice, and have potential for bridging the gap between paradigms. This strategy can also be applied to examination of behavioural change after MBIs (Singh et al. 2004).

5. Efforts should also continue to be expended that carefully examine the psychological and physiological changes that accompany the *practice and process* of mindfulness; such a strategy is much more likely to reveal commonalities with Western empirical concepts and to build sounder bridges between Buddhist and Western psychologies than employing *a priori* assumptions about mindfulness.

In conclusion, the beginning of a paradigm shift seems evident in new forms of concurrent scientific exploration of the subjective and objective (Thompson 2007; Varela, Thompson and Rosch 1991). Perhaps one of most important benefits that mindfulness itself can contribute to mindfulness research is that we may learn to cultivate a patient, intentional awareness of the present moment and of our own minds in the very work that we are conducting.

NOTE

1. Disclosure: the first author (P. Grossman) is co-author of the FMI.

REFERENCES

BAER, R. A. 2011. Measuring mindfulness. *Contemporary Buddhism* 12: 241–261.

BAER, R. A., D. B. SAMUELS, and E. L. B. LYKINS. 2011. Differential item functioning on the Five Facet Mindfulness Questionnaire is minimal in demographically matched mediators and nonmediators. *Assessment* 18: 3–10.

BAER, R., G. SMITH, and K. ALLEN. 2004. Assessment of mindfulness by self report: The Kentucky inventory of mindfulness skills. *Assessment* 11: 191–206.

BAER, R., G. SMITH, J. HOPKINS, J. KRIETEMEYER, and L. TONEY. 2006. Using self-report assessment methods to explore facets of mindfulness. *Assessment* 13: 27–45.

BAER, R. A., G. T. SMITH, E. LYKINS, D. BUTTON, J. KRIETEMEYER, S. SAUER, E. WALSH, D. DUGGAN, and J. M. G. WILLIAMS. 2008. Construct validity of the Five Facet Mindfulness Questionnaire in meditating and non-meditating samples. *Assessment* 15: 329–42.

BATCHELOR, S. 1997. *Buddhism without beliefs: A contemporary guide to awakening.* New York: Riverhead Books.

BAUMEISTER, R., K. VOHS, and D. FUNDER. 2007. Psychology as the science of self-reports and finger movements. Whatever happened to actual behavior? *Perspectives on Psychological Science* 2: 396–403.

BODHI, B. 1994. *The noble eightfold path: The way to the end of suffering.* 2nd ed. Kandy, Sri Lanka: Buddhist Publication Society, First Published in 1984.

BODHI, B. trans. 2000. *The connected discourses of the Buddha: A new translation of the Samyutta Nikaya.* Boston, MA: Wisdom.

BROWN, K. W., and R. M. RYAN. 2003. The benefits of being present: Mindfulness and its role in psychological well-being. *Journal of Personality and Social Psychology* 84: 822–48.

BUCHHELD, N., P. GROSSMAN, and H. WALACH. 2001. Measuring mindfulness in insight meditation (vipassanā) and meditation-based psychotherapy: The development of the Freiburg Mindfulness Inventory (FMI). *Journal for Meditation and Meditation Research* 1: 11–34.

BUDDHADĀSA BHIKKHU. 1988. *Mindfulness with breathing: A manual for serious beginners.* Boston, MA: Shambhala.

BUSH, M. 2011. Mindfulness in higher education. *Contemporary Buddhism* 12: 183–197.

CARRIERE, J. S., J. A. CHEYNE, and D. SMILEK. 2008. Everyday attention lapses and memory failures: The affective consequences of mindlessness. *Consciousness and Cognition* 17: 835–47.

CHEYNE, J., J. CARRIERE, and D. SMILEK. 2006. Absent-mindedness: Lapses of conscious awareness and everyday cognitive failures. *Consciousness and Cognition* 15: 578–92.

CHRISTOPHER, M. S., S. CHAROENSUK, B. D. GILBERT, T. J. NEARY, and K. L. PEARCE. 2009. Mindfulness in Thailand and the United States: A case of apples versus oranges? *Journal of Clinical Psychology* 65: 590–612.

CHRISTOPHER, M., and B. GILBERT. 2007. Psychometric properties of the Kentucky Inventory of Mindfulness Skills (KIMS) and the Mindful Attention Awareness Scale (MAAS) among Thai Theravada Buddhist monks. Retrieved from Pacific University Oregon website. http://commons.pacificu.edu/sppfac/2/

DAVIS, K. M., M. A. LAU, and D. R. CAIRNS. 2009. Development and preliminary validation of a trait version of the Toronto Mindfulness Scale. *Journal of Cognitive Psychotherapy* 23: 185–97.

DREYFUS, G. 2008. Attention and the regulation of ethically relevant mental states: An Abhidharmic view. Presentation at Mind and Life Summer Research Institute, June 6–12, 2008. Garrison, NY.

DREYFUS, G., and E. THOMPSON. 2007. Asian Perspectives: Indian theories of mind. In *The Cambridge handbook of consciousness*, edited by P. D. Zelazo, M. Moscovitch, and E. Thompson. New York: Cambridge University Press.

FRESCO, D. M., M. T. MOORE, M. VAN DULMEN, Z. V. SEGAL, J. D TEASDALE, H. MA, and J. M. G. WILLIAMS. 2007. Initial psychometric properties of the Experiences Questionnaire: A self-report survey of decentering. *Behavior Therapy* 38: 234–46.

GETHIN, R. 1998. *The foundations of Buddhism*. Oxford: Oxford University Press.

GROSSMAN, P. Forthcoming. Defining mindfulness by 'how *poorly* I *think* I pay attention in everyday awareness' and other intractable problems for psychology's (re) invention of mindfulness. *Psychological Assessment*.

GROSSMAN, P. 1983. Respiration, stress, and cardiovascular function. *Psychophysiology* 20: 284–300.

GROSSMAN, P. 2008. On measuring mindfulness in psychosomatic and psychological research. *Journal of Psychosomatic Research* 64: 405–8.

GROSSMAN, P. 2010. Mindfulness for psychologists: Paying kind attention to the perceptible. *Mindfulness* 1: 87–97.

GROSSMAN, P., and C. J. WIENTJES. 2001. How breathing adjusts to mental and physical demands. In *Respiration and emotion*, edited by Y. Haruki, I. Homma, A. Umezawa, and Y. Masaoka, 43–55. New York: Springer.

HANH, T. N. 1998. *The heart of the Buddha's teaching: Transforming suffering into peace, joy, and liberation*. New York: Broadway Books.

HARGUS, E., C. CRANE, T. BARNHOFER, and J. M. G. WILLIAMS. 2010. Effects of mindfulness on meta-awareness and specificity of describing prodromal symptoms in suicidal depression. *Emotion* 10: 34–42.

HAYES, S. C., and J. C. PLUMB. 2007. Mindfulness from the bottom up: Providing an inductive framework for understanding mindfulness processes and their application to human suffering. *Psychological Inquiry* 18: 242–8.

IRELAND, J. D. trans. 1997. *The Udana: Inspired utterances of the Buddha*. translated from the Pali. Kandy, Sri Lanka: Buddhist Publication Society.

KABAT-ZINN, J. 1990. *Full catastrophe living: Using the wisdom of your body and mind to face stress, pain, and illness*. New York: Dell Publishing.

KABAT-ZINN, J. 2003. Mindfulness-based interventions in context: Past, present, and future. *Clinical Psychology: Science and Practice* 10: 144–56.

KABAT-ZINN, J. 2005. *Coming to our senses: Healing ourselves and the world through mindfulness*. New York: Hyperion.

KHEMA, A. 1989. Supreme efforts: III. Aware and awake. http://www.vipassana.com/meditation/khema/hereandnow/awake_and_aware.php.

LAU, M. A., S. R. BISHOP, Z. V. SEGAL, T. BUIS, N. D. ANDERSON et al. 2006. The Toronto mindfulness scale: Development and validation. *Journal of Clinical Psychology* 62: 1445–67.

LEIGH, J., S. BOWEN, and G. A. MARLATT. 2005. Spirituality, mindfulness and substance abuse. *Addictive Behaviors* 30: 1335–41.

LINEHAN, M. M. 1993. *Cognitive-behavioral treatment of borderline personality disorder.* New York: Guilford.

MAYO, J., O. WHITE, and H. J. EYSENCK. 1978. An empirical study of the relation between astrological factors and personality. *Journal of Social Psychology* 105: 229–36.

ÑĀNAMOLI, B., and B. T. BODHI. trans. 2000. *The middle length discourses of the Buddha. A translation of the Majjhima Nikaya.* 2nd ed. Boston, MA: Wisdom Press.

PAGNONI, G., M. CEKIC, and Y. GUO. 2008. Thinking about not-thinking': Neural correlates of conceptual processing during Zen meditation. *PLoS ONE* 3: e3083.

PHILLIPSON, E., P. A. MCCELAN, C. E. SULLIVAN, and N. C. ZAMEL. 1978. Interaction between metabolic and behavioral respiratory control during hypercapnia and speech. *The American Review of Respiratory Disease* 117: 903–9.

REISE, S. P., and N. G. WALLER. 2009. Item response theory and clinical measurement. *Annual Review of Clinical Psychology* 5: 27–48.

ROSENBERG, L. 1998. *Breath by breath: The liberating practice of insight meditation.* Boston, MA: Shambhala.

SCHOOLER, J. W. 2002. Re-representing consciousness: Dissociations between experience and meta-consciousness. *TRENDS in Cognitive Sciences* 6: 339–4.

SEGAL, Z. V., J. M. G. WILLIAMS, and J. D. TEASDALE. 2002. *Mindfulness-based cognitive therapy for depression.* New York: Guilford Press.

SINGH, N., G. LANCIONI, A. WINTON, R. WAHLER, J. SINGH, and M. SAGE. 2004. Mindful caregiving increases happiness among individuals with profound multiple disabilities. *Research in Developmental Disabilities* 25: 207–18.

SMALLWOOD, J., E. BEACH, J. W. SCHOOLER, and T. C. HANDY. 2008. Going AWOL in the brain: Mind wandering reduces cortical analysis of external events. *Journal of Cognitive Neuroscience* 20: 458–69.

SOLLOWAY, S. G., and W. P. FISHER. 2007. Mindfulness practice: A Rasch variable construct innovation. *Journal of Applied Measurement* 8: 359–72.

TEASDALE, J. D., R. G. MOORE, H. HAYHURST, M. POPE, S. WILLIAMS, and Z. V. SEGAL. 2002. Meta-cognitive awareness and prevention of relapse in depression: Empirical evidence. *Journal of Consulting and Clinical Psychology* 70: 278–87.

THOMPSON, E. 2007. *Mind in life: Biology, phenomenology, and the sciences of mind.* Cambridge, MA: Harvard University Press.

THOMPSON, E., and F. J. VARELA. 2001. Radical embodiment: Neural dynamics and consciousness. *TRENDS in Cognitive Sciences* 5: 418–25.

VAN DAM, N. T., M. EARLEYWINE, and A. BORDERS. 2010. Measuring mindfulness? An item response theory analysis of the mindful attention awareness scale. *Personality and Individual Differences* 49: 805–10.

VAN DAM, N. T., M. EARLEYWINE, and S. DANOFF-BURG. 2009. Differential item function across meditators and non-meditators on the Five Facet Mindfulness Questionnaire. *Personality and Individual Differences* 47: 516–21.

VAN DAM, N. T., S. C. SHEPPARD, J. P. FORSYTH, and M. EARLEYWINE. 2011. Self-compassion is a better predictor than mindfulness of symptom severity and quality of life in mixed anxiety and depression. *Journal of Anxiety Disorders* 25: 123–30.

VARELA, F., E. THOMPSON, and E. ROSCH. 1991. *The embodied mind: cognitive science and human experience.* Cambridge MA: MIT.

WALACH, H., N. BUCHHELD, V. BUTTENMULLER, N. KLEINKNECHT, and S. SCHMIDT. 2006. Measuring mindfulness—the Freiburg Mindfulness Inventory (FMI). *Personality and Individual Differences* 40: 1543–55.

MEASURING MINDFULNESS

Ruth A. Baer

The commitment to evidence-based practice in clinical psychology requires scientific investigation of the effects of treatment and mechanisms of change. Empirical evidence suggests that mindfulness-based treatments provide clinically meaningful improvement for people suffering from many important problems, including depression, anxiety, pain, and stress. However, the processes of change that produce these beneficial outcomes are not entirely clear. Central questions include whether mindfulness training leads to increases in the general tendency to respond mindfully to the experiences of daily life, and if so, whether these changes are responsible for the improvements in mental health that are often observed. Answering these questions requires methods for assessing mindfulness. Several tools for this purpose are now available and early evidence suggests that they are useful and informative, despite shortcomings that require additional work. This paper summarizes the rationale for mindfulness questionnaires, the methods used to construct them, and research findings on their utility. Challenges related to maintaining consistency with Buddhist conceptions of mindfulness while applying psychological research methods to the study of its assessment are discussed.

Measuring mindfulness

The field of clinical psychology is increasingly committed to science as a foundation for clinical practice. This commitment requires that assessment and treatment of persons seeking help for psychological difficulties must be guided by the best scientific literature. Whenever possible, clinicians engaged in evidence-based practice provide treatments with strong scientific support for their efficacy. Newly developed treatments are considered experimental until scientific evidence of their effectiveness has been published in peer-reviewed journals. Standards of effectiveness may vary with the conditions and populations being studied, and the optimal methods for demonstrating effectiveness are topics of ongoing discussion. In general, however, empirically oriented clinical psychologists agree that scientific research is the most reliable source of knowledge about the best ways to alleviate psychological suffering. Empirical research is also essential for insuring that our treatments are not harmful and for understanding the aspects of mind and brain that underlie the alleviation of suffering.

Scientific study of the effectiveness of treatment requires measurement of the problems for which people seek help. As the commitment to scientific evidence in clinical psychology has grown, so has the array of methods available to measure the severity of unpleasant symptoms and maladaptive behaviours, such as depression, anxiety, disordered eating, substance abuse, and many others. A large body of literature demonstrates that many psychological difficulties can be treated effectively. Typically, this means that participants in treatment show significant and meaningful reductions in the symptoms for which they sought help. In some cases, it means that treatment leads to meaningful increases in quality of life, or reductions in stress, in spite of an incurable condition such as a chronic illness. In accordance with the rules of scientific evidence, research designs usually provide a strong indication that the improvements were attributable to the treatment, rather than to extraneous factors such as the passage of time or placebo effects.

Until recently, research on the effectiveness of psychological treatments focused primarily on *whether* they lead to improved mental health. However, as confidence in the effectiveness of psychological treatments has grown, attention has increasingly turned to the processes that account for *how* these treatments work. For example, numerous studies show that a variety of treatment approaches lead to substantial reductions in depression. But why is this so? Is it because people's thinking patterns become less distorted, or because their relationships with others become healthier, or because they become more actively engaged in rewarding activities? Answering such questions allows us to increase the effectiveness of treatment by refining the components that are responsible for therapeutic change and de-emphasizing or letting go of components that do not contribute to improvement. Thus, studies that measure the severity of symptoms before and after treatment are necessary but not sufficient. Understanding how treatments work requires that the hypothesized processes of change must be measured. Thus, if a treatment approach is designed to relieve depression by teaching people to think in less distorted ways, then studies of this treatment should measure the extent of distortion in people's thinking before and after treatment, and should examine whether the degree of change in distorted thinking is related to the degree of improvement in depression.

Within scientific clinical psychology, mindfulness-based treatments have generated considerable interest. Although more familiar treatments are effective for many people, some participants show only partial improvement or no improvement. Thus, the need for additional work is recognized. Approaches that propose new ideas and methods may be welcomed, especially if their theoretical and conceptual basis is well articulated and preliminary evidence suggests that they are effective. Empirical study of mindfulness-based approaches is relatively recent; however, the literature is growing rapidly and suggests that interventions such as mindfulness-based stress reduction (MBSR; Kabat-Zinn 1982, 1990) and mindfulness-based cognitive therapy (MBCT; Segal, Williams, and Teasdale 2002), among others, produce clinically significant improvements for people suffering from many important problems, including depression, anxiety, pain, and stress. Treatments that integrate mindfulness training with a variety of other strategies,

242

such as dialectical behaviour therapy (DBT; Linehan 1993) and acceptance and commitment therapy (ACT; Hayes, Strosahl, and Wilson 1999) also have strong empirical support for their efficacy.

However, it is not entirely clear *how* mindfulness-based treatments produce their beneficial outcomes. Addressing this question requires measuring the processes of change that are believed to account for the benefits of mindfulness training. It seems reasonable to assume that teaching participants to practice mindfulness meditation or mindfulness skills should cultivate their ability to respond mindfully to the experiences of daily life, including sensations, cognitions, and emotions, as well as sights, sounds, and other environmental stimuli. In turn, increased mindfulness in daily life is believed to lead to reductions in suffering (Goldstein and Kornfield 1987). Because a scientific approach requires that we test these assumptions empirically, researchers have begun to ask, 'Does mindfulness training lead to increased mindfulness in daily life?' and 'is this why mindfulness-based interventions are beneficial?' These questions cannot be answered without methods for measuring mindfulness. Although this task appears very challenging, psychologists have begun to consider how it might be done.

Methods for assessing psychological variables

Psychologists have developed many methods for assessing human behaviours, characteristics, and psychological functions. Some of these methods are more applicable than others to the study of mindfulness. For example, direct observation by trained observers has contributed greatly to the understanding of many forms of overt behaviour, such as types of play in young children, self-harm in developmentally disabled persons, and ways of arguing in married couples, among numerous others. Mindfulness is probably not well suited to such methods because it is not readily observable by others. Physiological markers of behaviours such as smoking, alcohol consumption, and drug use can be assessed in willing participants with breath or urine tests. However, no such markers of mindfulness in daily life have been identified. Scanning technologies can be used to study the brains of people who practice mindfulness meditation. Although these methods are yielding fascinating results in both long-term meditators and participants in mindfulness-based interventions, it is not clear that brain scans can be used to quantify the general tendency to be mindful in daily life. Computer-based or other cognitive tests can provide objective measures of a wide range of abilities. This approach has been used in several studies of mindfulness and some researchers have reported associations between mindfulness training and improvements in capacities such as sustained attention and working memory (Jha, Krompinger, and Baime 2007; Jha et al. 2010). However, findings are mixed, and although these capacities may be related to mindfulness, it does not appear that mindfulness is synonymous with sustained attention, working memory, or other previously recognized cognitive capacities. An objective test of mindfulness has not been developed.

Another assessment strategy is to ask people to describe their thoughts, feelings, or likely behaviours in response to open-ended questions or vignettes. Responses are recorded and transcribed and then can be analysed by trained coders. The Measure of Awareness and Coping in Autobiographical Memory (MACAM; Moore, Hayhurst, and Teasdale 1996) uses these methods to assess decentring, which is closely related to mindfulness. The psychological literature defines decentring as the ability to observe thoughts and feelings as transitory mental events that do not necessarily reflect reality, truth, or self-worth, are not necessarily important, and do not require particular behaviours in response. The MACAM is a vignette-based interview in which participants are asked to imagine themselves in several mildly distressing situations, such as waiting for a friend who does not show up for a lunch date. They are asked to recall specific occasions from their own lives that are brought to mind by the emotions that the vignettes generated, and to describe these occasions in detail, including their feelings in the situation and how they responded to them. Trained coders rate the responses for the extent to which they demonstrate a decentred stance, defined as awareness of thoughts and feelings as separate from the self. Lower ratings are given for descriptions that suggest being swamped or immersed in undifferentiated thoughts and feelings (feeling 'awful') whereas higher ratings are given for noticing specific thoughts and feelings and recognizing that they can step back from them or let them go. Research shows that the MACAM can be scored reliably and that scores are related in theoretically meaningful ways to important variables, such as recovery from depression and likelihood of experiencing a future episode. Further, the meta-awareness assessed by this procedure has been shown to change with participation in a mindfulness program (Hargus et al. 2010). However, the MACAM is difficult and time-consuming to use. It requires a lengthy one-on-one interaction with a trained interviewer as well as trained coders to rate the responses. These difficulties prompted the recent development of a self-report questionnaire to assess decentring.

Self-report questionnaires are popular for several reasons. They are convenient and efficient and can provide reliable and valid information if they are well constructed for the populations in which they will be used. They serve a vital role in psychological research because many of the variables of interest to clinical psychologists, such as thoughts, emotions, and other mental processes, are observable primarily by the person experiencing them. The most practical way to learn about these psychological variables is to ask people about them. Questionnaires provide a means of asking systematically, in ways that are standardized to permit comparisons between individuals and within individuals over time. Psychologists have developed countless questionnaires over a period of decades. They measure a huge variety of psychological variables, ranging from the relatively narrow (eating expectancies) to the very broad (personality). Many such questionnaires have been used in outcome studies of mindfulness to assess reductions in stress, anxiety, and depression; increases in self-coherence, resilience, and self-compassion; and to predict drop-out from mindfulness programmes. A set of principles and procedures guides the development and evaluation of psychological questionnaires (see Clark and Watson 1995, for an overview). In recent years these methods have been applied to the development of questionnaires designed to measure mindfulness itself. Several mindfulness questionnaires are now available in the published literature. Like most questionnaires, they consist of series of statements (known as items) that respondents rate according to how well each statement describes themselves, often on a scale of 1–5 in which 1 = *not at all true of me*, 3 = *moderately true of me*, and 5 = *very true of me*. Most mindfulness questionnaires are designed to assess the general tendency to be mindful in daily life.

The development of mindfulness questionnaires

What are we measuring?

The first step in constructing a questionnaire is to develop a detailed description of the variable to be measured, usually based on a comprehensive review of the relevant literature. This step is uniquely challenging in the case of mindfulness. Because most psychologists are not Buddhist scholars, the development of mindfulness questionnaires has relied largely on literature written by psychologists who have studied mindfulness or by teachers who have worked to make mindfulness accessible to non-Buddhist Westerners. Several psychologists have noted that the meaning of mindfulness is subtle and elusive and that defining it in precise terms is difficult (Block-Lerner, Salters-Pednault, and Tull 2005; Brown and Ryan 2004). However, numerous definitions and descriptions of mindfulness are available. Perhaps the most well known is an operational definition provided by Kabat-Zinn (1994) who describes mindfulness as 'paying attention in a particular way: on purpose, in the present moment, and nonjudgmentally.' In a later paper, Kabat-Zinn (2003) also suggests that mindfulness includes 'an affectionate, compassionate quality within the attending, a sense of openhearted, friendly presence and interest.' Brown and Ryan (2003) define mindfulness as 'the state of being attentive to and aware of what is taking place in the present.' Similarly, Marlatt and Kristeller (1999) define mindfulness as 'bringing one's complete attention to the present experiences on a moment-to-moment basis.' They also suggest that mindfulness involves observing experiences 'with an attitude of acceptance and loving kindness.' In a somewhat more elaborated description, Segal, Williams, and Teasdale (2002) state that ' . . . in mindfulness practice, the focus of a person's attention is opened to admit whatever enters experience, while at the same time, a stance of kindly curiosity allows the person to investigate whatever appears, without falling prey to automatic judgments or reactivity.' They also note that mindfulness can be contrasted with behaving mechanically, or without awareness of one's actions, in a manner often called *automatic pilot*. Bishop and colleagues (2004) suggest that mindfulness includes bringing 'nonelaborative awareness to current experience' with an orientation of 'curiosity, experiential openness, and acceptance.' While any of these definitions may leave out some significant elements, all seem to capture at least some of the qualities that mindfulness teachers would recognize as important.

Instructions that are commonly used in teaching mindfulness classes provide another source of information about the nature of mindfulness, especially for questionnaire developers, who are often interested in assessing the skills that contemporary mindfulness-based treatments are teaching. These treatments use a variety of methods to teach mindfulness. Some are formal meditation practices whereas others are less formal exercises for cultivating mindfulness in everyday life. Several instructions are common to most mindfulness practices. Participants are typically encouraged to focus their attention on stimuli that are observable in the present moment, such as the sensations and movements of breathing or sounds that can be heard in the environment. If thoughts, emotions, urges, or sensations arise, participants are instructed to observe them closely, and, as best they can, without judgment. Brief, covert labeling of observed experiences, using words or short phrases, is sometimes suggested. For example, participants might silently say, 'thinking,' 'aching,' or 'sadness is here' as their experiences come and go. When practicing mindfulness in daily life, participants are encouraged to bring moment-to-moment awareness to ordinary activities such as eating, walking, or washing dishes, and to gently return their attention to this activity when it wanders away. They are typically asked to bring an attitude or stance of acceptance, allowing, openness, curiosity, kindness, and friendliness to all observed experiences, even if they are unpleasant or unwanted.

Most mindfulness questionnaires are based on definitions, descriptions, and instructions such as these. Many include items that provide examples of the tendency to notice, observe, or pay attention to internal or external present-moment experiences. Items that describe awareness of ongoing activity are very common. Most mindfulness questionnaires also include items that describe taking an accepting, non-judgmental, non-reactive, or non-avoidant stance toward observed experiences. Some include responding to observed experiences with curiosity, kindness, or openness and some include items about noting or labelling observed experiences with words. Most of these questionnaires treat mindfulness as a dispositional or trait-like variable that is roughly consistent over time and across situations. However, it is assumed that the tendency to respond mindfully to daily life experiences is subject to change with practice. Indeed, a central purpose of these questionnaires is to assess changes occurring over the course of a mindfulness-based intervention or a long-term mindfulness practice.

Principles of questionnaire construction

An important principle governing the construction of questionnaires is that, in most circumstances, they should be usable by ordinary people. The general population includes a wide range of education levels and reading skills. Some people may have little knowledge of the variable being measured. For example, although many people probably have idiosyncratic understandings of depression, most are not familiar with the technical terms and diagnostic criteria currently used by mental health professionals. Therefore, depression questionnaires typically use ordinary language to assess common experiences that represent elements of depression, such as feeling sad or guilty, feeling like a failure, having trouble sleeping or concentrating, or losing interest in things, among others. Most people can rate how well such items describe themselves, regardless of their knowledge of or experience with depression.

A related principle of questionnaire design is that each item should assess only one characteristic or idea. For example, 'I avoid social gatherings because I don't like making conversation' is potentially problematic because it contains two distinct topics (avoiding social gatherings and disliking conversation) that might be differentially true for some people. Although some will find this item easy to rate, others may find it puzzling if, for example, they like conversation but avoid social gatherings for another reason, or if they attend gatherings in spite of conversation difficulties. Responses to items like this can be difficult to interpret.

A common practice in writing questionnaires is to include items that directly describe the variable to be measured as well as items that describe its opposite or its absence. For example, the tendency to experience anger can be assessed with items such as 'I am short-tempered' and 'I get irritated easily' or with items such as 'I keep my cool' and 'it takes a lot to make me angry.' With the latter type of item (known as reverse-scored), the scorer reverses the rating before it is added to the total so that high scores consistently reflect a greater tendency to be angry (ratings of 1 are changed to 5, while 5 is changed to 1, and so on). Experts have long recommended that questionnaires include both directly worded and reverse-scored items so that tendencies to be acquiescent or oppositional can be balanced (Nunnelly 1967; Paulhus 1991). Reverse-scored items are very common; however, they can occasionally be problematic. For example, if poorly written they can cause confusion, especially if they create double negatives (is it not true of me that I don't always keep my cool?). In some cases, reverse-scored items may not measure the same concept as directly worded items (Rodebaugh, Woods, and Heimberg 2007). On balance, however, reverse-scored items are generally believed to serve useful purposes.

Since a single item that uses simple language to assess a single idea cannot capture all of the relevant content for any important psychological variable, questionnaires typically have multiple items. For example, the most commonly used questionnaires that assess depression and anxiety each have about 20 items. Ratings are summed to quantify the extent to which the respondent is depressed or anxious. The need for ordinary language also can create the false impression that the resulting questionnaire is simplistic or superficial. In reality, extensive knowledge of the variable in question is needed to write items that represent it in simple terms.

To a large extent, the developers of mindfulness questionnaires have endeavoured to follow the principles just described. Many have assumed that it is useful to assess mindfulness in ordinary people, most of whom have no explicit knowledge of mindfulness or experience with meditation. This assumption is based on the idea that mindfulness is an inherent human capacity that (like most human capacities) varies in the general population, even in the absence of mindfulness training. That is, some people are naturally inclined to be mindful in daily life, some are inclined to be quite unmindful much of the time, and others fall in the middle of the range. As Kabat-Zinn (2003) stated, 'We are all mindful, to one degree or another, moment by moment.' However, it is not useful to ask people explicitly to rate how mindful they are, because they are likely to have idiosyncratic understandings (or no understanding) of what this term means. Instead, ordinary language must be used to describe common and recognizable experiences that are consistent with mindfulness (or a lack of mindfulness), such as noticing sensations in the body, doing something without paying attention, or trying to avoid unpleasant thoughts. That is, the use of everyday language is intended to insure that respondents need not have an understanding of mindfulness in order to complete the questionnaire. They need only to understand the language of each item. Reverse-scored items have been found to be useful for this purpose, perhaps because experiences of mindlessness (doing things automatically) are easily recognizable for most people. Finally, because mindfulness appears to have several elements or facets, an individual item cannot cover all of the relevant content (awareness, non-judging, non-reactivity and so on). Instead, ratings of many items are summed to provide an indication of the respondent's general tendency to be mindful in daily life.

Because writing good items is both difficult and critically important, questionnaire developers commonly ask independent experts to rate the quality of their items on several dimensions. Most developers of mindfulness questionnaires have asked experienced mindfulness teachers or practitioners to rate their items for clarity and for how well they represent the meaning of mindfulness in ordinary language. Items with poor evaluations by experts are usually modified or deleted. The questionnaire is then administered to large groups of respondents and scores are analysed with a variety of statistical methods. Items may be added, deleted, or modified during this process. In this way, most questionnaires evolve over several iterations. The version that is published in a peer-reviewed journal has typically been extensively studied. Following is a brief description of the mindfulness questionnaires that have been published so far. Table 1 lists these with examples of items from each.

Published mindfulness questionnaires

The Freiburg Mindfulness Inventory (FMI; Buchheld, Grossman, and Walach 2001) is a 30-item questionnaire assessing non-judgmental present-moment observation and openness to negative experience. The original version was developed with participants in mindfulness meditation retreats and (it is important to note) was designed for use with experienced meditators. Thus, the meaning of some items may be unclear to persons without meditation experience. A later version (Walach et al. 2006) consisting of 14 of the original items, was developed for use with nonmeditating populations. The items shown in Table 1 appear on both versions.

The Mindful Attention Awareness Scale (MAAS; Brown and Ryan 2003) is a 15-item instrument measuring attention to and awareness of present-moment experience in daily life. Items describe characteristics that are inconsistent with mindfulness, such as acting on automatic pilot, being preoccupied, and not paying attention to the present moment. Ratings are then reversed so that high scores represent high levels of mindfulness.

TABLE 1
Published mindfulness questionnaires and example items

Freiburg Mindfulness Inventory
I am open to the experience of the present moment.
I sense my body, whether eating, cooking, cleaning, or talking.
When I notice an absence of mind I gently return to the experience of the here and now.

Mindful Attention Awareness Scale
I find myself doing things without paying attention. (R)
I break or spill things because of careless, not paying attention, or thinking of something else. (R)
It seems I am "running on automatic" without much awareness of what I'm doing. (R)

Kentucky Inventory of Mindfulness Skills
When I'm walking, I deliberately notice the sensations of my body moving.
I'm good at findings the words to describe my feelings.
When I do things, my mind wanders off and I'm easily distracted. (R)
I tell myself that I shouldn't be feeling the way I'm feeling. (R)

Cognitive and Affective Mindfulness Scale - Revised
I am able to focus on the present moment.
I am preoccupied by the past. (R)
I am able to accept the thoughts and feelings I have.

Southampton Mindfulness Questionnaire
When I have distressing thoughts or images, I am able just to notice them without reacting.
When I have distressing thoughts or images, I judge the thought or image as good or bad. (R)
When I have distressing thoughts or images, in my mind I try and push them away. (R)

Five Facet Mindfulness Questionnaire
(This is a composite of the preceding five questionnaires and includes items from each.)

Philadelphia Mindfulness Scale
I am aware of what thoughts are passing through my mind.
When someone asks how I'm feeling, I can identify my emotions easily.
I tell myself that I shouldn't have certain thoughts. (R)

Toronto Mindfulness Scale
I was curious to see what my mind was up to from moment to moment.
I was receptive to observing unpleasant thoughts and feelings without interfering with them.
I approached each experience by trying to accept it, no matter whether it was pleasant or unpleasant.

Note: R = reverse-scored item

The Kentucky Inventory of Mindfulness Skills (KIMS; Baer, Smith, and Allen 2004) is a 39-item instrument designed to measure four elements of mindfulness: observing present-moment experiences, describing (applying verbal labels), acting with awareness, and accepting present-moment experiences without judgment. It was based largely on the conceptualization of mindfulness skills in DBT, although efforts were made to be consistent with descriptions of mindfulness in MBSR and MBCT and with writings by meditation teachers such as Goldstein and Kornfield (1987), Gunaratana (2002) and Rosenberg (1998).

The Cognitive and Affective Mindfulness Scale–Revised (CAMS-R; Feldman et al. 2007) is a 12-item questionnaire designed to measure attention, awareness, present-focus, and acceptance and non-judgment of thoughts and feelings in general daily life.

The Southampton Mindfulness Questionnaire (Chadwick et al. 2008) is a 16-item instrument designed to measure elements of mindfulness when unpleasant thoughts and images arise, including mindful observation, letting go, non-aversion, and non-judgment.

The Five Facet Mindfulness Questionnaire (FFMQ; Baer et al. 2006) is a 39-item composite of the five instruments just described. Empirical and statistical procedures were used to identify and select the items from these questionnaires with the strongest psychometric properties. The FFMQ measures five elements of mindfulness: observing, describing, acting with awareness, non-judging of inner experience, and non-reactivity to inner experience.

The Philadelphia Mindfulness Scale (PHLMS; Cardaciotto et al. 2008) is a 20-item questionnaire designed to measure two dimensions of mindfulness: awareness and acceptance. Awareness items assess noticing or observing of internal and external experiences. Acceptance items assess non-judging and openness to experience and refraining from attempts to escape or avoid them.

The Toronto Mindfulness Scale (Lau et al. 2006) measures the attainment of a mindful state during an immediately preceding mindfulness exercise. Participants first practice a 15-minute meditation exercise and then rate the extent to which they were mindful of their experience during the exercise. The TMS includes two factors: curiosity about (or interest in) inner experiences and decentring from experiences (awareness of them without being caught up in or carried away by them). A modified version of the TMS (Davis, Lau, and Cairns 2009) made small changes to the items in order to measure the same tendencies in general daily life. For example, instead of 'I was curious about each of my thoughts and feelings as they occurred' this version reads, 'I am curious about each of my thoughts and feelings as they occur.'

Evaluating mindfulness questionnaires

The published literature provides encouraging evidence that the mindfulness questionnaires just described are reasonably sound. For example, scores for most of them are significantly correlated with each other. This suggests that their authors have similar (though not identical) conceptions of the general nature of mindfulness in daily life. An exception to this pattern is the original version of the Toronto Mindfulness Scale, which does not measure mindfulness in daily life, but instead measures mindfulness during a particular mindfulness exercise. Most mindfulness questionnaires are correlated with psychological characteristics that, theoretically, should be related to mindfulness. For example, because mindfulness includes allowing thoughts to come and go on their own time, it should be negatively correlated with thought suppression (the tendency to try to get rid of unwanted thoughts). Similarly, mindfulness involves a particular type of attention to emotions and therefore should be positively correlated with emotional intelligence. Research consistently supports these patterns (Baer et al. 2006; Brown and Ryan 2003). A recent neuroimaging study (Way et al. 2010) found significant negative correlations between self-reported mindfulness (measured with the MAAS) and amygdala activity (which is associated with depression), providing preliminary evidence that self-reported mindfulness is associated with objectively measured brain activity.

Participants in MBSR and MBCT have shown significant increases in mindfulness scores over the course of treatment, suggesting that they are learning to be more mindful in daily life (Carmody and Baer 2008; Kuyken et al. 2010). In MBSR participants, Carmody and Baer (2008) found that improvements in self-reported mindfulness (as measured by the FFMQ) were strongly correlated with time spent in home mindfulness practice (as recorded in weekly diaries) and with the extent of reduction in psychological symptoms and stress. Statistical analyses suggested that the increase in mindfulness skills brought about by home practice was responsible for the observed improvements in psychological health. These findings provide the first empirical evidence for the idea that practicing mindfulness leads to increased mindfulness in daily life, which in turn reduces psychological suffering. Similarly, depressed persons who completed MBCT showed increases in mindfulness skills (measured with the KIMS) that predicted reduced depression 15 months later (Kuyken et al. Forthcoming).

Other evidence for the validity of mindfulness questionnaires comes from studies of long-term meditators, who have shown higher scores than non-meditators on several of these measures (see Baer, Walsh, and Lykins 2009, for a review). A recent comparison of meditators and non-meditators (Baer et al. 2008) found that the development of mindfulness skills in daily life (as measured by the FFMQ) appeared to be responsible for the improved psychological wellbeing that was associated with extent of meditation experience. Overall, the research literature suggests that data from mindfulness questionnaires show patterns that are consistent with theoretical expectations. Thus, they appear to be useful tools for studying the nature of mindfulness and are providing important information about the fruits of mindfulness training for psychological functioning.

However, mindfulness questionnaires have also been met with skepticism. Some of the objections to mindfulness questionnaires apply to all self-report instruments. Questionnaires can be subject to biases in which respondents misrepresent themselves, either deliberately or unconsciously. In the case of mindfulness questionnaires, people who recognize the mindfulness-consistent response may rate themselves as highly mindful, regardless of their true tendencies, especially if the circumstances create a demand for such a pattern. Experienced meditators, for example, may wish to create the impression that their practice has made them very mindful, or they may genuinely perceive that it has, when in reality their tendency to be mindful is weaker than they report. Similarly, participants in MBSR or MBCT, who have just spent eight weeks engaged in the intensive practice of mindfulness meditation, may show a deliberate or unconscious bias toward reporting large increases in their tendency to be mindful, regardless of the real effects of treatment.

While such biases are possible, it is unlikely that they account for the promising findings with mindfulness questionnaires. Response biases have been recognized for decades and psychologists have studied them extensively. Substantial response biases are observed primarily in settings where important personal consequences (such as gaining custody of one's children or being hired for a desirable job) depend on the findings of the assessment. When responses are anonymous or confidential and have no consequences for participants, distortion appears to be rare (Costa and Mccrae 1992b). The mindfulness literature shows that many participants are willing to provide data that are inconsistent with positive biases. For example, in studies that include home practice times, the average amount of self-reported home practice is often much less than was recommended. Furthermore, although outcomes for MBSR are generally positive, some studies show only small effects, suggesting that participants who experienced little benefit are willing to say so. Research in other areas of psychology shows that self-reports often are significantly correlated with other methods of assessment. Self-reported personality traits are correlated with reports by spouses or peers, regardless of the desirability of the trait (warmth, altruism, hostility, impulsiveness; Costa and McCrea 1992a). Self-reported alcohol use corresponds reasonably well with both biochemical markers and spousal reports of drinking (Del Boca and Darkes 2003). This is especially encouraging because of the potential for response biases when people report on their alcohol use. To the extent that self-reports and other methods disagree, it should not be assumed that self-reports are necessarily less accurate. Biochemical markers can be influenced by extraneous factors. Reports by others, even if they know the person well, are not always based on the same information that is available to the self-reporter. Overall, the literature suggests that self-reports are generally useful. The recent mindfulness literature suggests that when they change during treatment, they predict important downstream consequences (Carmody and Baer 2008; Kuyken et al. 2010).

A related concern that is more specific to mindfulness questionnaires is that, even when respondents are being honest and candid, they are unable to report accurately on their own tendency to be mindful because they are unaccustomed to noticing these aspects of their own functioning. As noted earlier, questionnaire developers have attempted to avoid this problem by writing items that use ordinary language to describe common experiences that most people recognize, even if they do not know that such experiences are consistent (or inconsistent) with mindfulness. For example, noticing how one's body is feeling, doing something without paying attention, and trying to get rid of negative thoughts appear to be familiar experiences, even for people with no mindfulness training. People should therefore be able to rate how often they have such experiences or how typical such experiences are for them. Research on mind-wandering shows that ordinary people are able to report on whether their minds were wandering at particular times during an experiment (Smallwood, McSpadden, and Schooler 2007), and that such reports correlate with cognitive measures such as how successfully they are able to generate random numbers (Teasdale et al. 1995). These findings imply that people can also report on such experiences in daily life.

An additional concern about mindfulness questionnaires is that knowledge and experience with mindfulness meditation may lead meditators and non-meditators to interpret the meaning of items in different ways. The use of ordinary language to describe common experiences is intended to circumvent this problem. However, empirical evidence suggests that items about noticing or observation of experiences (see the *observing* scales from the KIMS and FFMQ) function differently in meditating and non-meditating samples. Meditators seem to interpret *observing* to mean attending to experience in a non-judgmental and non-reactive way (consistent with mindfulness), whereas non-meditators appear to interpret *observing* as attending to experience in ways that might (or might not) be highly judgmental and reactive. These findings suggest that the *observing* items may provide misleading or confusing findings in non-meditating samples and should be used with caution. Modification or deletion of *observing* items may be helpful in the development of future mindfulness questionnaires.

Another recent study of meditators and non-meditators (Van Dam, Earleywine, and Danoff-Burg 2009) reported statistical evidence of differential item functioning for many FFMQ items. However, these findings are questionable on several grounds and a subsequent study (Baer, Samuel and Lykins, forthcoming) did not replicate them. Moreover, it is possible that differences between meditators and non-meditators in ways of understanding particular items are not always problematic. A similar pattern probably occurs for many psychological characteristics for which self-report questionnaires are well established. For example, people who have experienced major depressive episodes may have much more subtle and nuanced understandings of what it means to feel guilty, worthless, or suicidal than people who have never been depressed. This does not prevent never-depressed persons from providing useful responses on depression questionnaires that can be directly compared to responses from currently or previously depressed persons.

Regardless of how this specific issue is resolved, these recent findings illustrate an important benefit of questionnaire development: conceptualizing the variable to be measured by writing questionnaire items and then testing them empirically provides evidence that contributes to refining the conceptualization, which in turn may lead to improved measurement strategies. In other words, we need research to reveal surprising results to understand better the underlying variable we are measuring, and how best to measure it. Efforts to assess mindfulness are very recent, compared with the assessment of long-recognized variables such as depression, anxiety, and personality. Thus, it is not surprising that some of these attempts have yielded unexpected findings.

In spite of their promising features, it is clear that mindfulness questionnaires are imperfect in a variety of ways. As noted earlier, the *observing* items appear to mean different things to meditating and non-meditating samples, especially when the non-meditators are undergraduate students. This has resulted in some anomalous findings. For example, in student samples, the *observing* scale from the FFMQ is positively correlated with both adaptive and maladaptive characteristics (openness to experience, emotional intelligence, psychological symptoms, thought suppression; Baer et al. 2006). In another recent study, smoking and binge drinking college students unexpectedly obtained higher scores on the Freiburg Mindfulness Inventory than non-drinking, non-smoking students (Leigh, Bowen, and Marlatt 2005). This difference was due to high levels of bodily awareness in the drinkers and smokers, again suggesting that non-meditating students may observe their bodily sensations in unmindful ways. In addition, the *describing* scales found on the KIMS and FFMQ are more relevant to some mindfulness training approaches than to others. The rationale for *describing* as an element of mindfulness questionnaires is that the tendency to say, 'Ah, sadness has arisen' or 'here are self-critical thoughts' reflects a mindful stance toward these experiences; they have been observed and noted in non-judgmental terms. However, describing is not uniformly emphasized in mindfulness training approaches, and the *describing* items do not necessarily capture the non-judging quality (it is possible to describe one's experiences judgmentally). Some authors also have expressed concern that the absence of a particular quality does not always imply the presence of its opposite (Grossman and Van Dam 2011), and that reverse-scored items are therefore problematic. While this is a valid concern, it does not apply to all variables. Although the absence of depression is not happiness (Reise and Waller 2009), a low rate of judging implies non-judging, and a low rate of 'doing things without paying attention' (Brown and Ryan 2003) implies a tendency to act with awareness. Thus, these particular reverse-scored items appear to be conceptually sound. The empirical evidence that they are problematic is debatable; however, the issue needs further study (Baer et al. forthcoming; Van Dam, Earleywine, and Danoff-Burg 2009).

Are questionnaires sufficient to the task of assessing mindfulness? It is widely acknowledged in psychology that most variables should be assessed with multiple methods. Convergence among methods increases confidence that we have measured what we intended to measure. Thus, alternatives to self-report for assessing mindfulness should be developed. The text analysis methods used by the MACAM to assess decentring (described earlier) might be adapted for the study of mindfulness (as in Hargus et al. 2010). Ongoing work on computer-based tasks and brain-based assessment may lead to useful indicators of the tendency to be mindful in daily life. However, it should not be assumed that alternative methods will necessarily be more accurate or more useful than self-reports. All assessment methods are subject to error. Biological markers can be influenced by factors other than the variable under study. They also provide little information about the perceived experience of being mindful. Computer-based tests may not be representative of the same capacity in daily life. For these reasons, it is also important that work continue on improving self-report methods for assessing mindfulness. Toward this end, the ongoing flurry of research using the currently available measures, though lamented by Grossman and Van Dam (2011) as potentially harmful to this field of study, is probably advantageous. It is likely to clarify the strengths and weaknesses of these measures, which in turn should stimulate new ideas about better ways to proceed. The development of new measures designed to rectify the weaknesses of earlier ones is common in the psychological assessment literature. Intense interest in mindfulness suggests that new methods for its assessment will appear over time.

Mindfulness questionnaires and Buddhist conceptions of mindfulness

An important concern about mindfulness questionnaires is that they may not adequately represent the meaning of mindfulness as it is described in the Buddhist tradition. Most questionnaire developers have made strong efforts to be consistent with mindfulness as described Western interventions (MBSR, MBCT, DBT, ACT) and related papers in the psychological literature, and sometimes with contemporary writings by teachers such as Goldstein, Kornfield, and Hanh, among others. However, most do not claim knowledge of original Buddhist texts or their direct translations. Thus, inconsistencies with the original Buddhist conceptions are probably inevitable, for several related reasons. First is the need for secularization of mindfulness, if it is to be accessible to Western populations. Secularization has made the benefits of mindfulness training much more broadly available than would otherwise be possible. However, secularization also may have led to understandings of mindfulness within psychology that do not entirely capture the detail and subtlety of Buddhist teachings. A related factor is the need to define mindfulness in ways that make it amenable to scientific study within the discipline of psychology. For this purpose, it must be described in clear psychological terms. Finally, as noted earlier, most psychologists are not Buddhist scholars and must rely on secondary sources for an understanding of the systems of Buddhist thought and practice in which mindfulness is embedded. These factors suggest two general sources of inconsistency between mindfulness questionnaires and Buddhist conceptions of mindfulness. First, the questionnaires may reflect intentional adaptations made by treatment developers who are knowledgeable and experienced in Buddhist meditation practices, in efforts to maximize feasibility and efficacy of mindfulness training for Western clinical populations. Second, questionnaires may include unintentional and unrecognized distortions of the Buddhist meanings of mindfulness stemming from incomplete knowledge of Buddhist writings.

Several approaches to this situation merit consideration. One is to increase communication between Buddhist scholars and psychologists working with mindfulness, as in this volume. The Buddhist tradition provides an incomparably rich source of knowledge about mindfulness, how it can be taught, and its role in the reduction of suffering. Thus, scholarly work on Buddhist texts and dialogues with teachers of mindfulness in the Buddhist traditions should play an important role in discussions of mindfulness in Western psychological science. It is possible that something important is lost when mindfulness is translated into Western psychological terms. If psychologists can understand more clearly what is lost, we may find ways to mitigate the losses and optimize our assessments and interventions, while maintaining a secular and scientific perspective.

It may also be helpful to remember the distinction between measuring a variable and manipulating it. When we measure a variable (such as mindfulness), we then examine how these measurements relate to other variables (thoughts, emotions, behaviours) and how they change with treatment. For some research purposes, an alternative to measuring mindfulness is to manipulate it. In these studies, we teach mindfulness or guide participants in practicing it and then assess emotions, cognitions, or behaviours soon afterwards. One recent study of this type (Sauer and Baer 2011) asked adults with borderline personality disorder who were in an angry mood to either ruminate or to practice mindfulness for eight minutes and then work on a difficult arithmetic task. Those who had practiced mindfulness persisted much longer in the difficult task than those who had ruminated. Studies like this do not attempt to measure mindfulness, and yet they provide important information about the effects of practicing mindfulness. However, because such studies are often conducted in experimental situations that are somewhat artificial, they tell us little about how mindfulness-based treatments improve mental health in daily life. Thus, both approaches (measuring and manipulating) are considered important methods of study.

Another approach to a lack of consistency with Buddhist conceptions of mindfulness is to recognize that science has its own rules and methods and its outcomes cannot always be predicted. Continued scientific work on the assessment of mindfulness and on mindfulness-based treatments may lead to a conceptualization of mindfulness that is more consistent with the original Buddhist teachings, especially if it is informed by ongoing dialogue with Buddhist teachers. On the other hand, psychological research may eventually suggest that the most helpful ways of conceptualizing and teaching mindfulness for Western clinical populations are not entirely consistent with the original Buddhist teachings. For example, DBT operationalizes mindfulness as a set of behavioural skills that were adapted from Zen practices (Linehan 1993) and do not require formal meditation. The KIMS (Baer, Smith, and Allen 2004), although generally consistent with many accounts of mindfulness, is based largely on this conceptualization of mindfulness skills. Grossman and Van Dam (2011) caution that operationalizing in these ways risks trivializing and banalizing the Buddhist conception of mindfulness. However, clinical experience shows that the mindfulness skills in DBT provide rich and complex experiences for clients that can be deeply meaningful and often transformative. These skills, and recent efforts to assess them, are consistent with the overarching goal of the science of clinical psychology: to maximize the effectiveness of treatments and the understanding of the processes through which they work. In this endeavour, empirical enquiry using the best methods available, and revising our methods when we discover something better, is consistent with the ethics both of the foundational tradition of Buddhism, and of our science.

Conclusions

Within scientific clinical psychology, any treatment that claims to improve mental health by teaching a particular set of skills is subject to evaluation on several dimensions. It is necessary to show (according to the rules of science in this area) that participation in the treatment not only does not harm, but also leads to improvements in mental health that are not attributable to chance. It is also important to determine whether participants are learning what the treatment providers are teaching. If participants are not learning these skills, but their mental health is improving, then the treatment is probably working in unanticipated ways and might be more effective if more time were spent on active ingredients. If participants are learning the skills, and their mental health is improving, it is possible that the skills that are explicitly taught are responsible for the improvements in mental health. However, it is also possible that these skills have little to do with the beneficial outcomes and that improved mental health is due to other components of treatment. If this is the case, the treatment will be more effective if more effort is devoted to the elements that are responsible for the observed improvement. In order to determine whether participants are learning what the treatment is teaching, and whether beneficial outcomes should be attributed to this new learning or to other factors, we cannot avoid the challenge of measuring the processes that may account for therapeutic change.

This is admittedly a difficult challenge in most circumstances. In the case of mindfulness-based treatments, it is especially challenging. Mindfulness originates in ancient Buddhist traditions and is described in texts written long before the advent of Western science and in unfamiliar languages. It appears that understanding what the original Buddhist literature means by 'mindfulness' is not a simple matter. Given these realities, it is unlikely that Western psychologists' current understandings of mindfulness completely capture Buddhist teachings. In spite of these difficulties, the research literature suggests that teaching mindfulness in the forms that pioneering Western teachers such as Kabat-Zinn, Linehan, Goldstein, Kornfield, and Salzberg have developed is beneficial in many ways and for many different problems and conditions. The commitment to scientific study requires that we apply the best available methods to understanding what we are teaching in mindfulness-based treatments, what our participants are learning, and how this new learning is helpful to them.

While contemplating these sobering responsibilities, let us acknowledge how far we have already come. Within only a few decades, potential benefits of mindfulness training have become available to huge numbers of Westerners, many of whom have been suffering from severe conditions, such as depression, chronic pain, and borderline personality disorder. Within even fewer years, enough scientific evidence has accumulated to suggest that mindfulness-based treatment approaches are probably effective in treating these conditions and many others. More recently, we are beginning to understand, in scientific and psychological terms, the processes through which these beneficial outcomes arise. None of this would be possible without the efforts of many teachers, scholars, researchers, and writers to make mindfulness accessible to the Western community. Adaptations from the original Buddhist teachings may be necessary, and unintended and unrecognized conceptual slippage may be hard to avoid. On balance, however, the benefits seem to outweigh the difficulties.

REFERENCES

BAER, R. A., D. B. SAMUEL, and E. LYKINS. 2011. Differential item functioning on the Five Facet Mindfulness Questionnaire is minimal in demographically matched meditators and nonmeditators. *Assessment* 18: 3–10.

BAER, R. A., G. T. SMITH, and K. B. ALLEN. 2004. Assessment of mindfulness by self-report: The Kentucky Inventory of Mindfulness Skills. *Assessment* 11: 191–206.

BAER, R. A., G. T. SMITH, J. HOPKINS, J. KRIETEMEYER, and L. TONEY. 2006. Using self-report assessment methods to explore facets of mindfulness. *Assessment* 13: 27–45.

BAER, R. A., G. T. SMITH, E. LYKINS, D. BUTTON, J. KRIETEMEYER, S. SAUER, E. WALSH, D. DUGGAN, and J. M. G. WILLIAMS. 2008. Construct validity of the five facet mindfulness questionnaire in meditating and nonmeditating samples. *Assessment* 15: 329–42.

BAER, R. A., E. WALSH, and E. L. B. LYKINS. 2009. Assessment of mindfulness. In *Clinical handbook of mindfulness*, ed., F. Didonna, 153–68. New York: Springer.

BISHOP, S. R., M. LAU, S. SHAPIRO, L. CARLSON, N. C. ANDERSON, J. CARMODY, Z. V. SEGAL et al. 2004. Mindfulness: A proposed operational definition. *Clinical Psychology: Science and Practice* 11: 230–41.

BLOCK-LERNER, J., K. SALTERS-PEDNAULT, and M. T. TULL. 2005. Assessing mindfulness and experiential acceptance: Attempts to capture inherently elusive phenomena. In *Acceptance and mindfulness-based approaches to anxiety: Conceptualization and treatment*, ed. S. M. Orsillo, and L. Roemer, 71–100. New York: Springer.

BROWN, K. W., and R. M. RYAN. 2003. The benefits of being in the present: Mindfulness and its role in psychological well-being. *Journal of Personality and Social Psychology* 84: 822–48.

BUCHHELD N., P. GROSSMAN, and H. WALACH. 2001. Measuring mindfulness in insight meditation and meditation-based psychotherapy: The development of the Freiburg Mindfulness Inventory (FMI). *Journal for Meditation and Meditation Research* 1: 11–34.

CARDACIATTO, L., J. D. HERBERT, E. M. FORMAN, E. MOITRA, and V. FARROW. 2007. The assessment of present-moment awareness and acceptance: The Philadelphia Mindfulness Scale. *Assessment* 15: 204–23.

CARMODY, J., and R. A. BAER. 2008. Relationships between mindfulness practice and levels of mindfulness, medical and psychological symptoms, and well-being in a mindfulness-based stress reduction program. *Journal of Behavioral Medicine* 31: 23–33.

CHADWICK, P., M. HEMBER, J. SYMES, E. PETERS, E. KUIPERS, and D. DAGNAN. 2008. Responding mindfully to unpleasant thoughts and images: Reliability and validity of the Southampton mindfulness questionnaire. *British Journal of Clinical Psychology* 47: 451–5.

CLARK, L. A., and D. WATSON. 1995. Constructing validity: Basic issues in objective scale development. *Psychological Assessment* 7: 309–19.

COSTA, P. T., and R. R. MCCRAE. 1992a. *NEO Personality Inventory–Revised: Professional manual*. Odessa, FL: Psychological Assessment Resources.

COSTA, P. T., and R. R. MCCRAE. 1992b. Normal personality assessment in clinical practice: The NEO personality inventory. *Psychological Assessment* 4: 5–15.

DAVIS, K., M. LAU, and D. CAIRNS. 2009. Development and preliminary validation of a trait version of the Toronto Mindfulness Scale. *Journal of Cognitive Psychotherapy* 23: 185–97.

DEL BOCA, F. K., and J. DARKES. 2003. The validity of self-reports of alcohol consumption: State of the science and challenges for research. *Addiction* 98 (suppl. 2): 1–12.

FELDMAN, G. C., A. M. HAYES, S. M. KUMAR, J. G. GREESON, and J. P. LAURENCEAU. 2007. Mindfulness and emotion regulation: The development and initial validation of the cognitive and affective mindfulness scale-revised (CAMS-R). *Journal of Psychopathology and Behavioral Assessment* 29: 177–90.

GOLDSTEIN, J., and J. KORNFIELD. 1987. *Seeking the heart of wisdom: The path of insight meditation*. Boston, MA: Shambhala Classics.

GROSSMAN, P., and N. T. VAN DAM. 2011. Mindfulness, by any other mame...: Trials and tribulations of *sati* in western psychology and science. *Contemporary Buddhism* 12: 219–239.

GUNARATANA, B. H. 2002. *Mindfulness in plain English*. Somerville, MA: Wisdom Publications.

HARGUS, E., C. CRANE, T. BARNHOFER, and J. M. G. WILLIAMS. 2010. Effects of mindfulness on meta-awareness and specificity of describing prodromal symptoms in suicidal depression. *Emotion* 10: 34–42.

HAYES, S. C., K. STROSAHL, and K. G. WILSON. 1999. *Acceptance and commitment therapy: An experiential approach to behavior change*. New York: Guilford.

JHA, A. P., J. KROMPINGER, and M. J. BAIME. 2007. Mindfulness training modifies subsystems of attention. *Cognitive, Affective, & Behavioral Neuroscience* 7: 109–19.

JHA, A. P., E. Z. STANLEY, A. KIYONAGA, L. WONG, and L. GELFAND. 2010. Examining the protective effects of mindfulness training on working memory capacity and affective experience. *Emotion* 10: 54–64.

KABAT-ZINN, J. 1982. An outpatient program in behavioral medicine for chronic pain patients based on the practice of mindfulness meditation: Theoretical considerations and preliminary results. *General Hospital Psychiatry* 4: 33–47.

KABAT-ZINN, J. 1990. *Full catastrophe living: Using the wisdom of your mind and body to face stress, pain, and illness.* New York: Delacorte.

KABAT-ZINN, J. 1994. *Wherever you go, there you are: Mindfulness meditation in everyday life.* New York: Hyperion.

KABAT-ZINN, J. 2003. Mindfulness-based interventions in context: Past, present and future. *Clinical Psychology: Science and Practice* 10: 144–56.

KUYKEN, W., E. WATKINS, E. HOLDEN, K. WHITE, R. S. TAYLOR, S. BYFORD, A. EVANS, S. RADFORD, J. D. TEASDALE, and T. DALGLEISH. 2010. How does mindfulness-based cognitive therapy work? *Behaviour Research and Therapy* 48: 1105–12.

LAU, M., S. BISHOP, Z. SEGAL, T. BUIS, N. ANDERSON, L. CARLSON, S. SHAPIRO, J. CARMODY, S. ABBEY, and G. DEVINS. 2006. The Toronto mindfulness scale: Development and validation. *Journal of Clinical Psychology* 62: 1445–67.

LEIGH, J., S. BOWEN, and G. A. MARLATT. 2005. Spirituality, mindfulness, and substance abuse. *Addictive Behaviors* 30: 1335–41.

LINEHAN, M. M. 1993. *Cognitive-behavioral treatment of borderline personality disorder.* New York: Guilford.

MARLATT, G. A., and J. L. KRISTELLER. 1999. Mindfulness and meditation. In *Integrating spirituality into treatment*, ed. W. R. Miller, 67–84. Washington DC: American Psychological Association.

MOORE, R. G., H. HAYHURST, and J. D. TEASDALE. 1996. Measure of awareness and coping in autobiographical memory: Instruction for administering and coding. Unpublished manuscript, University of Cambridge.

NUNNALLY, J. C. 1967. *Psychometric theory.* New York: McGraw Hill.

PAULHUS, D. L. 1991. Measurement and control of response bias. In *Measures of personality and social psychological attitudes*, ed. J. P. Robinson, P. R. Shaver, and L. S. Wrightsman, 17–59. San Diego, CA: Academic Press.

REISE, S. P., and N. G. WALLER. 2009. Item response theory and clinical measurement. *Annual Review of Clinical Psychology* 5: 27–48.

RODEBAUGH, T. L., C. M. WOODS, and R. G. HEIMBERG. 2007. The reverse of social anxiety is not always the opposite: The reverse-scored items of the social interaction anxiety scale do not belong. *Behavior Therapy* 38: 192–206.

ROSENBERG, L. 1998. *Breath by breath.* Boston, MA: Shambhala.

SAUER, S., and R. A. BAER. 2011. Effects of mindfulness and rumination following an angry mood induction in individuals with borderline personality disorder. Manuscript under review.

SEGAL, Z. V., J. M. G. WILLIAMS, and J. D. TEASDALE. 2002. *Mindfulness-based cognitive therapy for depression: A new approach to preventing relapse.* New York: Guilford.

SMALLWOOD, J., M. MCSPADDEN, and J. SCHOOLER. 2007. The lights are on but on one's home: Meta-awareness and the decoupling of attention when the mind wanders. *Psychonomic Bulletin and Review* 14: 527–33.

TEASDALE, J. D., B. H. DRITSCHEL, M. J. TAYLOR, and L. PROCTOR. 1995. Stimulus-independent thought depends on central executive resources. *Memory and Cognition* 23: 551–9.

VAN DAM, N. T., M. EARLEYWINE, and S. DANOFF-BURG. 2009. Differential item functioning across meditators and nonmeditators on the five facet mindfulness questionnaire. *Personality and Individual Differences* 47: 516–21.

WALACH, H., N. BUCHHELD, V. BUTTENMULLER, N. KLEINKNECHT, and S. SCHMIDT. 2006. Measuring mindfulness—the Freiburg mindfulness inventory (FMI). *Personality and Individual Differences* 40: 1543–55.

WAY, B. M., D. J. CRESWELL, N. I. EISENBERGER, and M. D. LIEBERMAN. 2010. Dispositional mindfulness and depressive symptomatology: Correlations with limbic and self-referential neural activity during rest. *Emotion* 10: 12–24.

ON SOME DEFINITIONS OF MINDFULNESS

Rupert Gethin

The Buddhist technical term was first translated as 'mindfulness' by T.W. Rhys Davids in 1881. Since then various authors, including Rhys Davids, have attempted definitions of what precisely is meant by mindfulness. Initially these were based on readings and interpretations of ancient Buddhist texts. Beginning in the 1950s some definitions of mindfulness became more informed by the actual practice of meditation. In particular, Nyanaponika's definition appears to have had significant influence on the definition of mindfulness adopted by those who developed MBSR and MBCT. Turning to the various aspects of mindfulness brought out in traditional Theravāda definitions, several of those highlighted are not initially apparent in the definitions current in the context of MBSR and MBCT. Moreover, the MBSR and MBCT notion of mindfulness as 'non-judgmental' needs careful consideration from a traditional Buddhist perspective. Nevertheless, the difference in emphasis apparent in the theoretical definitions of mindfulness may not be so significant in the actual clinical application of mindfulness techniques.

It appears to have been T. W. Rhys Davids who first translated the Buddhist technical term *sati* (in its Pali form) or *smṛti* (in its Sanskrit form) by the English word 'mindfulness'. We cannot be sure quite what considerations led Rhys Davids to choose this word, since so far as I know he nowhere reveals them. The dictionaries he would have had before him— Monier Williams 1872, Childers 1875, Böhtlingk and Roth 1855–1875 [1]—would have suggested such translations as 'remembrance, memory, reminiscence, recollection, thinking of or upon (any person or thing), calling to mind' (from Monier Williams 1872), since this was the usual everyday meaning of the then more familiar Sanskrit term *smṛti*. It is true that for the verb *smarati*, Monier Williams gives the following as the initial range of meanings: 'to remember ... to recollect, call to mind, bear in mind, think of, think upon, be mindful of', and this may have suggested the translation 'mindfulness'. Yet Childers' 1875 Pali dictionary gives merely 'recollection', adding, perhaps mindful that he was here dealing with a Buddhist technical term, 'active state of mind, fixing the mind strongly upon any subject, attention, attentiveness, thought, reflection, consciousness'; for the expression *upaṭṭhitā sati* he gives 'presence of mind' and for *satipaṭṭhāna* he gives 'fixing the attention, earnest meditation'. Of course, there is no reason to assume that 'mindfulness' is necessarily a particularly surprising translation of *sati*; the OED records the use of the English 'mindfulness' in the sense of 'the state or quality of being mindful; attention; memory (*obs.*); intention, purpose (*obs.*)' from 1530 (*www.oed.com*).

It is clear, however, that the early translators of Buddhist texts were uncertain quite how to render *sati* as a Buddhist technical term, since words like 'remembrance' and 'memory' did not seem quite to fit what was required by its Buddhist usage. The earliest rendering I have been able to find is Gogerly's 1845 'correct meditation' for *sammā-sati* in the context of the eightfold path.[2] In 1850, Spence Hardy explained 'smirti' as 'the faculty that reasons on moral subjects, the conscience' (1850, 442). Three years later in his *Manual of Buddhism*, in several places he leaves the term untranslated (1853, 412, 413), but explains *satipaṭṭhāna* as 'four subjects of thought upon which the attention must be fixed, and that must be rightly understood' (1853, 497) and *sati* as a constituent of awakening (*sambojjhaṅga*) as 'the ascertainment of truth by mental application' (1853, 498) and, in his index, as simply 'conscience' (1853, 531). It is easy to be dismissive of these early 'missionary' explanations and translations as inadequate and based on misunderstanding, yet both Gogerly and Spence Hardy spent many years in Ceylon, were proficient in Sinhala and had close dealings with both lay and monastic Buddhists; thus their renderings and explanations are likely to reflect at least impressions derived from those interactions.

In 1881, T. W. Rhys Davids published translations of seven *suttas* from the Dīgha and Majjhima Nikāyas. His translation of the *Mahāparinibbāna Sutta* suggests some uncertainty about the correct rendering of *sati*. We find *sati* as 'mental activity' (Rhys Davids 1881, 9, 14, 63), as simply 'thought' (1881, 63); while the *satipaṭṭhānas* are also the 'earnest meditations' (1881, 62, 63).[3] Yet it is perhaps already clear that 'mindfulness' had become Rhys Davids' preferred translation. In his introduction to the translation of the *Dhammacakkappavattana Sutta* he comments of *sammā-sati* in the context of the eightfold path:

> *sati* is literally 'memory,' but is used with reference to the constantly repeated phrase 'mindful and thoughtful' (*sato sampajāno*); and means that activity of mind and constant presence of mind which is one of the duties most frequently inculcated on the good Buddhist. (Rhys David 1881, 145)

In his 1899 translation of the first volume of the Dīgha Nikāya he uses 'mindful(ness)' more or less consistently,[4] but it is only with his 1910 translation of the *Mahāsatipaṭṭhāna Sutta*[5] that Rhys Davids offers more developed consideration of the term. In the introduction to his translation he makes several points. He suggests that 'the doctrine' expounded in the *sutta* 'is perhaps the most important, after that of the Aryan Path, in early Buddhism' and that the *sutta* remains 'in frequent and popular use among those Buddhists who have adhered to the ancient faith'. On the issue of what 'mindfulness' is, he comments simply that '[t]his Suttanta will show', but goes on to offer certain observations about the term. He suggests that while *sati* is etymologically 'memory', in the Buddhist context this is 'a most inadequate and misleading translation' since *sati* has here become 'the memory, recollection, calling-to-mind, being-aware-of, certain specified facts':

> Of these the most important was the impermanence (the coming to be as the result of a cause, and the passing away again) of all phenomena, bodily and mental. And it included the repeated application of this awareness, to each experience of life, from the ethical point of view. (Rhys David 1910, 322)

Here Rhys Davids seems to be highlighting one of the repeated refrains of the *Mahāsatipaṭṭhāna* Sutta that stresses how the practice of *satipaṭṭhāna* involves watching how things 'come to be' and how they 'pass away'. Rhys Davids next offers some comparative reflections on Buddhist and Christian spirituality:

> When Christians are told: 'Whether therefore ye eat or drink, or whatsoever ye do, do all to the glory of God,' a way is shown by which any act, however lowly, can, by the addition of a remembrance (a Sati), be surrounded by the halo of a high moral enthusiasm; and how, by the continual practice of this remembrance, a permanent improvement in character can be obtained. The Buddhist idea is similar. But the remembrance is of what we should now call natural law, not of a deity. This has been made a cornerstone of the system of ethical self-training. The corresponding cornerstone in the West is conscience; and indeed, so close is the resemblance in their effects that one scholar has chosen 'conscience' as a rendering of Sati;—wrongly, we think, as this introduces a Western idea into Buddhism. (Rhys David 1910, 323)

Whether Rhys Davids has correctly characterized either Buddhist of Christian practice here is no doubt a matter for debate. Nonetheless, from the perspective of early Buddhist texts it is not hard to see what prompted Rhys Davids to draw the comparison he did: the message of *Mahāsatipaṭṭhāna Sutta* might be summed up as 'if you consistently "remember" what it is you are doing in any given moment, you will truly see what it is you are doing; and in truly seeing what it is you are doing, those of your deeds, words and thoughts that are motivated by greed, hatred and delusion will become impossible for you'. The association of 'mindfulness' with 'conscience', however, and its characterization as a kind of ethical intuition is not what has been emphasized or brought out in the definitions that have been current more recently in the context of mindfulness-based cognitive therapy, for example, which tend to stress that mindfulness is a 'non-judgemental' kind of observation.

Leaving this issue aside for the moment, it seems clear at least that with Rhys Davids' translation of the *Mahāsatipaṭṭhāna Sutta*, 'mindfulness' soon became established as the only possible English translation of *sati*. To name but a few significant works, it is the translation used by Chalmers in his partial translation of the Majjhima Nikāya (1926), by Mrs C. A. F. Rhys Davids and F. L. Woodward in their translation of the Saṃyutta Nikāya (1917–1930); by E. M. Hare and F. L. Woodward in their translation of the Aṅguttara Nikāya (1932–1936); and perhaps most significantly by Bhikkhu Ñāṇamoli's in his highly influential translation of Buddhaghosa's *Visuddhimagga*, first published in 1956 and reprinted many times.

So far we have primarily been considering the pioneering scholarly translations of early Buddhist texts. The influence on these of any perspective from actual Buddhist practice is limited, although we cannot rule out that Rhys Davids was influenced in his understanding of *satipaṭṭhāna* by his contact with monks in Ceylon. With Ñāṇamoli's *Path of Purification* (1964), however, we touch directly on the tradition of western monastic practitioners of Buddhism in general, and in particular on a tradition that has identified 'mindfulness' as the 'heart of Buddhist meditation', to use the title of Nyanaponika's important and influential book first published in 1954 (Nyanaponika 1962, 14). This is not the place to attempt to trace the history of this particular tradition in full. But what seems clear is that it is this tradition that lies behind the particular modern western reception of Buddhist meditation that has led to the adoption of both the term 'mindfulness' and certain practices in the context of modern psychotherapy. In broad terms the tradition can be traced from such Burmese meditation teachers as Mahāsī Sayādaw (1904–1982) and U Ba Khin (1899–1971); the former's instructions in meditation were one of the formative influences on Nyanaponika's own understanding of mindfulness and meditation.[6] Nyanaponika developed his initial interest in mindfulness meditation under the influence of two Ceylonese monks Kheminda Thera and Soma Thera. The latter published a translation of the *Satipaṭṭhāna Sutta* and its commentary in 1941 (Soma 1967) after completing a period of meditation practice in Burma in 1936–1937 and returning to Ceylon to spend a period at the Dodanduwa Island Hermitage established by Nyanatiloka (1878–1957) in 1911 (Nyanatusita and Hecker 2008, 36). Nyanaponika himself spent a period practising meditation in Burma with Mahāsī Sayādaw in the early 1950s.[7]

Nyanaponika in fact offers an account of mindfulness that is influenced by his understanding of the technical account of the process of perception (*citta-vīthi*) found in developed Theravāda systematic thought (*abhidhamma*). Mindfulness, he tells us, is no 'mystical' state; rather

> In its elementary manifestation, known under the term 'attention', it is one of the cardinal functions of consciousness without which there cannot be perception of any object at all. (Nyanaponika 1962, 24)

Nyanaponika does not say which, if any, technical Pali term 'attention' corresponds to. In a note (1962, 112) he indicates that he is referring to a stage in perception known as *āvajjana*, 'turning towards (the object)'. Certainly in technical *abhidhamma* terms this is among the barest kinds of attention there is; curiously in *abhidhamma* terms the mental quality of *sati* is not in fact present at this stage in the process of perception, something that Nyanaponika, who certainly had a sound grasp of *abhidhamma*, must have been well aware of. What he is perhaps referring to is the *abhidhamma* understanding of 'bringing to mind' or 'paying attention' (*manasikāra*), which is a feature that is understood to be present in all acts of awareness; moreover, how we initially turn our attention towards objects of perception, despite its being below the threshold of conscious control, is understood to play a crucial part in conditioning our subsequent emotional responses to objects of perception; that is, as governing whether we do in fact respond with 'mindfulness'.[8] What Nyanaponika seems to be suggesting here is that the manner of our initial attention to objects of perception is the seed of mindfulness. Although he goes on to distinguish clearly between this initial 'attention' and 'right mindfulness' (*sammāsati*), he nevertheless subsequently focuses on 'Mindfulness in its specific aspect of "bare attention" ' (Nyanaponika 1962, 30).

In discussing 'bare attention' Nyanaponika contrasts it with our habit of judging what we perceive from the point of view of self-interest; rather than being concerned with a disinterested assessment of how things truly are, we will see objects 'in the light of added subjective judgements' that are bound up with our preconceived sense of ourselves, our personality and ego (Nyanaponika 1962, 32–4). For Nyanaponika, bare attention is a way of beginning to counteract this process whereby with every act of awareness we reinforce certain habits of mind; it is a way of beginning to see things from a different perspective.

Nyanaponika's understanding of mindfulness as bare attention appears to have been widely influential. And while he may have been careful to present it as merely an elementary aspect of the practice of mindfulness and to distinguish it from a fuller understanding of mindfulness proper—right mindfulness as a constituent of the eightfold path—there has sometimes been a tendency for those who have written on mindfulness subsequently to assimilate it to 'bare attention'.

The tradition was disseminated and developed in the West by a number of meditation teachers and writers, including Jack Kornfield (b. 1945) and Joseph Goldstein (b. 1944), to name but two. It is, then, a tradition of Buddhist meditation that bases itself on a particular approach to the *Satipaṭṭhāna Sutta* and identifies this approach as what is meant by the traditional Buddhist term 'insight' (*vipassanā*).

Jack Kornfield in his useful anthology of the teachings of 'living Buddhist masters' (including one woman, Achaan Naeb, lest the term 'master' be read as not gender inclusive) introduces mindfulness as 'the one quality above all others' that is 'key to practice' in the development of wisdom:

> The most direct way to understand our life situation, who we are and how we operate, is to observe with a mind that simply notices all events equally. This attitude of non-judgmental, direct observation allows all events to occur in a natural way. By keeping attention in the present moment, we can see more and more clearly the true characteristics of our mind and body process. (Kornfield 1977, 13)

This provides a good example of an emerging working definition of 'mindfulness'. The key characteristics of this definition are that mindfulness is non-judgmental, direct observation of mind and body in the present moment, along with a claim that this kind of observation is peculiarly efficacious.

The use of Buddhist 'mindfulness' practices in the context of western clinical psychotherapy emerged in the 1980s and early 1990s and is associated above all with the name of Jon Kabat-Zinn and his work at the Stress Reduction Clinic (founded in 1979) and Center for Mindfulness in Medicine, Health Care, and Society (founded 1995) at the University of Massachusetts.[9] Jon Kabat-Zinn's 'mindfulness-based stress reduction' (MBSR) in turn fed into the development of 'mindfulness-based cognitive therapy' (MBCT) (Segal, Williams and Teasdale 2002). The direct Buddhist influences on Kabat-Zinn's approach to MBSR are clear from a number of his writings: certainly the tradition of insight and mindfulness meditation we have been discussing above is one of the major influences, although he also cites other Buddhist meditation practices and his early papers refer to contemplative traditions other than Buddhist.[10] Over the last 20 years the use of MBSR and MBCT as a clinical psychotherapy in America and Europe has grown considerably. In this context, the Buddhist origins of mindfulness, although not exactly a secret, are often underplayed or even not mentioned at all; the approach is practical and what is emphasised is the therapeutic usefulness of mindfulness rather than its Buddhist credentials, although these are sometimes alluded to. Thus in the introduction to *The mindful way through depression* (2007), Williams, Teasdale, Segal, and Kabat-Zinn talk of the clinical use of meditative practices,

> to cultivate a particular form of awareness, known as mindfulness, which originated in the wisdom traditions of Asia. These practices ... have been part of Buddhist culture for millennia ... We soon discovered that the combination of Western cognitive science and Eastern practices was just what was needed to break the cycle of recurrent depression. (Williams et al. 2007, 5)

Segal, Williams and Teasdale's earlier *Mindfulness-Based Cognitive Therapy for Depression* (2002), on the other hand, mentions 'Buddhist mindfulness meditation' only once in passing (2002, 44), although it does recommend for further reading at the conclusion guides to (Buddhist) insight meditation.[11]

How one views the adaptation of Buddhist mindfulness practice to a modern clinical context for the treatment of stress and depression will depend on one's particular perspective. From one sort of Buddhist perspective, the abstraction of mindfulness from its context within a broad range of Buddhist meditative practices might seem like an appropriation and distortion of traditional Buddhism that loses sight of the Buddhist goal of rooting out greed, hatred and delusion. From a different Buddhist perspective, it might seem to be an example of 'skill in means' (*upāya-kauśalya*): it provides a way of giving beings the opportunity to make a first and important initial step on the path that leads to the cessation of suffering. From yet another perhaps still Buddhist perspective that might be characterised as 'modernist', it strips Buddhism of some of its unnecessary historical and cultural baggage, focusing on what is essential and useful. A non-Buddhist perspective might regard the removal of the unnecessary historical and cultural baggage as finally revealing the useful essence that had hitherto been obscured by the Buddhist religion. Finally we might regard the coming together of practices derived from Buddhism with the methods of modern western cognitive science as affording a true advance that supersedes and renders redundant the traditional Buddhist practices. As observers of social history, we might also see it as an example of a change from a cultural situation where we turn to religion to heal our souls to one where we turn to medicine and science.

This is not the place to consider the significance of all these possible attitudes in depth. Whatever attitude we adopt towards it, a particular understanding of and approach towards mindfulness has emerged in the context of MBSR and MBCT; and given the acknowledged Buddhist provenance of mindfulness in general, it seems worth considering whether its translation from ancient India to the modern clinical 'mindfulness centre' has been straightforward or what, if anything, may have been lost in translation.

A full consideration of this question would require discussion not only of the understanding of mindfulness, but of the specific practices used in both the Buddhist and clinical context; this is beyond the scope of the present discussion which will be limited to certain aspects of the understanding of mindfulness.

While some recent discussions of mindfulness in the context of modern psychotherapy problematize its definition, perhaps the most often cited definition is Kabat-Zinn's own succinct 'operational' definition: 'Mindfulness means paying attention in a particular way: on purpose, in the present moment, and non-judgmentally.'[12] A slightly fuller definition that is also cited is:

> [A] kind of nonelaborative, nonjudgmental, present-centered awareness in which each thought, feeling, or sensation that arises in the attentional field is acknowledged and accepted as it is. (Bishop et al. 2004, 232)

As I have already suggested, the essential elements of such a definition can be seen in the characterizations of mindfulness that have emerged in the explicitly Buddhist context of writings by Nyanaponika and Kornfield.

To find a similarly succinct definition of mindfulness in the texts of early Buddhism is not so easy. Such definitions as there are are rather different in character. In response to the question 'what is the faculty of *sati*?' we are told that someone who has *sati* 'possesses perfect *sati* and understanding: he is someone who remembers and recollects what was done and said long before' (S V 197–98).

Another early response to a direct question about the characteristics of *sati* is found in the *Milindapañha* (Mil 37–38) where it is explained that *sati* has two characteristics (*lakkhaṇa*): 'calling to mind' (*apilāpana*) and 'taking possession' (*upagaṇhana*). Thus *sati* is explained as calling to mind wholesome and unwholesome qualities such that the meditator is in a position to know which qualities are the ones he should pursue and which are the ones he should not; this is likened to the manner in which a king's treasurer constantly reminds the king of his glory and property. Secondly, *sati* is said to follow the outcome of qualities and so to know which qualities are beneficial and which are not with the result that the meditator can remove those which are not helpful and take possession of those which are helpful; this is likened to the manner in which a king's adviser keeps the king informed about what is and is not beneficial.

The early Abhidhamma literature (see Dhs 16) lists a number of terms that are intended to illustrate the nature of *sati* and which are of some interest: recollection (*anussati*), recall (*paṭissati*), remembrance (*saraṇatā*), keeping in mind (*dhāraṇatā*), absence of floating (*apilāpanatā*), absence of forgetfulness (*asammussanatā*).

These ancient definitions and the Abhidhamma list of terms seem to be rather at odds with the modern clinical psychotherapeutic definition of mindfulness, and even perhaps with the more recent Buddhist definitions of mindfulness offered by way of exposition of the practice of *satipaṭṭhāna*.

Of course, such differences in the definition of mindfulness might simply reflect the fact that there have been in the history of Buddhist thought and practice somewhat different and even conflicting approaches to and conceptions of mindfulness. While not wishing to discount this possibility, I think it is also possible to suggest ways in which these early definitions complement what we can glean from other early Buddhist discussions of mindfulness; in this way we can perhaps arrive at a fuller and more complete appreciation of the early Buddhist understanding.

The key element in the early definitions, it seems to me, is that they take the sense of *sati* as 'remembering' seriously. The basic idea here is straightforward: if one is instructed to observe the breath and be aware whether it is a long breath or short breath, one needs to remember to do this, rather than forget after a minute, five minutes, 30 minutes, and so forth. That is, one has to remember that what it is one should be doing is remembering the breath. There is a further dimension to this remembering implied by my use of the expression 'what one is supposed to be doing'. That is in the specific context in which the practice of mindfulness is envisaged by ancient Buddhist texts, in remembering that one should remember the breath, one is remembering that one should be doing a meditation practice; in remembering that one should be doing a meditation practice, one is remembering that one is a Buddhist monk; in remembering that one is a Buddhist monk, one is remembering that one should be trying to root out greed, hatred and delusion. Conversely, in forgetting the breath, one is forgetting that one is doing a meditation practice; in forgetting that one is doing a meditation practice, one is forgetting that one is a Buddhist monk; in forgetting that one is a Buddhist monk one is forgetting that one is trying to root out greed, hatred and delusion. This seems to me to make sense of such traditional Buddhist meditations as recollection (*anussati*) of the qualities of the Buddha, the Dhamma and the Sangha, which the texts themselves seem keen to include within the broad framework of mindfulness practice.

I do not want to suggest by this that mindfulness is conceived in terms of a series of conscious and discursive reflections along these lines, but simply that ancient Buddhist texts understand the presence of mindfulness as in effect reminding us of who we are and what our values are. Incidentally, despite the definitions of mindfulness used in the context of MBSR and MBCT, it seems that certainly in practice mindfulness must have something of this quality here also, otherwise it is difficult to see how a patient would have the motivation to sustain the exercises in mindfulness.

There is a further aspect of *sati* as remembering that is, I think, hinted at by especially the *Milindapañha* characterization of *sati* as calling to mind various good and bad, beneficial and unbeneficial qualities. That is, when, for example, I am happy, it is difficult to remember what it feels like to be unhappy; conversely when I am unhappy, it is difficult to remember what it feels like to be happy. In such circumstances, I will be more likely to identify with passing moods and feelings, which may result in their being reinforced and in my being thrown mentally off course or balance. If on, the other hand, I remember when I am happy what it feels like to be unhappy, I am less likely to be thrown when the feeling passes, and more likely to be sympathetic to those around who are not so happy. If I remember when I am unhappy what it feels like to be happy, I may be more able to cope with the feeling until it passes, and less resentful of those around me who are happy. In similar vein, if I lack mindfulness, I may forget how particular patterns of behaviour make me feel and so repeat them. But if I truly remember that last time I acted in such a way it resulted in unpleasant feelings, then it may become more difficult to continue to indulge those patterns of behaviour. Such observations allow us to make some sense of a traditional Buddhist emphasis on *sati* as 'remembering'. It is perhaps worth noting in this context the findings cited by Segal, Williams and Teasdale (2002, 28–30) that suggest a significant factor in the relapse into depression may be the way in which someone vulnerable to depression tends to get lost in a sad mood, which may then provoke habitual patterns of negative thinking.

Two of the Abhidhamma terms given in explanation of mindfulness point towards mindfulness as something rather more than simply present-centered awareness of each thought, feeling, or sensation that arises. These terms are 'absence of floating' (*apilāpanatā*) and 'absence of forgetfulness' (*asammussanatā*). The former term is explained by a simile: absence of floating is to be contrasted with a state when the mind bobs about like a gourd floating on the surface of water; mindfulness, by contrast, plunges into the object of awareness.[13] The second term allows us to make a clearer connection with a semantic range of usage in English that parallels in good measure usage in Pali and Sanskrit. That is, absence of forgetfulness appears to refer not so much to having a good memory for facts and information, as to not being absentminded and forgetful. The term is related in Buddhist texts to two expressions in Pali, *muṭṭhā sati* and *upaṭṭhitā sati*, that literally mean 'mindfulness that is confused' and 'mindfulness that is at hand', but which can perhaps be rendered more idiomatically and even exactly as 'absentmindedness' and 'presence of mind'.[14] Mindfulness for Buddhist texts, it seems, thus has something of the quality of being 'on the ball'.

Let us now turn to one of the classic developed Buddhist definitions of mindfulness, namely that found in the exegetical texts of the Theravāda tradition.

> *Sati* is that by means of which [the qualities that constitute the mind] remember, or it itself is what remembers, or it is simply remembering. Its characteristic is not floating, its property absence of forgetting, its manifestation guarding or being face to face with an object of awareness; its basis is steady perception or the establishing of mindfulness of the body, and so on. Because of its being firmly set in the object of awareness, it should be seen as like a post and, because it guards the gates of the eye and other senses, as like a gatekeeper. (Vism XIV, 141)

We have already dealt with the aspects of remembering, absence of forgetting and not floating highlighted here; 'being face to face with an object of awareness' is straightforward in terms of the kind of definition of mindfulness found both in the context of modern insight meditation and MBSR and MBCT; seeing mindfulness as like a post because of its being firmly set in the object of awareness seems simply to reinforce its characteristic of not floating about.

Mindfulness's manifestation as 'guarding' and as 'like a gatekeeper' seems to allude to a passage describing the 'guarding of the gates of the senses' which is often repeated in the early texts as a prelude to the establishing of mindfulness and clear understanding:

> And how does a monk guard the gates of the senses? In this, when he looks at a visible object with his eyes, he does not hold on to the general experience nor particular aspects. Since someone who lives with the sense of sight unchecked might be affected by longing and discontent, by bad, unwholesome qualities, he tries to practise checking the sense of sight; he guards it, and achieves restraint. When he hears a sound with his ears... smells a smell with his nose... tastes a taste with his tongue... touches an object with his body... is conscious of a thought in his mind, he does not grasp at the general experience nor at particular aspects. Since someone who lives with the mind unchecked might be affected by longing and discontent, by bad, unwholesome qualities, he tries to practise checking the mind; he guards it, and achieves restraint. (See, for example, D I 70)

A simile found elsewhere (S IV 194) likens mindfulness directly to a gatekeeper guarding a city (the body) with six gates (the senses). The characterization of mindfulness as guarding and as like a gatekeeper seems closely related to mindfulness in its capacities of remembering and presence of mind. The suggestion seems to be that if we have mindfulness then we will remember what it is that we should be doing in a given moment (watching the breath, say, or paying attention to posture), and thus when perceptions, feelings, states of mind and emotions that might interfere with this arise, we will have the presence of mind not to let them overcome our minds and take hold.

The statement in the standard Theravāda exegetical definition of mindfulness that its basis is 'steady perception' or 'the establishing of mindfulness of the body, and so on' situates the cultivation and development of mindfulness in the kinds of practice that are set out in the *Satipaṭṭhāna Sutta*. A full exposition of the *Satipaṭṭhāna Sutta* is not possible in the present context, and I shall confine myself to a few observations.

In the first place, it would seem that the taking of the *Satipaṭṭhāna Sutta* as a succinct manual of insight (*vipassanā*) meditation as opposed to calm (*samatha*) meditation is a modern Buddhist reading rather than a traditional one. Neither the term *vipassanā* nor *samatha* in fact occurs in the Sutta, while a number of other Suttas which elaborate the practice of *satipaṭṭhāna* quite clearly integrate it with the practice of absorption (*jhāna*) and concentration (*samādhi*), which come to be seen as emblematic of *samatha* practice; the 'Discourse on mindfulness of the body' (M III, 88–99) presents *precisely* the practices set out in the section of the *Satipaṭṭhāna Sutta* concerned with the body as a basis for the attainment of absorption. The stock description of the manner in which a monk watches body as body, feelings as feelings, mind as mind and qualities as qualities in establishing mindfulness, comments that the monk 'overcomes his longing for and discontent with the world'. Buddhaghosa's fifth-century CE commentary on the *Satipaṭṭhāna Sutta* notes that this phrase can be understood as indicating the abandoning of the five hindrances—the basic obstacles to the attainment of absorption—by means of concentration (Gethin 2001, 49–53).[15] I am not here concerned with trying to establish an original and authentic interpretation of the *Satipaṭṭhāna Sutta*, only with establishing that there is clear evidence in the Pali sources of a traditional reading of the *Satipaṭṭhāna Sutta* as setting out both calm and insight practice, and little explicit indication before the twentieth century that it has been read exclusively in terms of the way of insight.

That watching the body as body with mindfulness should involve overcoming one's longing for and discontent with the world might suggest that mindfulness is envisaged as something rather more sustained and developed than mere bare attention or present moment non-judgmental observation; it suggests that a prerequisite for true mindfulness is watching from the vantage point of a relatively still and peaceful state of mind.

It is possible that 'non-judgmental' should be interpreted as implying a relatively still and peaceful state of mind. This raises the question of what is meant by non-judgmental in the context of the MBSR and MBCT understanding of mindfulness. As we have seen, for Nyanaponika it is clear that what is problematic in the context of mindfulness are our habitual judgments and opinions about how we and others are; being non-judgmental is about making space for a different perspective on how things are. This clearly bears some comparison with the way in which in the context of MBCT 'non-judgmental' mindfulness might counteract the problem of the 'ruminative mind' (Segal, Williams and Teasdale 2002, 33–37). Yet from a traditional Theravāda Buddhist perspective an unqualified emphasis on mindfulness as 'non-judgmental' might be seen as implying that being non-judgmental is an end in itself and that all states of mind are somehow of equal value, that greed is as good as non-attachment, or anger as friendliness. In fact, in the context of MBSR and MBCT, being 'non-judgmental' seems largely to be advocated as a practical stance rather than a final vision of the nature of things, while the question of the ultimate 'value' of our fleeting mental states takes us into complex areas of Buddhist thought and philosophy where different Buddhist traditions may express themselves differently. Yet something of a practical common ground of Buddhist psychology might be expressed by saying that although—or precisely because—the aim is to rid ourselves of greed, hatred and delusion, getting angry with and hating our own greed, hatred and delusion when they arise, or conversely, becoming pleased with and attached to our own non-attachment, friendliness and wisdom when they arise, is clearly something of a trap. And it is perhaps precisely this kind of practical approach that those who pioneered MBSR and MBCT intended to highlight by characterising mindfulness as 'non-judgmental'.

To return to the more general question of a possible distinction between proper mindfulness and simple observation of what is going on, this is perhaps also implied by the way in which the Buddhist definition quoted above draws attention to the fact that the basis of mindfulness is 'steady perception' or 'the establishing of mindfulness of the body, and so on'. That is, steady and clear observation, the bare practice of watching the body as body, do not of themselves guarantee or constitute the presence of real mindfulness; rather they set up the conditions that will conduce to its arising.

That mindfulness is seen as entailing the accomplishment of a sustained presence of mind is perhaps brought out by a particularly vivid simile (S V, 170). Mindfulness of the body is likened to the case of a man who must pay attention to a bowl brim full of oil that he is carrying on his head. The man must do this before a crowd that has gathered to watch the most beautiful girl of the land as she dances and sings; and as the man moves between the girl and the crowd with bowl on his head, he is followed by another man with a drawn sword who, if he spills so much as a drop of the oil, will cut of his head. In such circumstances, it is suggested, the man will pay very careful attention to the bowl of oil on his head and not be distracted by the crowd or girl; with a similar quality of attention the monk should cultivate mindfulness of the body.

I would like to conclude by making a few comments about the way in which mindfulness has been presented as the key practice of Buddhist meditation. As we have seen, this is linked first of all to the notion that it is insight meditation that is the quintessential form of Buddhist meditation and that it is the practice of mindfulness that lies at the heart of insight meditation. I have already suggested that this does not seem to reflect a traditional Theravāda perspective.[16] In the present context two further points seem worth making.

First, the singling out of the practice of mindfulness is in part based on a problematic translation of the characterization of the four ways of establishing mindfulness at the beginning of the Satipaṭṭhāna Sutta as a path that is ekāyana (D II, 290; M I, 55). All the early English translations of the Satipaṭṭhāna Sutta opt for interpreting ekāyana as characterizing the four ways of establishing mindfulness as the *only* path leading to the purification of beings.[17] While the precise interpretation of the expression remains obscure, it seems clear that what it does not mean is 'only', and that it probably means 'going to just one place' or 'single' as opposed to forked and can thus be rendered 'direct': 'this path leading to the purification of beings, namely the four ways of establishing mindfulness, is direct and clear' (Gethin 2001, 59–66).

Secondly, while the practice of mindfulness is certainly regarded as important in early Buddhist accounts of meditation, it is nonetheless always presented as one among several qualities that need to be equally balanced. This is nowhere more so than in the context of the *Satipaṭṭhāna Sutta* itself.

In a number of places in the Nikāyas the Buddhist path is summed up in terms of accomplishing the four ways of establishing of mindfulness through abandoning the five hindrances, and then developing the seven constituents of awakening.[18] Indeed it is possible to read the *Satipaṭṭhāna Sutta* precisely as an expansion of this short statement in so far as the fourth and final stage of establishing mindfulness (watching qualities as qualities) involves first seeing the that the five hindrances have been abandoned and then culminates in the development of the seven constituents of awakening and the understanding of the four noble truths: suffering, its origin, its cessation and the path leading to its cessation. That final awakening is seen precisely as a function of the seven constituents of awakening working in balance rather than as issuing from just the practice of mindfulness, say, or of some other quality, is well illustrated by a discussion of which of the seven constituents of awakening one should try to cultivate when the mind is depressed or dull (*līna*), and which one should try to cultivate when the mind is excited or overactive (*uddhatta*). When the mind is depressed, then is not the right time to develop tranquillity, concentration and equanimity; to do so would be like throwing wet grass on to a small fire that one wants to blaze up. It is, however, the right time to develop investigation of qualities, strength, and joy—just as one should throw dry grass on to a small fire that one wants to blaze up. When the mind is excited, then is not the time to develop investigation of qualities, strength and joy; to do so would be like throwing dry grass on to a great fire that one wants to put out. It is, however, the right time to develop tranquillity, concentration and equanimity—just as one should throw wet grass on to a great fire that one wants to put out. As for the constituent of awakening that is mindfulness, it is appropriate to cultivate this in all of the above circumstances. Thus while mindfulness is distinctive in so far as it can help whether the mind is dull or overactive, it nevertheless remains just one of seven constituents of awakening.

The MBSR and MBCT conception of mindfulness derives in significant part from a particular modern Buddhist tradition of mindfulness. From the perspective of the account of *sati* found in early Buddhist sources, this modern conception does seem to centre on something of a minimalist definition of mindfulness. The traditional Buddhist account of mindfulness plays on aspects of remembering, recalling, reminding and presence of mind that can seem underplayed or even lost in the context of MBSR and MBCT. Yet this may in part simply be a consequence of the particular succinct *definitions* of mindfulness highlighted in the context MBSR and MBCT. For the Buddhist tradition and for MBSR and MBCT, 'mindfulness' is part of a set of practices, and practices can have particular effects whatever our preconceived ideas and theories about them. That is, in its application in a clinical context, further aspects of mindfulness may well manifest and be relevant.

NOTES

Abbreviations: A = *Aṅguttara Nikāya*; As = *Atthasālinī*; D = *Dīgha Nikāya*; Dhs = *Dhammasaṅgaṇi*; M = *Majjhima Nikāya*; Mil = *Milindapañha*; Nett = *Nettippakaraṇa*; S = *Saṃyutta Nikāya*; Vism = *Visuddhimagga*. Editions are those of the Pali Text Society

1. The seventh volume containing the entries for *smar* and *smṛti* was published between 1872 and 1875.
2. Gogerly's translation of portions of the *Dhammacakkappavattana Sutta* as found in the Mahāvagga of the Vinaya (Vin I 8–14) was first published as part of a piece entitled 'On Buddhism' (Gogerly 1845, 23–25); it was subsequently reprinted in Gogerly (1908, 65–66), and is referred to in Rhys Davids (1881, 144).
3. This 1881 translation of the *Mahāparinibbāna Sutta* was reprinted, apparently without any modification, in Rhys Davids (1910, 71–191); for these translations see 85, 89, 130 ('intellectual activity'), 130 ('thought'), 128, 129 ('earnest meditations'). T.W. Rhys Davids, *Buddhism: Being a sketch of the life and teachings of Gautama, the Buddha* was first published in 1877 (London) and subsequently revised and reprinted many times; I have only had access to an 1882 edition (London: SPCK) in which he refers to sati by way of 'right mindfulness' (108), 'four earnest meditations' (172) and 'recollection' (173).
4. He translates *sato sampajāno* as 'mindful and self possessed' throughout.
5. Rhys Davids (1910, 322–46).
6. See Bodhi (1995, 12); Nyanaponika (1962, 85–107).
7. Bodhi (1995, 12). Other works which shaped the early western Buddhist reception of mindfulness include Shattock 1958 (which gives an account of the author's training in the Mahāsi Sayādaw insight method), and Thích Nhất Hạnh (1976).
8. 'But what determines this impulsion with respect to wholesomeness or unwholesomeness? Adverting and determining. For when at [the point of] adverting [the mind] has adverted appropriately and at [the point of] determining [the mind] has determined appropriately, it cannot be that an unwholesome impulsion will occur; [and similarly] when at [the point of] adverting [the mind] has adverted inappropriately and at [the point of] determining [the mind] has determined inappropriately, it cannot be that a wholesome impulsion will occur.' (As 277–78: *idaṃ pana javanaṃ kusalattāya vā akusalattāya vā ko niyāmetī ti? āvajjanaṃ c' eva votthappanañ ca. āvajjanena hi yoniso āvajjite votthappanena yoniso vavatthāpite javanaṃ akusalaṃ*

bhavissatī ti aṭṭhānam etaṃ. āvajjanena ayoniso āvajjite voṭṭhappanena ayoniso vavatthāpite javanaṃ kusalaṃ bhavissatī ti pi aṭṭhānam etaṃ ubhayena pana yoniso āvajjite vavatthāpite ca javanaṃ kusalaṃ hoti, ayoniso akusalan ti veditabbaṃ.)

9. See Kabat-Zinn (1990, 1993). Interestingly OED (*www.oed.com*) now cites a specialized use of 'mindfulness': 'Esp. with reference to Yoga philosophy and Buddhism: the meditative state of being both fully aware of the moment and of being self-conscious of and attentive to this awareness; a state of intense concentration on one's own thought processes; self-awareness'. One of the earliest citations it gives for this usage is Rowe (1983), a book by a clinical psychologist about the treatment of depression; the passage cited (p. 182) comes from a section about the use of mindfulness meditation in dealing with depression.

10. For a recent discussion of the Buddhist influences on Kabat-Zinn, see Gilpin (2008, 232). In addition to Theravāda 'Insight Meditation', Kabat-Zinn (1982, 34) and Kabat-Zinn, Lipworth, and Burney (1985, 165) also cite Soto Zen, and yogic practices expressed in the writings of Krishnamurti, Vimila Thakar, and Nisargadatta Maharaj.

11. Segal, Williams and Teasdale (2002, 325) refers to Goldstein and Kornfield's *Seeking the heart of wisdom: The path of insight meditation.*

12. Kabat-Zinn, (1994, 4); cited, for example, by Segal, Williams and Teasdale (2002, 40).

13. As 147, 405; for a fuller discussion of the term *apilāpanatā* see Gethin (2001, 38–39).

14. Cf. Anālayo (2003, 48).

15. For discussion of mindfulness in the context of *samatha* see Kuan (2008, 58–80).

16. On this see also Cousins (1996).

17. We find 'the one and only path' (Rhys Davids 1910, 327); 'this is the only way' (Soma 1967, 1); 'there is this one way' (Horner 1954, 71).

18. D II 83; III 101; S V 108, 160–1; A III 387; V 195; Nett 94; see Gethin (2001, 58–9, 169, 172, 258).

REFERENCES

ANĀLAYO. 2003. *Satipaṭṭāna: The direct path to realization.* Birmingham: Windhorse.

BISHOP, S. R., M. LAU, S. SHAPIRO, L. CARLSON, N. D. ANDERSON, J. CARMODY, Z. V. SEGAL, S. ABBEY, M. SPECA, D. VELTING, and G. DEVINS. 2004. Mindfulness: A proposed operational definition. *Clinical Psychology: Science and Practice* 11: 230–41.

BODHI, BHIKKHU. 1995. Life sketch of venerable Nyanaponika. In *Nyanaponika: A farewell tribute,* edited by Bhikkhu Bodhi, 8–14. Kandy, Sri Lanka: Buddhist Publication Society.

BÖHTLINGK, O. v., and R. ROTH. 1855. *Sanskrit-Wörterbuch.* St. Petersburg: Buchdruckerei der Kaiserlichen Akademie der Wissenschaften.

CHALMERS, R. 1926. *Further dialogues of the Buddha.* London: H. Milford.

CHILDERS, R. C. 1875. *A dictionary of the Pāli language*. London: Trübner & Co.

COUSINS, L. S. 1996. The Origins of Insight Meditation. *The Buddhist Forum* 4: 35–58.

GETHIN, R. M. L. 2001. *The Buddhist path to awakening: A study of the Bodhi-Pakkhiyā Dhammā*. Oxford: Oneworld.

GILPIN, R. 2008. The use of Theravāda Buddhist practices and perspectives in mindfulness-based cognitive therapy. *Contemporary Buddhism* 9: 227–51.

GOGERLY, D. 1845. On Buddhism. *Journal of the Ceylon Branch of the Royal Asiatic Society* 1: 7–28.

GOGERLY, D. 1908. The books of discipline. In *Ceylon Buddhism being the collected writings of Daniel John Gogerly*, edited by Arthur Stanley Bishop, 45–100. Colombo: Wesleyan Methodist Book Room.

HARDY, R. S. 1850. *Eastern monachism*. London: Partridge and Oakey.

HARDY, R. S. 1853. *A manual of Budhism: In its modern development*. London: Partridge and Oakey.

HARE, E. M., and F. L. WOODWARD. 1932–1936. *The Book of the gradual sayings*. 5 vols. London: Pali Text Society.

HORNER, I. B. 1954–1959. *Middle length sayings*. 3 vols. London: Pali Text Society.

KABAT-ZINN, J. 1982. An outpatient program in behavioral medicine for chronic pain based on the practice of mindfulness meditation. *General Hospital Psychiatry* 4: 33–47.

KABAT-ZINN, J. 1990. *Full catastrophe living: Using the wisdom of your body and mind to face stress, pain, and illness*. New York: Delacorte Press.

KABAT-ZINN, J., L. LIPWORTH, and R. BURNEY. 1985. The clinical use of mindfulness meditation for the self-regulation of chronic pain. *Journal of Behavioral Medicine* 8: 163–90.

KORNFIELD, J. 1977. *Living Buddhist masters*. Santa Cruz: University Press.

KUAN, TSE-FU. 2008. *Mindfulness in early Buddhism: New approaches through psychology and textual analysis of Pali, Chinese, and Sanskrit sources*. London: Routledge.

MONIER-WILLIAMS, M. 1872. *Sanskrit-English dictionary etymologically and philologically arranged*. Oxford: The Clarendon Press.

ÑĀṆAMOLI. 1964. *The path of purification (Visuddhimagga) by Bhadantācariya Buddhaghosa*. Colombo: Semage.

NYANAPONIKA. 1962. *The heart of Buddhist meditation: A handbook of mental training based on the Buddha's way of mindfulness*. London: Rider & Company.

NYANATUSITA, BHIKKHU, and H. HECKER. 2008. *The life of Nyanatiloka Thera*. Kandy, Sri Lanka: Buddhist Publication Society.

RHYS DAVIDS, C. A. F., and F. L. WOODWARD. 1917–1930. *The book of the kindred sayings*. 5 vols. London: Pali Text Society.

RHYS DAVIDS, T. W. 1881. *Buddhist suttas*. Oxford: Clarendon Press.

RHYS DAVIDS, T. W. 1899. *Dialogues of the Buddha*. Vol. 1. London: Henry Frowde.

RHYS DAVIDS, T. W. 1910. *Dialogues of the Buddha*. Vol. 2. London: Henry Frowde.

ROWE, D. 1983. *Depression: The way out of your prison*. London: Routledge & Kegan Paul.

SEGAL, Z. V., J. M. G. WILLIAMS, and J. D. TEASDALE. 2002. *Mindfulness-based cognitive therapy for depression: A new approach to preventing relapse*. New York: Guilford Press.

SHATTOCK, E. H. 1958. *An experiment in mindfulness.* London: Rider & Co.

SOMA THERA. 1967. *The way of mindfulness: The Satipaṭṭhāna sutta and commentary.* 3rd ed.. Kandy, Sri Lanka: Buddhist Publication Society.

THICH NHAT HANH. 1976. *The miracle of mindfulness: A manual of meditation.* Boston, MA: Beacon Press.

WILLIAMS, J. M. G., J. D. TEASDALE, J. KABAT-ZINN, and Z. V. SEGAL. 2007. *The mindful way through depression: freeing yourself from chronic unhappiness.* New York: The Guilford Press.

SOME REFLECTIONS ON THE ORIGINS OF MBSR, SKILLFUL MEANS, AND THE TROUBLE WITH MAPS

Jon Kabat-Zinn

The author recounts some of the early history of what is now known as MBSR, and its relationship to mainstream medicine and the science of the mind/body connection and health. He stresses the importance that MBSR and other mindfulness-based interventions be grounded in a universal dharma understanding that is congruent with Buddhadharma but not constrained by its historical, cultural and religious manifestations associated with its counties of origin and their unique traditions. He locates these developments within an historic confluence of two very different epistemologies encountering each other for the first time, that of science and that of the meditative traditions. The author addresses the ethical ground of MBSR, as well as questions of lineage and of skillful 'languaging' and other means for maximizing the possibility that the value of cultivating mindfulness in the largest sense can be heard and embraced and cultivated in commonsensical and universal ways in secular settings. He directly addresses mindfulness-based instructors on the subject of embodying and drawing forth the essence of the dharma without depending on the vocabulary, texts, and teaching forms of traditional Buddhist environments, even though they are important to know to one degree or another as part of one's own development. The author's perspective is grounded in what the Zen tradition refers to as the one thousand year view. Although it is not stated explicitly in this text, he sees the current interest in mindfulness and its applications as signaling a multi-dimensional emergence of great transformative and liberative promise, one which, if cared for and tended, may give rise to a flourishing on this planet akin to a second, and this time global, Renaissance, for the benefit of all sentient beings and our world.

As I will recount a bit further along, mindfulness-based stress reduction (MBSR) was developed as one of a possibly infinite number of skillful means for bringing the dharma into mainstream settings.[1] It has never been about MBSR for its own sake. It has always been about the M. And the M is a very big M, as I attempt to describe in this paper.

That said, the quality of MBSR as an intervention is only as good as the MBSR instructor and his or her understanding of what is required to deliver a truly mindfulness-based programme. Much of what is said here, both in this paper, and in the entire issue of the journal is meant to reinforce our collective inquiry into what is involved in maintaining the highest standards of understanding and practice in delivering such programmes in the years ahead, given the exponential rise in interest and activity in this burgeoning field and its attendant risks and opportunities. By necessity, the perspective offered here is inevitably personal, shaped by my own experience over the past four decades. I offer it in the hope that it will prove useful to others and also to further dialogue concerning the meanings and essence of mindfulness, its value and promise in the wider world, the pitfalls attendant with such aspirations, and the challenges we face individually and collectively in the future in developing novel and hopefully skillful avenues and vehicles for moving the bell curve of our society toward greater sanity and wellbeing. In this sense, MBSR was conceived of and functions as a public health intervention, a vehicle for both individual and societal transformation.

When I wrote *Full Catastrophe Living*, nine years after starting the Stress Reduction Clinic, it was very important to me that it capture the essence and spirit of the MBSR curriculum as it unfolds for our patients. At the same time, I wanted it to articulate the dharma that underlies the curriculum, but without ever using the word 'Dharma' or invoking Buddhist thought or authority, since for obvious reasons, we do not teach MBSR in that way. My intention and hope was that the book might embody to whatever degree possible the dharma essence of the Buddha's teachings put into action and made accessible to mainstream Americans facing stress, pain, and illness. This is plainly stated in the Introduction, where I did not shy away from explicitly stating its Buddhist origins. However, from the beginning of MBSR, I bent over backward to structure it and find ways to speak about it that avoided as much as possible the risk of it being seen as Buddhist, 'New Age,' 'Eastern Mysticism' or just plain 'flakey.' To my mind this was a constant and serious risk that would have undermined our attempts to present it as commonsensical, evidence-based, and ordinary, and ultimately a legitimate element of mainstream medical care. This was something of an ongoing challenge, given that the entire curriculum is based on relatively (for novices) intensive training and practice of meditation and yoga, and meditation and yoga pretty much defined one element of the 'New Age.'

Before the book was published, I asked a number of colleagues that I respected to endorse it. Among those I asked was Thich Nhat Hanh, whom I didn't know at the time except through his writings, and in particular, his little book, *The Miracle of Mindfulness* (Hanh 1975), which had a certain plainness and simplicity to it that I admired. In this case, more than hoping for any kind of endorsement, I thought I would simply share with him the direction we were taking and get his sense of it. I didn't actually expect a response. However, he did respond, and offered a statement that I felt showed that he had grasped the essence of the book and the line it was trying to walk. What's more, he expressed it in such an elegant and affirming way that I felt it was a gift, and that it would be disrespectful, having asked for it, not to use it. However, I did think twice about it. It precipitated something of a crisis in me for a time, because not only was Thich Nhat Hanh definitely a Buddhist authority, his brief endorsement used the very foreign word *dharma* not once, but four times. Yet what he said spoke deeply and directly to the essence of the original vision and intention of MBSR. I wondered: 'Is this the right time for this? Would it be skillful to stretch the envelope at this point? Or would it in the end cause more harm than good?' In retrospect, these concerns now sound a bit silly to me. But at the time, they felt significant.

At the same time, I found myself pondering whether such concerns might not have become a bit outmoded by then. Perhaps by 1990 there was no longer such a strong distinction between the so-called New Age and the mainstream world. So many different so-called counter-cultural strands had penetrated the dominant culture by then that it was hard to make any binary distinctions about what was mainstream and what was fringe. Advertising alone was materializing and commercializing everything, exploiting even yoga and meditation for its own ends. In the process, it was breaking down conventional stereotypes while simultaneously creating new ones. The world was shifting rapidly, even before the impending global emergence of the internet with its constantly accelerating onslaught of information and its effects on our minds and our pace of life. Perhaps there was no longer as big a risk of our work being identified with a 'lunatic fringe.' Perhaps there was already enough evidence in support of the efficacy of MBSR to open the door at least a bit to expanding the ways in which I could articulate its origins and its essence—not so much to the patients, but to the growing number of health professionals becoming interested in mindfulness and its clinical applications. Perhaps it was important to be more explicit about why it might be valuable to bring a universal dharma perspective and means of cultivating it into the mainstream world.[2]

And so, in the end, I decided to use Thich Nhat Hanh's words and to put them up front, with his permission, as the preface to the book. It was a simple extension of something I had already been doing for many years when giving lectures (at medical and psychiatry grand rounds) at medical centres around the country, as well as in public talks. In the mid 1980s I had begun using a series of slides that included a photograph of the great Buddha statue in Kamakura, Japan, and finding simple and matter-of-fact ways to articulate for professional and lay audiences the origins and essence of those teachings—how the Buddha himself was not a Buddhist, how the word '*Buddha*' means one who has awakened, and how mindfulness, often spoken of as 'the heart of Buddhist meditation,' has little or nothing to do with Buddhism per se, and everything to do with wakefulness, compassion, and wisdom. These are universal qualities of being human, precisely what the word *dharma*, is pointing to. The word has many meanings, but can be understood primarily as signifying both the teachings of the Buddha and the lawfulness of things in relationship to suffering and the nature of the mind.

Now, more than 30 years after the founding of the Stress Reduction Clinic, the very existence of this special issue, as well as so many other interfaces at which such conversations and studies are taking place (see Kabat-Zinn and Davidson 2011), is evidence that a deeper conversation, coupled with increasingly robust scientific investigations, is ensuing. We can observe an accelerating confluence of dharma with mainstream medicine, healthcare, cognitive science, affective neuroscience, neuroeconomics, business, leadership, primary and secondary education, higher education, the law, indeed, in society as a whole, in this now very rapidly changing world. Such developments have major implications, of course, for the kinds of training required to skillfully deliver mindfulness-based interventions in a range of different environments without omitting or denaturing their dharma essence. We shall return to this question in the final section of this paper.

By now, everybody is familiar with the graphs that show the exponential rise in the number of scientific papers each year on the subject of mindfulness (see Introduction, Figure 1). It is profoundly gratifying that a whole family of what are now called mindfulness-based interventions, such as MBCT, MBRP, MBCP, MB-EAT, MBEC[3] and many more have developed for specific purposes and are making profound and continually expanding contributions to the alleviation of suffering and to our deepening understanding of the nature of the human mind and heart.

For our work to be most skillful, it is important for us to inquire deeply into the inevitable limitations of our individual perspectives and to articulate the tension, mystery, and potential for continually deepening our understanding and furthering the evolution of our collective interests and activities on the basis of the kinds of perspectives expressed by the contributors to this special issue.

It is my hope that people attracted to this field will come to appreciate the profound transformative potential of the dharma in its most universal and skillful articulations through their own meditation training and practice. Mindfulness can only be understood from the inside out. It is not one more cognitive-behavioural technique to be deployed in a behaviour change paradigm, but a way of being and a way of seeing that has profound implications for understanding the nature of our own minds and bodies, and for living life as if it really mattered (Kabat-Zinn 2003). It is primarily what Francisco Varela termed a first-person experience. Without that living foundation, none of what really matters is available to us in ways that are maximally healing, transformative, compassionate, and wise. Of course, ultimately there is no inside and no outside, only one seamless whole, awake and aware.

> A human being is a part of the whole, called by us 'universe', a part limited in time and space. He experiences himself, his thoughts and feelings as something separated from the rest—a kind of optical delusion of his consciousness. This delusion is a kind of prison for us, restricting us to our personal desires and to affection for a few persons nearest to us. Our task must be to free ourselves from this prison by widening our circle of compassion to embrace all living creatures and the whole nature in its beauty. Nobody is able to achieve this completely, but the striving for such attainment is in itself a part of the liberation, and a foundation for inner security.
>
> Albert Einstein
> New York Times, March 29, 1972

Motivation

As I reflect on it now, from the very beginning there was for me one primary and compelling reason for attempting to bring mindfulness into the mainstream of society. That was to relieve suffering and catalyse greater compassion and wisdom in our lives and culture. In my view, it is still the primary benefit that will accrue to us if the momentum continues, and the investigation and adaptation of mindfulness writ large (see below for what I mean by this) succeeds in maintaining its full depth, integrity, and potential. However, the mystery of how this came about, or how anything comes about, is in some sense opaque. Even having played a role in its unfolding, I find the indeterminacy and impersonal yet very personal nature of it mysterious. What is more, I am not sure it can be told entirely accurately as one fixed and definitive story or pathway—it strikes me as requiring a set of Feynman diagrams of various recollected trajectories. One would need to sum over all the stories, memories, records, and artefacts from that time to even approximate the actual truth of things. I love that.

It certainly wouldn't be summing over just my life, and just my memories either, but over the lives and memories and relationships and yearnings of my colleagues and friends who came to be involved in the early years of the Stress Reduction Clinic, as well as the stories and pathways of all the people far and wide who are now engaged in one way or another in working at the various interfaces that this special issue of the journal represents. As I see it, we are all participants in this mysterious unfolding process that may actually have no precise beginning, and no end either. The various involvements, participation, and caring on the part of the contributors to this issue and of our colleagues near and far, and on the part of the readers of this issue imply that we all carry some degree of responsibility for the integrity of the dharma as it is reflected in our lives and work. That, it seems to me, is the best way to keep it alive and to guard its integrity and vitality, by carrying it in our own individual hearts in our own individual ways, which we share as colleagues and as a distributive global sangha of overlapping, if not entirely commonly shared perspectives, concerns, and purpose. I sometimes describe this interconnectedness as Indra's Net at work (Kabat-Zinn 1999). It may be an apt metaphor for the interconnectedness of the universe, but its essence remains deliciously mysterious.

In what follows, I offer a few of the narrative threads that have been important to me in pondering the unfolding of MBSR and which reflect the distributive and multiplicative elements that give it value—for myself and for many others, priceless value. It will be a non-linear, impressionistic, somewhat reflective recounting of these various threads. Perhaps, taken together in the spirit in which they are offered, they may come into focus and illuminate some of the larger themes and challenges we are facing in the rapidly growing field of mindfulness-based interventions and their roles in medicine, psychology, science, and the wider society.

In addition to the primary motivation discussed above, there were a number of secondary motivations that drew me to pursue this path. These included its potential for elucidating and deepening our understanding of the mind/body connection via new dimensions of scientific investigation, and also, the possibility of developing a form of right livelihood for myself at a particular juncture in my life, as well as, if successful, right livelihood for possibly large numbers of others who would be drawn to work of this kind because of its potential depth and authenticity. And there was also the fact of being in love with the beauty, simplicity, and universality of the dharma, and coming to see it as a worthy and meaningful pathway for a life well lived, a life of devotion to the potential for awakening and the alleviation of suffering, and thus, full circle to the original motivation.

Envisioning the possible

I started what was originally called the Stress Reduction and Relaxation Program in September 1979. It didn't come out of a vacuum ... there were many years of pondering and meditating and inward and outward wandering before it arose as a possibility in my mind. Once established in the hospital, within a few years, it got renamed the Stress Reduction Clinic to normalize it by emphasizing that it was a clinical service, like any other, in the Department of Medicine. We were proud of the brand new hospital signs that pointed the way to our clinic, one small indicator of having blended into the mainstream of healthcare. Later, as more and more programmes started forming based on our work, we came to speak of our work in a more generic form as MBSR, or *mindfulness-based stress reduction*. From the start, it was motivated by a strong impulse on my part, as recounted below, to bring my dharma practice together with my work life into one unified whole, as an expression of right livelihood and in the service of something useful that felt very much needed in the world.

Even as a graduate student at MIT (1964–1971), I had been pondering for years 'what is my job with a capital J,' my 'karmic assignment' on the planet, so to speak, without coming up with much of anything. It was a personal koan for me and became more and more a continuous thread in my life day and night as those years unfolded. 'What am I supposed to be doing with my life?' I kept asking myself. 'What do I love so much I would pay to do it?' I knew it wasn't to continue in a career in molecular biology, much as I loved science and knew I would be disappointing my Nobel Laureate thesis advisor at MIT, Salvador Luria, and my father, himself an accomplished scientist. I was first exposed to the dharma at MIT, of all improbable places, in 1966, and started a daily meditation practice from that point on (Kabat-Zinn 2005a, 2005b). Meanwhile, I did what I could to find work, especially after I was married and, with my wife, Myla, had started a family. That included two years as a faculty member in the Biology Department at Brandeis University teaching molecular genetics and a science for non-science majors course (which was an opportunity for teaching meditation and yoga as pathways into a first-person experience of biology), and then a stint as Director of the Cambridge Zen Center under the Korean Zen Master, Seung Sahn, where I was also his student and a Dharma teacher in training. I was also teaching large mindful yoga classes weekly in a church in Harvard Square, and exploring other things, such as offering occasional meditation training and yoga/stretching workshops for athletes, especially runners.

In 1976, I went to work at the almost brand-new University of Massachusetts Medical School.[4] All the while, my koan about what I was really supposed to be doing with my life in terms of right livelihood was unfolding in the background.

On a two-week *vipassanā* retreat at the Insight Meditation Society (IMS) in Barre, Massachusetts, in the Spring of 1979, while sitting in my room one afternoon about Day 10 of the retreat, I had a 'vision' that lasted maybe 10 seconds. I don't really know what to call it, so I call it a vision. It was rich in detail and more like an instantaneous seeing of vivid, almost inevitable connections and their implications. It did not come as a reverie or a thought stream, but rather something quite different, which to this day I cannot fully explain and don't feel the need to.

I saw in a flash not only a model that could be put in place, but also the long-term implications of what might happen if the basic idea was sound and could be implemented in one test environment—namely that it would spark new fields of scientific and clinical investigation, and would spread to hospitals and medical centres and clinics across the country and around the world, and provide right livelihood for thousands of practitioners. Because it was so weird, I hardly ever mentioned this experience to others. But after that retreat, I did have a better sense of what my karmic assignment might be. It was so compelling that I decided to take it on wholeheartedly as best I could.

Pretty much everything I saw in that 10 seconds has come to pass, in large measure because of the work and the love of all the people who found their way to the Stress Reduction Clinic once it was born, wanting to contribute their own unique karmic trajectories and loves to the nascent and then continually unfolding enterprise of MBSR, the wellbeing and longevity of which were always in some sense tentative and uncertain, because of the vagaries of medical school and hospital politics (one foot on a roller skate, the other on a banana peel, I used to say).

It struck me in that fleeting moment that afternoon at the Insight Meditation Society that it would be a worthy work to simply share the essence of meditation and yoga practices as I had been learning and practicing them at that point for 13 years, with those who would never come to a place like IMS or a Zen Center, and who would never be able to hear it through the words and forms that were being used at meditation centres, or even, back in those days, at yoga centres, which were few and far-between, and very foreign as well.

A flood of thoughts following the extended moment filled in the picture. Why not try to make meditation so commonsensical that anyone would be drawn to it? Why not develop an American[5] vocabulary that spoke to the heart of the matter, and didn't focus on the cultural aspects of the traditions out of which the dharma emerged, however beautiful they might be, or on centuries-old scholarly debates concerning fine distinctions in the Abhidharma. This was not because they weren't ultimately important, but because they would likely cause unnecessary impediments for people who were basically dealing with suffering and seeking some kind of release from it. And, why not do it in the hospital of the medical centre where I happened to be working at the time? After all, hospitals do function as 'dukkha magnets' in our society,[6] pulling for stress, pain of all kinds, disease and illness, especially when they have reached levels where it is impossible to ignore them (Kabat-Zinn 2005c). What better place than a hospital to make the dharma available to people in ways that they might possibly understand it and be inspired by a heartfelt and practical invitation to explore whether it might not be possible to do something *for themselves* as a complement to their more traditional medical treatments, since the entire raison d'être of the dharma is to elucidate the nature of suffering and its root causes, as well as provide a practical path to liberation from suffering? All this to be undertaken, of course, without ever mentioning the word 'dharma.'

The early years

With the aim of bridging these two epistemologies of science and dharma, I felt impelled to point out in the early years of MBSR the obvious etymological linkage of the words *medicine* and *meditation* and articulate for medical audiences their root meanings (Bohm 1980; Kabat-Zinn 1990). In that context, it felt useful to adopt the already established terminology of self-regulation (Shapiro 1980) and describe meditation operationally, in terms of the self-regulation of attention (Goleman and Schwartz 1976). From there, it was commonsensical, if not axiomatic, to point out that much of the time we are barely present in our own bodies and lives as they are unfolding, and so have not cultivated interior resources available to us that might be of profound benefit...such as the wise, discerning, embodied, and selfless aspects of awareness itself. The intention and approach behind MBSR were never meant to exploit, fragment, or decontextualize the dharma, but rather to *recontextualize* it within the frameworks of science, medicine (including psychiatry and psychology), and healthcare so that it would be maximally useful to people who could not hear it or enter into it through the more traditional dharma gates, whether they were doctors or medical patients, hospital administrators, or insurance companies.

And because naming is very important in how things are understood and either accepted or not, I felt that the entire undertaking needed to be held by an umbrella term broad enough to contain the multiplicity of key elements that seemed essential to field a successful clinical programme in the cultural climate of 1979. *Stress reduction* seemed ideal, since pretty much everybody can relate to that instinctively, even though 'reduction' is a something of a misnomer. The term *stress* also has the element of dukkha embedded within it. In fact, some Buddhist scholars translate the term 'dukkha' in Buddhist texts as 'stress' (see, for example, Thanissaro Bhikkhu 2010). Moreover, there was already a growing literature related to the psychophysiology of stress reactivity and pain regulation (Goleman and Schwartz 1976; Melzack and Perry 1975; Schwartz, Davidson and Goleman 1978). But as more than one participant in MBSR has exclaimed on occasion after a few weeks in the programme: 'This isn't stress reduction. This is my whole life!' New evidence in fact demonstrates that chronic stress exerts potentially deleterious health effects on the brain, on one's behaviour, and on cognitive abilities across the entire lifespan, with particular windows of heightened vulnerability (Lupien et al. 2009). Chronic stress has also been shown by Nobel Laureate Elizabeth Blackburn to increase the rate of degradation of the telomers at the ends of all of our chromosomes, and thus accelerate biological aging at the cellular and sub-cellular level, leading to a significant shortening of the lifespan (Epel et al. 2004).

As things developed, it increasingly felt that something more was needed to differentiate our approach from many programmes that also used the term stress reduction or stress management but that had no dharma foundation whatsoever. So at a certain point in the early 1990s, it seemed sensible to formally begin calling what we were doing mindfulness-based stress reduction (MBSR) although, in point of fact, we had been referring to what we did as training in 'mindfulness meditation' from the very beginning in the scientific papers coming out of the Stress Reduction Clinic (Kabat-Zinn 1982; Kabat-Zinn and Chapman-Waldrop 1988; Kabat-Zinn, Lipworth, and Burney 1985; Kabat-Zinn et al. 1986). The term mindfulness meditation had already been used several times in the psychological literature (Brown and Engler 1980; Deatherage 1975).

The early papers on MBSR cited not just its Theravada roots (Kornfield 1977; Nyanaponika 1962), but also its Mahayana roots within both the Soto (Suzuki 1970) and Rinzai (Kapleau 1965) Zen traditions (and by lineage, the earlier Chinese and Korean streams), as well as certain currents from the yogic traditions (Thakar 1977) including Vedanta (Nisargadatta 1973), and the teachings of J Krishnamurti (Krishnamurti 1969, 1979) and Ramana Maharshi (Maharshi 1959). My own primary Zen teacher, Seung Sahn, was Korean, and taught both Soto and Rinzai approaches, including the broad use and value of koans and koan-based 'Dharma combat' exchanges between teacher and student (Seung Sahn 1976). This form contributed in part to the element of interactive moment-by-moment exchanges in the classroom between teacher and participant in which they explore together in great and sometimes challenging detail direct first-person experience of the practice and its manifestations in everyday life. This salient feature of MBSR and other mindfulness-based interventions has come to be called 'inquiry' or dialogue[7] (Kabat-Zinn 2005d; Ocok 2007; Williams et al. 2007).

Some works not cited in the early papers but that made a significant impression on my appreciation of the dharma at that time and how it could be articulated in a simple and colloquial vocabulary included *Meditation in Action* (Trungpa 1969), *The Miracle of Mindfulness* (Hanh 1976), and *The Experience of Insight* (Goldstein 1976). Early studies that helped contextualize the work of MBSR within the nascent framework of scientific research into meditation and its potential clinical applications included the early papers of Dan Goleman and Richard Davidson (Davidson and Schwartz 1976; Goleman and Schwartz 1976); the work of Benson (Benson 1976), and the work of Roger Walsh, including his seminal 1980 paper (Walsh 1977, 1978, 1980).

Naming what we were doing in the clinic *mindfulness-based* stress reduction raises a number of questions. One is the wisdom of using the word *mindfulness* intentionally as an umbrella term to describe our work and to link it explicitly with what I have always considered to be a universal dharma that is co-extensive, if not identical, with the teachings of the Buddha, the Buddhadharma. By 'umbrella term' I mean that it is used in certain contexts as a place-holder for the entire dharma, that it is meant to carry multiple meanings and traditions simultaneously, not in the service of finessing and confounding real differences, but as a potentially skillful means for bringing the streams of alive, embodied dharma understanding and of clinical medicine together. The intention was for it to be commonsensically relevant and accessible enough to benefit potentially anybody who might be overwhelmed by suffering and sufficiently motivated to undertake a certain degree of hard work in the form of a daily mindfulness practice in the *'laboratories'* of the MBSR programme and of life itself. The challenge for the participants was to just do the work from week to week, in other words, to practice the curriculum as it was being unfolded, and see what would happen. The emphasis was always on awareness of the present moment and acceptance of things as they are, however they are in actuality, rather than a preoccupation with attaining a particular desired outcome at some future time, no matter how desirable it might be (see Cullen 2006, 2008). One major principle that we committed to was, and still is, never asking more of our patients in terms of daily practice than we as instructors were prepared to commit to in our own lives on a daily basis.

It always felt that the details concerning the use of the word *mindfulness* in the various contexts in which we were deploying it could be worked out later by scholars and researchers who were knowledgeable in this area, and interested in making such distinctions and resolving important issues that may have been confounded and compounded by the early but intentional ignoring or glossing over of potentially important historical, philosophical, and cultural nuances— issues that may yet be shown to be critical to a deeper understanding of the mind and its relationship to the brain and body, as is implied in many of the papers in this volume, as well as a deeper understanding of the dharma itself, as the subject is excavated so elegantly and eloquently in the scholarly papers in this issue from various classical Buddhist perspectives. This special issue is perhaps only a first step to just the kind of dialogue necessary to remind us all of the need for both fidelity and imagination in furthering the work of the dharma in the world in an ever-widening circle of settings and circumstances, including business, leadership, education, etc.

In the early years, I did find great support for the direction I was taking in the writings of Nyanaponika Thera (1962) and in particular, what I thought of at the time, and still do, as an extremely elegant encapsulation of the centrality of mindfulness. In his words, Mindfulness, then, is

the unfailing master key for *knowing* the mind, and is thus the starting point;

the perfect tool for *shaping* the mind, and is thus the focal point;

the lofty manifestation of the achieved *freedom* of the mind, and is thus the culminating point.

Seen in this way, mindfulness is the view, the path, and the fruit all in one.

I also felt that it was more important to describe mindfulness in considerable detail in the early scientific papers on MBSR and cite its various origins in various contemplative traditions, rather than to offer a definitive and concise definition. And when I did offer definitions of mindfulness, as I did repeatedly in professional talks, and later, in books, they were *operational* definitions, not meant to be definitive statements in absolute accord with the Abhidharma or any other classical teaching that tended to limit it to the mind state that knows and remembers whether or not the attention is on the selected object of attention, or any other aspects of remembering, as described in this volume by a number of contributors (Dreyfus, Gethin, Olendzki). My training in Zen consistently emphasized non-dual awareness transcending subject and object, akin to what John Dunne refers to in this issue as an innatist perspective, and what I believe Nyanaponika meant by the 'lofty manifestation of the achieved freedom of the mind.' What seemed called for, practically speaking, was an instrumental and operational emphasis on what is actually *involved* in the gesture of awareness, to use Francisco Varela's elegant phrase (Depraz, Varela and Vermesch 1999; Varela, Thompson and Rosch 1991). Thus, several variants of oft-quoted working definitions were expressed at different times: (a) paying attention in a particular way: on purpose, in the present moment, and non-judgmentally (Kabat-Zinn 1994); (b) the awareness that arises from paying attention, on purpose, in the present moment, and non-judgmentally (Kabat-Zinn 2005e). No single definition of mindfulness was given in *Full Catastrophe Living*. Instead, I chose to describe it operationally from many different angles depending on context. In some sense, the entire book is a definition of mindfulness.

On the issue of 'memory' as an intrinsic element of *sati*, I have always felt that one natural function of present moment awareness is to remember the immediate past. Thus, the element of *retention* that Georges Dreyfus emphasizes in his paper did not seem either necessary or useful to feature in a working definition of mindfulness in the West, given how cognitive we tend to be already, and how little we experience the domain of being (in the present moment) without any agenda other than to be awake and without the lenses of our likes and dislikes and opinions, which are usually colouring and filtering direct experience. Thus, the strong emphasis on *non-judgmental awareness* in the operational definitions. Non-judgmental does not mean to imply to the novice practitioner that there is some ideal state in which judgments no longer arise.

Rather, it points out that there will be many many judgments and opinions arising from moment to moment, but that we do not have to judge or evaluate or react to any of what arises, other than perhaps recognizing it in the moment of arising as pleasant, unpleasant, or neutral (the second foundation or establishment of mindfulness). This can lead naturally to the directly experienced discovery that the liberative choice in any moment either to cling and self-identify or not is always available, always an option, and perhaps to a further discovery that non-clinging sometimes happens spontaneously through the intrinsic liberative quality of pure awareness, with no effort whatsoever.

For this reason, and a personal affinity with the various streams of Chan and Zen, there was from the very beginning of MBSR an emphasis on non-duality and the non-instrumental dimension of practice, and thus, on non-doing, non-striving, not-knowing, non-attachment to outcomes, even to positive health outcomes, and on investigating beneath name and form and the world of appearances, as per the teachings of the *Heart Sutra*, which highlight the intrinsically empty nature of even the Four Noble Truths and the Eightfold Path, and liberation itself and yet are neither nihilistic nor positivistic, but a middle way (see Kabat-Zinn 2003, 2005f; Wallace and Hodel 2008). The emphasis in Chan on direct transmission outside the sutras or orthodox teachings (Luk 1974) also reinforced the sense that what is involved in mindfulness practice is ultimately not merely a matter of the intellect or cognition or scholarship, but of direct authentic full-spectrum first-person experience, nurtured, catalysed, reinforced and guided by the second-person perspective of a well-trained and highly experienced and empathic teacher. Therefore, MBSR was grounded in a non-authoritarian, non-hierarchical perspective that allowed for clarity, understanding, and wisdom, what we might call essential dharma, to emerge in the interchanges between instructor and participants, and within the meditation practice of the participant as guided by the instructor. And indeed, quite intentionally, we give a great deal of guidance in the meditation practices of MBSR in the early weeks of the programme, in class and on the guided meditation CDs.

A concrete example of the middle way orientation in MBSR can be felt in the way the instructor relates to the participants and to the entire enterprise. Although our patients all come with various problems, diagnoses, and ailments, we make every effort to apprehend their intrinsic wholeness. We often say that from our perspective, as long as you are breathing, there is more 'right' with you than 'wrong' with you, no matter what is wrong. In this process, we make every effort to treat each participant as a whole human being rather than as a patient, or a diagnosis, or someone having a problem that needs fixing. MBSR is grounded altogether in a non-fixing orientation and approach. It is less about *curing* and more about *healing*, which I define as *a coming to terms with things as they are* in full awareness. We often see that healing takes place on its own over time as we align ourselves with what is deepest and best in ourselves and rest in awareness moment by moment without an attachment to outcome. Or, alternatively and in all probability, seeing and not judging, to whatever degree possible, how strongly we *are* attached to a particular outcome, and then bringing that quality of awareness into all aspects of our lives, work, and relationships as best we can.

The fact that attending in this way with consistency and stability is actually the hardest work in the world for human beings doesn't make it any less attractive or important. We might say that if mindfulness does not in some sense become our *default mode*, then its opposite, mindlessness or unawareness, will certainly retain that role. The inevitable result is to be caught up in a great many of our moments in a reactive, robotic, automatic pilot mode that has the potential to easily consume and colour our entire life and virtually all our relationships. One of the major discoveries of MBSR is that our patients realize this in dramatic ways and become motivated to live a life of greater awareness that extends far beyond the eight weeks they are in the programme. That greater awareness includes, of course, our intrinsic interconnectedness as beings, and so the possibility of greater spontaneous compassion toward others and toward oneself. For many, it also includes formal meditation becoming an ongoing feature of one's daily life, often for years and decades after the initial experience of MBSR.

MBSR and other mindfulness-based interventions modeled on it are intrinsically a participatory engagement... we invite the patient to *participate* in his or her own movement toward greater levels of health and wellbeing, starting from the actuality of the present circumstance, whatever it might be. It is invitational, and depends on the patient's willingness to tap into those profound innate resources we all have by virtue of being human, the capacities for learning, growing, healing, and transformation inherent in the systematic cultivation of awareness itself and its sequelae. We think of this as *participatory medicine* at its best: the healthcare team brings its resources to the table, and the patient/participant brings his or hers as well (Kabat-Zinn 2000). We pour energy, in the form of attention, into what is 'right with us' in the present moment (which requires *recognition* that there may indeed be something 'right' with us) and let the rest of the hospital and the healthcare team take care of what is 'wrong.' It is a worthy division of labour, and a good place to start the process of reclaiming the full dimensionality of one's being and embodying it in everyday life, whatever else one might have to come to terms with, all of which is an intimate part of 'the curriculum' of the practice in any event.

In the Spring of 1979, after the vision I experienced on the retreat at IMS, I met individually with three physicians in the hospital, the directors of the primary care, pain, and orthopedic clinics, to try to find out how they viewed their work, what their clinics' successes were with their patients, and what might be missing in the hospital experience, both for their patients and for themselves. When I asked what percentage of their patients they felt they were able to help, the response was typically 10–20%. I was astonished, and asked what happened to the others. I was told that they either got better on their own, or never got better. So I asked whether they would be open to referring their patients, when appropriate, to a programme that would teach them to take better care of themselves as a complement to whatever the healthcare system was or was not able to do for them. It would be based on relatively intensive training in Buddhist meditation without the Buddhism (as I liked to put it), and yoga. Their responses were very positive. On the basis of those meetings, I proposed that a programme be set up under the auspices of ambulatory care in the hospital, which would take the form of an eight-week course to which physicians would refer patients they were seeing who they felt were not responding to their treatments, and were in some sense, falling through the cracks of the healthcare system (really in large measure a disease-care system) and not getting any or full satisfaction from their healthcare. And so, MBSR came into being in the Fall of 1979, and those first three very forward thinking clinic directors, Tom Winters, Bob Burney and John J. Monahan exclusively referred the first few cycles of patients until word spread further into the medical community within the hospital and then out into the larger medical community as well. Within the year, the Chief of Medicine, James E. Dalen, suggested it become part of the Department of Medicine. We were invited wholeheartedly into the mainstream. This was before the new signs went up in the hospital, of course.[8]

Ethics

The question is sometimes raised about the ethical foundation of MBSR. Are we ignoring that fundamental aspect of the Dharma in favour of just a few highly selected meditation techniques, again, decontextualizing elements of a coherent whole? My view is that we are not. First, it is inevitably the personal responsibility of each person engaging in this work to attend with care and intentionality to how we are actually living our lives, both personally and professionally, in terms of ethical behaviour. An awareness of one's conduct and the quality of one's relationships, inwardly and outwardly, in terms of their potential to cause harm, are intrinsic elements of the cultivation of mindfulness as I am describing it here.

At the same time, it seems to me that an ethical foundation is naturally built into the structure and setting of MBSR in a number of different ways. For instance, within the context of medicine and healthcare, we already have in place a profound framework and professional code of conduct in the Hippocratic tradition, founded on the principle of *primum non nocere*, to first do no harm, and to put the needs of the patient above one's own. Such principles are axiomatic and foundational within the context of MBSR, whether it is offered in a hospital setting, or elsewhere. Of course, a degree of mindfulness is required even to sense that one might actually be doing harm, either by commission or, more subtly, by omission.

We also encourage a work environment in the clinic and the Center for Mindfulness in which we depend not only on our own awareness but also on each other's awareness, candour, and willingness to communicate about challenging circumstances to keep us individually and collectively honest. It is built into the fabric of how we see our work and commitment to our patients, our colleagues, and ourselves. Moreover, as noted earlier (see note 6), the Hippocratic Oath in some sense is mirrored in the Bodhisattva Vow to attend completely to the suffering and liberation of an infinite number of beings before attending to one's own. From the non-dual perspective, the infinite number of beings and oneself are not separate, and never were. This perspective can and needs to be taken seriously, and gently supported by explicit intentions regarding how we conduct ourselves both inwardly and outwardly.

In this way, and also for cultural reasons having to do with how common it is in our society to profess a moral stance outwardly that one does not adhere to inwardly, it feels appropriate in our environment that the ethical foundation of the practice be more implicit than explicit, and that it may be best expressed, supported, and furthered by how we, the MBSR instructor and the entire staff of the clinic, embody it in our own lives and in how we relate to the patients, the doctors, the hospital staff, everybody, and of course, how we relate to our own interior experience. Ultimately, the responsibility to live an ethical life lies on the shoulders and in the hearts of each one of us who chooses to engage in the work of mindfulness-based interventions. It too is a distributive Dharma responsibility. And the first line of defence in terms of potential transgression or betrayal is always awareness of one's own motivations and emotions, and the universal tendencies of grasping, aversion, delusion, and 'selfing' which can so easily colour our moments and blind us to root causes of suffering that we might be participating in unwittingly.

It has always felt to me that MBSR is at its healthiest and best when the responsibility to ensure its integrity, quality, and standards of practice is being carried by each MBSR instructor him or herself. That is not to turn it into an ideal or a burden, but rather to keep it very real and close to our everyday experience held in awareness with kindness and discernment. In my experience, which is certainly limited and circumscribed, the shouldering and embodiment of this responsibility has been the case with MBSR teachers around the world to an extraordinary degree. To my mind, when each of us who cares about this work, who loves this work, takes care of the dharma through our practice and our love, then the dharma that is at the heart of the work flourishes and takes care of itself. Tended by each member of the Sangha of instructors, practitioners, researchers, everybody . . . it defines a distributive responsibility that turns out to be a great joy and a continued invitation to have there be no separation between one's practice and one's life. Some mindfulness teachers who are also physicians have characterized this stance as the foundation of *professionalism* in medicine, and boldly point out its potential for developing a more compassionate and less stressed and error-prone healthcare system (Epstein 1999; Krasner et al. 2009; Sibinga and Wu 2010).

Lineages and training for teachers of mindfulness-based interventions

The early years of MBSR and the development of other mindfulness-based clinical interventions were the province of a small group of people who gave themselves over to practicing and teaching mindfulness basically out of love, out of passion for the practice, knowingly and happily putting their careers and economic wellbeing at risk because of that love, usually stemming from deep first-person encounters with the dharma and its meditative practices, usually through studying with Buddhist teachers from well-defined traditions and lineages, and/or Asian teachers in other traditions that value the wisdom of mindfulness, such as Sufism, the yogas, Vedanta, and Taoism. Fortunately, there are even more options in this era, for those who wish to pursue them, to study and practice with such respected teachers in the root traditions of Asia, as well as with seasoned Western Buddhist Dharma teachers, and, of course, to sit long retreats at wonderful Dharma centres both in Asia and in the West.[9] I personally consider the periodic sitting of relatively long (at least 7–10 days and occasionally much longer) teacher-led retreats to be an absolute necessity in the developing of one's own meditation practice, understanding, and effectiveness as a teacher. In terms of the 'curriculum' of mindfulness training, to become an MBSR teacher, it is a laboratory requirement. But while participating in periodic long retreats may be necessary and extremely important for one's own development and understanding, by itself it is not sufficient. Mindfulness in everyday life is the ultimate challenge and practice. Of course, the two are complementary and mutually reinforcing and deepening. And once again, we can remind ourselves that ultimately there is no separation between them, because life itself is one seamless whole.

The practice of mindfulness is a lifetime's engagement. Growth, development, and maturation as a mindfulness practitioner and teacher of mindfulness are a critical part of the process. It is not always painless. As we know from direct experience, self-awareness can be exceedingly humbling. Thus, the motivation to persevere and face what needs facing and work with it wisely and compassionately must mature as well in the process. This brings us to some critical concerns regarding the teaching of mindfulness in non-Buddhist settings and the mental models or maps that instructors of mindfulness-based interventions might use to navigate by in those settings.

The trouble with maps—a note to mindfulness-based instructors

First, I want to say that there is nothing wrong with maps. I love maps, and can pore over them for hours. They are incredibly useful, absolutely essential at times, and wonderfully pleasurable for some people to contemplate endlessly. I am one of those people. Such contemplation can lead to great insight. But, as the saying goes, they are not the territory. This is hugely relevant for teaching MBSR and other mindfulness-based interventions.

Since all mindfulness-based interventions are based on relatively intensive training in awareness in the context of a universal dharma framework (and as I have been asserting here, not different in any essential way from Buddhadharma), the various maps of the territory of the dharma can be hugely helpful to the MBSR instructor in certain ways. Paradoxically, they can also be hugely interfering and problematic.

The biggest problem is that not only is the map not the territory, but that it can seriously occlude our ability as a mindfulness-based instructor to see and communicate about the territory in any original and direct way—a direct transmission if you will, outside the formal teachings, and thus, an embodiment of the real curriculum. Our internal map, if we are unaware of it, or strongly attached to it, can unwittingly impose just such a coordinate system for the patient/participant that can lead to idealizing a goal to be realized or attained, rather than letting realization and attainment take care of themselves. Our job is to take care of the territory of direct experience in the present moment and the learning that comes out of it. This suggests that the instructor is continually engaged in mapping the territory inwardly through intimate first-person contact and discernment, moment by moment, all the while keeping the formal dharma maps of the territory in mind to whatever degree we may feel is valuable, but not relying on them explicitly for the framework, vocabulary, or vehicle for working with what is most salient and important in the classroom in any moment. Some of this will naturally be thought-based, but a good deal of it will be more intuition-based, more embodied, more coming out of the spaciousness of *not-knowing* rather than out of a solely conceptual knowing. This can be quite challenging unless the formal dharma maps are deeply engrained in one's being through practice, not merely cerebral and cognitive.

For example, in the context of the emotional safety we attempt to establish within the MBSR classroom, to suggest that a person look directly into the experience of pain and bring awareness to the sensations in the body, whatever they are, and simply rest in that awareness without having to do anything brings the person right into the practice with beginner's mind. No map necessary. Just the invitation to look and perhaps see, listen and perhaps hear, sense and perhaps feel, thus cultivating an exquisite intimacy or familiarization with actual experience as it is unfolding. Of course, it is a radical act, and huge amounts of support and guidance are necessary to keep the person engaged in such a practice, even for the briefest of moments at first, and this is why mindfulness-based interventions such as MBSR are delivered in a group setting as 'courses' over an extended period of time, for the purpose of letting just such a learning curve and a deepening of stability and insight develop in a context of total support which is none other than sangha (Santorelli 1999). In the case of pain, the instructor might, as we often do in the MBSR classroom to reinforce the participants' motivation and understanding of the transformative potential of the mind/body connection, cite recent supportive evidence, in this case from studies such as those demonstrating that: (1) Zen meditators show structural brain changes (in terms of cortical thickness) related to decreased sensitivity to thermal pain in pain-related brain regions using fMRI (Grant et al. 2010); and (2) that long-term meditators using an open focus of attention, in other words, putting out the welcome mat for whatever arises in the field of awareness, what we call choiceless awareness in MBSR, showed reductions in self-reported unpleasantness but not of intensity in response to a thermal pain stimulation (Perlman et al. 2010). Under other circumstances, as part of the didactic element of MBSR that addresses specific background issues and research findings relevant to the participants in the program (Kabat-Zinn, 1982; Kabat-Zinn, 1990), we might cite other studies of brain changes seen with MBSR training (Hölzel et al. 2010; Hölzel et al. 2011), or of improved quality of life, depression, and fatigue in people with multiple sclerosis (MS) after MBSR training (Grossman et al. 2010).

It doesn't take long for novices to the practice of mindfulness to notice that the thinking mind has a life of its own, and can carry the attention away from both the bare attending to sensation in the body and from any ability to rest in awareness with whatever is arising. But over time, with ongoing practice, dialogue, and instruction, it is not unusual for even novice practitioners to see, either spontaneously for themselves or when it is pointed out, that the mind indeed does have a life of its own, and that when we cultivate and stabilize attention in the body, even a little bit, it often results in apprehending the constantly changing nature of sensations, even highly unpleasant ones, and thus, their impermanence. It also gives rise to the direct experience that 'the pain is not me,' and thus the option of non-identification not only with the sensations, but also with any attendant inflammatory emotions and thoughts that might be arising within the attending and the judging of the experience. Thus we become intimate with the nature of thoughts and emotions, and mental states such as aversion, frustration, restlessness, greed, doubt, sloth and torpor, and boredom, to name a few, which constitutes the territory of the third foundation of mindfulness, without ever having to mention the classical map of the four foundations of mindfulness, nor the five hindrances, nor the seven factors of enlightenment.

For that matter, when we work with people in a medical or psychological setting, using 'stress' and the suggestion that 'stress reduction' might be possible as the core invitational framework, we can dive right into the experience of dukkha in all its manifestations without ever mentioning dukkha; dive right into the ultimate sources of dukkha without ever mentioning the classical etiology, and yet able to investigate craving and clinging first-hand, propose investigating the possibility for alleviating if not extinguishing that distress or suffering (cessation), and explore, empirically, a possible pathway for doing so (the practice of mindfulness meditation writ large, inclusive of the ethical stance of śīla, the foundation of samadhi, and, of course, prajñā, wisdom—the eightfold noble path) without ever having to mention the Four Noble Truths, the Eightfold Noble Path, or śīla, samadhi, or prajñā.

In this fashion, the Dharma can be self-revealing through skillful and ardent cultivation via formal and informal practice in the supportive context of dialogue, inquiry, and skillful instruction, which are themselves all one seamless whole. We can speak of and reinforce attending to the experience of change and impermanence since they are self-evident, and develop a collective appreciation of them through engaging in the dialogues and conversations among the class participants. The law of impermanence reveals itself without any need to reference a Buddhist framework or lens for seeing it. The same is true for all four noble truths—perhaps better spoken of as the four realities (Gethin 1998). The same is true for *anattā* although this one is trickier and scarier, and needs to be held very gently and skillfully, letting it emerge out of the participants' own reports of their experience rather than stated as a fact. Often it begins with the realization, not insignificant, that 'I am not my pain,' 'I am not my anxiety,' 'I am not my cancer,' etc. We can easily ask the question, well then, who am I? This is the core practice of Chinese Chan (Sheng-Yen 2001), Korean Zen (Buswell 1991; Seung Sahn 1976), Japanese Zen (Kapleau 1965), and also of Ramana Maharshi (1959). Nothing more is needed . . . . Just the question and the questioning . . . the inquiry and investigation into the nature of self, not merely through thought, but through awareness itself.[10]

In the same way, we can be loving and compassionate as teachers/ instructors/ and guides, and introduce practices to cultivate lovingkindness, especially toward oneself in times of contraction and mental seizures, as well as compassion, joy, and equanimity, without any mention of the Four Immeasurables, or necessary recourse to the classical ways in which these are cultivated. The same is true for generosity, gratitude, and other positive mental states.

This all is to say that it can be hugely helpful to have a strong personal grounding in the Buddhadharma and its teachings, as suggested in the earlier sections. In fact, it is virtually essential and indispensible for teachers of MBSR and other mindfulness-based interventions. Yet little or none of it can be brought into the classroom *except in essence*. And if the essence is absent, then whatever one is doing or thinks one is doing, it is certainly not mindfulness-based in the way we understand the term.

This means that we cannot follow a strict Theravadan approach, nor a strict Mahayana approach, nor a strict Vajrayana approach, although elements of all these great traditions and the sub-lineages within them are relevant and might inform how we, as a unique person with a unique dharma history, approach specific teaching moments in both practice, guided meditations, and dialogue about the experiences that arise in formal and informal practice among the people in our class. But we are never appealing to authority or tradition, only to the richness of the present moment held gently in awareness, and the profound and authentic authority of each person's own experience, equally held with kindness in awareness.

This orientation within mindfulness-based interventions has elements of the Chan approach of non-doing and non-striving, the so called 'method of no method,' and of the paradoxical 'Dharma combat' dialogue and inquiry mentioned earlier, so characteristic of the lineages of Seng-Ts'an and Hui Neng, the third and sixth Zen Patriarchs of the Chan tradition in Six and Seventh Century China (Kabat-Zinn 2010; Luk 1974; Mu Soeng 2004; Sheng-Yen 2001; Suzuki 1956). All maps are laid aside as an act of love and wisdom, meaning that we no longer have any attachment to what they portray, and are thus able to exemplify and embody the essence of the territory of being human in all its dimensionalities, while transmitting to others through our direct seeing and honouring of their intrinsic Buddha nature that there is indeed, nowhere to go, nothing to do, and nothing to attain . . . the gateway to any authentic attainment. This is all intrinsic to any mindfulness-based intervention, what we might call its *marrow*.

How then might we understand the whole question of lineage, especially the *lineage* of your patients and clients, because their lineage is very likely to start with you, their teacher. What do you understand as your own lineage? What nurtured your dharma practice and understanding early on? What nurtures them now? Perhaps the dharma in its largest and most universal sense and language, whatever the particulars of your dharma history, is your lineage. Skillful means might require that you take responsibility for the whole of it, wordlessly, with perhaps an interior smile, not of self-satisfaction or secrecy, or attainment of anything at all, but of delight that the real lineage is formless, and with eyes of wholeness and a heart of kindness, know that literally everything and everybody is already the Buddha, already the patriarchs, already the dharma, already your teacher. You have nothing to do except give it away, and the only way you can do that is to give yourself away. No charge for this, it and you being already free.

> . . . . by watching yourself in your daily life with alert interest with the intention to understand rather than to judge, in full acceptance of whatever may emerge, because it is here, you encourage the deep to come to the surface and enrich your life and consciousness with its captive energies. This is the great work of awareness; it removes obstacles and releases energies by understanding the nature of life and mind. Intelligence is the door to freedom and alert attention is the mother of intelligence.
>
> Nisargadatta Maharaj (1973)
> Quote on the last page of the MBSR workbook

NOTES

1. In the present context, to recognize the universal character and applicability of the dharma, I am using the term with a lower-case "d" except in those very specific circumstances where it signifies the traditional Buddhist teachings within an explicitly Buddhist context.
2. From the start, there were times that I thought of what we were doing in the stress reduction clinic as a kind of guerilla theatre within medicine and healthcare and the hospital, and in a larger sense, engaging with those universes in an ongoing dance resembling the martial art of aikido, with its characteristic give and take, entering and blending, and its unswerving aims of vigilance, groundedness, fluidity, and appropriate application of focused energy, all in the service of wisdom in difficult circumstances—the wisdom of non-harming and peaceful resolution of conflicting interests.

3. Mindfulness-Based Cognitive Therapy (Segal, Teasdale and Williams 2002), Mindfulness-Based Relapse Prevention (Bowan, Chawla and Marlatt 2011); Mindfulness-Based Childbirth and Parenting (Bardacke, forthcoming); Mindfulness-Based Eating Awareness Training (Kristeller, Baer and Quillian-Wolever 2006); Mindfulness-Based Elder Care (McBee 2008).

4. I went to work as a research associate and later, post-doctoral fellow in the Anatomy and Cell Biology Department, in the lab of a fellow named Rob Singer, who is now at the Albert Einstein College of Medicine. I took that job because I needed work, we had an indirect MIT connection, and, to sweeten the deal, he promised me that I could also participate in teaching gross anatomy to the first year medical students, which meant being one step ahead of the students in doing the actual cadaver dissections. As a yoga teacher and also someone who was interested in what is called *maranasati* or mindfulness of death, that was a 'to die for' experience. And so I went to work in Rob's lab. The back story is that I met with Rob originally at the suggestion of someone I did not know, but who introduced himself as a friend of one of my brothers, and then proceeded to tell me what I should be doing with my life, as if he knew and I didn't, which turned out to be more correct than I would ever have imagined. His name was Earl Etienne. He was a young full professor of physiology at UMass Medical School, wise, worldly, a truly amazing being. Many years later, he showed up at a medical grand rounds I gave on MBSR at the California Pacific Medical Center. I spotted him in the audience and spontaneously dedicated the talk to him and publically expressed my gratitude for his essential catalytic role in my being at UMass in the first place. If I had not already been there, it is doubtful that MBSR, at least as it is presently configured, would have come into the world. To me, this is one of an infinite number of examples of the interconnectivity of emergences, and how empty it is to reify an independent entity that would feel the need to claim individual credit for any complex emergence. It may be correct as far as it goes, but it is never the whole story. Perhaps any whole story is so complex it can never be completely known. Tragically, Earl Etienne died young, several years later.

5. I thought of it in those terms at the time. Now I am not quite sure what adjective to use. Secular might do, except that it feels dualistic, in the sense of separating itself from the sacred; I see the work of MBSR as sacred as well as secular, in the sense of both the Hippocratic Oath and the Bodhisattva Vow being sacred, and the doctor/patient relationship and the teacher/student relationship as well. Perhaps we need new ways of 'languaging' our vision, our aspirations, and our common work. Certainly it is only a matter of 'American' in the US. Each country and culture will have its own challenges in shaping the language to its own heart-essence without denaturing the wholeness of the dharma.

6. Hospitals are not the only dukkha magnets in society—schools, prisons, and the military could also be described this way. Now there are growing movements to bring mindfulness into K-12 education (Burnett and Cullen 2010; Grossman et al. 2010; Kaiser-Greenland 2010), into the military (Jha et al. 2010; Stanley and Jha

2009; Stanley et al. 2011), and into prisons (Menahemi and Ariel 1997, Phillips 2008; Samuelson et al. 2007).

7. Saki Santorelli contributed in profoundly creative and incisive ways to this form of inquiry in MBSR.

8. Twenty years later, as recounted in his powerful and illuminating contribution to this special issue, Saki Santorelli found himself facing the institutional dissolution of the Stress Reduction Clinic. Remarkably, he steered a path through cycles of chaos, uncertainty, and loss to a new and even more vigorous life, a veritable phoenix rising out of the ashes. The marvel and gratitude of all of us who cared about the clinic's fate and its role in the world is boundless.

9. Here I am using the verb 'to sit' as an umbrella term to cover the entire range of formal and informal practices and the moment by moment experiencing of anything and everything arising from engaging in the retreat.

10. Studies of MBSR suggest that mindfulness training can influence and modulate different modes of self-referencing in anatomically distinct networks, one medial, one lateral, within the cerebral cortex (Farb et al. 2007). Such findings may ultimately contribute to a richer understanding within psychology of the term 'self' and its meanings, and thus a new and deeper appreciation of its functional expressions and relativistic and dynamical nature. This in itself could transform the field of psychology.

REFERENCES

BARDACKE, N. Forthcoming. *Mindful birthing: Training the mind, body and heart for childbirth and beyond.* New York: Harper Collins.

BENSON, H. 1975. *The relaxation response.* New York: Morrow.

BOWEN, S., N. CHAWLA, and G. A. MARLATT. 2011. *Mindfulness-based relapse prevention for addictive behaviors.* New York: Guilford Press.

BURNETT, R., and C. CULLEN. 2010. The mindfulness in schools project. http://www.mindfulnessinschools.org.

BUSWELL, R. E., JR. 1991. *Tracing back the radiance: Chinul's Korean way of zen.* Honolulu: University of Hawaii Press.

BOHM, D. 1980. *Wholeness and the implicate order,* 19–26. London: Routledge Kegan Paul.

BROWN, D. P., and J. ENGLER. 1980. A Rorschach study of the stages of mindfulness meditation. *Journal of Transpersonal Psychology* 12: 143–92.

CULLEN, M. 2006. Mindfulness: The Heart of Buddhist Meditation? A Conversation with Jan Chozen-Bays, Joseph Goldstein, Jon Kabat-Zinn, and Alan Wallace. *Inquiring Mind* 22: 4–7 ff.

CULLEN, M. 2008. On mindfulness. In: *Emotional awareness: A conversation between the Dalai Lama and Paul Ekman,* 61–3. New York: Times Books.

DEATHERAGE, G. 1975. The clinical uses of mindfulness meditation techniques in short-term psychotherapy. *Journal of Transpersonal Psychology* 2: 133–44.

DEPRAZ, N., F. J. VARELA, and P. VERMERSCH. 1999. The gesture of awareness: An account of its structural dynamics. In *Investigating phenomenal consciousness*, ed. M. Velmans, 121–36. Amsterdam: John Benjamins.

EPEL, E. S., E. H. BLACKBURN, J. LIN, F. S. DHABHAR, N. E. ADLER, J. D. MORROW, and R. M. CAWTHON. 2004. Accelerated telomere shortening in response to life stress. *Proceedings of the National Academy of Sciences, USA* 101: 17312–15.

EPSTEIN, R. M. 1999. Mindful practice. *Journal of the American Medical Association* 282: 833–9.

FARB, A. S., Z. V. SEGAL, H. MAYBERG, J. BEAN, D. MCKEON, Z. FATIMA, and A. K. ANDERSON. 2007. Attending to the present: Mindfulness meditation reveals distinct neural modes of self-referencing. *Social Cognitive and Affective Neuroscience* 2: 313–22.

GETHIN, R. 1998. *The foundations of Buddhism.* Oxford: Oxford University Press.

GOLDSTEIN, J. 1976. *The experience of insight: A natural unfolding.* Santa Cruz: Unity Press.

GOLEMAN, D. J., and G. E. SCHWARTZ. 1976. Meditation as an intervention in stress reactivity. *Journal of Consulting and Clinical Psychology* 44: 456–66.

GRANT, J. A., J. COURTEMANCHE, E. G. DUERDEN, G. H. DUNCAN, and P. RAINVILLE. 2010. Cortical thickness and pain sensitivity in Zen Meditators. *Emotion* 10: 43–53.

GROSSMAN, L., M. COWAN, and R. SHANKMAN. 2010. Mindful schools. http://www.mindfulschools.org.

GROSSMAN, P., L. KAPPOS, H. GENSINCKE, M. D'SOUSA, D. C. MOHR, I. K. PENNER, and C. STEINER. 2010. MS quality of life, depression, and fatigue improve after mindfulness training: a randomized trial. *Neurology* 75(13): 1141–49.

HANH, T. N. 1975. *The miracle of mindfulness: A manual on meditation.* Boston, MA: Beacon.

HÖLZEL, B. K., J. CARMODY, K. C. EVANS, E. A. HOGE, J. A. DUSEK, L. MORGAN, R. K. PITMAN, and S. W. LAZAR. 2010. Stress reduction correlates with structural changes in the amygdala. *Social Cognitive and Affective Neuroscience* 5(1): 11–17.

HÖLZEL, B. K., J. CARMODY, M. VANGEL, C. CONGLETON, S. M. YERRAMSETTI, T. GARD, and S. W. LAZAR, 2011. Mindfulness practice leads to increases in regional gray matter density. *Psychiatry Research Neuroimaging* 191(1): 36–43.

JHA, A. P., E. A. STANLEY, A. KIYONAGO, L. WONG, and L. GELFAND. 2010. Examining the protective effects of mindfulness training on working memory capacity and affective experience. *Emotion* 10: 54–64.

KABAT-ZINN, J. 1982. An out-patient program in Behavioral Medicine for chronic pain patients based on the practice of mindfulness meditation: Theoretical considerations and preliminary results. *General Hospital Psychiatry* 4: 33–47.

KABAT-ZINN, J. 1994. *Wherever you go, there you are.* 4. New York: Hyperion.

KABAT-ZINN, J. 1990. *Full catastrophe living.* 163. New York: Dell.

KABAT-ZINN, J. 1999. Indra's net at work: The mainstreaming of Dharma practice in society. In *The psychology of awakening*, ed. G. Watson, S. Batchelor, and G. Claxton, 225–49. London: Random House/Rider.

KABAT-ZINN, J. 2000. Participatory medicine. *Journal of the European Academy of Dermatology and Venereology* 14: 239–40.

KABAT-ZINN, J. 2003. Mindfulness-based interventions in context: Past, present, and future. *Clinical Psychology Science and Practice* 10: 144–56.

KABAT-ZINN, J. 2005a. Dying before you die. In *Coming to our senses*. by J. Kabat-Zinn, 486–90. New York: Hyperion.

KABAT-ZINN, J. 2005b. Dying before you die–deux. In *Coming to our senses*. by J. Kabat-Zinn, 491–3. New York: Hyperion.

KABAT-ZINN, J. 2005c. Dukkha magnets. In *Coming to our senses*. by J. Kabat-Zinn, 130–3. New York: Hyperion, .

KABAT-ZINN, J. 2005d. Dialogues and discussions. In *Coming to our senses*. by J. Kabat-Zinn, 448–50. New York: Hyperion.

KABAT-ZINN, J. 2005e. *Coming to our senses*. by J. Kabat-Zinn, 108. New York: Hyperion.

KABAT-ZINN, J. 2005f. *Coming to our senses*. by J. Kabat-Zinnm, 172–83. New York: Hyperion.

KABAT-ZINN, J. 2009. Foreword. In *Clinical handbook of mindfulness*, ed. F. Didonna, xxv–xxxiii. New York: Springer.

KABAT-ZINN, J. 2010. Foreword. In *Teaching mindfulness*. by D. McCown, D. Reibel, and M.S. Micozzi, xix–xxii. New York: Springer, .

KABAT-ZINN, J., and A. CHAPMAN-WALDROP. 1988. Compliance with an outpatient stress reduction program: Rates and predictors of completion. *Journal of Behavioral Medicine* 11: 333–52.

KABAT-ZINN, J., and R. J., DAVIDSON, eds. 2011. *The mind's own physician: A scientific dialogue with the Dalai Lama on the healing power of meditation*. Oakland, CA: New Harbinger.

KABAT-ZINN, J., L. LIPWORTH, and R. BURNEY. 1985. The clinical use of mindfulness meditation for the self-regulation of chronic pain. *Journal of Behavioral Medicine* 8: 163–90.

KABAT-ZINN, J., L. LIPWORTH, R. BURNEY, and W. SELLERS. 1986. Four year follow-up of a meditation-based program for the self-regulation of chronic pain: Treatment outcomes and compliance. *Clinical Journal of Pain* 2: 159–73.

KAISER-GREENLAND, S. 2010. *The mindful child*. New York: Free Press.

KAPLEAU, P. 1965. *The three pillars of Zen*. Boston, MA: Beacon.

KRASNER, M. S., R. M. EPSTEIN, H. BECKMAN, A. L. SUCHMAN, B. CHAPMAN, C. J. MOONEY, and T. E. QUILL. 2009. Association of an educational program in mindful communication with burnout, empathy, and attitudes among primary care physicians. *Journal of the American Medical Association* 302: 1284–93.

KRISTELLER, J. L., R. A. BAER, and R. QUILLIAN-WOLEVER. 2006. Mindfulness-based approaches to eating disorders. In *Mindfulness-based treatment approaches: A clinician's guided to evidence base and applications*, ed. R. Baer, 75–91. San Diego, CA: Elsevier.

KORNFIELD, J. 1977. *Living Buddhist masters*. Santa Cruz: Unity.

KRISHNAMURTI, J. 1969. *Freedom from the known*. New York: Harper and Row.

KRISHNAMURTI, J. 1979. *The wholeness of life*. New York: Harper and Row.

LUK, C. 1974. *The transmission of the mind outside the teaching*. New York: Grove Press.

LUPIEN, S. J., B. S. MCEWEN, M. R. GUNNAR, and C. HEIM. 2009. Effects of stress throughout the lifespan on brain, behavior, and cognition. *Nature Reviews: Neuroscience* 10: 434–45.

MAHARSHI, R. 1959. *The collected works of Ramana Maharshi*, edited by A. Osborne. New York: Weiser.

MCBEE, L. 2008. *Mindfulness-based elder care.* New York: Springer.

MELZACK, R., and C. PERRY. 1975. Self-regulation of pain: The use of alpha feedback and hypnotic training for the control of chronic pain. *Experimental Neurology* 46: 452–69.

MENAHEMI, A., and E. ARIEL. 1997. *Doing time, doing Vipassana,* Karuna Films Ltd. http://www.karunafilms.com/Dtdv/Distribution.htm

MU, SOENG. 2004. *Trust in mind: The rebellion of Chinese Zen.* Boston, MA: Wisdom.

NISARGADATTA, M. 1973. *I Am That.* Vol. 1 and 2. Bombay: Chetana.

NYANAPONIKA, T. 1962. *The heart of Buddhist meditation.* 24. San Francsico: Weiser.

PERLMAN, D. M., T. V. SALOMONS, R. J. DAVIDSON, and A. LUTZ. 2010. Differential effects on pain intensity and unpleasantness of two meditation practices. *Emotion* 10: 65–71.

PHILLIPS, J. 2008. *Letters from the Dhamma brothers: Meditation behind bars.* Onalaska, WI: Pariyatti Press.

SAMUELSON, M., J. CARMODY, J. KABAT-ZINN, and M. A. BRATT. 2007. Mindfulness-based stress reduction in Massachusetts correctional facilities. *The Prison Journal* 2: 254–68.

SANTORELLI, S. F. 1999. *Heal thy self: Lessons on mindfulness in medicine,* 45–50. New York: Bell Tower, NY.

SCHWARTZ, G. E., R. J. DAVIDSON, and D. J. GOLEMAN. 1978. Patterning of cognitive and somatic processes in the self-regulation of anxiety: Effects of meditation versus exercise. *Psychosomatic Medicine* 40: 321–8.

SEGAL, Z. V., J. M. G. WILLIAMS, and J. D. TEASDALE. 2002. *Mindfulness-based cognitive therapy for depression.* New York: Guilford Press.

SEUNG SAHN. 1976. *Dropping ashes on the Buddha.* New York: Grove Press.

SHAPIRO, D. H. 1980. *Meditation: Self-regulatory strategy and altered state of consciousness.* New York: Aldine.

SHENG-YEN. 2001. *Hoofprint of the ox: Principles of the Chan Buddhist path as taught by a modern Chinese master.* Oxford: Oxford University Press.

SIBINGA, E. M., and A. W. WU. 2010. Clinician mindfulness and patient safety. *Journal of the American Medical Association* 304: 2532–3.

STANLEY, E. A., and A. P. JHA. 2009. Mind fitness: Improving operational effectiveness and building warrior resilience. *Joint Force Quarterly* 55: 144–51.

STANLEY, E. A., J. M. SCHALDACH, A. KIYONAGA, and A. P. JHA. 2011. Mindfulness-based mind fitness training: A case study of a high stress pre-deployment military cohort. *Cognitive and Behavioral Practice.* DOI: 10.1016/j.cbpra.2010.08.002.

THANISSARO, BHIKKHU. 2010. http://www.accesstoinsight.org/tipitaka/sn/sn38/sn38.014.than.html. http://www.accesstoinsight.org/ptf/dhamma/sacca/index.html.

TRUNGPA, C. 1969. *Meditation in action.* Boston: Shambhala.

UCOK, O. 2007. Dropping into being: Exploring mindfulness as lived experience. 5th annual international conference on Mindfulness for Clinicians, Researchers and

Educators: Integrating Mindfulness-Based Interventions into Medicine, Health-care and Society, Worcester, MA. Manuscript in preparation.

VARELA, F. J., E. THOMPSON, and E. ROACH. 1991. *The embodied mind: Cognitive science and human experience.* Cambridge: MIT.

WALLACE, B. A., and B. HODEL. 2008. *Embracing mind: The common ground of science and spirituality*, 121–3. Boston: Shambhala.

WALSH, R. N. 1977. Initial meditative experiences I. *Journal of Transpersonal Psychology* 9: 151–92.

WALSH, R. N. 1978. Initial meditative experiences II. *Journal of Transpersonal Psychology* 10: 1–28.

WALSH, R. N. 1980. The consciousness disciplines and the behavioral sciences: Questions of comparison and assessment. *American Journal of Psychiatry* 137: 663–73.

WILLIAMS, J. M. G., R. CRANE, J. SOULSBY, M. BLACKER, F. MELEO-MEYER, and R. STAHL. 2007. The inquiry process–aims, intentions and teaching considerations. Personal communication.

Index

Page numbers in **bold** type refer to **figures**
Page numbers in *italic* type refer to *tables*
Page numbers followed by 'n' refer to notes

INDEX

CAMS-R (Cognitive and Affective Mindfulness Scale - Revised) 250
Candrakīrti 87n
canonical perspective 19–39
Carmody, J.: and Baer, R.A. 251
Carruyo, L. 193
Center for Contemplative Mind in Society 10, 184–5, 187
Center for Mindfulness in Medicine, Health Care and Society 200–17, 294
Chah, A. 100
Chan tradition 299
change: and *dukkha* 92, 104–5; propositional and implicational 114–15, 123
Chaskalson, M.: and Teasdale, J.D. 6–7, 89–102, 103–24
Cheng, A. 189
Childers, R.C. 263
Chogyam Trungpa 186, 188
Christopher, M.: and Gilbert, B. 220
City Meditation Crew 189
clear comprehension (*sampajañña*) 29, 33–5, 37n, 50, 51
Cognitive and Affective Mindfulness Scale - Revised (CAMS-R) 250
cognitive dimensions 41–54
cognitive effort 78, 82
cognitive science 4
Cognitive Therapy (CT) 8, 125–42; Beck's cognitive model 128–30, **129**; collaborative therapeutic alliance 128, 130; and depression 128–9; development 127; empirical investigation 128, 131; essential present moment 137; goal-orientation 133–4; individual case formation 132–3; languages 134–5; learning process 138–9; MBCT contribution 131–2; MBIs congruences 136–40; MBIs' differences 131–6; methodologies 134; mind map 137; negative automatic thoughts 128; persistent distress 137; theoretical framework 128, 129–30; training trajectory 135–6; underlying theory 127; verbal interventions 138
Columbia University 186
compassion 62, 151–2, 171, 223; cultivation 147–9, 151–3; definition 144–5; and healing process 145–7; and suffering 143–55; suffering landscape 149–51
Compassion Focused Therapy (Gilbert) 171

comprehension: clear (*sampajañña*) 29, 33–5, 37n, 50, 51
concentration 28, 49, 158–9; right 224; sustained in leadership lessons 213–14
conciliation: wisdom and leadership 212–13
conditionality: and *dukkha* 92–3
confidence 61
conscience: consciousness 61; suspension 59
consciousness 47, 48, 57, 67, 68, 69; applied thought 63; delusion 59, 60, 61, 63; modalities 57–62; universals 58–9
construction 55–70
contact 58, 62
contemplation 21
contemplative education 185–97
Contemplative Studies Initiative (Brown University) 190
Contemporary Buddhism 1–2, 203

Dakpo Tashi Namgyel 79–80, 85, 86
Dalai Lama 144
Davidson, R. 290
daydreaming 228
decentring 244
decision 59
delusion 181–2; consciousness 59, 60, 61, 63
denotations and connotations 220–3
depression 126–9, 143, 145–7, 149, 150–4, 227, 242, 254, 268; Beck's cognitive model 128–30, **129**; and Cognitive Therapy 128–9; *dukkha* 92; Niagara falls analogy 146, **146**
Dewey, J. 183
Dhammacakkappavattana Sutta 264
dharma (*dhamma*) 14, 20–1, 24, 33, 35–6, 44, 56–8, 173–4, 206–8, 282–4, 287–8, 294, 296, 298; evaluative characterization 56–7
Dharmakīrti 74, 77
Dialectical Behavior Therapy (DBT) 257
Discourse on the Forms of Thought 161
distress: persistent and Cognitive Therapy 137
disturbing thoughts: dealing mechanisms 161–4
Dreyfus, G. 6, 7, 41–54, 78–9, 82, 107, 188, 291
dukkha 288, 298; anguish 90; change 92; change strategies 104–5; and conditionality 92–3; Dependent Origination 104; depression 92; and ignorance 93; incompleteness 90; mind

INDEX

Teasdale, J.D.: and Chaskalson, M. 6–7, 89–102, 103–24; Segal, Z. and Williams, M. 111, 117, 131, 160
Third Noble Truth 99
thoughts: applied 59; disturbing 161–4; sustained 59, 63
Three Jewels 173–4
Thurman, R. 186, 187, 189
time travelling 77, 82
Toronto Mindfulness Scale (TMS) 250, 251
tranquility 61
Tsongkhapa 50

UMass Memorial Health Care (UMMHC) 200
understanding 169
universal unwholesomes 58, 59–60
universals: consciousness 58–9; wholesome 58, 61
Universities: Alberta 192; American 192; Arizona 192; Brown (Contemplative Studies Initiative) 190; Columbia 186; Harvard 185, 188; Maryland 193; Massachusetts Medical School (UMMS) 11, 200, 202, 287; Missouri-Columbia Law School 194; Naropa 186; Roger Williams School of Law 194, 196; State (New York) 189; Syracuse 189; Toronto 186–7; Washington 193
unwholesome occasionals: consciousness 58, 60–1
unwholesomes: universal 58, 59–60
upaṭṭhāna (setting up, establishing) 25, 33
upāya (skilful means) 167, 268

Van Dam, N.T.: and Grossman, P. 12, 219–39
Varela, F. 284, 291
Vassar College 193
Vasubandhu 49, 73; Abhidharmakósa 6, 66–7, 73

vipassanā meditation 51,157–8, 163, 273
virtue 169, 170
Visuddhimagga (Buddhaghosa) 25, 37n, 266
Vitakkasaṇṭhāna Sutta 9, 161, 163
volition 58, 62

wakefulness: and Second Noble Truth 120
Walking on Lotus Flowers (Batchelor) 158
Walsh, R. 290
Wapner, P. 192–3
way of being 116–18
wholesome occasionals 58, 61–2
wholesome universals 58, 61
wieldiness 61
Williams, J.M.G.: and Kabat-Zinn, J. 1–18
Williams, M.: Segal, Z.; and Teasdale, J.D. 111, 117, 131, 160
wisdom 32–3, 62, 67; conciliation and leadership 212–13
Working Group on Contemplative Mind in Society 186
working memory: concept 7, 107–10; and consciousness 108; implicational 111, 113, 115–16, 117; and mindfulness 107–8; propositional 111

yoga 20
Yogācāra philosophy 73

Zajonc, A. 184, 191
Zen 9, 157–9, 163, 165–6, 171, 173, 291, 292, 297
Ziegler, J. 188, 196
Zlotnick, D. 194, 196